HYPERCOMPETITION

HYPERCOMPETITION

MANAGING THE DYNAMICS OF STRATEGIC MANEUVERING

RICHARD A. D'AVENI
WITH ROBERT GUNTHER

FOREWORD BY IAN C. MACMILLAN

THE FREE PRESS
A Division of Macmillan, Inc.
NEW YORK

Maxwell Macmillan Canada
TORONTO

Maxwell Macmillan International
NEW YORK   OXFORD   SINGAPORE   SYDNEY

The Free Press
A Division of Macmillan, Inc.
866 Third Avenue, New York, N. Y. 10022

Maxwell Macmillan Canada, Inc.
1200 Eglinton Avenue East
Suite 200
Don Mills, Ontario M3C 3N1

Macmillan, Inc. is part of the Maxwell Communication
Group of Companies.

Printed in the United States of America

printing number
1   2   3   4   5   6   7   8   9   10

Library of Congress Cataloging-in-Publication Data

D'Aveni, Richard A.
    Hypercompetition : managing the dynamics of strategic maneuvering /
Richard A. D'Aveni, with Robert Gunther.
      p. cm.
    ISBN 0–02–906938–6
    1. Strategic planning. 2. Competition. I. Gunther, Robert E.
    II. Title.
HD30.28.D375 1994
658.4′012—dc20   93–42423
                                                              CIP

Figures I–1 (p. 8) and I–2 (p. 12) are based on research by Ian C. MacMillan. In
"Controlling Competitive Dynamics by Taking Strategic Initiative." Academy
of Management *Executive* 2, no. 2 (1988): 111–18.

To Ross and Gina, the son and daughter
who have lit up my life with their joy and intelligence,
and
To Michele, the daughter I'll never get to know
but always regret not having the chance,
I love you all.

CONTENTS

FOREWORD

It has become clear from the rumblings and soul-searching in the field of competitive strategy that a revolution is brewing. Managers and strategy researchers are discovering that existing models of strategy are nearly obsolete in the intensity of today's fast-paced competition. Some have called for a more dynamic approach, even questioning the sustainability of competitive advantage in this new environment. But so far, this revolution-waiting-to-happen has had no leader. Now it has.

In this book Richard D'Aveni offers a powerful model that addresses the emerging realities of competing in intense and dynamic environments, what he describes as "hypercompetition." Revolutionary technology, globalization, new business methods, radically new communication and information-processing techniques, flexible manufacturing equipment, and low-cost foreign labor are all conspiring to heat up markets everywhere in the world. Hypercompetition is an environment of intense change, in which flexible, aggressive, innovative competitors move into markets easily and rapidly, eroding the advantages of the large and established players.

Hypercompetition represents a fundamental shift in thinking necessary for coping with these changes. Whereas managers and researchers have operated on the assumption that companies should try to *sustain* their advantages, D'Aveni, for the first time, shows that no organization can build a competitive advantage that is sustainable. Every advantage erodes. So in this environment the company must actively work to *disrupt* its own advantages and the advantages of competitors. Efforts to sustain advantage in the current business environment may actually undermine the true competitiveness of the firm. If you accept this view of reality—and D'Aveni makes a thoroughly convincing case for it—this represents a turning point in the development of strategic thinking.

A generation of managers exhorted to sustain advantages or increase commitment by investing in large plants or equipment may find this book surprising. We have been taught to seek consistency and long-term strategies, but D'Aveni shows that this makes companies more inflexible and predictable in this environment. Today's strengths become tomorrow's weaknesses so quickly that sustaining advantages is nearly impossible. We have been taught to select one of the generic strategies, such as being a differentiator or low-cost producer. But firms using new manufacturing technologies and product designs actually maneuver between these positions or occupy both positions at once. We have been taught that large companies have monopoly power, but we see the growing power of small, flexible firms. We have been taught that entry barriers sustain advantage, but D'Aveni shows how aggressive firms are beating down entry barriers right and left. We have been taught that companies can become more profitable by being more cooperative, but he shows how reaching oligopolistic bargains decreases a firm's long-run competitiveness. He suggests that profits from all the traditional advantages are a short-lived fantasy that dissolves in the face of even a single hypercompetitive (usually foreign) rival.

D'Aveni clears away the cobwebs of theories that are no longer relevant in dynamic markets. He makes it clear why these strategies fail and proposes a new model and new techniques to take their place. He provides insights into the dynamic movement of competition through a series of "escalation ladders" in four arenas of competition. At every step along the way, he backs up the discussions with vivid examples of corporate actions to illustrate the dynamic evolution of competition. Finally, he provides a series of tools for managers to use in analyzing competition in their industries and describes a set of "New 7-S's" companies are using to succeed in hypercompetition.

For those who think hypercompetition is something that only happens to high-tech industries, this book will be a wake-up call. It chronicles the spread of hypercompetition into such unlikely industries as toys, cat food, grains, and hot sauces. In fact, Jeffrey Williams, in his insightful article on the sustainability of advantages, had cited hot sauces as an example of a slow-moving industry. But, as D'Aveni discusses, even here the advantage of the industry leader for over one hundred years is now under attack by aggressive competitors. If your industry is not in hypercompetition today, there is a good chance it will be tomorrow.

This book forces us to rethink how we study strategy, how we teach it to students, and how we practice it. It provides the basis for a wide variety of research studies and a textbook for students who wish to extend their understanding of competition beyond the foundation work of Michael Porter. It offers a training manual for managers out on the front lines of competitive actions who want to outmaneuver those using traditional strategic methods. The book enables managers to use intellectual judo to take advantage of the weaknesses created by traditional strategic thinking. Finally, the book poses a challenge to U.S. policymakers and antitrust regulators. Just as hypercompetition undermines traditional strategic thinking, it also makes traditional antitrust policy obsolete.

To tackle issues of theory, practice, and policy in a single book is nothing short of a monumental task. Richard D'Aveni is the ideal person to take it on. He brings an extensive knowledge of current business practice tempered by the broader perspective of theory. I have had the pleasure of working with him on research projects and supporting his work for nearly a decade. He has an impeccable academic record of careful, systematic, and relevant research. We also have shared consulting clients among the Fortune 500 corporations. So I know Richard has a close association with and concern for management practice. You too will find that what he has to say is directly applicable to current strategic action and that this book is on the cutting edge of strategic thinking worldwide.

This book has the power to revolutionize how we study, practice, teach, and regulate strategy. It is so relevant, so timely, and so close to the reality of today's competition that no manager can ignore it. Anyone who hopes to survive and succeed as a competitor into the year 2000 and beyond should be interested in the principles and approaches described in this book.

Ian C. MacMillan
George B. Taylor Professor of Entrepreneurial Studies
Director, Sol C. Snider Entepreneurial Center
The Wharton School of the University of Pennsylvania

PREFACE

NEW REALITIES OF HYPERCOMPETITION

In the old days in science, the universe was fairly simple. Nearly every science museum has a huge, old model of the solar system in which all the movements of the planets are represented with clockwork gears. Then we realized that reality was much more complex. All motion was relative. The universe is a system in dynamic motion and flux with all motion being determined by the forces of inertia, complex gravitational interactions of heavenly bodies and even unseen gaseous clouds, random collisions, millions of asteroids, and the overall movement of galaxies toward the outer boundaries of the universe.

Business has also entered an age of new realities. It is essential to understand and take advantage of the dynamic motion and flux of our global markets and technological breakthroughs. In this book I examine four traditional sources of competitive advantage and explain how each is eroded by the unrelenting maneuvering of companies. I describe how this maneuvering has resulted in a new type of competition, which I call "hypercompetition." Then I examine a system of seven strategies for competing in this environment, the "New 7-S's" (whose title is derived from McKinsey's original 7-S's). Unlike the original 7-S's, the New 7-S's are designed to help firms cope with hypercompetition by creating and controlling the dynamic fluxes in their marketplaces through intentionally disrupting the status quo and using hypercompetitive methods to one's own advantage.

Hypercompetition results from the dynamics of strategic maneuvering among global and innovative combatants. It is a condition of rapidly escalating competition based on price-quality positioning, competition to create new know-how and establish first-mover advantage, competition to protect or invade established product or geographic markets, and competition based on deep pockets and the creation of even deeper pocketed alliances. In hypercompetition the frequency, boldness, and aggressiveness of dynamic movement by the players accelerates to create a condition of constant disequilibrium and change. Market stability is threatened by short product life cycles, short product design cycles, new technologies, frequent entry by unexpected outsiders, repositioning by incumbents, and radical redefinitions of market boundaries as diverse industries merge. In other words, environments escalate toward higher and higher levels of uncertainty, dynamism, heterogeneity of the players, and hostility.

Under these conditions, it would seem that the most logical course for most American firms would be to liquidate or exit their industries because sustained advantage is impossible and low profitability would seem to be inevitable. American corporations will be forced to ask themselves, Why are we in business, to make profits or build the U.S. economy? As more and more industries go hypercompetitive, boards of directors will have to ask whether their companies will just give up because Wall Street doesn't want to invest when the going gets tough or fight to survive in this much harsher world. Competing in hypercompetition is a tremendous challenge, but it is better than the alternative—a downward spiral of declining U.S. competitiveness and market position. To stop this spiral, we must rethink why our post–World War II corporate giants are failing, how our concepts of good strategy have failed us, and what we must do to win in the dynamic world of the next millennium.

THE NEW STRATEGIC TOOLS FOR COPING WITH HYPERCOMPETITION

My goal is to provide managers with a better understanding of the process of competitive strategic maneuvering and to help them make better strategic decisions in a world of dynamic motion where no action or advantage can be sustained for long. In doing so, I point out weaknesses in many of the traditional "myths" that underlie strategies used in today's America. Strategic concepts such as fit, sustainable advantage, barriers to entry, long-range planning, the use of financial goals to control strategy implementation, and SWOT analysis all fall apart when the dynamics of competition are considered.

This book is designed to help managers understand hypercompetitive markets and act effectively and aggressively in them. Each chapter concludes with a section on management challenges that explores some of the implications of the discussion for management decisions. In addition, several sections of the book focus more intently on describing the application of the principles examined. This is both to illustrate the discussion and to demonstrate the usefulness of these approaches.

Throughout the book, examples of actual companies are used to illustrate the dynamic strategic interactions discussed in the text. On occasion, this book cites companies that appear to be doing poorly or succeeding well at a given point in time. It is important to note (with the human penchant for ranking and categorizing) that these examples should not be viewed as simplistic attempts to single out "winners" or "losers," nor are they a reflection of the current performance of these firms, because one of the fundamental premises of this book is that everything changes. A poor performer today may be a star tomorrow, and a stellar company may be brought quickly down to Earth if it fails to keep moving forward. Moreover, I have worked with publicly available information, so new facts may come to light. I would like to make it clear from the outset that this is not an attempt to assess the excellence of companies, but rather to describe and illustrate effective strategies for hypercompetitive markets.

This book discusses many aggressive strategies, but this discussion should not be misconstrued as encouraging companies to break any laws, particularly not antitrust laws. Each company's situation is different. Each industry has unique characteristics. So, it is impossible to say whether the tactics discussed here are universally applicable. Companies should be sure to check with their attorneys before pursuing any strategy to ensure that it is in compliance with the law.

I also present two key tools managers can use to apply this new strategic approach to competition in their own industries:

Four Arenas Analysis

The first four chapters of Part I offer a model for understanding competition based on dynamic maneuvering in four arenas of competition, each based on a different competitive advantage that is continuously destroyed and recreated by the dynamic maneuvering of hypercompetitive firms. Chapter 5 offers an explicit exploration of how this Four Arena model can be used to analyze an industry, competitor, or specific competitive move. This Four Arena analysis is used to determine the position of companies in each of the four arenas, while a Four Lens analysis is used to determine the impact of a single strategic action in each of the arenas. MBA students and managers in executive programs at the Tuck School, after having studied earlier drafts of this book, have used these analyses to clarify their firms' next move or to anticipate the next moves of competitors.

The New 7-S's Analysis

After Part II discusses why hypercompetitive markets are different, Part III then describes the New 7-S's, a set of approaches that can be used to change the company's position in the arenas and disrupt the balance of power by restarting the cycle within each arena or shifting to a new arena. A New 7-S's analysis can be used to analyze industries and competitors and to identify one's own strengths and weaknesses in meeting the challenges of hypercompetition.

THE NEW IDEOLOGY OF HYPERCOMPETITION

Hypercompetitive methods like those presented in the New 7-S's highlight a basic tension in the U.S. view of business. On the one hand, Americans are afraid of the power of large companies and try through regulations to keep them in line. On the other hand, Americans believe in the Darwinian struggle of free-market competition, preferring to see the efficient and creative win. Depending on one's viewpoint, those who use hypercompetitive tactics can be perceived as (1) using aggressive, strong-arm tactics that force the "small guy" out of the market, or (2) striving to provide the best product at the best price with the most convenience and service to the public. Thus, *hyper* competitive actions also have been paradoxically called *anti* competitive.

Traditionally, American corporations have sought to establish monopolies and stable oligopolies, but these have become increasingly scarce in a world of numerous global competitors. Some strategists have proposed openly cooperative arrangements (such as alliances) as an escape from hypercompetition, hoping that cooperation will help them avoid the difficult and dangerous competitive struggle inherent in constantly moving forward to build new temporary advantages. This strategy is a return to the past, a last attempt to create a genteel and less competitive environment. As discussed in Chapters 10 and 11, cooperation in hypercompetitive markets ultimately is not sustainable and leads to more intense levels of competition.

Similarly, hypercompetition has undermined the usefulness of U.S. antitrust laws. These laws, designed to promote competition, now actually have become obstacles to the aggressive competition that is demanded in hypercompetition. As discussed in Chapter 11, the restraints designed to limit the power of once monopolistic or oligopolistic companies now are holding back the most aggressive and successful U.S. companies in world markets. Companies such as American Airlines and Wal-Mart have been charged by competitors or government regulators with antitrust violations.

Maintaining existing antitrust regulations in hypercompetition is like driving a Model T on an expressway. It worked in the old environment but now is a threat to the survival of U.S. firms in aggressive global competition. Similarly, maintaining a "chivalrous" view of strategy and competition focused on seeking profits by reducing competition is likewise unsuited to the rigors of the all-out war of hypercompetition.

In sum, America must resolve its conflicts about competition. It must define what constitutes "fair" competition in a way that fits with the harsh realities of hypercompetition. This book proposes some new antitrust laws and strategic views that help do just that.

THE ORIGIN OF THE HYPERCOMPETITION CONCEPT

I have heard from executives about the challenges of wrestling with hypercompetition during executive education courses taught at the Tuck School at Dartmouth and the Wharton School of the University of Pennsylvania. These managers have seen their formerly brilliant strategies turn to dust and have felt growing uncertainty about the best way to meet the future. These executives have also helped to extend and clarify my models in the crucible of real-world experience.

I also owe a debt to the many brilliant strategy researchers and thinkers who identified key features of this emerging environment or laid the foundation for our knowledge of strategy. These include Ian C. MacMillan, James Brian Quinn, Donald Hambrick, Michael Porter, Peter Drucker, Tom Peters, Gary Hamel, Kenichi Ohmae, C. K. Prahalad, George Stalk, Karl von Clausewitz, Sun Tzu, Liddell Hart, and many others. When ideas have become so well known that they are "general knowledge" among educated and savvy business executives, I don't credit the ideas to every author who has ever mentioned one. Instead, I hope that, by describing the bigger picture of how all these specific pieces of the theory come together, I have done more than just restate the ideas of others. I build on their work to design a new dynamic strategic theory that is accessible to managers and deals with the current business environment. As Sir Isaac Newton once said, "If I have seen further, it is by standing upon the shoulders of giants."

Building upon the insights of researchers who have pointed out the weaknesses of current static approaches to strategy, I have proposed a new framework using a more dynamic view. As one of the first, if not the first, model of this type, it can without doubt be further refined by more extensive and rigorous research. But its basic structure and approach have much to offer as a tool for understanding strategy.

I have based my thinking on many theories, particularly those developed by the economist Joseph Schumpeter. I have also built on the work of his predecessors and followers, those whom Robert Jacobson has identified in a recent article in the *Academy of Management Review* as the Austrian School.[1] This respected but little-known group of scholars created a school of thought that emphasizes the competitive processes occurring within marketplaces, not the static structure of industries. Their ideas have gone largely unnoticed or unused by industrial economists and strategists who relied on the static structure-conduct-performance model until Michael Porter's book *The Competitive Advantage of Nations.*[2] In this book and a recent article in the *Strategic Management Journal,*[3] Porter published his latest views, suggesting that the dynamics of the marketplace are crucial to strategic theory because the most competitive firms were those spawned by "vigorous domestic rivalry." He noted that nations that encouraged unvarnished local rivalry and avoided limiting vigorous competition tended to perform best. In addition, the recent work by Ming-Jer Chen[4] and Ken G. Smith, Curtis Grimm, and Martin Gannon,[5] which looked at short-term tactical responses to strategic maneuvering, stimulated me to look for longer-term trends and cycles that develop as firms maneuver against each other many times over sustained periods of time.

The strategic concepts underlying this book generally are consistent with the tenets of the Chicago School of Industrial Economics (even though the book doesn't necessarily subscribe to all the beliefs of that school of thought). I agree with Chicago's view that natural market processes maintain competition better than government intervention, but only in hypercompetitive markets. (With markets increasingly moving into hypercompetition, Chicago may have been slightly ahead of its time.) But while Chicago sees static efficiency resulting from market competition, I stress another view. Chicago and I agree that markets correct themselves because, even though some companies may seem to have an inordinate amount of power at a particular moment in time, that power will erode due to the entry and the force of firms fighting for dominance. However, I do not expect static efficiency or a stable equilibrium to result in hypercompetition. Instead, I argue in the appendix that four types of dynamic efficiency result. Stable equilibria are impossible because constantly shifting technology, global competitors, and strategic positioning will result in frequent or almost constant disequilibrium in which new entrants and established competitors disrupt the balance of power and gain temporary superiority.

Thus, many people's ideas have contributed to my effort to develop a new, more dynamic view of strategy. This book has deep intellectual and economic roots that have not been extensively applied to strategy before but that offer a fresh view of strategy with vastly different implications about competitive advantage, methods of competing, and even the definition of strategy itself.

I would also like to thank the many individuals who contributed specifically to the development of this project. I especially thank Ian C. MacMillan for his pathbreaking work, his willingness to share ideas concerning the instability of competitive advantage, and his personal support for the project. David Ravenscraft provided valuable assistance on the antitrust implications of this book's thesis. I would like to thank research assistants Greg Berzolla, Henri Bichet, Greg Capitolo, Ravi Kushan, Evan Ladouceur, Steve Mendola, Brett Rome, and Joanne Tower Roth for their efforts in collecting information. Several students in a seminar at the Tuck School contributed much-appreciated critiques to the book. They are Christopher C. Andrysiak, Jennifer D. Baldwin, Serkan V. Bektas, Henri Bichet, Elizabeth S. Buchan, Marshall F. Cooper, Evan D. Ladouceur, Lucyna A. Litorowicz, Christina M. Takoudes, Myra J. Wonisch, Daniel P. Jacques III, Julie B. Lang, Lisa Leslie-Henderson, Laura A. Posten, John R. Roesset, Joanne Tower Roth, Marat H. Shinkarev, Thomas Wisniewski, and Tracey A. Wyatt. Bette Snyder, Jim Fries, Tom Labruna, Karen Sluzenski, and Jonathan Brown, the professional staff at Dartmouth's Feldberg Library, did the library research that provided stacks of information on specific company actions, and Peg McGann kept this project moving through many phases of its development. I thank them for their very valuable assistance. My wife Anne's continuing support, love, and help on this project were greatly appreciated. I would like to acknowledge my literal debt to Wharton's Sol C. Snider Center for Entrepreneurial Studies and the Amos Tuck School of Business Administration for their support of this project.

Finally, if it were not for James Brian Quinn's support and his introduction of me to Bob Wallace of The Free Press, this manuscript would not be as well thought out or polished as it is today. I want to thank Brian, Bob Wallace, and the rest of The Free Press staff for their generous and thorough contributions to this book. They made a big difference.

Although I am a special consultant to the Federal Trade Commission, the contents of this book and the opinions contained herein represent the views of the author only, not the policy or views of the Federal Trade Commission.

RICHARD A. D'AVENI
Hanover, New Hampshire

INTRODUCTION

W e have seen giants of American industry, such as General Motors and IBM, shaken to their cores. Their competitive advantages, once considered unassailable, have been ripped and torn in the fierce winds of competition. Technological wonders appear overnight. Aggressive global competitors arrive on the scene. Organizations are restructured. Markets appear and fade. The weathered rule books and generic strategies once used to plot our strategies no longer work as well in this environment.

The traditional sources of advantages no longer provide long-term security. Both GM and IBM still have economies of scale, massive advertising budgets, the best distribution systems in their industries, cutting-edge R&D, deep pockets, and many other features that give them power over buyers and suppliers and that raise barriers to entry that seem impregnable. But these are not enough anymore. Leadership in price and quality is also not enough to assure success. Being first is not always the same as being best. Entry barriers are trampled down or circumvented. Goliaths are brought down by clever Davids with slingshots.

This book provides insights into this process of the destruction of traditional advantages and the building of an entirely new set of advantages. It charts the evolution of industries through a series of competitive moves and countermoves that we label "dynamic strategic interactions." We look at these dynamic strategic interactions in four arenas of competition: (1) cost and quality competition, (2) timing and know-how competition, (3) competition for the creation and destruction of strongholds, and (4) competition for the accumulation and neutralization of deep pockets. As firms have made moves and countermoves in each arena, they have sought to destroy, neutralize, or render obsolete their rivals' competitive advantages. Traditional approaches to strategy stress "creation of advantage"; we take the alternative view that strategy is also the creative destruction of the opponent's advantage.

1

Competition in these four arenas has grown increasingly aggressive and rapid. While there are many complex interactions among firms, one can observe patterns of movement and response, punches and counterpunches, in each of these arenas.

HYPERCOMPETITION

While cost and quality, timing and know-how, strongholds, and deep pockets have always played a role in competition, the difference today is the speed and aggressiveness of interaction in these arenas. Part I of the book will examine patterns of interactions in each arena and show how they have taken on an increased ferocity and speed. This creates an environment of hypercompetition—an environment in which advantages are rapidly created and eroded.

Microsoft is a hypercompetitive firm. It has moved from a dominance in operating systems to a strong position in applications programs. Although *Business Week* reported that Microsoft held 90 percent of the market for personal computer operating systems in 1992, Microsoft sank $100 million into developing the next generation of programming, Windows.[1] Then it moved from that success to developing Windows NT, using an operating system that will replace its own MS-DOS. Instead of trying to protect its advantage with DOS, Microsoft is actively trying to erode it. It knows that if it doesn't, a fast-moving competitor will. Microsoft realizes that its success with MS-DOS, Windows, and many applications programs doesn't guarantee that it will lead in the next generation of software. Even though its large size can be an advantage, Microsoft is far from invincible. Critical markets remain in the hands of competitors. *Business Week* reported that Novell still held 70 percent of the networking market in early 1993.[2] In just one year, Clarisworks won 77 percent of the $50 million integrated software market for Apple Macintosh computers, which Microsoft had held virtually by itself, according to *Business Week.*[3] Microsoft CEO Bill Gates commented in a 1993 interview, "This is a hypercompetitive market. Scale is not all positive in this business. Cleverness is the positive in this business."[4] Success depends not so much on how large the company is but rather on moving aggressively to the next advantage.

The airline industry is another industry that is clearly in hypercompetition. American Airlines is both a cause of the hypercompetition and one of the most successful players in this environment. It has developed a series of temporary advantages that have made it a leader in the industry. Competitors duplicated these services fairly quickly, but American was already moving on to its next innovation. Instead of trying to sustain an advantage, American focuses on jumping to new advantages.

In May 1981 the airline launched its frequent-flyer program, AAdvantage, creating a trend that rapidly swept across the industry. American's SABRE reservation system gave it an advantage in keeping track of bonus miles for the program. It took some time, but other carriers developed their own frequent flyer programs. No problem, because American had already moved on to extend its frequent-flyer program to cover rental mileage, hotels, and flights on British Airways. In 1987 American—this time following the lead of other airlines—hooked up with Citibank to offer a credit card that also earned frequent-flyer points. It offered a frequent flyer gold card with additional perks for high-mileage travelers. In 1990 American broke new ground again when it began offering other outlets for frequent-flyer miles, including rebates on cars, computers, jewelry, and financial services. For trans-Atlantic flights, American now boasts extra-roomy seats, personal video players, lobster fajitas, and award-winning wines. Even so, there is intense price competition in the industry, some of which was driven by American's announcement of new fare structures in 1992.

As CEO Robert Crandall commented in a 1992 *Business Week* article, "This business is intensely, vigorously, bitterly, savagely competitive."[5] American's success depends on moving quickly from one advantage to the next.

American's leadership in the industry, like all advantages in hypercompetition, is precarious. Smaller, nimble competitors such as Southwest Airlines and Reno Air used their cost advantages to drive down the price of travel to a point where American could not follow. In 1993, after three years of losses in its airline business, Crandall announced that he was cutting routes, retiring planes, and downsizing the work force. American may have been unable to move quickly enough to its next advantage. According to an article in *The New York Times,* it appeared that there is "the real possibility that Crandall built the wrong kind of airline for the 1990's: a high-cost carrier that provides plenty of customer service."[6]

While Gates and Crandall perceive their moves as geared to serving customers better, creating new advantages, and surviving in bitterly contested markets, their competitors and the government have scrutinized and criticized the actions of both companies as being anticompetitive. Microsoft is the target of a several-year probe of anticompetitive behavior by the Federal Trade Commission.[7] American has been sued by competitors for predatory pricing, and Crandall had to face a Senate committee to explain American's actions in 1992.[8]

These are two divergent views of competition. The government's view that society is best served by limiting aggressive competition may be outdated; this question is examined in more detail in the appendix to this book. The traditional approach of limiting aggressive competition no longer creates the benefits it was intended to create. In global markets hypercompetition cannot be stopped or slowed by national regulations. The escalation in the four arenas described in Part I is a market phenomenon that is inevitable and that cannot be artificially stopped by government regulation without adverse effects on the competitiveness of America's best companies. If U.S. companies are forced to compete with one hand tied behind their backs, they will have a much harder time succeeding in a world where they face global competitors whose governments support their hypercompetitive behavior.

HYPERCOMPETITION IS WIDESPREAD

It is not just fast-moving, high-tech industries, such as computers, or industries shaken by deregulation, such as the airlines, that are facing this aggressive competition. There is evidence that competition is heating up across the board, even in what once seemed the most sedate industries. From software to soft drinks, from microchips to corn chips, from packaged goods to package delivery services, there are few industries that have escaped hypercompetition. As Jack Welch, CEO of General Electric, commented in 1992, "It's going to be brutal. When I said a while back that the 1980s were going to be a white-knuckle decade and the 1990s would be even tougher, I may have understated how hard it's going to get."[9]

There are few industries and companies that have escaped this shift in competitiveness. Competition is escalating in several arenas of competition described in Part I of this book. Once placid firms are now fighting harder on price and quality, timing of entry and creation of new technical and business know-how, invasion and defense of product/market strongholds, and the use of deep pockets. Even such seemingly comatose industries as hot sauces or such commodity strongholds as U.S. grain production have been jolted awake by the icy waters of hypercompetition.

Competition on price and quality has intensified across a wide range of markets. Industries such as electric lamps, gasoline engines, refrigerators, paper products, and broiler chickens have faced moderate pressure, with prices dropping at annual rates of 0.7 percent to 2.8 percent. Industries such as home electronics, microwave ovens, integrated circuits, electronic wristwatches, and computers have faced intense price pressures, with prices falling at an annual rate of as much as 29 percent in the early 1980s.[10]

Powerful brands, once considered a "sustainable" advantage, have been shaken in the winds of hypercompetition as quality has been driven up and price driven down. This increases the volatility of competition. In 1992 brands such as Kraft Cheese slashed prices 8 percent, Frito-Lay cut prices on snack foods by as much as 15 percent, and Marlboro shocked the industry and investors by announcing price cuts. Procter & Gamble lowered its diaper prices by 12 percent as a result of increasing pressure from private-label brands.[11]

Competition on timing and know-how has intensified. Product life cycles and design cycles have been compressed, and the pace of technological innovation has increased. New models of computers that once had product life cycles of five years now turn over every six months; car models that once were introduced every decade are now changed in five years or less. Design time for new models of cars has been cut almost in half, from 5 1/2 years to 3 years. Even an industry that has seen few product launches in more than a century is suddenly heating up.

The hot-sauce industry—in which McIlhenny's Tabasco sauce has had a seemingly unshakable 125-year hold on the market—has been cited as an example of a "slow-cycle" industry and a demonstration that "first-mover advantage is highly sustainable" in some industries.[12] But a *Wall Street Journal* article comments in 1993 that "Tabasco's hot-sauce hegemony is being threatened as never before."[13] Rival companies are developing new tastes that are weakening McIlhenny's hold on the market. *The Journal* reports that McIlhenny's Tabasco's market share slipped from 32.5 percent during a thirteen-week period in 1989 to 27.5 percent during a comparable period in 1992. Private-label rivals nearly doubled their share of the market in the same period. For the year ending November 1992, second-place Red Hot had gained more than 25 percent of the market compared to 28 percent for Tabasco, and smaller rivals were gaining rapidly.

Entry barriers, which once exerted a stabilizing force on competition, have fallen in the face of the rapid changes of an information age, leaving companies exposed to the full force of hypercompetition. Economies of scale, product differentiation, capital investments, switching costs, access to distribution channels, and government policy have all weakened as barriers to competitors, as will be discussed in Chapter 3. Even such seemingly unassailable government-sanctioned monopolies as telecommunications, postal services, and electric power generation have been broken by consumer pressure, changes in regulations and shifts in technology.

The international grain industry was once dominated by U.S. growers. But aggressive foreign competitors knocked down U.S. grain exports by 24 percent from 1981 to 1991. A combination of farm subsidies by foreign governments, and high-tech advances in new high-yield grains and fertilizers has shifted the rules of competition. The traditional U.S. response to the decline—dumping surplus and propping up prices—no longer works in this environment. With growing world grain production, U.S. attempts to control the market had little or no effect—except to reduce American grain production by 7 percent during the 1980s.[14]

Market definitions are also shifting. Consulting companies, which are helping other organizations to deal with intensifying competition, are facing similar pressures of their own. Consulting firms are developing know-how that moves them into new markets, and innovations in the scope and structure of consulting companies are rapidly imitated. Andersen Consulting's computer consulting is facing new challenges from hardware manufacturers such as IBM, and Unisys has expanded its consulting to include management consulting and business process reengineering to create an all-in-one consulting practice. This in turn has placed greater competitive pressure on McKinsey & Company and Boston Consulting Group. Andersen faces great risks in redefining itself, and if it succeeds, it will only face a more intense competitive battle against a wider set of big, well-established firms. As a *Business Week* article comments, "About all Andersen can be sure of is that if it does succeed, there will be plenty of competitors feverishly drafting one-stop consulting plans of their own."[15]

Deep pockets, which were once a powerful source of advantage, have increasingly been susceptible to being outmaneuvered by rivals. Firms are joining together to create alliances to give them the deep pockets to take on more powerful rivals. Many companies have used such alliances to take on larger, more powerful competitors. Small companies have used such alliances to ride into the Fortune 500. They have also used a variety of other legal and competitive tactics to undermine the advantage of larger companies.

Intel grew to dominate the chip-making industry through its alliance with IBM. Eventually however, it became so powerful that IBM joined forces with Apple and Motorola to work on the next generation of chips. This alliance will help the three companies compete against Intel and also against the Japanese companies with deep-pocketed alliances based on keiretsus such as NEC. It is one of many shifting alliances among companies that compete against other groups of firms.

Intense competition is also reflected in the competitive rhetoric of corporate leaders. S. Robert Levine, CEO of Cabletron—one of the hottest companies developing and selling computer network technology—reportedly ends his pep talks to sales recruits by plunging a combat knife into a beach ball emblazoned with the name of the company's rival.[16] *Fortune* reports that Mitchell Leibovitz, CEO of the highly successful auto parts store Pep Boys, burns and buries baseball caps bearing his competitors' corporate logos and videotapes the process to show to his employees.[17] He also reportedly keeps a collection of snapshots of rival stores that Pep Boys has helped drive out of various locations. Pep Boys more than doubled its sales to over $1.1 billion between 1986 and 1993.

The presence of just one hypercompetitive firm, or even the threat of entry by just one hypercompetitive firm, is enough to drive the industry into hypercompetition. Other competitors are forced to react to the advances of the hypercompetitive firm. As their advantages are eroded, they must react to create new advantages or lose their position in the market. Their responses then force the initial aggressor to build new advantages. This restarts an endless cycle.

As can be seen from the above discussion, hypercompetition requires a fundamental shift in the focus of strategy. Instead of seeking a sustainable advantage, strategy in hypercompetitive environments now focuses on developing a series of temporary advantages. Instead of trying to create stability and equilibrium, the goal of strategy is to disrupt the status quo.

The need for this shift in strategic direction has been recognized by groundbreaking work on "strategic intent" by Hamel and Prahalad and other researchers on strategy.[18] This work has indicated a new focus for strategy, but it has yet to be shaped into a truly dynamic approach to the creation and destruction of traditional advantages. Nor has it developed into a coherent theoretical framework that ties together competencies, capabilities, and tactics. This is the goal of this book.

NEW WAYS OF THINKING ABOUT COMPETITIVE ADVANTAGE
Every Advantage Is Eroded

The pursuit of a sustainable advantage has long been the focus of strategy. But advantages last only until competitors have duplicated or outmaneuvered them. As will be seen in the discussions of Part I, protecting advantages has become increasingly difficult. Once the advantage is copied or overcome, it is no longer an advantage. It is now a cost of doing business. Ultimately the innovator will only be able to exploit its advantage for a limited period of time before its competitors launch a counterattack. With the launch of this counterattack, the original advantage begins to erode (see Figure I–1), and a new initiative is needed.

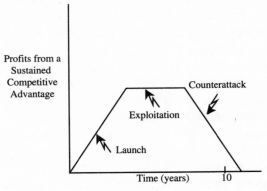

FIGURE I–1
EVERY ADVANTAGE ERODES EVENTUALLY

As shown in Figure I–1, the cycles for launching and exploiting initiatives (new product introductions, for example) offer only a limited window of opportunity during which the firm can earn profits. Eventually, at the end of the cycle, the advantage is eroded by a counterattack. The competitive advantage of the firm is then lost. In the past, competitive advantage has always eroded, but it used to be over longer product life and product development cycles. Traditional strategic thinking has been to find ways to extend the plateau in Figure I–1. Companies like IBM, GM, and Caterpillar all developed entry barriers and power over buyers and suppliers that extended for decades. But, as described in Part I, these cycles have compressed, and maintaining a sustainable advantage has become increasingly difficult. Obviously, advantages in cost and quality or timing and know-how are eroded by the actions of competitors. But even such seemingly unbeatable advantages as geographic or market entry barriers and deep pockets are proving to be little match for aggressive and innovative competitors, as examined in Chapters 3 and 4 of Part I.

Sustaining Advantage Can Be a Deadly Distraction

Of course, if companies *can* extend these plateaus of sustainable advantage, they can reap profits. So what is the harm of trying to sustain an advantage for as long as possible? In an environment in which advantages are rapidly eroded, sustaining advantages can be a distraction from developing new ones. It is like shoveling sand against the tide rather than moving on to higher ground.

Trying to sustain an existing advantage is a harvest strategy rather than a growth strategy. It is designed to milk what assets you have now rather than to seek new assets to build on. Even in high-growth markets old advantages based on old assets may not be the ones that will be the source of future success. A strategy of sustaining the advantage created by your existing assets creates a danger of complacency and gives competitors time to catch up and become strong.

The declining power of brands, described above, may be a result of firms seeking to sustain their static competitive strategies. Companies have rested upon the sustainable advantage of brand equity rather than building new advantages. Gillette's success at rebuilding its brand through the launch of the Sensor razor and Lever Brothers' success with Lever 2000 soap show the power of brands if they are coupled with a dynamic competitive strategy.

Both companies were able to shake up the status quo of their industries. Gillette introduced a technologically superior, upscale razor in a market dominated by disposables. Lever combined moisturizing, deodorizing, and antibacterial qualities into one bar of soap, crossing over the traditional divisions among products in the industry. "This proves people want new brands, especially in a category like soap that's saturated with old ideas," commented Al Ries, chairman of the marketing firm Trout & Ries, on the launch of Lever 2000.[19]

Gillette, in particular, didn't stand still after Sensor's success, but introduced a radically redesigned Sensor for women and a new line of personal care products. The company's relentless pursuit of new advantages left some observers bewildered. As the *Economist* commented in describing Gillette's launch of "a better version" of the Sensor razor in Europe: "Analysts were mystified. The original Sensor is still selling well."[20] But Gillette has learned that rather than milk its current advantage for all it is worth, it must move on to its next advantage—or its competitors will.

Attempting to sustain an old advantage can eat up resources that should be used to generate the next move, thereby inviting attack by savvy competitors who realize that complacency has set in. Sustaining advantage is effectively a defensive strategy designed to protect what a firm has. In hypercompetition the better defense is often a strong offense.

Digital Equipment Corporation tried to sustain its advantage in minicomputers. It had posted a 31 percent average growth rate from 1977 to 1982 by focusing on the minicomputer. But the company clung so tenaciously to its advantage in minicomputer technology that it failed to develop a strong position in the emerging markets for microcomputers and personal computers. As CEO Kenneth Olsen commented in a 1984 *Business Week* article, "We had six PCs in-house that we could have launched in the late '70s. But we were selling so many [Vax minicomputers], it would have been immoral to chase a new market."[21] By 1992 *Business Week* notes, DEC had "ousted" Olsen and took $3.1 billion in charges over two years, to cut 18,000 jobs and close 165 facilities.[22] Its pursuit of a sustainable advantage may have left it without the series of temporary advantages it needed to thrive in a hypercompetitive market where competitors just destroyed Digital's advantage by outmaneuvering it.

Even such a successful competitor as Matsushita, which has been cited as a paradigm of successful management and competition, stumbled in hypercompetitive markets by not moving on to new advantages. *The Wall Street Journal* reported consolidated pretax earnings in 1992 tumbled by 39 percent. *The Journal* notes, "To ensure its long-term health, what Matsushita really needs to do is start looking for new areas of growth. Yet the company traditionally has been a laggard at developing pathfinding new products with world-wide appeal. . . . Matsushita also hasn't been aggressive in developing an emerging new wave of products combining consumer electronics with computers and telecommunications, even though it produces most of the components."[23] Even for the largest and most successful of competitors, past advantages are no guarantee of future success.

The Goal Is Disruption, Not Sustaining Advantage

If companies are not seeking a sustainable competitive advantage, what is the goal of strategy in hypercompetitive environments? The primary goal of this new approach to strategy is disruption of the status quo, to seize the initiative through creating a series of temporary advantages.

If a company's goal is to sustain advantage, it tries to create an equilibrium in its industry at a point at which it has an advantage. Part I will demonstrate the futility of this approach. In hypercompetition, however, the company's goal is to disrupt the industry to create new advantages and erode those of competitors. By creating a series of these disruptions, companies can keep one step ahead of their competitors, moving from one temporary advantage to the next.

A survey of the fifty oldest U.S. companies found that they have persisted not by exploiting a single advantage but "by ceaselessly altering and renewing their technologies and products and sometimes, too, their capital structures." These oldest companies have done more than survive; they outperformed the Standard & Poor 500 in 1991. To take just one example, the oldest U.S. public company, the Dexter Corporation began as a cloth mill in 1767, moved to turning rope into wrapping paper, and then moved to producing teabags and meat casings, as well as automotive gaskets. It is now moving into new areas such as aerospace and medical fabrics.[24]

Strategies such as "stick to your knitting" and "build off your core competence" may maximize short-run performance and profitability by using the same assets over and over again. But these approaches do not provide the guidance for true long-run survival. While they may generate short-term profits, these strategies ultimately leave companies with a tired, out-dated asset base that is not adapting to the future. Instead a new approach is needed.

Seizing the Initiative with a Series of Small Steps

As competitive cycles have shortened, the need to rapidly develop new advantages has increased. It has become more important for companies to focus on generating their next advantages even before their current advantages erode. The traditional goal of strategists has been to find a grand and long-term strategy that sustains itself for years or even decades. Today this is becoming rare, if not impossible. The grand, long-term strategy is often outmaneuvered, so it rarely wins. It often takes too long to create the assets needed to pull off this grand strategy. By the time a firm has the assets in place, they are obsolete or the circumstances have changed so much that new and better alternative strategies have emerged. The days where it is possible to do five- and ten-year strategic plans are coming to an end as changes hasten. It is the rare industry where a firm can predict how technology, customers, regulation, competition will look in ten years. Even five years is difficult. In 1988, who knew that, by 1993

- Russia would be a new capitalist market?
- One of the leaders of the Japanese juggernaut, Matsushita, would stumble?
- Chrysler and Ford would reseize the initiative in the car industry?
- Cold fusion may instead be for real?

Just to name a few of the surprises over the last five years.

Instead of long-range plans and enduring competitive advantages, a succession of small, often easily duplicated strategic attacks are more typically used in rapidly changing hypercompetitive environments. By stringing together a series of these short-term advantages, the firm can effectively create a long-term sustainable advantage in the marketplace (see Figure I–2).

Both Microsoft and American Airlines have used a series of initiatives to keep bringing their customers back into the fold. Although many of these innovations have been copied by the competition, the steady stream has helped these companies succeed. If Microsoft had rested on its laurels

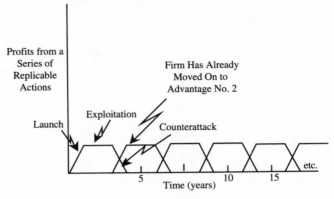

FIGURE I–2
A SERIES OF SHORT-LIVED ACTIONS ADD UP TO A
SUSTAINED ADVANTAGE

with MS-DOS in the way that Digital clung to the minicomputer, it would have been laying off employees rather than continuing to expand.

American's advantages were even more easily copied. At each stage in the development of American's strategy, competitors moved in and duplicated American's advantage. But by the time the competitors arrived on the scene, American had already built a new advantage through its next innovation. So American, even with its reservation system, has been successful through a series of nonsustainable or imitated actions. Its advantage resulted because it did them first and frequently.

These moves were not a random series of actions. Each created an advantage or disrupted the marketplace by destroying an advantage of its competitors. American seized the initiative by finding ways to serve its customers better than other carriers. It did so by identifying the business traveler as a customer for the first time, searching for new opportunities within its current markets, and shifting the rules of competition from competition on price and service to competition on perks. Each of these actions by American forced competitors onto the defensive because they had to rise to the challenge or be left behind.

OLD WAYS OF THINKING ABOUT
COMPETITIVE ADVANTAGE

To be effective in times of change, strategy must look to an industry's future. It must provide an understanding of possible moves and countermoves of rivals and offer a map of where the interactions between competitors might be headed. This requires a dynamic view of strategy.

Static models of strategy provide an invaluable set of tools for analyzing the competitive environment and position of a firm at any point in its evolution. They identify some of the key sources of advantage at a given point in time. As firms maneuver to create these advantages and erode the advantages of competitors, these static models provide important insights. However, they fail to recognize competitive advantage as a fluid and dynamic process. Advantages that worked in an industry's past only continue to work in a relatively static environment.

Static Views of Competitive Advantage

Static views of strategy attribute competitive advantage to success in four key arenas of competition. These are price and quality, timing and know-how, strongholds, and deep pockets. These arenas form the starting point for our discussion of dynamic strategic interactions and success in hypercompetitive markets.

ADVANTAGE 1: COST AND QUALITY

The simplest view of competitive advantage is that firms compete on efficiency (affecting costs and reducing price) or on product characteristics desired by customers (affecting quality and increasing price). Profits are derived from two sources: (1) minimizing costs or increasing price to increase margins or (2) increasing sales volume to improve capacity utilization and spread fixed costs over greater volume. This is a very simple accounting-based view of where profits come from.

Porter outlines three generic strategies for creating advantage that are consistent with the accountants' view of the sources of profits.[25] The first is overall cost leadership. Under this strategy, the firm stresses efficiency and reduces its costs so it can underprice and outsell competitors. This is a low-margin, high-volume strategy. The second strategy, differentiation, is to create a product with distinctive qualities that are perceived as being unique. This added quality allows the firm to sell at a premium price to customers who desire such quality and who will pay for it. The third strategy, focus, relies on segmentation of the marketplace. By concentrating on a small part of the market, the firm carves out a niche that no direct competitors serve as well, allowing the firm to sell a premium-priced product with high quality to a small but appreciative number of customers. The focus strategy is a high-margin, low-volume approach.

A more dynamic model of price-quality advantages would consider how competitors will react and maneuver around the price-quality positions that rivals stake out. It will ask, how do firms change their price-quality ratio (value to customer) or their relative positions over time to create advantage? Companies move from one position to the next and competitors respond to their moves.

In his more recent work Porter himself recognizes the instability of these generic strategies and the need for more dynamic models to explain the competitive dynamics of price and quality. In *The Competitive Advantage of Nations*, he notes that sources of price-quality advantage are constantly evolving. "The firm competing with a differentiation strategy, for example, must find a stream of new ways to add to its differentiation, or, minimally, improve its effectiveness in differentiating in old ways."[26] The creation and destruction of cost-quality advantages will be examined in Chapter 1.

ADVANTAGE 2: TIMING AND KNOW-HOW

Another model suggests that competitive advantage is based on the unique assets and knowledge of the firm, which can be used to earn "rents," or abnormal profits, by charging customers for the use of those assets and knowledge.[27] The timing (duration and growth) of these "rents" determines the value created by a firm for its shareholders.

Under this model the firm gains advantage by creating *unique* assets or knowledge of value to customers. The uniqueness of the resource allows the firm to increase its prices. If customers want its know-how or if they need its assets, they have nowhere else to go. To be unique, the firm has to be the first to develop knowledge or assets that no one else has.

This model doesn't describe how these rents decline as competitors replicate the advantage, nor does it provide an understanding of how competitors will compete and what they will do to replicate the uniqueness of an opponent's assets or knowledge. A more dynamic view recognizes that there is a big distinction between the value created for shareholders by an investment that creates a "home run" (one shot that is a very profitable effort over a long duration) versus the value created by a multiple "base hit" approach (several shots, each with its own small impact, that add up to the same stream of returns that a home run would generate), even if the net present value of the two are the same. Both the home run and the base hit approaches could produce the same overall return for shareholders. But they are very different approaches to strategy and have different effects on the firm, on competitive rivalry, and on society. The home run approach may set the company up for future failure if it is riskier and harder to execute than the base hit approach.

This dynamic process of innovation and imitation of unique assets will be examined in Chapter 2, where it will become clear that it is much harder to create a home run than a series of base hits.

ADVANTAGE 3: STRONGHOLDS

Another view of competitive advantage asserts that firms earn profits if they can restrict the number of competitors through creating a stronghold surrounded by entry barriers that block competitors out of a marketplace, industry, segment, or geographic region. Free entry leads to pure competition and lower profits. Advantage is created by raising entry barriers that exclude potential players or limit buyers and suppliers who might enter the industry through vertical integration. Porter identifies six major barriers to entry: economies of scale, product differentiation, capital requirements, switching costs, access to distribution channels, and cost disadvantages (other than scale).[28] The firm's advantage derives largely from monopolizing protected strongholds with high entry barriers.

A more dynamic view of advantage considers how strongholds are created and eroded over time. Rivals can maneuver to circumvent or overcome entry barriers. Then the incumbent firm is forced to respond to this new entrant. Porter's model provides a valuable framework for competitor analysis, but it does not lay out any view of what specific actions are likely to be undertaken. For example, if the firm increases its power over suppliers too much, what will the suppliers do? If the firm increases its power over dealers, what does the dealer alienation mean to the firm's long-run future?

While Porter's approach relies heavily on the strength of entry barriers, traditional entry barriers have become much more vulnerable to attack because of severe changes in the business environment, as will be described in Chapter 3. Trade barriers can be shifted by agreements and trading zones. Barriers such as high-tech investments can be minimized through research consortia or alliances. Economies of scale can be undermined by advances in the production process; product differentiation barriers can be undermined by rapid design cycles. A dynamic view looks at why strongholds fall or fail, and it looks at the series of moves and countermoves that result from building and breaking them, as examined in Chapter 3.

ADVANTAGE 4: DEEP POCKETS

In its simplest form the military model of competition analogizes competing firms to warring armies. It asserts that competitive advantage is derived from a larger resource base and the superior concentration of force inherent in this large resource base against a smaller foe. The larger firm can crush the smaller one by brute force since it can sustain greater losses and invest more resources in the battle for customers. This model is based on common sense and centuries of experience in fighting wars, especially wars of attrition, which are fought until the last man is left standing.

The view that bigger is better is simplistic. Every company that has deep pockets today started out as a small company. Companies change their resource levels. A relatively small company such as Honda rapidly became a giant with deep pockets. A small company may also unseat a giant through clever tactics, as PepsiCo was able to grow from a small player to rival Coca-Cola.

Bigger firms do enjoy some advantages over smaller companies, but they must use their additional resources effectively or lose them. A company with deep pockets may have more options in developing strategic interactions, but more options do not guarantee success. The building and erosion of the deep-pocket advantage will be examined in Chapter 4.

BEYOND STATIC COMPETITIVE ADVANTAGE

The theories of strategy and competitive advantage described above have been helpful in focusing the attention of managers and researchers on strategic decisions. But have they enabled managers to improve their strategic viability? As Gary Hamel and C. K. Prahalad note, strategy, as it is currently practiced, may be a distraction from real strategic action.

As "strategy" has blossomed, the competitiveness of Western companies has withered. This may be coincidence, but we think not. We believe that the application of concepts such as "strategic fit" (between resources and opportunities), "generic strategies" (low cost vs.

differentiation vs. focus), and the "strategy hierarchy" (goals, strategy, and tactics) have often abetted the process of competitive decline.[29]

Static models of strategy describe competition at one point in time. This is effective in an environment in which changes are slow and sustaining advantage is the goal. But in hypercompetition, where change is rapid and the goal is disruption, effective strategy has to have a more dynamic focus. Strategy requires a theory that pays attention to the sequential moves and countermoves of competitors over long periods of time. As competition has heated up, this dynamic interaction among competitors has become the key to competitive success. Success depends not on how the firm positions itself at a certain point in time, but on how it *acts* over long periods of time. So the shift from static thinking to dynamic focus is crucial to understanding strategy in the long run.

Michael Porter recognized this need in a 1991 speech in which he noted, "The frontiers of the strategy field lie in integrative frameworks that address the dynamics of strategy choice over time, and which help us better understand the strategy/organization interface."[30]

A dynamic view is based on three major principles. The first is that all actions are really interactions. This is examined below in the discussion of dynamic strategic interactions. The second principle is that all actions are relative. The value, risks, and effectiveness of every move must be seen in relation to the actions of competitors. The third is that competitors need to project out the long-term trends and trajectories of competitive maneuvers to see how they evolve and to understand where these actions lead. Simply looking at one or two interactions is not enough. These trajectories are examined later in this introduction.

Dynamic Strategic Interactions

In a basketball game a team's performance is much more than a composite of the stats of individual players. It is how the players understand the game and react to the opposing team that determines their scoring ability. It is a rapid series of moves and countermoves that propel the game forward.

In the discussion of strategy in the following chapters, these moves and countermoves are labeled "dynamic strategic interactions." In each dynamic strategic interaction one firm acts to gain a temporary advantage over its competitor. The competitor then responds to neutralize that advantage or to build a new advantage. The first company is forced to respond to this new action. Each interaction modifies the nature of competition between firms, often moving the industry to more intense levels of competition. Through these moves and countermoves companies attempt to disrupt the status quo in the industry to gain advantage.

The term *interactions*, as opposed to *actions*, is key to the understanding of strategy presented here. Economists have long recognized the interdependence of firms in oligopolies, industries with a small number of large players. Under such conditions the success of a strategy depends on how competitors interact. Economists, however, have overlooked the interdependency of firms in fragmented industries, those with a large number of small players. These firms are just as engaged in interactions in struggling over markets, niches, or even specific customers.

These are *dynamic* strategic interactions because, as mentioned above, these interactions evolve over long time frames. The organizations that survive and thrive over decades don't remain static. They change their position in the marketplace and undertake new initiatives or change their strategic focus to outmaneuver the competition. They maintain a flexible posture that allows them to be dynamic.

No single play will work in all situations. Instead the team with resources that allow for flexible responses and a variety of moves over the course of the whole season will most likely win. Even the specific resources needed to achieve flexibility will change over time as firms compete to become more flexible than others. Thus, dynamic competitive advantage is not due to a single item. Winning results from many nonsustainable plays. Once used, each play loses its effectiveness because it becomes known to competitors, so winning depends on having a deep bench, the imagination to invent new plays, and the flexibility to be able to carry out those plays in an unpredictable way.

Strategy Is Relative

There are no absolutes in strategy. A company's competitive position and the sustainability of its advantage are related to the moves of its competitors. For example, consider Figure I–3. Is position A the low-cost producer? The answer depends on where competitors are positioned. If competitor B is positioned in the upper right (B_1), the answer is yes. A offers the low-price–low-quality product, while B offers the premium product. If,

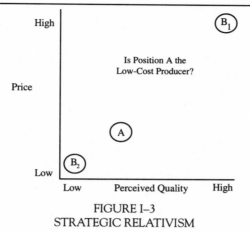

FIGURE I–3
STRATEGIC RELATIVISM

on the other hand, the competitor is in position B_2, the answer would be no. Here, A offers the premium-priced–high-quality product.

Moreover, A can become the low-cost producer without changing its strategy at all. Look what happens when B switches from position B_2 to position B_1. Without doing anything, firm A has now suffered a change in its strategic position. When Frank Perdue brought heavily advertised, premium-priced chickens into the poultry market, he transformed other branded chickens into low-cost producers. Without moving an inch, their relative position had been transformed.

This movement by competitors also affects the *sustainability* of a given strategy. Competitors' moves determine whether a given high- or low-cost position will produce profits for a long or short period of time. If competitors do not act aggressively to respond to a company's actions, then it can enjoy the competitive advantage it has gained. But if competitors act quickly to neutralize the company's advantages, then it will also have to adjust its strategy to meet these new assaults. Suppose a firm is at B_1 in Figure I–3. It looks like a premium-priced–high-quality differentiator. However, if several firms move into that position, the initial firm is no longer differentiated, and its old differentiation advantage is lost because of the relative position of its competitors.

Relativity is important because a given price-quality strategy cannot be labeled as "low cost" or "differentiated" without knowing the positions of competitors. Once labeled, the strategy still may change because of changes in the actions of competitors or in the environment. A specific advantage cannot be labeled "sustainable" without considering whether competitors will allow the advantage to be sustained.

Trajectories in Four Arenas of Competition

The strategic position of a firm is not only relative to the position of competitors, it must also be taken in the context of the historical sequence of interactions undertaken by competitors. Each action is embedded in a series of actions that can affect counterresponses in ways that are unforeseen. So it is possible to win the battle and lose the war. For example, JFK may have won the Cuban missile crisis, but the long-run effect was to motivate the Soviets to undertake the most massive buildup of nuclear arms in their history, leading to nuclear parity with the United States by the early 1970s.

The same is true in business. The traditional doctrine for business strategy is that a firm should use its competitive advantage (its strength) to attack where the competitor lacks an advantage (its weakness). Hardly anyone would disagree with this piece of common sense. Using strength against weakness is the clearest way to gain superiority in a marketplace. Only a fool would attack the strength of a competitor. Only an even bigger fool would attack with his weakness.

This doctrine is, however, faulty if one considers the dynamics of strategic interaction. Consider a tennis match between two players with strong forehands and weak backhands. Player No. 1, following traditional strategy, uses his strength (forehand) to attack his opponent's weakness (his backhand). This strategy appears to work brilliantly over the short term.

But consider what happens after two hundred volleys. Thanks to all the practice from player no. 1, player no. 2 has now improved his backhand. Player no. 1 suddenly is facing an opponent with a strong forehand *and* a strong backhand. At the same time player no. 1 has become very predictable; he will always play to his opponent's backhand. The winning strategy for the short term ultimately results in disadvantage and loss in the long run.

Now consider what happens when an American consumer electronics company uses traditional doctrine against an opponent. Each has several hundred or even a thousand products, the equivalent of numerous volleys in a tennis match. The American company learns to apply its strength against weakness and is rewarded for it in the short run. But the opponent wins the war because he builds new competitive advantages as his weaknesses are tested and rectified. Thus, it is crucially important to track the volleys between firms. Otherwise, a firm will win the battle and lose the war.

As outlined above, traditional theories of strategy define four dimensions of competitive advantage for which firms compete. These dimensions provide a useful framework for tracking the dynamic strategic interactions among competitors over long periods of time and for understanding the evolution of industries. As mentioned above, these arenas are based on competition with respect to

- cost and quality
- timing and know-how
- strongholds
- deep pockets

Part I of this book will examine in detail how each of these sources of traditional competitive advantage play out over decades, based on two years of research on hundreds of industries and considerable anecdotal evidence from extensive case studies. This section describes common patterns of moves and countermoves as competitors struggle to gain control in each of these arenas. Below is a brief outline of the trends of these moves and countermoves in each arena.

THE TREND IN THE COST AND QUALITY ARENA

The first arena is competition based on cost and quality. Product positioning can be a source of strategic advantage. Usually firms compete by offering differing levels of quality at different prices because if they all offer the same-price and -quality product, they will have created a commodity market. When quality is not a factor, firms are forced to engage in price wars because this is the only dimension in which they can compete. As hypercompetition escalates, firms use new dimensions of quality and service to differentiate themselves. Some firms try to cover all the ground between being a high-priced–high-quality differentiator and low-priced–low-quality cost leader by becoming full-line producers. For example, General Motors offers products that range from Chevys to Cadillacs, and Microsoft makes DOS, Windows, and NT software.

But competitors still have room to join the industry at the high end or low end with niche or outflanking strategies. The competition often moves to these areas. Moves into the upper and lower segments of the market then raise the top of the market or lower the bottom of it. Firms also attempt to carve out specialty markets to fill holes in the middle. The full-line competitor must respond by raising quality or lowering price. This tends to drive the costs down and quality up until the industry approaches the point of "ultimate value." This is the optimal ratio of cost and quality that can be delivered by firms seeking to offer high-quality–low-priced goods. As all firms in the industry converge on this point, advantages become increasingly difficult to develop, because all firms have the same ratio of price and quality and the same product offerings. Thus, price war ironically reemerges after a series of hypercompetitive maneuvers are played out to avoid a price war among firms that initially offered very similar products.

When American restructured its fares for "value pricing" in April 1992, lowering coach fares by as much as 38 percent, it touched off a violent price war. A month later Northwest announced a two-for-one promotion, and American responded with a 50 percent cut in fares. On the quality side companies have offered new seating arrangements and improved amenities to set themselves apart from the competition. These advantages are, of course, quickly copied by competitors. Once the cost-quality advantage is eroded, the company must move on to the next one.

THE TREND IN THE TIMING AND KNOW-HOW ARENA

One way to escape this cycle of competition on price and quality is to enter a new market or launch a new product. Timing of market entry and the know-how that allows entry form the second arena for competitive interaction. A first mover can seize control of the market but often invests heavily in establishing a product or service that can be imitated and improved upon by competitors. To foil the imitators, the first mover may create impediments to imitation. But the followers then attempt to overcome these impediments. The followers become faster at imitation, forcing the first mover to change tactics. The first mover may then use a strategy of leapfrogging innovations, building on large technological advances that require entirely new resources and know-how. This makes it harder for an imitator to develop the same resources, but eventually the imitators do catch up. This forces the first mover to seek new leapfrog moves, which become more expensive and risky with each leap.

These cycles of innovation and imitation eventually lead to a market in which the last available leapfrog move is exploited and imitated and continuing the leapfrogging strategy becomes unsustainable because the cost of the next-generation leapfrog is too high. At this point, even if a new technological leapfrog jump can be made, it takes so long that competitors have time to catch up. In addition, when imitators become very fast at imitating, the first mover doesn't have time to recapture its investment in R&D. Thus, as can be seen in the personal computer industry, technology-based first mover advantage still ends up converting what was once a market of many differentiated products into a market that is largely a price-competitive market.

Microsoft has introduced a series of new products, building on its know-how. But the costs of development continue to rise. Windows cost one hundred million dollars, and analysts expected that Microsoft's new database, Cirrus, could lose money for years because of its high costs of development.[31] American Airlines' innovations, even its computerized reservation system, have been copied by competitors. Some entrepreneurial travel agents have even reverse-engineered the data output by computer reservation systems to produce analyses of fare changes that benefit their corporate clients. This has eliminated American's listing advantage and helps customers to defeat American's efforts to manage its "yield," forcing it to come up with new innovations to stay ahead of competitors.

THE TREND IN THE STRONGHOLDS ARENA

As the move toward ultimate value and rapid imitation tends to level the playing field, competitors seek to gain advantage by creating strongholds that exclude competitors from their turf. By creating entry barriers around a stronghold in a certain geographic region, industry, or product market segment, the firms try to insulate themselves from competitive attacks based on price and quality or innovation and imitation.

While firms build entry barriers that keep others out of their markets, this tactic is rarely sustainable over the long run. Entrants eventually find ways to circumvent entry barriers. After building a war chest in their own strongholds, competitors can fund forays into the protected strongholds of others. These expeditions usually provoke a response from the attacked companies. Such responses often go beyond defensive actions in the attacked market by leading to a counterattack against the initiating firm's stronghold. These attacks and counterattacks often erode the strongholds of both players. This process can be seen on a large scale in globalized markets where huge businesses based on one continent attack the strongholds of large companies based on other continents until it becomes hard to tell whether competitors are American or Japanese (or any other nationality) anymore. As entry barriers have come down and markets integrate, the playing fields again begin to level out and the old competitive advantages provided by having a protected stronghold are no longer viable.

In launching its NT software, Microsoft is using the momentum of its stronghold in DOS operating systems to invade Novell's stronghold of networking software. Competitors are countering with their own software. Each change in systems shakes up the market boundaries. For example, the launch of Windows allowed Microsoft to gain ground in spreadsheets from market leader Lotus. The battle to invade Microsoft's core market has yet to begin, but the world has not yet seen how IBM and Apple will seek to regain the initiative from Microsoft.

American Airlines has used its stronghold in the United States to move into European markets. From 1988 to 1992, it increased its overseas revenues from 12 percent to 26 percent.[32] Although European governments have responded by trying to protect their national airlines, the European Community has begun long-haul deregulation. This promises to increase opportunities for American Airlines and other U.S. competitors. In response British Airways is seeking entry opportunities into the United States via acquisition. If this process continues, one global airline market will eventually emerge with only a few very large players dominating the trunk lines between continents.

THE TREND IN THE DEEP-POCKETS ARENA

After firms exhaust their advantages based on cost and quality, timing and know-how, and after their strongholds have fallen, they often rely upon their deep pockets. The fourth arena in which firms try to develop strategic advantage is based on financial resources. Well-endowed firms can use their brute force to bully a small competitor. These large firms have greater endurance, using their resources to wear down or undercut their opponents. But the small competitors are not completely defenseless. They can call upon government regulations, develop formal or informal alliances, or step aside to avoid competition with the deep-pocket firm. With these moves and countermoves, or even with the erosion of resources over time, the large firm eventually loses its deep-pocket advantage. When small firms build their access to resources through joint ventures or alliances, power tends to equalize and balance out, and large-scale global alliances of megacompetitors create the business equivalent of King Kong versus Godzilla. Eventually the deep-pocket advantage is neutralized.

American Airlines' deep pockets have given it an advantage in price wars with competitors, but American's size has also made it vulnerable because of the high operating costs associated with managing an older, more complex, and geographically dispersed fleet. Although much smaller than American, Southwest has a 43 percent cost advantage over its larger competitor, allowing it to continue to expand its services. Similarly, Microsoft's deep pockets, built on the profits from DOS and Windows, have been used for research to build the next generation of software, but the alliance between IBM and Apple creates a very formidable deep pocket for funding the design of the next generation of software.

THE BIG PICTURE: ESCALATION LADDERS AND HYPERCOMPETITION
Two Types of Escalation

Research of the trajectories within each arena of competition reveals two types of escalation. The first is the escalation within each arena. As outlined in the discussion of trends in each arena, moves lead to counter-moves, and the competition continues to escalate. Firms move to higher and higher levels of conflict in each arena, as if they are escalating up a ladder with each rung representing the new level of competition intro-duced by the last competitive maneuver. So, for example, firms escalate by increasing the level of quality or lowering the price of their goods. They also escalate their efforts to develop new know-how, move faster, invade or create new strongholds, and build deep pockets. Part I of the book will examine this process of escalation in each of the four arenas. It will look at the strategic insights provided by each of the four static views of competi-tive advantage, and it will consider the implications of a long-term dy-namic view of the moves and countermoves that are typically observed.

There is a second type of escalation going on as well. As described above, escalation occurs across arenas, as illustrated in Figure I–4. Compa-nies may begin competing on cost and quality until they exhaust the ad-vantages of that arena. They then move on to know-how in the second arena until the benefits of these advantages are too expensive. They then attempt to create strongholds to limit the competition, but these strong-holds are eventually breached. This leads to the use of deep pockets, wherein size is an advantage until firms deplete their resources or find alli-ances to balance off the resources of competing alliances. As discussed below, this is only one possible scenario for movement across arenas.

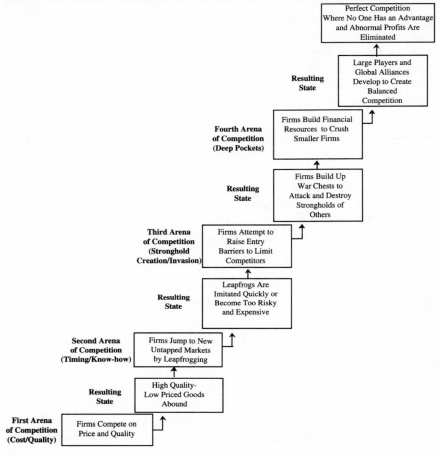

FIGURE I-4
ONE SCENARIO FOR THE ESCALATION OF CONFLICT ACROSS
ARENAS OF COMPETITION

Jumps across arenas can also be much less orderly, moving back and forth into arenas that offer the best possible opportunities for creating new advantages and seizing the initiative.

Figure 1–4 points out that the evolution of an industry makes it increasingly harder to gain and maintain strategic advantage. As firms reach the top of the figure, they approach a "perfectly competitive" market. Every firm must offer low price and high quality, so no one has the advantage. Imitation happens so rapidly that everyone offers almost the same product line, and no one has a serious first mover advantage. Firms compete to develop know-how that competitors don't have, but they find that know-how (as well as products) can be imitated. Global competition has eroded traditional strongholds, so eventually no one has the advantage of a well-protected safe haven. Finally, the deep-pocket advantage is eroded through global alliances and joint ventures until resources are no longer unequal. Firms move up the ladders one step at a time, arriving at a place where no competitor ever intended to go and no one has an advantage.

Although, for convenience, this flow is described as a sequential process, it is often much less orderly than this description would suggest. Some industries follow these patterns fairly closely, but some compete in multiple arenas and at different levels of each arena simultaneously. Some industries get stuck at one level of an escalation ladder for years, and others skip right over that level, depending upon the aggressiveness of competitors in each industry. Thus, in the real environment there is significantly more complexity. The more simplified description here is designed to emphasize relationships within and among the arenas and to stress the broader trends in competition based on these four traditional sources of competitive advantage. This is done for the sake of clarity, not to suggest that the real progression toward a perfectly competitive environment is anywhere near this predictable.

Hypercompetition: Movement toward, but Failure to Reach, Perfect Competition

As illustrated in Figure I–4, competition escalates in and across these four arenas, moving from a state of relatively less competition to a state of perfect competition wherein no player has an advantage in any of the four arenas and all firms compete on price until no one makes any profits. What this points out is that different grades or levels of competition exist in an industry over time. Figure I–5 illustrates the various levels that industries may go through.

American corporations have traditionally sought established markets wherein sustainable profits were attainable. They have done so by looking for low or moderate levels of competition. Low and moderate-intensity competition occurs if a company has a monopoly (or quasi monopoly protected by entry barriers) or if competitors implicitly or explicitly collude, allowing each other to "sustain" an advantage in one or more industries or market segments. Collusion or cooperation, while it can be useful in limiting aggressiveness, is limited because there is incentive to cheat on the collusive agreement. An aggressive player can escalate up one or more of

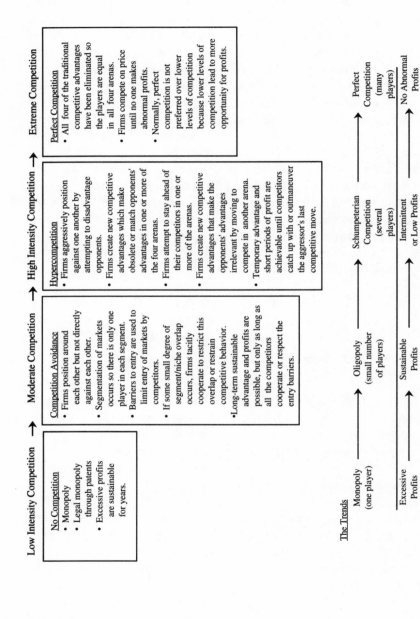

Low Intensity Competition → Moderate Competition → High Intensity Competition → Extreme Competition

No Competition
- Monopoly
- Legal monopoly through patents
- Excessive profits are sustainable for years.

Competition Avoidance
- Firms position around each other but not directly against each other.
- Segmentation of markets occurs so there is only one player in each segment.
- Barriers to entry are used to limit entry of markets by competitors.
- If some small degree of segment/niche overlap occurs, firms tacitly cooperate to restrict this overlap or restrain competitive behavior.
- Long-term sustainable advantage and profits are possible, but only as long as all the competitors cooperate or respect the entry barriers.

Hypercompetition
- Firms aggressively position against one another by attempting to disadvantage opponents.
- Firms create new competitive advantages which make obsolete or match opponents' advantages in one or more of the four arenas.
- Firms attempt to stay ahead of their competitors in one or more of the arenas.
- Firms create new competitive advantages that make the opponents' advantages irrelevant by moving to compete in another arena.
- Temporary advantage and short periods of profit are achievable until competitors catch up with or outmaneuver the aggressor's last competitive move.

Perfect Competition
- All four of the traditional competitive advantages have been eliminated so the players are equal in all four arenas.
- Firms compete on price until no one makes abnormal profits.
- Normally, perfect competition is not preferred over lower levels of competition because lower levels of competition lead to more opportunity for profits.

The Trends

Monopoly (one player) → Oligopoly (small number of players) → Schumpeterian Competition (several players) → Perfect Competition (many players)

Excessive Profits → Sustainable Profits → Intermittent or Low Profits → No Abnormal Profits

FIGURE I–5
DIFFERENT LEVELS OF COMPETITION WITHIN AN INDUSTRY

the escalation ladders in the four arenas and gain advantage. Entry and mobility barriers are destroyed by firms seeking the profit potential of industries or segments with low or moderate levels of competition. Gentlemanly agreements to stay out of each other's turf fall apart as firms learn how to break the barriers inexpensively.

As competition shifts toward higher intensity, companies begin to develop new advantages rapidly and attempt to destroy competitors' advantages. This leads to a further escalation of competition into hypercompetition, at which stage companies actively work to string together a series of temporary moves that undermine competitors in an endless cycle of jockeying for position. Just one hypercompetitive player (often from abroad) is enough to trigger this cycle.

No matter what pattern competitors follow through the escalation ladders, it is the speed and intensity of the movement that characterizes hypercompetition. At each point firms press forward to gain new advantages or tear down those of their rivals. This movement, however, takes the industry to faster and more intense levels of competition. The most interesting aspect of this movement is that, as firms maneuver and outmaneuver each other, they attempt to neutralize each other's advantage in all four arenas. This means that they are constantly pushing toward perfect competition, where no one has an advantage. However, while firms push toward perfect competition, they must attempt to avoid it because profits are not at all possible in perfectly competitive markets. In hypercompetitive markets it is possible to make temporary profits. Thus, even though perfect competition is treated as the "equilibrium" state in static economic models, it is neither a desired state nor a sustainable state from the perspective of corporations seeking profits. They would prefer low and moderate levels of competition but often settle for hypercompetitive markets because the presence of a small number of aggressive foreign corporations won't cooperate enough to allow the old, more genteel levels of competition that existed in the past; for example, the old nonaggressive competition among the Big Four U.S. car companies and planned obsolescences that existed before foreign competitors entered the U.S. market. Part II examines the nature of environments in more detail and how hypercompetition develops when the companies involved often do not desire it.

In one sense, it might seem that hypercompetition is just a faster version of traditional low- and moderate-intensity patterns of competition, but that is like saying that a hurricane is a faster form of summer breeze. The key strategies for survival and success are different. Low- and moderate-intensity competition, which is relatively static for long periods of time, is characterized by long periods of advantage disrupted infrequently by breakthroughs or actions that erode that advantage. Hypercompetition, on the other hand, is characterized by short periods of advantage punctuated by frequent disruptions. The focus thus shifts from managing advantages to effectively managing disruption.

NEW RULES FOR HYPERCOMPETITION: THE NEW 7-S'S

In hypercompetition success depends on developing a series of new advantages that disrupt (not sustain) the status quo and that cope with other firms trying to disrupt the status quo. But what is it that allows companies to rapidly and continuously identify and develop new advantages? What is it that allows them to successfully compete in hypercompetitive environments? Part III explores how firms navigate through this hypercompetitive environment by using a new set of principles, designated as the New 7-S's. These strategic principles are quite different from those of the traditional 7-S's.

The Failure of Fit: McKinsey's Old 7-S Framework

McKinsey's 7-S framework[33] says that competitive advantage arises from creating a proper "fit" among key organizational characteristics and focusing these characteristics on one purpose or mission. This requires a fit between the organization's strategy and environment as well as the proper fit among seven key internal factors. These factors are structure, strategy, systems, style, skills, staff, and superordinate goals. These 7-S's can be seen as a way to implement and create the four traditional competitive advantages (cost-quality, timing–know-how, strongholds, and deep pockets).

Fit implies a sense of permanence. It is concerned with maintaining a steady state rather than guiding the constant evolution of new advantages. It is also very predictable, making the company an easy target for competitors. If the organization is so tightly galvanized around a single objective, it can tend to make a firm less flexible and unable to change strategy or the rest of the 7-S's to meet new needs. In hypercompetition today's fit becomes obsolete and easy to outmaneuver.

Competitors can also turn the 7-S formula against the firm. When they try to outmaneuver the company, they can easily read its capabilities and weaknesses, given the current configuration of the 7-S's. Firms need to prepare for hypercompetition in an entirely different way.

The New 7-S's

Our examination of successful hypercompetitive firms revealed that many utilized some or all of a new set of approaches—the New 7-S's. These are

- superior Stakeholder Satisfaction
- Strategic Soothsaying
- positioning for Speed
- positioning for Surprise
- Shifting the rules of competition
- Signaling strategic intent
- Simultaneous and Sequential strategic thrusts

The New 7-S's are concerned with the ability of the company to create disruption, seize the initiative, and create a series of temporary advantages like those shown in Figure I–2. The first two of these S's—stakeholder focus and strategic soothsaying—are concerned with establishing a vision for how to disrupt the market. This includes setting goals, setting the firm's disruption strategy, and identifying some core competencies necessary for the firm to create specific disruptions. The second two—speed and surprise—are focused on key capabilities that can be applied across a wide array of actions intended to disrupt the status quo. The final three—shifting the rules, signaling, and simultaneous and sequential strategic thrusts—are concerned with disruptive tactics and actions in hypercompetitive environments.

Traditional strategic planning has focused only on planning moves in specific markets rather than developing new markets and new approaches. The traditional goal has been to sustain advantage rather than disrupt the market and develop a series of temporary advantages. This has led to a very different approach to strategy.

VISION: GOALS AND COMPETENCIES FOR DISRUPTION

The first two S's provide the vision and core competencies for disruption. They define the source of new advantages and ways to achieve them. Superior *stakeholder satisfaction* is the key to winning each dynamic strategic interaction with competitors. The process of developing new advantages or undermining those of competitors begins with an understanding of how to satisfy customers. By discovering ways to satisfy customers, the company can identify its next moves to seize the initiative. But customers are not the only stakeholders that must be satisfied. By empowering employees, the company can gain the internal motivation and vision needed to carry out those moves. It was American Airlines' understanding of the business traveler and its motivated work force that allowed it to create the business class and to implement its series of advantages. It was Microsoft's understanding of customers and its motivated work force that allowed it to develop Windows and other successful software systems.

Strategic soothsaying is a process of seeking out new knowledge necessary for predicting or even creating new temporary windows of opportunity that competitors will eventually enter but that are not now served by anyone else. These opportunities can be found by creatively combining products, understanding trends in the business environment that will open up new opportunities, and serving new customer markets with the existing capabilities of the firm. Microsoft's development of NT software resulted from a combination of reading current market needs and creating new opportunities, and it is already working on the next generation of operating system, Cairo, due in 1995.

These two S's differ from conventional thinking about advantage in that they argue that the source of advantage is the ability to win each dynamic strategic interaction with competitors. This is achieved by finding how to satisfy the customer in a way that is new or superior to old methods. This requires two competencies: (1) motivated, empowered workers at all levels of the organization, and (2) knowledge of the future or an ability to create the future. Together these allow the hypercompetitive firm to disrupt the market by creating new opportunities and by making old methods of serving the customer obsolete.

CAPABILITIES FOR DISRUPTION

To quickly take advantage of the vision identified by the first two S's, the company needs to develop the capability for disruption through the next two S's—*speed* and *surprise*. These capabilities can be used across a series of dynamic strategic interactions. By pre-positioning the company's organizational capabilities for speed and surprise, the firm creates the ability to react quickly to opportunities in the environment or to proactively outmaneuver competitors at every stage of the dynamic strategic interactions between companies.

Because advantages are eroded quickly, capabilities for speed and surprise are vital to seizing the initiative. Speed and surprise are needed to take advantage of opportunities, to move quickly against competitors, or to respond to a competitor's attack. Speed is also a key part of competitive advantage, because it enhances the ability to serve customers and to choose the moment in time that the firm will enter the market (e.g., as a first mover or a fast follower). Surprise is also crucial to success. The longer the first mover can delay entrance by competitors into the market by stunning them with a surprise attack, the more time there is to create a strong position and make gains before the competition responds and forces movement onto the next market, product, or new method of competing.

Competitors are becoming increasingly savvy. They are running numerous SWOT analyses (i.e., studies of the Strengths, Weaknesses, Opportunities, and Threats facing the other players in their industry) as a routine way to predict competitors' behaviors. Like radar, this awareness has made creating surprise much more difficult. The company must develop its own radar-jamming or stealth mechanisms to avoid this radar, and they must have the ability to send up decoys to throw the opponent off the track.

American's computer reservation system has given it the ability to rapidly rework its fare structures and perks for customers, surprising its competitors. Microsoft's combination of operating systems and applications programs has led to complaints that it has an inside track on new operating systems that aid its development of applications. Although the company claims it shares information about new systems with competitors, it has still managed to move quickly into new markets, gaining 60 percent of the market for applications for software that works with Windows.

These two S's suggest that advantage during each dynamic strategic interaction rests in organizational capabilities that allow firms to outmaneuver competitors by surprising or being faster than competitors are. Since firms can only create a temporary advantage with each new move to satisfy customers (according to vision created by the first two S's), firms must strike quickly and without warning as a way to keep these temporary advantages open for as long as possible.

TACTICS FOR DISRUPTION

The final three S's are concerned with tactics or punch/counterpunches used in a hypercompetitive environment. *Shifting the rules of competition* is concerned with actions that redefine the battlefield. By shifting the rules of the game, the company creates new opportunities to satisfy customers. The company finds new ways of satisfying customers that transform the industry, such as adapting the personal computer to serve the mainframe computing industry or inventing the disposable razor to transform the market for standard razors. These shifts are not always the result of technological innovations. For example, Dell's shift to mail-order sales of PCs shifted the rules in that industry. American Airlines' restructuring and simplification of its fare structures reshaped pricing in the airline industry. Microsoft's creation of Windows also shifted the rules and created new markets for applications programs that the company was ready to fill, and it changed the nature of competition between IBM-compatible personal computers and Apple systems.

Signals—verbal announcements of strategic intent—are important preludes to more powerful actions. Signals can stall the actions of competitors or create uncertainty that erodes their will to defend against attacks. They can preannounce or fake aggressive offensive moves that alter the behavior of competitors. Thus, signals can be used to disrupt the status quo and interactions between companies and thereby create an advantage. Software companies sometimes announce new systems that are years away from completion. The companies claim that these preannouncements of "vapor ware" are designed to aid applications developers. But competitors complain that preannouncements lead customers to wait for the new program rather than buy competitors' products that have made it to market more quickly.

Simultaneous and sequential strategic thrusts are the use of a series of actions designed to stun or confuse competitors, disrupting the status quo to create new advantages or erode those of competitors. Whereas traditional strategic actions have been treated one at a time, actions in hypercompetition are used in combinations that are difficult to unravel and difficult to defend against. These thrusts move on several geographic or market fronts simultaneously. By manipulating competitors' reactions using a series of simultaneous or sequential actions, they result in the initiating company's advantage. Simultaneous and sequential strategic thrusts are used by hypercompetitive firms to harass, paralyze, induce error, or block competitors.

American Airlines has used a sequential set of thrusts designed to lock in business travelers and force competitors to constantly play catch-up ball just to stay even with American. It has also used a simultaneous approach. While pinning U.S. competitors down in a battle for domestic market share, American has quietly been expanding into Europe by buying up computer reservation systems and looking for potential acquisition targets.

These three S's suggest that winning a dynamic strategic interaction has to do with how the traditional interaction between competitors is attuned to using (1) signals, (2) new competitive methods that shift the rules, and (3) simultaneous and sequential actions that manipulate or mold the actions of competitors.

Sustaining the Unsustainable: A New Form of Competitive Advantage

In sum, the only sustainable competitive advantage is based in the knowledge that these New 7-S's provide about how to manage dynamic strategic interactions with competitors. For too long, firms have defined advantage as finding ways to sustain and extend the profit plateaus in Figure I–1 by using one or more of the traditional competitive advantages. However, as this becomes increasingly more difficult due to hypercompetition, it becomes important to shift focus toward knowledge and skills relevant to

1. launching multiple unsustainable initiatives (as shown in Figure I-2) and
2. using them to outmaneuver the old competitive position of rivals by taking advantage of the dynamic and relativistic properties of strategic positioning (illustrated in Figure I–3).

Thus, in hypercompetition, the new emphasis is on using dynamic strategic interactions to neutralize the opponent's previous advantage by making it obsolete, irrelevant, or nonunique. As hypercompetition speeds up, the plateaus in Figure I–2 will get shorter in duration and lower in height. Instead of maximizing profits as the sole goal of corporations, hypercompetition will necessitate new goals, including (1) maximizing the opponents' losses while minimizing one's own losses or (2) living with low profits while aiming at maximizing market share and domestic employment to build the wealth of the nation through having high employment with significant disposable income.

Taken to its logical conclusion, hypercompetition will escalate until there is some stabilizing force in world markets, such as transnational regulations. This prospect, even if it may be considered desirable, seems unlikely at this point. In the meantime truly hypercompetitive firms will eventually compete by getting better and better at the New 7-S's until only those firms who are good at these New 7-S's survive and there is no longer any competitive advantage provided by their use. At that point the New 7-S's will become necessities for survival, and firms will have to seek a new source of advantage or live with even shorter plateaus than those shown in Figure I–2, making it even more ridiculous to set profits as the goal of the firm.

IMPLICATIONS FOR THEORY, MANAGEMENT, AND POLICY

The Twilight of Traditional Strategic Doctrines: Chivalry Is Dead

Just as the codes of chivalry are no longer effective in modern warfare, so the pursuit of sustainable advantage may be an anachronism in an age of hypercompetition. Before, rivalry often was held in check by the tacit co-operative agreements, norms of behavior, or barriers to entry that allowed dominant firms to sustain their advantage in exchange for a tacit promise not to decimate the underdog by aggressively competing to wipe it out. Today the forces that allowed companies to sustain their advantages are now rapidly eroding, and competitors are no longer as polite and well-mannered. As competitive rivalry continues to increase, companies can no longer follow the genteel traditions of the past. Chivalry is dead.

The new code of conduct is an active strategy of disrupting the status quo to create a series of unsustainable advantages. Its focus is on controlling the dynamic evolution of the industry as firms progress up the escalation ladders in each arena. Its focus is on using the New 7-S's to move forward to the next level of competition. This is not an age of defensive castles, moats, and armor. It is rather an age of cunning, speed, and surprise. It is not an age of ancestral fiefdoms but rather an age of shifting borders and the nouveau riche.

It may be hard for some to hang up the chain mail of sustainable advantage after it has appeared to serve so well through so many battles. But hypercompetition, a state in which sustainable advantages are no longer possible, is now the only level of competition that can occur. Changing technology, information availability, and globalized competitors are forcing firms to race up the escalation ladders in each of the four arenas of competition. Firms can't afford to be left behind. Just as changing technology, information, and global contact were root causes for the fall of communism, they will also cause profound changes in capitalism. Competition will differ in the 1990s and beyond. So too will the nature of competitive advantage. Welcome to the world of hypercompetition.

HYPERCOMPETITION AND ESCALATION TOWARD PERFECT COMPETITION IN FOUR ARENAS OF COMPETITION

CHAPTER 1

HOW FIRMS OUTMANEUVER COMPETITORS WITH COST-QUALITY ADVANTAGES

TRADITIONAL VIEWS OF COST-QUALITY ADVANTAGES

Cost and quality are the staples of competitive positioning. As discussed, Porter identified three generic strategies based on cost and quality advantages: overall cost leadership, differentiation, and focus strategies.[1] The cost-leadership strategy involves offering a mass-marketed, low-priced, low-quality product. The differentiation strategy involves offering a premium-priced, high-quality good, and the focus strategy targets a premium-priced product for a smaller niche audience with a special definition of what is high quality. While there has been much discussion of strategic positioning using cost and quality, this chapter offers an overview of the *process* of the evolution of this competition.

The traditional, static understanding of the relationship between cost and quality and competitive advantage is based on accounting approaches, such as those popularized by the DuPont model. According to this model, the company's return on equity (ROE) is a function of its margins, sales volume, and the financial policy of the firm. As shown in the equation below, ROE is related to (1) profits/sales (also called operating margins or return on sales, often labeled ROS), (2) volume (high sales volume given the firm's asset investment), and (3) assets/equity (which is equal to $1 - $ debt/equity, a major part of the financial policy of the firm). Thus:

$$\text{ROE} = \text{profits/equity} = \text{ROS} \times \text{sales/assets} \times (1 - \text{D/E})$$
$$\text{or (margins)} \times \text{(volume)} \times \text{(financial policy)}$$

Porter's low-cost strategy achieves profits through a high-volume, low-margin approach, while his other two strategies are low-volume, high-margin approaches to generating profitability. Under this view of competitive advantage, firms compete for the high-volume market primarily through cost improvement, and they compete for lower-volume markets primarily through quality improvements. For all three strategies profits are produced by improving margins and/or volume.

Useful Insights from the Cost-Quality View of Competitive Advantage

This view of competitive advantage has proven highly useful. Kenichi Ohmae provides an example of the kind of strategic analysis that can be done using this view. In his set of "profit diagrams" in *The Art of Strategic Thinking*,[2] he demonstrates a systematic way to look for margin- and volume-improving strategies based on cost and quality. A machine-tool company had asked him how it could improve the profitability of the products in its line. Ohmae developed a diagram to address the question of how the profitability of a certain product can be increased. The diagram outlines a series of decisions managers must make in deciding how to increase profits. For example, the first choice in raising profits is to lower product costs, increase pricing, or increase volume. If managers decide to raise prices, they can do so by raising the market price or reducing margins for distributors. Sales volume can be increased by boosting market share, expanding the market segment, or moving into new segments. Each decision thus leads to a new set of choices, and ultimately to a set of actions to boost quality or decrease cost.

In addition, Ohmae recommends assessing whether each component of a product needs to be changed, analyzed, or left alone, depending upon whether it is more or less costly and of lower or higher quality than the component used by the firm's best and fiercest competitor. Product costs and quality can be improved by changing design, reducing fixed costs, or cutting variable costs, through value analysis (VA) and value engineering (VE). Value analysis and engineering are methods of reverse-engineering the product from the perspective of both the customer and manufacturing costs. Each component of a firm's product is identified and redesigned or eliminated to reduce cost (via value engineering) or increase quality (via value analysis) to the customer. Value engineering and analysis are used whenever the components of a firm's product are inferior or too costly compared to the components of the best products in the marketplace. In sum, according to this view, advantage is created by the components contained in the product and the price and attributes of the product as a whole. Advantage is said to exist when the product offers the correct combination of price and quality. Product positioning at a given point in time matters.

Critique of Traditional View

While this analysis captures the fundamental relationship between cost and quality, it is reactive rather than proactive. The model considers competitors only to the extent that they shape market conditions and the current benchmark levels of price and quality. This view does not look at potential competitive responses and future actions in the market. Ohmae himself cautions that competitor positions should be considered. "No product is sold in the desert or on the moon; manufacturers' prices and the various competitive segments they serve are determined in a competitive environment," he warns. "What if all manufacturers in the market are producing similar high-quality products and offering them to the market at a relatively low price (i.e., with narrow profit margins)? In this case, it would be disastrous for the company to modify Product A's design in order to reduce costs . . . because the seemingly lower quality product would be driven out of the market by the low-priced, high-quality products already competing for the customer's favor."[3] But even here he is concerned primarily with current competitor positions rather than *future actions*. This analysis sees the market at one point in time rather than examining how it evolves over long periods of time. There is no dynamic aspect to the profit improvement and product component analyses suggested by Ohmae and discussed earlier.

While Porter examines some movement within industries, even he does not consider *how* cost-quality positioning evolves. He presents an extensive discussion of competitor analysis and tools for analyzing the future evolution of the industry, including product life cycles and changing buyer behaviors. But competition on cost and quality are viewed from the more static position of the generic strategies. As he notes, one of the primary risks of the generic strategies is for "the value of the strategic advantage provided by the strategy to erode with industry evolution."[4]

The Dynamic View

It is our contention that the risk posed by evolution that Porter mentions has become so great that it can no longer be considered as an afterthought to strategic thinking. Competition is so intense and markets are so dynamic and volatile that this evolution has become the dominant force in strategic action. Companies can no longer count on succeeding by choosing a generic strategy. The most important aspect of competition is, not current position, but the changes created by the dynamic interaction between rival firms. Thus the position of the firm offers only a temporary advantage. It is the firm's ability to manage a series of interactions successfully that determines the success of the company.

Over long periods of time, companies are forced to shift their cost (and price) and quality positions. Industries readjust their minimum acceptable level of quality and maximum acceptable price required to be a player in the marketplace. There are revolutions in quality that raise standards and then new revolutions that shatter those standards. There are innovations in product or process technology that drive dramatic improvements in quality or reductions in cost. These cycles of change are growing progressively shorter. Advances in information, manufacturing, and basic technology have accelerated so quickly that many processes and products now have lives of three months or less before they become obsolete.

DYNAMIC STRATEGIC INTERACTIONS AND THE ESCALATION LADDER

We begin this chapter with the most primitive of all economic situations—the case where two companies make the same product (with the same quality) and thus are forced to compete on price. We see how this simple situation escalates into price wars, then differentiated markets, then full-line producers, and then niche strategies, as competitors try to avoid the brutality of price wars. A sophisticated movement toward offering progressively higher customer value evolves. Like the force of gravity, the overall process of moves and countermoves tends to draw the industry back toward a price-competitive market after all the firms focus on imitating or outmaneuvering earlier moves. At some point everyone must move toward high quality and low cost to survive, and many firms offer the same range of product variety. Thus, the dynamics of competitive interaction cause product price and quality to cease to be opportunities for gaining advantage over competitors.

The individual players might be better off if they didn't escalate the competition toward this situation. But the dynamics of their interaction force them along this path. If one of them were to drop out of the competition, the other would gain a temporary advantage. Each one cannot trust the other to de-escalate the conflict. This course is set in motion the minute the two players step into the arena of competing on price and quality.

We have observed during our research that firms interact competitively at each step of the way so as to escalate the conflict. This series of dynamic strategic interactions defines each step or level of competition within the cost (and price)-quality arena. We will observe each dynamic strategic interaction between players, looking at how it was caused by the previous dynamic strategic interaction and at how it leads to the next level of interaction. Overall, each step moves the industry up the "escalation ladder" toward a situation in which cost and quality are no longer a source of competitive advantage.

What Is Quality?

When we discuss quality here, we are referring to "perceived quality" of consumers. This can sometimes be very close to more concrete measures of quality (all of which are defined by consumers), but for some products consumers just don't take the time to carefully assess quality, particularly for products that are low investment. Some consumers may be relatively unconcerned about costs for a product for which quality is the fundamental concern or a product such as a tube of toothpaste for which the cost is small enough not to matter much. Differences in customer perceptions can distort the broader view of price and quality presented here. Perceived quality also changes over time as customer preferences shift. A concern with automobile luxury shifts to a concern with gas mileage during the oil-strapped 1970s and then becomes an obsession with safety in the 1980s and 1990s.

From a marketing standpoint such broad approximations leave much to be desired. From an economic viewpoint the approximation of referring to "quality" as a clearly defined characteristic is one that is taken as a given in most models. We assume that there is a general standard of quality in an industry and that consumers are concerned about both price and quality. At the level of analyzing an individual company or industry, on the other hand, differences in perception of quality can be key and should be given careful consideration.

What is even more important is that these differences in the perception of quality and changes in the view of quality can be put to good use by companies searching for advantages. These quality perceptions change, and differences can provide key points of leverage in influencing the dynamic process of competition. As we will discuss in considering stakeholder satisfaction and strategic soothsaying in Part III, keeping in touch with emerging needs of customers and identifying new ways to meet those needs or emerging needs are essential strategies in hypercompetitive markets.

The First Dynamic Strategic Interaction: Price Wars

Unlike some other longer-lasting competitive moves, price changes can be very rapidly imitated, leading to all-out price wars. These conflicts can be particularly intense if the two firms have different costs, making it easier for one of them to cut prices. This encourages firms to compete by seeking cost reductions. Thus, price wars result when quality is not a factor. In Figure 1–1, if all firms are at point C, price moves downward. Price wars are not so simple, however. There are, for example, some interesting strategies for fighting price wars, which we consider below.

ALL-OUT WAR: TYLENOL'S HEADACHE

Typically a price war looks like the situation that occurred when Datril took on Tylenol in the pain reliever market. Datril offered the same-formula medicine for a lower price, capturing half of Tylenol's sales in test

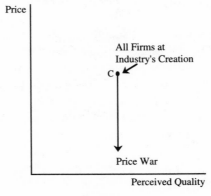

FIGURE 1–1
WHEN QUALITY ISN'T A FACTOR

markets in 1975. But Tylenol responded aggressively by lowering its price and launching its first ad campaign. Tylenol, which had as much as 37 percent of the analgesic market at one time, could fight with lower prices because of its economies of scale. As a result, Datril ended up with less than 1 percent of the market.[5] But the battle was not without damage. In the process Tylenol gave up millions in profits.

However, less aggressive alternatives are available. Competitors can use restraint, hidden price wars, and phantom price wars to avoid a head-to-head confrontation on prices.

RESTRAINT

In purely competitive markets price should fall to the marginal cost of the lowest-cost producer, who would normally be expected to expand to capture market share from higher-cost producers until it fills all of its capacity. Ultimately the lowest-cost producer should capture 100 percent of the market if he expands capacity to meet demand.

There are several reasons why industries don't always evolve this way. Antitrust regulations discourage single-player dominance in most industries. Often the low-cost producer has inadequate resources to build the capacity to cover the entire industry. Even if the firm has the resources, it might not want to take on the risk of putting all its eggs in one basket. To avoid problems of demand fluctuations such as those created by seasonality or business cycles, the company might restrict its capacity and raise its prices above its own costs, thereby leaving some market share for a second or third player. This forces some of the risk of demand fluctuations onto the higher-cost players and concedes the unattractive niches to competitors. This strategy satisfies the pressure on the low-cost producer for short-term profits and allows the company to share the market with a smaller, higher-cost player for antitrust reasons.

If the low-cost producer does not capture the entire market, the second- or third-lowest-cost producers move into this opening with goods at their higher costs. This depends on the capacity of the next two or three players compared to the demand for the product beyond what is fulfilled by the lowest-cost player in the industry. In such cases, the small number of competitors makes it easy for firms to tacitly collude to keep prices up. The low-cost producer may raise his price to the cost of the second- or third-low-cost producer. This keeps everyone happy, except the customer. Of course, this collusion has to be implicit, because an explicit agreement would violate antitrust laws.

HIDDEN PRICE WARS

If, as suggested by our discussion of restraint, prices in the industry have equalized at a point above the costs of the lowest-cost producer, this allows room for more subtle price wars: disguised price wars and phantom price wars.

In *disguised price wars*, financing, installation and repair services, or re-placement parts can be used to adjust the final price of the product up or down without changing its initial offering price. The initial price is kept high, but the company offers incentives that reduce the actual price. This might be an airline that provides frequent-flier points, an automaker offer-ing zero-percent financing, or a manufacturer who provides lower-cost re-placement parts or a better delivery schedule to cut the buyer's inventory costs.

In *phantom price wars*, the initial price is kept low, but it is made up for by higher prices for using the product. For example, a car may have a low sticker price but high costs for replacement parts and maintenance, or Polaroid may offer lower instant camera prices but higher film costs than Kodak, or vice versa.

These strategies often create switching costs for the customer. Cus-tomers with frequent-flier points, trade-in allowances, or a design based on nonstandard replacement parts will be less price sensitive on their second purchases. The features that link the customers to the original supplier raise the perceived value of the product. This begins to shift the focus of competition from price to quality and service.

THE PERILS OF PRICE WARS

There is a strong incentive to move away from price wars. As we saw in Tylenol's battle with Datril, price wars are brutal. They are the economic equivalent of the game of holding one's breath to see who turns blue first. The individual with the greatest lung capacity wins, but both end up weakened and exhausted. (See Chapter 4 on deep pockets for more about this aspect of dynamic strategic interaction.)

Price wars produce profits only if costs are kept well below the price during the war. The war can generate big losses because, once the weak firms are driven out of the market by a price war, the survivors often can't recapture losses created by the war by raising prices after the war is over. If customers have no brand loyalty and no switching costs (sunk capital or personal investments related to the product that are lost if the customer changes products), any subsequent increase in price will lead to defections.

In addition, it is often hard to contain the losses from a price war once one has begun. Seizing and holding market share is crucial for gaining economies of scale and to spread out fixed costs over a large volume. So all firms will try to keep their prices at the lowest possible levels to gain economies of scale to further lower their costs. However, this squeezes profit margins in the short run. The squeeze isn't too bad when the demand is greater than industry capacity, but it can be severe, leading to huge losses, when the demand drops below industry capacity.

This puts the company involved in price-competitive markets at the mercy of fluctuations in demand. When demand declines, the price war will worsen and a shakeout often occurs. This is not a favorable situation for the long-term success of most firms. It drives many firms to seek a higher level of competition—on both price and quality—thereby escalating the conflict one more notch on the escalation ladder.

The Second Dynamic Strategic Interaction: Quality and Price Positioning

GENERIC STRATEGIES EVOLVE

To escape the price war, companies differentiate themselves by quality as well as by price. Some firms move from point C in Figure 1–2 to what Porter calls the low-cost producer position (L), offering a lower price and a lower-quality product. Others become what Porter calls differentiators

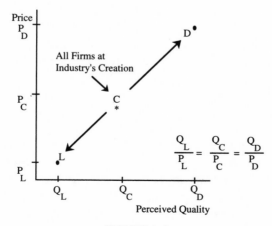

FIGURE 1–2
GENERIC STRATEGIES

(position D), offering a product with a premium price and higher perceived quality.

As shown in Figure 1–2, the value (quality-price ratio) remains constant across the high and low ends of the line in the graph. The low-cost producer and differentiator firms serve fundamentally different groups of customers, but they offer similar value in the sense that customers get the level of quality they are willing to pay for.

For commodity products, the movement to D and L may seem impossible. It would appear that these industries should stay locked in perpetual price wars. But in most commodity industries, such as steel and paper, resourceful organizations have found ways to differentiate their products based on quality or service. While traditional U.S. and Japanese steelmakers wrestled to cut the costs of their products, the U.S. minimills quietly changed the rules of the game. The minis can produce specialty steels from scrap metal much more quickly and cheaply than the large steel mills. Advances in technology that improved the output of these small mills have made them a more serious threat to the large U.S. mills than the Japanese. From 1980 to 1990, their share of the domestic market has risen from 28 percent to 37 percent.[6]

Through downstream vertical integration Kimberly-Clark transformed itself from a lumber and paper company into a consumer-products company. It differentiated specific brands of bathroom tissues, sanitary napkins, and disposable diapers. The company moved out of the price wars in the commodity paper and pulp industry into more stable markets where it could compete on both quality and price.

The desirability of each position (L vs. D) depends on the number of firms that move into each position, the size of the customer base desiring products at that price-quality level, the ability of others to enter the market segment later, and changes in the economy or demographics that might shift customer preferences from high- to low-priced goods or vice versa.

WITHIN-SEGMENT POSITIONING

Once these positions are staked out clearly, a new form of competition results. If there is more than one firm at each position, there can be smaller price and/or quality skirmishes at each position. The value (ratio of quality to price) offered by groups of firms within each position could vary, so some customers may start moving toward the firm that offers the higher

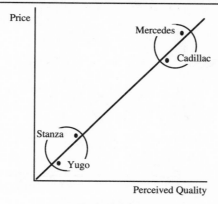

FIGURE 1–3
WITHIN-SEGMENT COMPETITION

value at that position. For example, within the luxury car segment of the auto market, the differentiator position, there are many competing manufacturers offering various combinations of price and quality. As indicated in Figure 1–3, within the differentiator position of the larger industry, some customers might perceive Mercedes as the differentiator compared to Cadillac's position. Within the low-cost producers, some customers might perceive Nissan's Stanza as a differentiator compared with Yugo.

BETWEEN-SEGMENT POSITIONING

Thus, the battle shifts to price and quality differentiation within each segment. However, this type of competition can escalate to even higher levels—competition between segments. This occurs in two ways. Either the distance between L and D can be reduced so that the two segments overlap (as shown in Figure 1–4) or the value offered by L or D can be improved (as shown in Figures 1–5a and 1–5b). The first method allows L to siphon off the low end of D's market or D to siphon off the high end of L's market. The second method forces (1) low-end consumers to decide whether they want to pay the lowest total price or get the highest value (quality per dollar) for their money (Figure 1–5a) and (2) high-end consumers to decide whether they want to buy the highest-overall-quality product or get the highest value (quality per dollar) for their money (Figure 1–5b). Thus, the next rung in the escalation ladder is reached by gradual extension of the methods used in the war on price and quality within each segment.

FIGURE 1–4
SEGMENT OVERLAP

The Third Dynamic Strategic Interaction: The Middle Path

BEING IN THE MIDDLE

The simplest way to outmaneuver firms at D or L is to try to move into the middle position (position M in Figure 1–6). This is not such a bad spot to be in, as long as the company can offer the same value as D and L. It can then draw away some of their customers, both low-end customers seeking slightly higher quality and high-end customers seeking slightly lower prices. As long as the overall value remains the same, customers are often willing to make some movement down or up along the constant value line shown in Figure 1–6. This suggests that being in the middle can be perilous

FIGURE 1–5A
DIFFERENTIATOR IMPROVES
VALUE

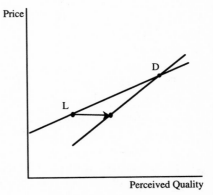

FIGURE 1–5B
LOW-COST PRODUCER IMPROVES
VALUE

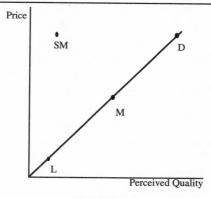

FIGURE 1–6
STUCK IN THE MIDDLE VS. BEING
IN THE MIDDLE

if it overlaps too much with the firms staking out the L and D positions. If provoked, firms in positions L and D may launch a two-front attack on firms in position M and squeeze it from both sides.

BEING STUCK IN THE MIDDLE

In contrast to being in the middle, a firm can be in even more trouble if it is positioned at SM in Figure 1–6. If the company is at point SM, at a lower value ratio, it will have a harder time competing, since it will be what Porter calls "stuck in the middle." The company may be able to carve out a niche for itself as a high-cost, low-quality player if it serves a niche that no one else is currently selling to or if it can offer something unique—like service or convenience—that compensates for the lower perceived quality of the product itself. But it is unlikely that it will survive at this point over the long haul unless it finds a way to make up for the high price of its low-quality goods with some unique service or attribute for a specialized niche of customers. Most customers will ask themselves why they should buy from SM when they can get higher quality at the same price from D or get the same quality for a lower price from L. In most cases only a few customers want the unique service or convenience of SM enough to trade off cost or quality. If SM can move to point M, with the same value ratio as the two extreme players, it has a better chance of staking out a viable segment of the market.

As noted above, the M position could provoke a response from D (who might reduce price) or from L (who might raise quality) to squeeze M out of the market. Thus, the M position can be unstable unless D and L are so far away in price and quality that they are in segments of the market that are not threatened by M. (For example, if L is a VW Beetle and D is a Rolls Royce, there is plenty of room for a Buick to stake out position M.) Even if M is not a defensible position, it might be a good offensive move. It disrupts the original positions of D and L and costs them money, perhaps even forcing D and L to move out of their original positions to make room for a determined, aggressive firm staking out position M. This strategy is also expensive for M and probably requires either deep pockets or a weak adversary to make it work.

If the distance between D and L is large, then there will be a hole in the middle where a new entrant can make inroads or a current player can move. If the distance between D and L is small, on the other hand, entrants can attack by outflanking at the high end or low end of the market. So whichever position competitors D and L take can be outmaneuvered, as we will see in the next two dynamic strategic interactions.

The Fourth Dynamic Strategic Interaction: Cover All Niches

A GIANT MAKER: THE FULL-LINE PRODUCER STRATEGY

Because of this threat of entry at the middle of the market, which would require costly defensive moves, companies such as D and L often try to protect themselves against this type of attack. This escalates the level of competition from battling over the positions of individual products to competing as full-line producers. Food companies, for example, have attempted to fill up the breakfast cereals market with numerous brands to fill all the niches, making it hard for anyone to enter the market with sufficient economies of scale by squeezing into the small remaining niches between existing brands. Again, the last dynamic strategic interaction (moving into the middle) causes an escalation by forcing firms to gain access to more of the market to make it harder for new entrants to find a niche in the middle.

General Motors was one of the originators of the full-line strategy. Customers can start with a Chevy and, as their income increases, move up through Pontiacs, Buicks, and Oldsmobiles to Cadillacs (see Figure 1–7). IBM also took this approach with its System/360 series in 1964, the first family of compatible computers that spanned the market from the high end to the low end. Six compatible processors were in the family, the biggest of which was fifty times faster than the smallest. And the company

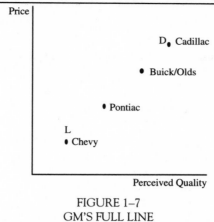

FIGURE 1–7
GM'S FULL LINE

continued to add more models to the line over the years. The 360 series set the standard for the industry for decades after its launch. Both GM and IBM serviced customers over their lifetime by encouraging trade-up to higher-and-higher-priced products. This full-line producer strategy has been so successful that it has built some of the largest firms (like GM and IBM) in the world.

DIFFICULTIES WITH FULL-LINE PRODUCER STRATEGIES

While there are obvious advantages to this approach, this strategy, like all others, is open to being outmaneuvered. In most industries firms cannot span the entire price-quality continuum, and customers don't trade up. There are, instead, distinct market segments with completely different critical success factors. In breakfast cereals, for example, the all-natural healthy breakfast segment opened up, allowing entry to segments that very few of the existing brands covered. In addition, in some industries, applying the same company name to a wide range of products can cause a confused image among consumers, as some lines of hotels are finding. For example, the use of a hotel's name on low-end inns has tainted the high end of the hotel chain, while the low-end inns aren't perceived as low-priced because of the high-end hotel name. Often this problem can be solved by applying different brand names to different segments of the market, as Honda did for its highest-end product, Acura. However, it is often difficult to be both a low-cost producer and a differentiator at the same time. It may be impossible, for example, to be both a low-cost producer of mass-merchandised chain saws for casual users while still providing the high-overhead services demanded by the professional end of the market. The casual market requires simple saws with a short useful life (approximately one hundred to two hundred hours of use over a lifetime). The professional market requires complex, powerful saws to cut down a wide variety of trees and useful lives of several thousand hours. Manufacturing methods and distribution outlets are so entirely different for the two markets that they would have to be done by entirely different subunits of the company, each recognizing the completely different critical success factors relevant to the segments.

The Fifth Dynamic Strategic Interaction: Outflanking and Niching

FILLING IN THE HOLES

Even when it is possible to pursue a full-line strategy, covering the market does not always prevent entry by competitors. While the full-line producer is forced to look at the big picture, smaller players can enter by focusing on small segments of the market. If there is sufficient room for growth within a single market segment, some companies may decide to stake out that point on the price-quality continuum and concede other positions to full-line competitors. Others will go to the extremes of the market, targeting the high end or low end not covered by the full-line producer.

Apple moved into the low end of the computer market with its personal computer, ultimately threatening IBM's position as a full-line mainframe producer. Big Blue also faced competition from smaller companies that carved out niches in mainframe markets. Finally, it was taken on in price on its own personal computer by a host of low-cost clone makers. IBM saw its hold on the world computer market drop from around 30 percent in 1985 to 21 percent in 1990, according to *Management Today*.[7] Similarly, Japanese automakers moved in on the low end of the U.S. auto market, starting below the low end of GM's line. They then moved up. More recently, Japanese automakers have seized the high end of the U.S. auto market (staking out ground just above GM's Cadillac but below the cost of foreign imports).

CREEPING UP AND DOWN

While niching and outflanking competitors are not a tremendous threat to the full-line producers at the outset, in the long run they can spread across the market like a forest fire, as was the case in the U.S. auto market. By

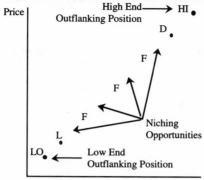

L = traditional low-cost producer position
H = traditional differentiator position
F = full-line producer's other products

FIGURE 1–8
TYPICAL ENTRY BY OUTFLANKING
AND/OR NICHING

establishing themselves in a small segment, they can move out to take over progressively larger portions of the market.

Competitors can either enter high and move down or enter low and move up (see Figure 1–8). They can also grab up any unoccupied space in the middle of the market. Large companies lose interest in these niche segments when they become too small to be profitable. Even then, smaller companies can still move in and make a profit in these niches. Eventually they can also become full-line producers as they fill in all the holes.

Some companies cannot or do not move out of their niche. For example, when Mercedes entered the U.S. auto market, it remained at the high end. BMW, Volvo, and Saab, on the other hand, entered at the high end and crept down, some more so than others.

At the opposite end of the spectrum, Volkswagen created and dominated the subcompact market with its Beetle but had trouble creeping up. The Rabbit took a nosedive, and VW's market share fell from 7.2 percent in 1970 to 2.6 percent in 1983.[8] Amidst rising costs and concerns about quality, VW was initially swept away by a wave of competitors who had entered the low-end niche with newer and less-expensive, high-mileage cars. These manufacturers, many of them Japanese, then proceeded to move up to higher ends of the market. Thus, VW's upward move was hindered more by implementation errors than by a weakness in the essential strategy.

Another example of high-end outflanking can be seen in the disposable diaper wars, as shown in Figure 1–9. (Perceived quality is noted in this

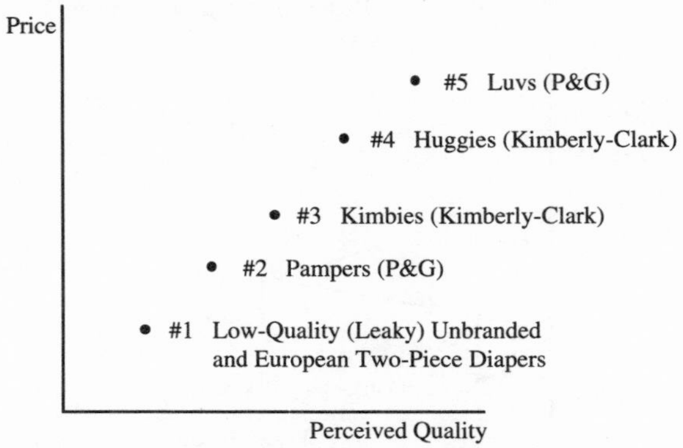

Price

• #5 Luvs (P&G)

• #4 Huggies (Kimberly-Clark)

• #3 Kimbies (Kimberly-Clark)

• #2 Pampers (P&G)

• #1 Low-Quality (Leaky) Unbranded
and European Two-Piece Diapers

Perceived Quality

Note: The numbers indicate order of entry.

FIGURE 1–9
CREEPING UP THE LINE IN DIAPERS

figure for illustrative purposes rather than as a reflection of a formal evaluation of consumer perceptions.) Procter & Gamble defined the market in 1961 with the introduction of Pampers, defeating several European-style two-piece diapers and unbranded low quality (leaky) diapers being tested in the U.S. market. Seven years later, Kimberly-Clark entered the market with Kimbies and quickly snatched 20 percent of the market share with its innovative designs, according to *The Wall Street Journal*.[9] But Kimberly-Clark rested on its laurels and shifted its focus away from innovation, allowing P&G's quality to catch up with Kimbies. Its sales plummeted, and the company debated whether to stay in the disposable market.[10] Kimberly-Clark staged a comeback in 1978, moving up in both price and quality with the introduction of Huggies. Two years later, Procter & Gamble followed suit with the introduction of Luvs. Luvs and Huggies fought for the same piece of the market. They continue to jockey for position in the market, constantly raising the upper end of the market by adding new features. In 1989, when Luvs introduced separate diapers for boys and girls, it surged past Huggies Supertrim to become the number one brand in food store sales. When Huggies got Muppet Babies, Luvs found Sesame Street baby characters.[11] The latest innovation has been diapers designed for specific stages in the child's development. There has also been recent competition on reducing environmental impact, resulting in competition to reduce waste.

At the same time, these diaper makers have increased the quality of the low end of the market by selling their excess capacity to generic brands distributed through supermarket chains. In addition, product features are often imitated and leakage is no longer a problem for the unbranded, low-end diapers. This has allowed these low-cost producers to move toward higher quality (i.e., the lower right-hand corner of Figure 1–9), making the whole market more price competitive. In response P&G and Kimberly-Clark are using heavy marketing of their diapers and the ceaseless introduction of new features. This has slowed, but not eliminated, this movement toward a commodity market.

The Sixth Dynamic Strategic Interaction: The Move toward Ultimate Value

Some of the new products designed to niche or outflank existing products carve out niches that overlap with those of existing competitors. Some firms creep up or down to consume more of the market from the full-line producer. This forces the existing competitors to respond by offering better values to the customers by lowering price, raising quality, or both. In addition, the aggressive firms find that it can be difficult to simply move up or down into the markets of the full-line producers unless they can offer either better quality or lower price than the full-line producers. This leads to the next dynamic strategic interaction: the move toward ultimate value.

Ultimate value is what economists refer to as "perfect competition," the point at which all players are driven down to similar levels of price and quality and no one has any competitive advantage. Competitors in some industries never reach this point, even though they are continually moving in the direction of lower costs and higher quality. Other industries arrive there briefly and then move off by restarting the cycle of competition or jumping to another one of the four arenas. Others freeze there for years if the firms hit the theoretical envelope for quality and cost improvement and if the firms are not very clever about how to move that envelope.

While the average competitor fights for niches along a common ratio of price and value ("You get what you pay for"), innovative firms can enter the market by providing better value to the customer ("You get more than what you pay for"). These companies offer lower cost *and* higher quality than their competitors (see Figure 1–10). This shift in value is like lowering the stick while dancing the limbo. All the competitors have to do the same dance with tighter constraints on both costs and quality.

For example, when Honda and other Japanese automakers brought a quality revolution to the auto industry, they redefined the levels of cost and quality in the field. American car companies were forced to redirect

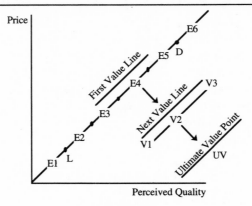

FIGURE 1–10
THE MOVE TOWARD OFFERING
ULTIMATE VALUE

their efforts to generating higher quality and slashing prices, either directly or through rebates. It brought them to a new and more intense level of competition.

The disposable diaper market is also moving in the same direction. As the market gets more price competitive, it is also moving toward higher levels of quality (less leakage, greater absorbency, greater thinness, etc.). The products are offering higher and higher value to customers as the competition between firms gets heated. As incremental product improvements are becoming more marginal, quality differences are disappearing between brands (because *everyone* offers high quality). But the competitors continue to make these incremental improvements as a means of gaining a temporary advantage.

This move toward higher value (lower-price, high-quality products) continues to approach the point UV on Figure 1–10, ultimate value. This UV position makes all other positions unviable. UV offers better quality for the same low price to customers seeking low prices, and it offers a lower price for the same high quality for those seeking quality. To survive, other firms are forced to move toward the UV point by lowering their prices and raising quality. This movement has been speeded up by practices such as the benchmarking of best-in-class competitors. Over time, the market becomes commodity-like when all firms evolve to the same low price and high quality position.

Of course, as we have noted, not all industries can be reduced to a single point of ultimate value. It seems very unlikely, no matter what technological advances are made in car production, that the auto industry would become a commodity-like industry. But a growing emphasis on quality in that industry has caused the line of competition to shift toward a position of ultimate value within each segment of the market. The segments may still fall along a line with a high end and a low end, but all producers along the way will offer a much better ratio of price and quality. Moreover, the line will continue to move toward the ultimate value corner of the graph (Figure 1–10), and many manufacturers will offer similar lines. At each step of the process, competitors seek a temporary advantage with new price and quality initiatives. Thus, the process of competition forces firms to offer a line of high-quality, low-priced goods that eventually make high quality and lower prices a *necessity* for survival. Competitive advantage is not created by price-quality positioning when this occurs.

Sometimes companies stop at what appears to be a point of ultimate value when they hit a technological barrier that prevents them from lowering cost or increasing quality. This allows other firms to catch up and creates an environment similar to perfect competition. But this situation is sometimes eroded after a period of time either by a technological breakthrough or through the application of new approaches to the product or service that restarts the movement toward UV. Whether the process of movement stops or continues, at some point in time everyone loses the ability to win by competing along the price and quality dimensions because differences between competitors become smaller and smaller. They also become harder and harder to achieve.

REVOLUTIONARY JUMPS TO THE ULTIMATE-VALUE POSITION

Sometimes the movement toward ultimate value occurs in a brief flash because of a single technological innovation, such as Pilkington's development of a new process for producing plate glass.

Before Pilkington's introduction of this technology, which floated a ribbon of glass on a bath of molten tin, glass purchasers had a choice between low-cost, low-quality sheet glass and high-cost, high-quality plate glass. The sheet glass was too crude to be used for such applications as shop windows, cars, and mirrors. Plate glass was made by grinding down sheet glass to make it smoother, but this was a very expensive and time-consuming process.

The development of Pilkington's new float process in the late 1950s transformed the industry. And Pilkington moved from being a participant in the sleepy world glass industry to being the largest glass manufacturer in the world, selling its products in more than thirty-three countries around the globe. It also exported its technology. Because of the high cost of developing the new process, Pilkington licensed the process to its competitors, and it soon became the standard for the industry, making the flat glass industry more of a one-segment commodity market offering only low-cost, high-quality flat glass.

This controversial strategy of giving away its advantage to its competitors generated substantial income for Pilkington, helping to assure its continued technological leadership in the industry for decades. Thus, one method for moving toward the ultimate value position is to look for revolutionary process innovations that simultaneously raise quality and lower price. As we will examine in Chapter 2, even technological innovations that increase quality and lower cost provide only a temporary advantage. Even if the innovator does not license the new process as Pilkington did, other competitors will eventually catch up or surpass this level of quality and cost, restarting the competition at a higher level.

TWO-STAGE MARCHES TOWARD ULTIMATE VALUE

Not all moves toward ultimate value occur with the rapidity of Pilkington's transformation of the flat glass market. It is hard to transform both price and quality at the same time (unless the company can use a process innovation such as Pilkington's). Improvements in quality very often strain costs, and reductions in price very often strain quality. Usually companies move from M to D or L, concentrating on cost or quality first, and then proceed toward ultimate value.

Whereas Pilkington's process innovation transformed both quality and price simultaneously in the industry, slower strategies call for a two-step process in changing these two factors. These two-step processes can work in two directions. The first approach is for the company to enter with a low quality and low price and then raise its quality, raising value while keeping price constant. The second approach is to enter with a high quality and high price and then lower costs and prices, raising value while holding quality constant.

When Toyota and Nissan entered the U.S. auto market, they were first low-cost producers. As they continued to lower their costs, they could then reinvest their profits to raise quality without raising price. This way they moved to a higher value point. Similarly, Gallo entered the wine industry with low-cost wines, then made incremental improvements to move to more upscale wines at popular prices, offering better and better value.

Another approach is to enter as a differentiator at the high end of the spectrum. Keeping quality high, the firm then reinvests profits to lower its costs and price. This also moves the industry toward a position of higher value.

DRIFTING TOWARD ULTIMATE VALUE

Some industries take neither a dramatic nor a steady, strategic route to ultimate value. They simply move toward it by a gradual drift. This even happens in industries that have reached an equilibrium, with low-cost producers staking out the low end, differentiators staking out the high end, and fringe players focusing on small segments in between.

Even in this apparent steady state, dynamic strategic interactions continue to work beneath the surface to move the segment toward higher value. The interactions within each segment create pressures for higher value. The low-cost producers try to outposition other low-cost producers. The winner is the one that can offer the highest quality for the lowest price. At the high end the differentiators continue to jockey for position, lowering price or raising quality, moving toward higher value. The pressures from these two small sets of interactions tend to move the entire industry toward the ultimate value point.

We can see this drift toward ultimate value in the competition among fast-food hamburger restaurants, as shown in Figure 1–11. As the industry emerged, McDonald's was at the lower end of the cost-quality spectrum, offering low-priced, moderate-quality food. Burger King raised the quality a notch by offering custom-made burgers ("have it your way") that were flame-broiled. Wendy's, and others, later entered with larger portions, salad bars, and higher quality at higher prices. (Of course, there are high- and low-end nichers in the fast-food hamburger industry, but we consider three to simplify this discussion.)

If McDonald's, Burger King, and Wendy's had originally positioned themselves at points far enough apart (points M1, B1 and W1 on Figure 1–11) so that they had their own separate niches, there might have been no "burger wars." But each firm's niche overlapped, so they competed for customers "on the margin," i.e., those who might switch between the competitors. So McDonald's, in response to the "have it your way" campaign, took on Burger King by offering more customization and variety without long waits, moving to M2. This variety was heightened with the entry of Wendy's and others who offered salads, chili, baked potatoes, and other goodies. By improving customization and product variety, McDonald's increased its overall quality. Burger King, competing directly with McDonald's on price, dropped price and increased variety to offer higher

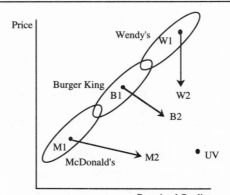

Note: The numbers indicate initial position
and subsequent movement.

FIGURE 1-11
THE DRIFT TOWARD ULTIMATE
VALUE IN FAST-FOOD HAMBURGER
INDUSTRY

quality, moving to B2. Wendy's, after establishing its quality leadership, moved to offering ninety-nine-cent value items and other strategies for reducing price, moving to W2. This process of dynamic strategic interaction has pushed the three restaurants toward the point of ultimate value. Although there are value distinctions among the three competitors, they act more and more like direct competitors in one niche.

In industries such as fast food, the point of ultimate value is not really a point. It is a direction that all firms constantly strive for because, in some circumstances, human ingenuity can constantly create new ways to move to higher levels of value. This is the concept behind Kaizen, the Japanese ideal of continuous quality improvement. Perfect competition still results in this situation, especially when all the competition is moving uniformly toward that point at the same rate. As long as no one has a substantial lead, high quality and low cost positioning provides no advantage. They become, however, necessities for survival.

The Seventh Dynamic Strategic Interaction: Escaping from the Ultimate Value Marketplace by Restarting the Cycle

As industries move toward ultimate value, profits are squeezed and competition intensifies. Competitors who are far from the UV point are doomed.

They can provide neither higher quality nor lower prices. As soon as customers discover this, these firms are history. The players that remain are battling for a single position, a small island of success. Price-quality positioning has led the industry back to a perfectly competitive, commodity-like market, where quality is a necessity, not a source of advantage.

Competitors begin to look for ways to escape from their profitless efforts. There are a variety of options for breaking free, but most of these options throw competitors into a new, more competitive cycle. Among the options are the following:

1. Shifting the graph: A company can shift the entire graph so that the UV position is either the low-cost producer or differentiator. By moving the benchmark for good quality or reasonable price, they make the UV point the middle or low or high end of the price-quality continuum. Then the cycle of cost-quality maneuvering begins again because a new value line is created. See Figure 1–12 for an example of creating a new differentiator position.
2. Redefining perceived quality: By changing the definition of perceived quality, a company can redefine the graph and create a new point of ultimate value. For example, quality in the auto industry shifted during the gas crisis to fuel economy but has now been redefined as safety and comfort. Again, this restarts the cycle of cost-quality maneuvering, using the new dimensions of quality.

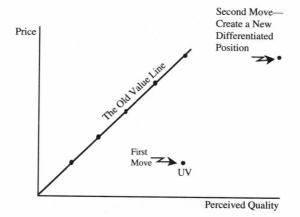

FIGURE 1–12
SHIFTING THE GRAPH TO
OUTMANEUVER FIRMS OFFERING
THE VALUE PRODUCT

3. Shift from product to service: One way to redefine product quality is to make service a key component of overall quality. The product-service bundle increases the value to the customer. In the early 1980s IBM made this shift in focus from making machines to providing software and high levels of service to customers. Intel used the better service offered by designing customized microchips to add value to its products. Again, this restarts the cycle of cost-quality maneuvering, using the new service dimensions to define quality.

4. Micromarketing and masscustomization: With advances in computing technology such as CAD/CAM and flexible manufacturing, companies can quickly tailor their product to many different customer needs. This provides virtually unlimited product differentiation. Again, product variety enhances the quality of the firm's overall offerings. This also restarts the cost-quality cycle from scratch.

The problem with all these approaches is that they are imitable and restart the cycle of the first six dynamic strategic interactions. And once all competitors have implemented them, they no longer provide any advantage. Moreover, the competitors are forced to escalate from lower levels to higher levels of competitiveness to keep from being left behind.

BEYOND COST AND QUALITY: NO PRODUCT POSITIONING ADVANTAGE IS SUSTAINABLE

Sometimes, when this point of ultimate value is reached, firms may turn to one of two strategies that abandon the market because the market seems too competitive to be profitable.

1. Product-line extensions: Just as service can enhance product quality, companies can also add new products to fill in excess distribution capacity. For example, McDonald's has gone into related items, such as breakfasts, chicken, and salads, and is experimenting with ribs and other items. Anheuser-Busch added Eagle Snacks to fill its beer-distribution capacity, and P&G continues to add new personal-care products to its product line so that it can serve its supermarket customers with a broader line. Thus, product variety becomes a new form of quality in the firm's overall offerings by providing customers more choices and options. A customer who perceives a high-quality meal as

a salad rather than a burger is offered high quality by this increase in variety.

2. Flight: When the going gets tough, one option is to move into a completely new industry or niche that is not so far down on the cost-quality competitive cycle. This option, which we will discuss in greater detail in the next chapter, gives the company more maneuvering room.

Ultimately, no cost-based price and quality advantage is sustainable. No matter how one defines quality (even if it contains a servicelike custom design or micromarketing methods), the cost-quality cycle will repeat itself. Each dynamic strategic interaction provides a firm with a temporary advantage, but it also forces the rest of the market to become more competitive. To break from the cycle of price wars, companies move toward price-quality competition. They then move toward covering all niches, which leads to outflanking and niching strategies by competitors. These dynamic strategic interactions push the industry toward providing products of ultimate value to the customer, making the industry more price competitive. Then new definitions of the product and quality appear, setting off a new cycle of dynamic strategic interactions (see Figure 1–13).

Although we portray this cycle as sequential, it may also be parallel. Two or three definitions of quality may be used at the same time. Also, some companies may skip steps along this ladder or be frozen at one rung temporarily. Firms proceed up the ladder at different speeds, depending upon the aggressiveness and quirks of the competitors in the industry and the potential for finding new types of quality and improving on old levels of quality and market characteristics. Nevertheless, this escalation ladder (illustrated in Figure 1–13) defines the rungs in the process and shows how one dynamic strategic interaction leads to the next. But competitors will climb up this ladder in many different ways.

HYPERCOMPETITIVE BEHAVIOR IN THE COST-QUALITY ARENA

Hypercompetitive firms attempt to (1) stay ahead of competitors who are attempting to catch up to or overtake them on the escalation ladder and (2) slow down competitors' efforts to overtake them without slowing down their own advancement up the escalation ladders. These hypercompetitive actions are efforts to avoid perfect competition (where

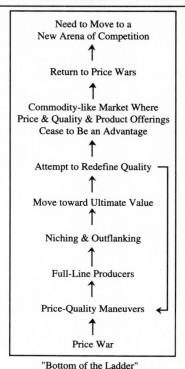

FIGURE 1–13
THE CYCLE OF PRICE- QUALITY COMPETITION—
MOVING UP AN ESCALATION LADDER

no one has an advantage) by rushing up the escalation ladder in Figure 1–13 or restarting it. Firms failing to be hypercompetitive are always playing catch-up so they never define the means of competition in their industry.

Hypercompetition in the Price and Quality Arena of Two Industries: Watches and Coffeemakers

Hypercompetitive behavior in the price-quality arena seems to be accelerating in many industries. From its sleepy roots in the mountains of Switzerland, for example, the watch industry has been shaken awake by hypercompetition. The center of watchmaking shifted from Switzerland to Japan in the early 1970s.[12] The Japanese producers, capitalizing on a low-paid workforce as well as the better quality of quartz oscillator technology, pursued a low-cost, high-quality strategy. But by the late 1970s Eastern watchmakers had driven up quality, offering low-cost, high-quality watches as well.

Even so, the low-cost, high-quality strategy of the Japanese began to cut into the Swiss market. In response two failing Swiss firms joined to form SMH, whose goal was to regain lost market share and "revitalize the Swiss watch industry."[13] The Swiss company created a manufacturing innovation of integrating the quartz movement into a plastic case. This process innovation gave the Swiss a cost advantage over the Japanese. It was used to introduce Swatch watches with an aggressive media campaign, a new type of quality based on fashion, and new distribution channels. Swatch sold fifty million watches in its first five years, switching the center of watchmaking back to Switzerland.

The watch industry remains segmented into premium and differentiators and low-cost watches. However, high-end players continue to fight based on reputation, and low-end players compete on both cost and quality. The introduction of Swatch shifted the low end of the curve to lower cost and higher quality. But there continues to be a broad spectrum of competition. One serious obstacle to the move toward a single ultimate value point is that in the watch industry, as in other fashion industries, price is a signal of quality. This factor tends to slow the industry's movement toward a single ultimate value point because a high-quality, low-priced product will still suffer from a lower perceived quality because of its reduced price tag.

The dynamic strategic interactions among the players in the coffeemaker industry appear to be moving at an even faster pace than in the watch industry. Companies have staked out positions along a full line of products from basic four-cup machines to combined coffeemakers and expresso machines. Companies such as Braun and Krups have staked out the high end of the industry, while others such as Mr. Coffee have taken the low end. Overall, however, the industry has been driven toward the ultimate value point. Because of the high level of variety in the industry, there continues to be competition along a broad spectrum. Coffee-machine buyers are strongly influenced by evaluators such as *Consumer Reports*, keeping all players on their toes as they compete to produce the highest-quality product (usually defined as the largest number of features) for the lowest price. Constantly shifting the rules by defining new levels of quality (through introducing new features) has become a key strategy in distinguishing competing products. Companies have added clocks, developed iced-tea makers, combined coffee grinders and coffeemakers, and brought out home expresso machines. But because these features are so easily imitated, the competition quickly reverts to price wars. A wide variety of filter shapes can provide opportunities for further sales to existing customers, but many generic brands also make filters. The entire industry faces threats from the outside that include instant coffee and microwave coffee bags. Some companies have found ways to jump out of price competition, at least for some of their sales. Melitta, for example, has found a new distribution channel by offering a custom coffeemaker as a premium for joining a Swedish coffee club.

Like many industries in today's competitive world, product-based advantages are fleeting in watches and coffeemakers. However, hypercompetitive firms continue to maneuver for temporary advantage by moving up the price-quality ladder faster than competitors and by restarting the cycle with new ways to redefine quality or find lower costs. In each of these industries, competitors pass through periods of price wars (perfect competition) for short periods of time but always find new ways to break out of that state. The hypercompetitive firms are the ones who set the price-quality pace that others must follow.

So hypercompetition occurs because it must. Each firm must follow the price-quality leader to survive, and the leader cannot afford to fall behind out of fear of losing its edge. On occasion, a hypercompetitive firm overtakes another on its way up the ladder, and competitors alternate playing leader. However, the truly hypercompetitive firms find ways to maintain their lead through a series of actions that give temporary advantage until others catch up. The alternative is to let others catch up, ending any form of advantage and resulting in a profitless, perfectly competitive industry.

Escalation to the Next Arena

Ultimately, as we have shown, this series of interactions drives the industry toward perfect competition. In a perfectly competitive environment, all companies offer a similar set of products at each price-quality point so that product features and price are no longer an advantage. To escape this arena of fierce competition on price and quality, companies try to escape by using innovative strategies to enter new markets that are not yet engaged in the price-quality maneuvering discussed in this chapter. Thus, hypercompetitive firms must engineer an escape from perfect competition by (1) moving up the escalation ladder in Figure 1–13 faster than competitors, so that others cannot catch up with their leading quality or price; (2) restarting the escalation ladder in Figure 1–13 by redefining quality in a way that others do not compete on yet; or (3) by moving to competition in the second arena: timing and know-how. It is in this new arena that they interact by selecting the timing of their entry into new markets with new products based on using the firm's technological and marketing know-how to innovate or imitate. We will consider this arena of competition and the second escalation ladder in the next chapter.

Management Challenges

The sequence of dynamic strategic interactions described in this chapter has many implications for management decisions. This outline of strategic moves and countermoves can help you understand where you are in the cycle in your industry and what your next step should be. It can also help you anticipate your competitors' next move. By seeing what's ahead, you can jump levels to speed the escalation of the cycle and catch your competitors off guard. Those who climb the ladder faster are always one step ahead of the competition, forcing the others to catch up with the new advantage created by moving up to the next step on the ladder. Or you can take action to slow down the competitors who want to jump past you.

Here are some of the major issues that managers face in taking control of this cycle:

- Are you in the middle or stuck in the middle?
- Which product segment (price-quality) is most attractive? Will it remain that way?
- Is someone building a full line in your industry or creeping up or down the line?
- How can you (or how will your competitors) try to move toward the ultimate value positions?
- Is it to your advantage to speed up the cycle? How can you do this? How much?
- Are you leading the industry up the ladder or following? Why?
- Who and what are setting the pace of escalation in your industry? Why?
- How can you redefine quality and restart the cycle?

Not all industries are at the same point along this cycle. Some move through each of these stages quickly, and others slowly. Some have potential to be temporarily frozen at one stage. Others don't. Some can be speeded up. Others can't. But most travel through the rungs on the escalation ladder in Figure 1–13 over the long run. By understanding these mileposts, you can take greater charge of your direction and face fewer surprises from competitors. In Part III of this book, we will develop several techniques and strategies for dealing with these management challenges and creating the types of temporary advantage that are available at each step of the escalation ladder in this arena of competition.

CHAPTER 2

HOW FIRMS OUTMANEUVER COMPETITORS WITH TIMING AND KNOW-HOW ADVANTAGES

In the preceding chapter we have seen how the cycle of competition in the price and quality arena drives firms relentlessly toward the point of ultimate value. One way for firms to escape from this cycle is to leap into a new market or jump to a new level of quality that is so improved that it represents entry into a new marketplace. These leaps are usually the product of timing and know-how advantages. A timing advantage is created by skills that allow a firm to be a first mover. A know-how advantage is the technological knowledge or other knowledge of a new method of doing business that allows the firm to create an entirely new product or market.

Arriving first to market with an innovative product can be a tremendously powerful strategy. Hoffmann-LaRoche was a tiny struggling chemical company that made a few textile dyes before it used a timing and know-how advantage to transform itself into a major pharmaceutical company. Hoffmann-LaRoche took a chance on producing vitamins, which had still to receive any recognition from the medical community. The company then moved into sulfa drugs in the 1930s and later to the production of tranquilizers (such as Librium and Valium). At each of these steps, it was the first to move into unproven territory. This strategy made it one of the world's largest and most profitable pharmaceutical companies.

Dr. An Wang also had a timing and know-how advantage that he put to use in creating the first office word processor to replace typewriters and other office equipment. This was not a breakthrough in hardware technology as much as it was an innovation in utilizing that technology with new software. Wang Laboratories grew very large and profitable based on this innovation but failed to sustain the momentum. Other companies leapfrogged past Wang. Hardware innovations, such as personal computers coupled with laser printers, replaced Wang's more cumbersome minicom-

71

puter. Wang filed for Chapter 11 protection in 1992.[1] In sum, unlike Hoffmann-LaRoche, Wang failed to improve its knowledge base to the degree necessary to maintain its momentum and dominance in the word processing market. The Wang example points out that know-how can be neutralized or made obsolete over time by aggressive competitors.

TRADITIONAL VIEWS OF TIMING AND KNOW-HOW ADVANTAGES

The Hoffmann-LaRoche and Wang examples illustrate that arriving first to market can give a company a substantial advantage. If the first-mover firm arrives long before competitors, it may be the only seller of a product or provider of a service, allowing it to charge a premium because of its status as a monopolist. In addition, being first can enhance the first mover's ability to control a market for long periods into the future. Sometimes first movers can exclude entrants, build brand equity, create for the product a large loyal following unlikely to switch, and achieve economies of scale and experience curve effects unavailable to later entrants.

The Hoffmann-LaRoche and Wang examples also illustrate that underlying the ability to be first is a composite of *unique intangible assets*: know-how. These include the technology necessary to build and manufacture the product, knowledge of unmet customer needs, and the marketing skills needed to introduce a new product quickly. Know-how can also be used to enter the market after the first mover. Advantages are derived from the development of know-how and its application as either a first mover or a later entrant.

The shareholder-value model of strategy, described by William Fruhan, explains why these advantages create value for shareholders.[2] According to this model, the timing advantage (or first-mover status) offers a unique asset or skill that can be used to earn "rents" (abnormal profits). As long as these assets/skills remain unique, the company can charge these high rents to customers who need them.

Even though the customer buys a product, it is really paying for the use of the firm's unique ability to build and design the product. Unlike the cost-quality view of competitive advantage in the previous chapter, this suggests that the components of the product and the product itself are rarely where the value is. The uniqueness of the intangible assets (i.e., the know-how) that are necessary to invent and make a product are what allow the firm (1) to charge more than the cost of the unique asset as a rent on the asset and (2) to take advantage of opportunities not open to other firms.

The duration and growth of these rents determine the value created by a firm for its shareholders. That value is the net present value of the future cash flows generated by investments to create the unique assets/skills. However, the duration of these cash flows rarely approaches perpetuity.

Once these intangible assets/skills are imitated or replaced with a new set that can be used to serve the same customer need, the first mover begins to lose its ability to charge high rents because the firm must compete with other firms seeking to rent similar assets to the same customers. Over time, followers insure that the assets/skills are no longer a resource that the firm can use to generate rents.

While Fruhan's analysis deals largely with one-shot developments such as Wang's office system, the erosion of rents leads to the ultimate conclusion that companies need to develop a series of advantages to succeed. As the rents of the first initiative begin to erode, the company must have a second initiative in progress or face the fate of Wang, whose original advantage was eroded before it had established a new one.

Resource-based Strategies: Pre-positioning and Strategic Postures Based on Intangible Assets

The firm's ability to push into new markets—especially in high-tech or industrial markets—is determined by its strategy in developing technology and other know-how and by its ability to exploit these intangible assets better than anyone else. By building unique tangible and, especially, intangible assets, the firm can position itself to take advantage of two different types of timing opportunities: being a first mover into new markets or a close follower of the actions of competitors. The way the company approaches the development of this experience base is critical in determining the type of offensive moves that the firm can mount.

How does the firm go about developing new know-how? The company can choose a revolutionary or an evolutionary strategy. The revolutionary strategy attempts to introduce a sharp, discontinuous technological change, while the evolutionary strategy works on a series of incremental improvements, either to the product or to the production process. The revolutionary strategy is the strategy of the first mover. The evolutionary strategy is the approach of second or later entrants into new markets. First movers, in particular, need a strong base of intangible technological resources to make big jumps in product design and manufacturing. Moreover, the firm's resource posture, especially its stocks of intangible resources, pre-positions the firm for entirely different types of strategic actions.

RESOURCE INVESTMENTS FOR REVOLUTIONARY LEAPFROGS

Investments in developing radically new technology or accumulating radically different skills and experience can be staggering. In high-tech industries, in particular, the company is sometimes required to "bet the firm" to move to the next stage in its technological development. The challenge is to assure that these investments are taking the firm in the right direction. The role of the strategist in planning for product markets is to decide in what direction to drive technology so that the firm can navigate from its current design to a future design that gives the maximum increase in value to the customer per dollar of development cost. Some technological advances will open up large new markets for new products, while other efforts will have little or no effect. The key is to drive the development of intangible assets such as technology and marketing or production know-how in the direction in which it will not hit a technological barrier, an unsolvable technical problem.

To make this decision, managers must analyze their markets and technology. As we will examine in our discussion of the New 7-S's in Part III, understanding stakeholders and looking ahead to changes in technology through strategic soothsaying are crucial to success as a first mover. Companies need to know the key attributes that their customers want and the limits of technology and know-how. They must overcome those limitations in a way that enhances the attributes desired by customers. A first-mover strategy that ignores customer needs will end up on the scrap heap with such revolutionary new products as Polaroid's "instant" movie camera and Federal Express's ZapMail. A strategy that fails to examine the shape of know-how barriers may cause the company to make costly investments in new technology that are impossible to achieve. As the scientist and inventor Sir Alastair Pilkington commented, "A large part of innovation is, in fact, becoming aware of what is really desirable. [Then you] are ready in your mind to germinate the seed of a new idea."[3]

Useful Insights from the Resource-based View of Competitive Advantage

BUILDING CORE COMPETENCY AROUND KNOW-HOW

The view that timing advantages are based on unique know-how advantages has produced several particularly important insights. Prahalad and Hamel, for example, reconceptualized the mission of firms as based on building up their core competencies (i.e., their underlying know-how) rather than on their product markets.[4] Honda is not a car company. It is a company whose mission is to dominate small engine design and knowledge about how to apply it to multiple products. In contrast, the less successful firms of Chrysler and GM have missions to be vehicle companies, wherein engines are just a component used in making them. Thus, Honda extends its product line by putting its world-class engines in cars, motorcycles, lawn mowers, recreational vehicles, motor bikes, snow blowers, snowmobiles, chain saws, and many other products. In contrast, GM extends its product line by making trucks, vans, and all sorts of cars, and Chrysler even out-sources its engine design and manufacturing. The main difference is that Honda focuses on building a knowledge base (about small engines), while the American firms focus on making products. As discussed earlier in this chapter, competitive advantage is rarely in the product; it comes from underlying knowledge that firms develop and exploit.

Consider another example. IBM's mission is to be a computer company. It makes chips and software for use in its computers. In contrast, NEC has emerged as a world leader in semiconductors and telecommunication technologies, which it applies to making mainframe computers, telephones, facsimile machines, and laptop computers. NEC's approach allows it to fully exploit its investment in know-how by using its know-how in several ways. IBM's approach leaves many potential applications of its technologies unfulfilled, inefficiently using its vast know-how and wasting some of its technological investment by not capitalizing upon it.

This view suggests that unlike physical assets, competencies do not deteriorate as they are used. Unless replicated by competitors, they should grow as they are used. Over time, core competencies can be combined to generate a whole new family of products. Canon combines its know-how in several areas (precision mechanics, fine optics, and microelectronics) to make several products (see Figure 2–1). Each time it uses its knowledge about precision mechanics, fine optics, and microelectronics, this knowledge base expands.

	Precision Mechanics	Fine Optics	Micro-electronics
Basic camera	■	■	
Compact fashion camera	■	■	
Electronic camera	■	■	
EOS autofocus camera	■	■	■
Video still camera	■	■	■
Laser beam printer	■	■	■
Color video printer	■		■
Bubble jet printer	■		■
Basic fax	■		■
Laser fax	■		■
Calculator			■
Plain paper copier	■	■	■
Battery PPC	■	■	■
Color copier	■	■	■
Laser copier	■	■	■
Color laser copier	■	■	■
NAVI	■	■	■
Still video system	■	■	■
Laser imager	■	■	■
Cell analyzer	■	■	■
Mask aligners	■		■
Stepper aligners	■		■
Excimer laser aligners	■	■	■

Every Canon product is the result of at least one core competency.

FIGURE 2–1
CORE COMPETENCIES AT CANON

Source: An exhibit from "The Core Competence from the Corporation," by Prahalad and Hamel (*Harvard Business Review*, May–June 1990). Copyright © 1990 by the President and Fellows of Harvard College; all rights reserved.

Under this view, firms are reconceptualized as portfolios of competencies that create many products and businesses, instead of as portfolios of products. Resources are allocated to building and exploiting competencies, not to SBUs (single business units) defined by the products they make. Top management's role is to build and transfer know-how from product SBU to SBU, carefully managing the usage of each competency to maximize its exploitation, to build its potential, and to plan for new competencies that secure the future. As such, top managers must monitor the value created for shareholders by the firm's intangible assets.

MONITORING THE VALUE OF INTANGIBLE ASSETS

Every firm has a "going-concern value." Part of this value is due to the cost of replicating the firm's physical assets. The rest is due to the value that is created by how these physical assets are used. This is the know-how of the firm; i.e., the management talent and intellectual assets used to employ the firm's physical assets. Based on appraisals and engineering studies, the replacement value of the physical assets can be calculated and subtracted out of the going-concern value of the firm. The value of these intangibles is the net present value of the rents on a firm's investments to create the unique intangible resources that we mentioned earlier in this chapter.

The simplest way to monitor the value of intangible assets is through Tobin's q, which is the market value of a firm's equity divided by the replacement value of its tangible assets. The intent of this measure is to capture the stock market's estimate of the value added by intangible assets (like technological know-how, management skill, and other core competencies) to the firm's physical asset base. (Sometimes Tobin's q is proxied with an easier number to get, the market value of equity divided by the net book value of the firm [from financial statements].) Figure 2–2 shows how firms can monitor their intangible resources (as estimated by the stock market) over time.

Competitor A is building its intangible assets relative to the rest of the industry, while competitor B is depleting them. Note that it was mentioned earlier in this chapter that core competencies don't deteriorate when used. They can, however, deteriorate if a firm's core competency loses its uniqueness or becomes obsolete. In Figure 2–2, competitor B no

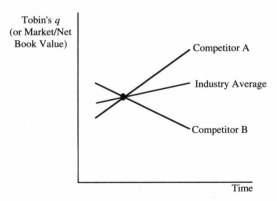

FIGURE 2–2
CHANGES IN INTANGIBLE RESOURCES
OVER TIME

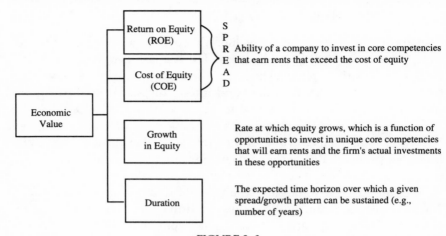

FIGURE 2–3
ECONOMIC VALUE IS DRIVEN BY THREE STRATEGIC LEVERS—SPREAD,
GROWTH, AND DURATION

longer has any unique know-how, and competitor A is outmaneuvering competitor B over time, obsoleting competitor A's know-how.

This analysis provides a view of whether the intangible assets of the firm are building or declining due to replication or obsolescence. However, it does not provide any detailed analysis about why this is occurring.

Based on a set of complex formulas and assumptions, which can be found in published articles on value creation,[5] several consulting firms produced a more extensive analysis designed to identify the source of the value created by a firm's physical and intangible assets. Figure 2–3 shows three levers that can be expected to create or destroy the economic value of the firm: spread, growth, and duration. Each of these is defined in Figure 2–3.

The formula that holds all of these together is:

$$\frac{Economic\ Value}{Book\ Value} = 1 + \frac{S}{k-g}\left(1 - \left(\frac{1+g}{1+k}\right)^n\right)$$

where S = spread between return on equity and cost of equity
k = cost of equity
g = equity growth rate
n = duration (number of years) beyond which $S = 0$ is assumed.

The formula itself isn't as important as recognizing that, while spread is the key determinant of value creation, a company can achieve different economic values by different combinations of spread, duration, and growth.

These three levers—spread, duration, and growth in equity—can be further linked to a comprehensive set of performance measures, as illustrated in Figure 2–4. The detailed components of two of the levers (spread and growth in equity) can be calculated using historical data from the firm's financial statements. With this data one can ask questions that reveal strategically important information.

Consider the following analysis of Dr Pepper versus Royal Crown Cola in 1975 and 1980. An analysis using Figure 2–4 would reveal that in both years, Dr Pepper (Dr P) was more successful at creating value than Royal Crown Cola (RCC). When you ask why by looking at the detailed breakdown of spread and equity growth in Figure 2–5, we see that Dr Pepper's equity growth and spread stayed high in both years, but Royal Crown Cola's equity growth and spread fell sharply.

RCC's declining value seems to be the result of falling operating margins and asset utilization. There was no or little disadvantage in the cost of equity or the contribution to ROE made by increasing the firm's leverage. Thus, through this analysis, we have found that financial decisions are not responsible for the declining value of the firm. Operating decisions are. This suggests that RCC's core competencies are losing their uniqueness. RCC's core competencies were its unique cola-based taste and its diet cola, which it introduced to the market first. However, competitors like Pepsi and Coke replicated these intangible assets, while they did not replicate Dr Pepper's taste. Coke's Mr. Pibb never took off (even though Coke thought it was a Dr Pepper fighter). RCC's niche was evaporating in the late 1970s because its core competency was no longer unique. Dr Pepper's niche was not threatened.

A more detailed analysis can be done. ROS can be broken down into ROS by product or division. Asset utilization can be broken down by asset type (e.g., inventory, receivables, plant and equipment, land, etc.) or by specific plant. Once the location of the eroding ROS or asset utilization is identified, it can often be linked to the erosion of uniqueness in specific intangible assets associated with the product, division, asset type, or specific plant.

Notice that this analysis of RCC did not provide any explicit analysis about the duration; that is, the amount of time that the spread would remain greater than zero. Calculation of duration is more problematic than calculation of growth and spread. Duration requires a projection into the

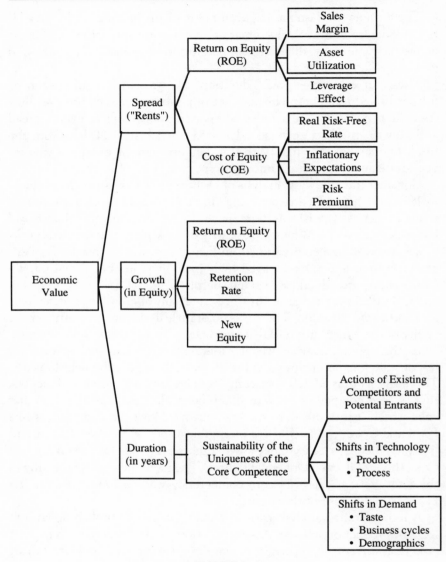

FIGURE 2–4
LEVERS OF ECONOMIC VALUE

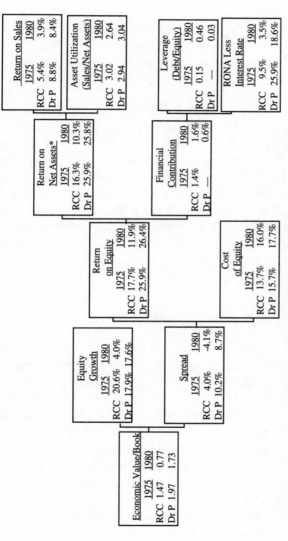

Definitions: (1) Return on equity is net income after preferred dividends divided by common equity.
(2) Return on net assets (RONA) is earnings before interest but after taxes divided by net assets.
(3) Return on sales is earnings before interest but after taxes divided by sales.

*Operating contribution only

Note: Values based on five-year weighted average performance, using the sum-over-sum method.

FIGURE 2–5

COMPARISON OF ROYAL CROWN COLA (RCC) WITH DR PEPPER (Dr P)

future, while the formula uses historical growth and spread data. Because the model provides no guidance on how the competitors may act in the future, the model necessarily provides a "naive" estimate of the firm's economic/book value that

- is based on historical growth and spread and
- assumes a duration (typically set at ten or fifteen years for the sake of analysis)

If a simple ten- or fifteen-year assumption is not used, some consultants inappropriately extrapolate how long the spread will stay above zero. According to Figure 2–5, Dr Pepper's spread declined 1.5 percent (from 10.2 percent to 8.7 percent) over five years. At this rate of decline (0.3 percent per year), it will remain above zero for approximately twenty-nine years. For extremely successful firms, some consulting firms that have used a similar model assume that the duration is infinite. This allows them, through mathematical derivation, to reduce the original model to a more simple model:

$$\frac{\text{Economic Value}}{\text{Book Value}} = \frac{\text{ROE–g}}{\text{COE–g}}$$

This simplification is rarely realistic, so further analysis is often done. The naive calculation of economic/book value (assuming historical spread, historical growth, and an arbitrary duration) can be compared to the market's estimate of the value of the firm's equity/book values. When the naive calculation is below the market's, one asks: Why does the market believe that the firm will do better than the historical assumptions used in the model? When the naive calculation is above the market's, one asks: Why does the market believe that the firm will do worse than the historical assumptions used in the model?

The answers to these questions often depend upon dynamic shifts in the future that make historical estimates of spread and growth and linear extrapolation of duration irrelevant or impossible. Thus, the dynamics of the future can only be guessed at when using the traditional models that are based on the economic rents created by unique intangible resources called core competencies.

TIMING-BASED STRATEGIES
AND DYNAMIC STRATEGIC INTERACTION

The timing of a firm's rents and cash outflows depends upon the timing of its competitors' movements into new markets and the timing of the firm's own development of new technology and other know-how. This often depends upon whether firms choose to make revolutionary or evolutionary product changes. Moreover, the timing of the rents and cash outflows depends upon which of these two strategies is chosen.

While the traditional models reviewed above (like Fruhan's) recognize that rents on intangible resources will decline as the uniqueness of the asset erodes due to imitation, they do not provide an understanding of how and when competitors neutralize the uniqueness of an opponent's resources. They do not provide guidance on how to preserve the uniqueness of the first mover's assets. They also do not distinguish between creating value by a single high-profit, one-shot effort versus a series of actions that aren't sustainable but that also produce the same cumulative value for shareholders. Moreover, while recognizing the importance of timing and know-how, they do not offer any prediction about the type of competitive countermoves that will be used. And they do not show how imitation occurs or when it can be impeded. Models based on the net present value of an innovation seem to focus on a "single-wave" picture of a one-shot know-how leap that generates cash for many years rather than on a successful strategy of several waves occurring sequentially or simultaneously, each lasting only temporarily. These models say only that, given the pattern of cash flows generated by a unique resource, its value to shareholders can be calculated.

A more dynamic view of strategy looks at the way competitors interact to build their own advantage through entry timing, the creation of know-how, and the methods used to erode the uniqueness of their competitors' resources. Ultimately this dynamic plays a greater role in shaping the firm's future rents than does the value of the expected cash flows from an investment viewed in isolation of the countermoves that might occur. While traditional financial models provide the ability to incorporate an estimate of the impact of countermoves, they provide no guidance about what these countermoves will be or why they will occur.

Thus, competition develops among firms with respect to (1) building their resource base (especially know-how) and destroying the uniqueness of the opponent's resource bases and (2) the timing of moves that emanate from use of that resource base—first mover versus follower. These moves and countermoves create an escalation ladder of dynamic strategic inter-actions in which firms enter markets, innovate, and imitate each other until they compete away all the unique advantage provided by know-how and other intangible assets.

The First Dynamic Strategic Interaction: Capturing First Mover Advantages

For every strategic move, the firm has a choice: to act first or to wait. Turning back to our struggle to escape the cycles of quality and price com-petition, a company may eventually find that the only way to move up is to move out. Entering a mature market puts the company right back in the press of intense competition. The only markets that offer relief from this competition are those that either don't exist yet or are virtually untapped.

Arriving first at the market, as we saw in the examples of Hoffmann-LaRoche and Wang, can offer a tremendous advantage. It also creates sig-nificant risks. If Hoffmann-LaRoche had been wrong about vitamins and later studies disproved their usefulness, its strategy could have cost it the firm. If the market did not adopt vitamins, Hoffmann-LaRoche could have been left with a very costly but useless product line. Wang suffered an even bigger risk commonly associated with being a first mover. It put all its eggs in one basket and failed to adapt to the subsequent moves of entrants in that market.

The advantages of being a first mover include the following:[6]

- *Response lags* In the time it takes for second movers to reach the market, the first mover can earn substantial rents as a temporary mo-nopolist.
- *Economies of scale* The first mover has time to achieve economies of scale before later entrants arrive. First movers tend to have signifi-cantly broader served markets.[7]
- *Reputation and switching costs* Establishing brand loyalty first, so fol-lowers must convince customers to bear the costs and risks of switch-ing to an untried, unknown late entrant's brand. The first mover is also helped by the cost of evaluating switching to a new product, which often leads to customers buying from the market leader.
- *Advertising and channel crowding* By the time later entrants arrive, it may be harder for them to find uncluttered advertising space and distribution networks.
- *User-base effects* Some products such as telephones increase in

value as the number of users increases. By arriving first, the innovator can set the standard and build a stable, large user base that provides funds for the next leap in products.

- *Producer learning* Moving down the production and technology experience curve faster than competitors.
- *Preemption of scarce assets* First movers have their choice of unique natural resources (e.g., Nickel Mines with the lowest extraction costs), valuable land (e.g., McDonald's restaurant locations), or shelf space (e.g., P&G's control of supermarket displays and shelving).

Empirical evidence from the PIMS database (containing almost six hundred consumer goods firms and thirteen hundred industrial goods firms) shows evidence that first movers earn the biggest profits for long periods of time when they move into industries with significant switching costs.[8] The advantage is strongest in industries with high product-purchase prices and low new-product sales and in high-value-added product markets. The first mover advantages are weakest in markets with high price competition, in which direct-sales-force expenditures are high and products are highly customized or service is important.[9] First movers in consumer goods industries, because of the generally low costs of purchases, appear to benefit most when there is consumer uncertainty regarding product quality and not much to be gained by a long and time-consuming search for information from sources like *Consumer Reports*. These are situations in which brand loyalty will be important. Because of the high purchase amount, first movers in industrial goods industries appear to benefit most when there are severe buyer-switching costs and unique patents that hold up over time and when they form strategic alliances with customers. Followers do better when there is a high retail purchase price for consumer goods and a low retail purchase price for industrial goods. Thus, where consumers find it easy to switch, followers benefit most.

First movers also benefit from ambiguity that makes it harder for competitors to unravel the source of advantage of the innovating firm. This makes it hard for competitors to determine which actions to imitate. In particular, process R&D (the results of which are usually much less visible than product R&D) can provide longer-lasting advantages.[10]

To be effective, first movers must develop some special know-how, including the following:

- *Innovation skills* Their R&D must be fast, innovative, risk-taking. Pilkington spent more than seven years and twenty-one million dollars to perfect its new float plate glass process. The results transformed the industry and assured Pilkington's dominance in it, but a failure would have been a major loss. Sony, from its start, bet the company on breakthroughs in technology, beginning with the development of a tape recorder after the war and gambling on creating the first pocket transistor radio. Sometimes the risks didn't pay off as well, as in the case of Beta video machines.

- *Customer knowledge* They must be intuitively in touch with the marketplace because market research usually doesn't work with completely new products. Customers cannot articulate a desire for products they have never seen.
- *Market penetration skills* Their marketing skills must be fast and good enough to gain quick market share after early product introduction, and they must have a brand name that is capable of sustaining a premium price large enough to recapture R&D investments before competitors move into the market.
- *Flexible manufacturing skills* Their manufacturing skills must be flexible enough so that new products can be introduced quickly and so that components can be created that are not available on the open market, increasing the element of surprise. First movers are often not organized to do routine mass production because their systems are designed to be flexible enough to switch from one new product to another.

Because these skills and knowledge are not easy to create, many firms choose to stand and wait rather than make the first move into the market. After observing what the first mover has done, other players countermove, as illustrated in the next dynamic strategic interaction, imitation.

The Second Dynamic Strategic Interaction: Imitation and Improvement by Followers

Being a first mover can be very risky. As we have examined above, the first mover faces substantial challenges. Customers do switch products. Brand loyalty can be overcome in consumer products industries, and switching costs can be circumvented in industrial products industries. Innovations diffuse among competitors. Diffusion is especially rapid when

- reverse engineering is easy
- equipment suppliers help transfer key technologies or other business know-how

- industry observers, trade associations, or collegial professional societies help transfer technologies and other business know-how
- buyers encourage other manufacturers to become qualified second or third sources
- personnel move to rival firms frequently
- leaks of secret information are commonplace and not punishable legally

Thus, first mover advantages are often very tenuous in nature, and they may not create the barriers to imitation that people commonly assume.

The risks of being a first mover can be minimized by being a close follower. Quite often imitators profit more from an innovation than the innovating firm. The product succeeds fabulously, but the company that first brings it to market is not the one to profit from it. Imitators do follow. One study found that 60 percent of patented successful innovations were imitated within four years, and the imitator's development costs were 35 percent less than the innovator's.[11] Another study found that major patented innovations could be imitated within three years in half of the 129 lines of business studied. For unpatented inventions the statistics were worse, with about 65 percent copied in a year or less.[12] Imitation barriers appear to be low.

Historically, Japanese firms have gained time and cost advantages in imitation due to acquisition of the know-how of competitors. Most advantage comes not from internal technology, but from external technology bought or copied from competitors.[13] In nearly three-hundred cases of links between U.S. and Japanese companies, more than 90 percent involved a transfer to Japan, according to a report by the National Academy of Sciences.[14] In Japan firms take about 25 percent less time and spend about 50 percent less money to carry out an innovation because of their use of external technology rather than inventing in-house. Moreover, this is true in all industries.[15]

Peter Drucker observed several advantages to following.[16] The follower allows the first mover to test the waters. It learns from the innovator's mistakes and can move in with a product better suited to the actual needs of the market. The imitator can avoid the tremendous expenses of development through reverse engineering and other methods. The imitator can focus its attention and resources on process technology rather than product technology, allowing it to produce a higher-quality product and/or to make the product more efficiently.

The follower also can take advantage of subsequent product or process innovations such as more powerful computers or chips, while the first mover may be locked into the technology at the time of the product's development because of sunk costs in research, manufacturing, distribution, and other areas. Thus, the close follower can arrive with a better product at a lower price.

A fast second mover or even a slow third mover can sometimes outperform the innovator. In some cases, such as Matsushita's VHS recorders, the follower wins. But in other cases, such as DuPont's Teflon, the innovator wins. See Figure 2–6 for other examples.

There are three things needed for the imitator to win: regimes of appropriability, dominant design paradigm, and complementary assets.[17] Appropriability is related to the strength of patents and other legal protection, as well as the difficulty for followers in using technology to invent around patents. If followers can enter before the emergence of a dominant design, they have a shot at offering their own design against that of the original innovator. The follower needs complementary assets such as marketing, manufacturing, and other capabilities that allow it to produce the new product.

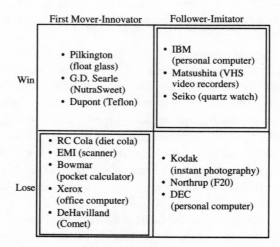

	First Mover-Innovator	Follower-Imitator
Win	• Pilkington (float glass) • G.D. Searle (NutraSweet) • Dupont (Teflon)	• IBM (personal computer) • Matsushita (VHS video recorders) • Seiko (quartz watch)
Lose	• RC Cola (diet cola) • EMI (scanner) • Bowmar (pocket calculator) • Xerox (office computer) • DeHavilland (Comet)	• Kodak (instant photography) • Northrup (F20) • DEC (personal computer)

FIGURE 2–6
TAXONOMY OF OUTCOMES FROM THE
INNOVATION PROCESS

Source: David J. Teece, "Profiting from Technological Innovation: Implications for Integration, Collaboration, Licensing and Public Policy," p. 187 in Chapter 9 (pp. 185–219) of *The Competitive Challenge: Strategies for Industrial Innovation and Renewal*, edited by David J. Teece (Cambridge, MA: Ballinger Publishing, 1987).

This strategy of imitation is not without its risks and challenges. Following can splinter the company's efforts by offering too many variants and improvements without a clear focus. Piecemeal following may result in a set of products that cannot be integrated into one unified system. Another risk is that the follower, who is looking at the competitor, may misread customer needs and trends. This may make the follower unable to follow or improve when customers needs change again. For the follower strategy to work, the follower has to gain market share before the first mover has taken over the market. The success of this strategy also depends on the ease of imitation of the product. Complex products, for example, are harder to reverse-engineer and imitate.

With longer development times and higher technology costs, it can take a long time for second movers to crank up to speed to enter a promising market. On the other hand, a follower who moves too quickly can incur many of the same costs and risks as the first mover without gaining the advantage of arriving in the market first.

Follower strategies work best when the first mover is unable to keep up with demand, is not satisfying all segments of customers or all varieties of customer needs, or has a product with a design flaw that can be corrected. For example, aspirin was hard on the stomach, so buffered aspirin could move in to take over the market for pain relievers. This "design flaw" also left the door open for more revolutionary innovations such as acetaminophen and ibuprofen.

It is not just technology that can be imitated but also services. For example, even as Dell Computer was cloning the technology of the IBM personal computer and offering it at a lower price with higher service, other competitors were imitating Dell's approach to direct marketing. Smaller companies entered the market with direct-mail operations, offering a little less service for substantially lower prices. Even large competitors such as Digital are entering the mail-order business or increasing their telephone support and service to users.[18]

Direct imitation of the first mover, however, sometimes produces a less than appealing product. Why should happy customers switch to a new product when they are satisfied with the product of the first mover? This creates a need for more elaborate forms of imitation to differentiate the imitator from the first mover. Several methods are used, including pure imitation, adding bells and whistles, stripping down, creating flanking products, and reconceptualizing the product, all of which are summarized in the next section.

ALTERNATIVE STRATEGIES FOR FOLLOWING

There are several strategies the imitator can use to overcome switching costs and brand loyalty and to make up for his late arrival and lack of novelty.[19] In some ways these strategies are similar to those discussed in cost-quality competition in the first arena, but they are different in their degree. An automaker might move in the first arena by producing different cars with gasoline engines, but a car company might move in the second arena by introducing electric or solar cars or minivans. Of course, the two arenas, as we noted in the introduction, are separated here only to clarify the interactions. Actions in one arena affect competition in the others; a strategy to differentiate the imitator obviously has an impact on quality and cost.

Among the strategies used to differentiate the second mover are

- *Pure imitation* Here the second mover uses superior know-how to make the same product at a lower price. This is, in one sense, price competition, as noted in the first arena. But to offer a lower price, particularly when the first mover already has a head start on the experience curve, the follower has to be able to cut its costs of development and production. This can be done through better manufacturing processes and technology, reduced R&D costs, and reduced marketing outlays.
- *Adding bells and whistles* A lower price is not the only way a follower can steal customers. Adding features to the product or service allows followers to gain ground in the existing market. For example, when Procter & Gamble introduced Crest, it was a basic no-nonsense, cavity-fighting toothpaste. But some followers realized that it is not how customers feel but how they look that is important. So Lever Brothers came out with Close-Up, adding new ingredients to freshen breath and whiten teeth. Lever then followed with Aim, combining both a gel and fluoride protection. Beecham then came out with Aqua-Fresh, a swirl of paste and gel to fight cavities and improve the user's social life at the same time. In Chapter 1, we saw a similar type of escalation in product features in the disposable diaper market, where basic diapers became better-quality diapers and then gender-specific diapers and finally age- and gender-specific diapers.
- *Stripping down* The reverse strategy is to take away options, creating a less-expensive model for a more focused market segment. Rather

than imitate the service and fare schedules of existing airlines, People Express stripped down air travel to its no-frills minimum—getting from point A to point B. It eliminated flight attendants, meals, and reservations to offer lower-priced flights to nonbusiness travelers. To take an example of a product that has been stripped down, consider the massive copier-printing machines, designed to print truckloads of documents, that were scaled down to create machines for a single office or a single person. This is the difference between the approach of Xerox and Savin.

- *Flanking products* Another strategy is to create products that serve the same purpose for the same or similar customers but in a slightly different way. This is a variation on the bells-and-whistles approach that can be used to outflank a competitor by creating products that are smaller, larger, contain fewer calories, are in smaller packages, or are more convenient. Sony, for example, used miniaturization to enter the low end of the electronics market, and it used larger sizes, such as its thirty-two-inch television, to take the high end. Head Ski's oversized tennis racket is another example of the use of a larger size to distinguish an imitative product. Other features that are frequently used to distinguish a product include reduced calories, as in Miller Lite or Stouffer's Lean Cuisine; convenience of purchase, such as Avon's door-to-door marketing of products to women; and repackaging, such as milk in small aseptic cartons or orange juice cartons with screw-on lids. These flanking strategies have become increasingly important in competitive strategy. They can help the company shift the rules of competition, one of the New 7-S's that we will explore in Part III.

- *Reconceptualized products* Instead of changing the product, the imitating firms sometimes change the uses of the product. For example, baking soda was once used primarily in cooking, but is now offered as laundry detergent, toothpaste, and refrigerator deodorant. Motorcycles are variously seen as inexpensive transportation, a vehicle for fun or recreation, or a status symbol of macho power and prestige. This reconceptualization strategy is also becoming increasingly important, as we will examine in our discussion of searching for new opportunities in Part III.

- *Branded products* When customers are not likely to search out new products because it is too time-consuming and they are unwilling to test new products because they fear they may be low quality, the follower can advertise, provide warranties, or give free samples or free demonstrations of the product to overcome consumer unwillingness to switch.

- *Compatible products* When the customer must incur a cost to switch to a new product, followers often make compatible products. Personal computers and peripheral devices are frequently IBM-compatible to encourage IBM users to switch. Even software products are now compatible. If all of a firm's word processing was done in Word Star, it can be converted to WordPerfect relatively easily with software provided by WordPerfect.

The wide range of options for imitators indicates the fertile field that second movers enjoy. But innovators, facing this threat, do not sit idly and watch their market share erode. They are forced to make countermoves, illustrated in the next dynamic strategic interaction.

The Third Dynamic Strategic Interaction: Creating Impediments to Imitation

First movers can anticipate imitators by using the above strategies before the followers do so. However, this is often not done. First movers are not set up to imitate themselves. Their R&D labs often are looking for new technologies, and their scientists are often insulted if asked to modify existing products instead of inventing new, exciting ones. Moreover, this anticipation strategy only engages the first mover in an activity it sought to avoid by being a first mover. That is, it wants to be involved in untapped markets so it can act as a monopolist with a novel product. It does not want to compete by covering all the niches and becoming a full-line producer. This only drains resources away from its core mission: innovation and invention. Thus, first movers often turn to other strategies to prevent or delay imitation.

In developing and marketing their products or services, first movers often create obstacles for imitators. There are several major impediments to imitation.[20] These are the smoke screens and roadblocks that pioneers use to delay the entrance of followers. The nine impediments are deterrent pricing, secret information or know-how, size economies, contractual relationships with suppliers, threats of retaliation, patents, bundled products, switching costs, and restrictive licensing. We will examine each of these in turn.

- *Deterrent pricing* By anticipating the follower in its pricing, the first mover can discourage entry. If the first mover sets its prices as shown in Figure 2–7, placing its price slightly above its costs, the competitor has an easier time matching the first mover's price than if the first mover had taken an initial loss, as shown in Figure 2–8. The introductory price in Figure 2–8 is below the actual costs of producing the product and is meant to deter entrants by forcing them to enter at such a low price that their introductory losses might be prohibitive. Later, the first mover can establish a "price umbrella" to recapture its investments in R&D and its losses due to product introduction. This umbrella, drawn from its monopoly power, allows the company to price far above its cost. As soon as followers enter, after overcoming the delay of the first mover's initial low price, the first mover begins dropping its price to slow their entry. Eventually the market reaches a point of price competition. Once the first mover develops a reputation for pricing in this manner (i.e., per Figure 2–8), imitators may learn that following will not be very lucrative.

- *Secret information* By keeping information or know-how secret, first movers can prevent imitators from snatching their ideas. Know-how (technical information that is based on specialized experience and not divulged in patents) makes it much harder for competitors to imitate.[21] Whether it is the "special sauce" on a McDonald's Big Mac, the formula for Coca-Cola, or the huge investment in software for American Airlines' SABRE reservations system, the know-how that the first mover has accumulated is kept from competitors for as

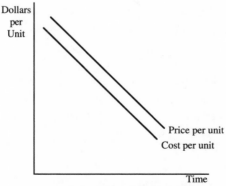

Note: For simplicity the learning curve
has been reduced to straight
lines by using a logarithmic scale.

FIGURE 2–7
SIMPLISTIC PRICING BASED ON COST
ASSUMING A LEARNING CURVE

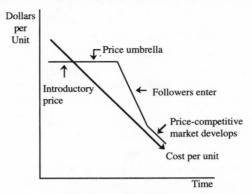

Note: For simplicity the learning curve
has been reduced to straight
lines by using a logarithmic scale.

FIGURE 2–8
ENTRY DETERRING AND UMBRELLA PRICING

long as possible. Ironically, firms often avoid patenting or copyright-
ing their secrets to keep them out of the public domain.

- *Size economies* If the first mover has gained economies of scale, then
  the later entrant must join the market at least at that scale if he
  wants to capture equivalent costs per unit. The cost of entering at
  that level may be too great for later entrants. This is a particularly
  effective deterrent if the remaining market for the product is too
  small to support another producer at the scale of the first mover.
  This means the first mover's large scale not only ups the ante for
  entering the market but also leaves little room for competitors to
  gain enough market share to be competitive.
- *Contractual relationships* The first mover's contractual relationships
  with suppliers or distributors may help lock out the follower from the
  market. If the follower cannot obtain necessary components or cannot bring his product to market, it is difficult for him to enter.
- *Threats of retaliation:* If the first mover threatens the entrant with
  retaliation, the follower may be more reluctant to enter the first
  mover's turf. We will examine various forms of retaliation to this
  type of turf invasion in more detail in the next chapter.
- *Patents* Patents provide an obvious defense against unwanted late
  entry by competitors. First movers often control the patents to a new
  product or process, making it more difficult (or sometimes even impossible) for competitors to imitate without infringing on the first
  mover's patent rights.

- *Bundled products* Bundled products are component systems that use a full line of pieces not made by the follower. If the follower cannot gain access to the components, then it cannot imitate the first mover.
- *Switching costs* Brand equity, customer loyalty, and other switching costs can make it hard for imitators to break into the market. Car companies such as GM and computer makers such as IBM have benefited from switching costs in the past. Brand loyalty and familiarity tended to keep buyers wedded to the first mover's products.
- *Restrictive licensing* First movers can use licensing to slow or restrict (but not eliminate) imitation in some locations by licensing their products to competitors but restricting them to specific geographic areas or regulating the timing of the followers' entry. But the drawback is that in each case the technology is transferred to the competitor. The resulting learning in the competitor's organization makes it easier for it to replicate the first mover's technological know-how.

The entrance of followers also may be delayed by response lags such as delays in retooling or gaining FDA approval for drugs. These lags can be anticipated by the first mover. Moreover, delays can be enhanced by keeping plans secret or guarding technological know-how, thereby delaying the competitor's awareness of the innovation and its understanding of the know-how needed to produce it. If the delay allows the first mover to establish itself firmly in the market, the second mover may have a diminished chance of entering.

But resourceful imitators do not sit idly by and accept these obstacles. Imitators have several incentives to enter the market as quickly as possible. First, it is easier to attract new customers than to woo customers away from the first mover. Second, by limiting the first mover's share of the market, the imitator can decrease the first mover's economies of scale and its experience curve effects and thereby decrease the resources the first mover can put into its next innovation. If the potential market is desirable enough, imitators will find a way to overcome these obstacles, as we can see in the next countermove, the fourth dynamic strategic interaction.

The Fourth Dynamic Strategic Interaction:
Overcoming the Impediments

Even when the first mover has scattered the path with obstacles, imitators can find ways to make countermoves in the market. Barriers to imitation tend to decay over time. This decay can be hastened by a technological breakthrough or through aggressive competition. This erosion can be slowed or reversed by continual reinvestment in know-how to increase the difficulty of imitation.[22]

In response to the nine impediments to imitation outlined above, here follows some actions that imitators take to overcome these barriers:

- *Deterrent pricing* If followers have sufficient resources, they may be able to match the first mover's prices, even during the period of its low introductory price. Particularly if the follower can develop process technology that reduces the cost of production, it may be able to match the first mover's prices at a much lower volume. This will force the first mover to drop its prices more quickly, reducing the profits earned by eliminating its price umbrella.

- *Secret information* By careful investigation, private information is often legally discovered, either by hiring away personnel from the first mover or by taking apart his products. Depending on the type of information, this may be more or less of a barrier. If a new fast-food chain wants to get a good idea of what's in the "special sauce" at McDonald's, it just buys a few Big Macs for chemical analysis or experiments to find an equivalent recipe. Even the Coca-Cola formula, which has never been replicated, has been hurt by the Pepsi Cola formula, developed by experimenting and adding more sweetness to a cola-based formula. On the other hand, a biotechnology company may have a stronger hold on secret information because of the complexity of the underlying technology, processes, and products (but such a hold is no longer as strong as companies think, as we will discuss in more detail when we examine entry barriers in Chapter 3).

- *Size economies* Some followers improve the product so they can enter at a higher price without the need for the lowest costs. Others improve the manufacturing process technology so they enter the market with a competitive price, even without economies of scale. By making the process more efficient, followers often quickly increase their scale and eventually overtake the first mover. Size economies also provide little protection if the market is growing faster than the capacity of the first mover to meet it. In this case, the first mover will not be able to fulfill the needs of the market, providing a ready entry point for an imitator. Other followers build up their scale in a protected geographic market and then enter another market with sufficient economies of scale to win. The entry of Japanese firms into the United States provides a good example of this process.

- *Contractual relationships* Contractual relationships with suppliers and distributors are overcome by finding or developing new suppliers or outlets for the product. If there is a demand, there will probably be suppliers and distributors to meet it. Also, upstream or downstream vertical integration by the imitator often eliminate the need for these contractual relationships.
- *Threats of retaliation* Frequently threats are not perceived as credible when push comes to shove. Some types of retaliation, such as price wars, can hurt the first mover as much as the follower by taking away funds that could be used for future innovation. In our discussion of signals in Part III, we will provide more detail about how companies make these threats credible.
- *Patents* A study of forty-eight innovations found that patents tend to increase imitation costs only by 11 percent (although they are more effective in some industries than others). Within four years 60 percent of the patented successful innovations had been copied. "Contrary to popular opinion," the study's authors concluded, "patent protection does not make entry impossible, or even unlikely."[23] Slight variations in the product are often not covered by patents. For example, adding an atom to a drug molecule can result in a "different" product with all the same pharmaceutical properties as the original. Close substitutes can also be developed, as when animal insulin was replaced by biogenetically produced human insulin for sale in the diabetic market. Patents also expire. In 1992, for example, patents were expiring on drugs that accounted for half of Upjohn's 1991 profits. Patents also don't provide protection in all parts of the world. Microsoft Corporation loses hundreds of millions of dollars each year to pirated software in other countries, with more than 75 percent of all software sales in many European and Asian nations coming from illegal copies.[24]
- *Bundled products* As in the case of contractual relationships, imitators sometimes overcome bundled products by vertical integration or through joint ventures. By gaining or obtaining the capacity to create or buy the components of the product, imitators can do the same kind of bundling. This gives the imitators the same access to components as the first mover, overcoming the obstacle of bundled products.
- *Switching costs* Not only can switching costs be overcome—through advertising, discounting, and direct comparisons that show the follower's product is better—high switching costs may actually be an attraction to new entrants. A recent study argued that markets with

high switching costs were more attractive to entrants because, once they gained a foothold in the market, they benefited from the same switching costs.[25] Thus, it was worth the effort to break through these barriers.

- *Restrictive licensing* As mentioned above, restrictive licensing doesn't stop the imitator and may actually give the following firm access to vital technology. The trick for the follower is to overcome the restrictions on the licensing. This can be done by developing its own international technology base to replicate the first mover's product or introduce the next generation of products, thereby eliminating the need for licensing.
- *Response lags* By improving internal processes and consistently advancing its technology, followers reduce the response lags due to internal constraints. External lags can also be mitigated. For example, the FDA clearance process can be accelerated for products that are "substantially equivalent" to existing drugs or for life-saving pharmaceuticals such as AZT. In this way the standard response lags are shortened considerably.

Thus, we see it is nearly impossible for the first mover to shut the door completely on imitators, a fact to which the personal computer market provides ample witness. So there is no safe haven where the first mover can rest on its laurels. The followers keep getting better at following, shortening the product life cycle and giving the first mover less time to recapture R&D investments through premium pricing within a price umbrella. The first mover is thus forced to sell at a higher and higher price if it is to recapture its R&D in less time. This makes financing a first-mover strategy more difficult and slows the rate at which it will preempt market share, a key goal of the first-mover strategy.

The eventual entrance of followers forces the first mover to react. For a while the first mover may try to make incremental improvements in its products to meet the imitator's challenge. But the imitator's resources are focused on incremental improvements, while the first mover is often more adept at more dramatic innovations. This leads to the next dynamic strategic interaction, wherein the first mover is forced to respond to the entrant after it successfully follows into the market. The first mover may try to fight new entrants on their own terms—becoming a low-cost producer and abandoning its innovative efforts by redirecting resources away from R&D to focus on lowering manufacturing costs. In such a case the first mover advantage is abandoned. But some first movers continue to push forward with the next generation of innovations to create a new advantage. To do this, they need to move to the next dynamic strategic interaction.

The Fifth Dynamic Strategic Interaction: Transformation or Leapfrogging

Eventually imitators become very good at imitating and overcoming the impediments thrown up by the first mover and achieve technical parity with the first mover, much as the Japanese consumer electronics giants, such as Matsushita, have moved from mere copying to mastering the technology for leadership in such new consumer electronics advances as HDTV and DAT. Over time, by learning to imitate the products, Matsushita has also imitated the intangible *resource base* (i.e., the know-how) of its competitors. At this point the first mover has lost any advantage it once had from its know-how, and the follower has the chance to take the leadership role. The first mover must then create a new set of intangible resources to win. This leads to either a *leapfrog* strategy or a *transformation* strategy.

Up to this point we have assumed that the first mover will continue to move ahead of the second mover. In fact, true competition is more complex. The second mover, as we noted, can move ahead of the first, forcing the first mover to catch up. This means, in effect, that the first mover becomes a follower. With roles reversed, hypercompetition still follows the pattern of moves and countermoves with each player trying to overtake the other. The interactions can thus become quite complex, as shown by Figure 2–9, which illustrates a series of three successive interactions between two competitors.

In the first interaction, the follower surpasses the first mover. Then (in interaction 2) the first mover catches up without surpassing the follower, allowing the follower the opportunity to jump ahead once again. Finally (in interaction 3), the first mover responds by overtaking the first mover, only to lose its lead once again. The first mover could retain the initiative throughout each interaction, the follower could seize the initiative and retain it, or it could move back and forth as in the above example. Eventually, after a series of such interactions, the players reach the fifth dynamic strategic interaction, where one or both players seek to put an end to this endless jockeying for position by leapfrogging the other player or transforming itself.

In the leapfrog strategy the company develops the resources to serve a

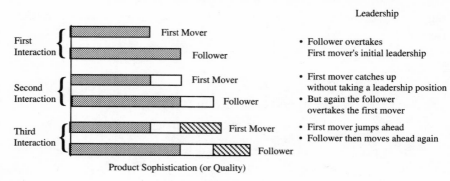

FIGURE 2–9
ILLUSTRATION OF A SITUATION WHERE A FIRST MOVER AND FOLLOWER
JOCKEY FOR LEADERSHIP

new customer or create an entirely new product. In the transformation strategy the company develops new resources that allow it to execute the strategy of its opponent and directly compete with the opponent on its own terms.

TRANSFORMATION OF THE RESOURCE BASE

For the first mover the transformation strategy strikes at the follower while it is still on the beach or beats it back into the ocean if it already has a substantial beachhead. This strategy requires a transformation on the part of the first mover. The first mover must shift from competing on technology or product know-how to competing on price and manufacturing know-how. The first mover also must match any incremental product improvements made by the follower. The primary questions at this point are how much it will cost to become a low-cost producer and whether there will be enough cash to fund future product R&D efforts.

This means the first mover has to find ways to become better at mass production and incremental product improvements. This requires a fundamental transformation of the first mover's culture and skills base, certainly no small undertaking.

Even if successful, the transformation strategy places the first mover in a war of attrition, a perfectly competitive environment. At the same time that it is improving its product and processes, the imitator is doing the same thing and is probably better at it. The follower is experienced at price competition and the incremental development of product improvements. With many similar products the market becomes increasingly price competitive. Competition focuses more on the price-quality arena and often evolves into a price war. The first mover is virtually indistinguishable from the followers (and vice versa), and price becomes the primary interest of consumers.

Compaq, fighting for its survival, transformed itself from a premium-priced innovator to a low-cost manufacturer. Compaq had built its reputation and market share by rolling out an IBM-compatible portable computer before IBM in 1982.[26] Compaq's engineering focus allowed it to create innovative products offering "better than IBM" PCs at premium prices. But the entry of low-cost, mail-order companies such as Dell and AST drove prices down at the same time that customers were becoming increasingly sophisticated in their computer purchases. Facing intense price competition, Compaq posted its first quarterly loss in the fall of 1991.[27] According to *Business Week,* Compaq's board ousted cofounder and CEO Rod Canion in 1991, and newly appointed CEO Eckhard Pfeiffer set about transforming the company to a low-cost clone maker.[28] He cut costs and slashed prices, making Compaq competitive with Dell and others, moved into new retail distribution channels, and drastically reduced cycle times for rolling out new products. In 1992 Compaq rolled out forty-five new models. *Business Week* reported that Compaq's ProLinea 386SX computer, for example, was less than half the price of a comparable DeskPro, its old model.[29] From 1991 to 1992, Compaq's share of the U.S. PC market shot up from 3.5 percent to 5.1 percent, according to *Fortune.*[30]

There are many risks to this strategy. Even though Compaq's sales in third-quarter 1992 increased by 50 percent, lower prices cut into its margins, according to *Fortune.*[31] Meanwhile, *Fortune* reported that Dell and AST cut their prices in response to Compaq's move, and even large competitors, including IBM, eyeing Compaq's success, are moving aggressively into the low end of the market, further heating up price wars. Although Compaq continues to differentiate itself on innovation, its transformation cuts into its resources and reputation for creating technological innovations. As *Forbes* asked in May 1992, "What is Compaq Computer Corp.? A clonemaker that sells on price or a market leader that sells on technological prowess? It's somewhere in between, and that's a dangerous place to be right now."[32]

Because of the competitive risks and organizational challenges posed by the transformation strategy, many first movers opt instead for leapfrogging strategies, choosing to switch rather than fight. Transformation is a retreat to fighting in the price-quality arena and may require deep pockets of the kind discussed in Chapter 4 on the deep-pockets arena.

LEAPFROGGING STRATEGIES: THE CREATION OF A NEW RESOURCE BASE

When markets become too crowded, the innovator often heads on to the next untapped frontier. But this strategy, as we will see, has its own danger:

Each leap is longer and requires greater expenditures to build new resources appropriate to the new market. Observation of leapfroggers indicates that each leap becomes more costly and more risky than the one before, until finally one giant mistake puts an end to the firm or the cost becomes too great and the firm runs out of cash.

> Sony is a leapfrogger. Early on, it built tape recorders and used the know-how and resources from that project to fuel its development and production of transistor radios. It brought out a pocket-sized transistor radio at a time when most radios were the size of a briefcase. Then Sony built on that success with the development of the Trinitron television in the late 1960s, and the superiority of the product made it a leader in that market. But many new entrants in the television market tended to force Sony into the very large and very small ends of the market. Sony then moved on to a new technology, creating the first consumer videocassette recorder in the world. Although Sony scientists believed their Beta system was technologically superior to the VHS format, Sony lost out in the marketing war to establish the standard for the industry. As the market was flooded with recorders and videotapes, Sony moved on to a new market—small, portable, personal listening devices, the first of which was the Walkman. Again, Sony used and extended its skills in miniaturization and audio technology to develop this next innovation.

As illustrated in Figure 2–10, with each innovation the company gained profits quickly while it controlled the market. When the profits from one product declined because of followers, Sony moved on to a new product, generating a new upward curve in profits. For each product Sony battles the problem of Matsushita and others entering as fast followers. Then, typically, later followers such as the Korean manufacturers enter with even lower costs.

The problem with a leapfrogging strategy is that each leap often takes more resources than the one before. First movers often pick the easy targets first. Thus, each subsequent jump is often steeper in its costs. Followers move in more quickly because they have gained skill at following and competing from previous attempts at imitating the first mover's product, contracting the cycle times from trough to trough more and more (as shown in Figure 2–10).[33] This limits the amount of time that the first mover has to recoup its R&D investment. As shown in Figure 2–10, the complexity of each successive innovation makes pushing the envelope more risky. In Sony's case, profits fluctuated to higher peaks and lower valleys with each new product, and the time from valley to valley got shorter. As more competitors entered the market, the fierceness of price competition intensified, further eroding profits. Thus, the risks to the company escalate with each new product. Eventually the leapfrog re-

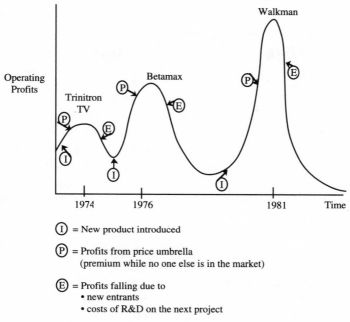

FIGURE 2–10
SHORTER CYCLES AND HIGHER AMPLITUDES ASSOCIATED
WITH INNOVATIONS AT SONY CORPORATION

sponse becomes unsustainable when new projects consume more funds than the company can raise, especially if profits can't be made due to fast imitation. Eventually the first mover is forced to "bet the company" on its latest project, or its leapfrogging hits a brick wall.

The risks of such a strategy at this point are staggering. Gordon Moore, cofounder of Intel, says his business "lived on the brink of disaster" as it moved from innovation to innovation in microchip technology, one step ahead of the competition. Moore said, "As soon as you could make a device with high yield, you calculated that you could decrease costs by trying to make something four times as complex, which brought your yield down again."[34] As each new microchip was developed, Intel had to take it quickly into production, forcing it to build both strong R&D and strong flexible production skills.

These risks increase as competitors have become more aggressive and faster. Intel's highly successful innovations in chip design have been increasingly pressured by fast and innovative followers such as Cyrix and by aggressive attempts by rivals making RISC-based chips to unseat Intel as the PC industry standard. At first, Cyrix introduced a clone of Intel's 486

chip in eighteen months, compared to a standard three- or four-year design cycle in the industry. The "workalike" chip is based on a different
design but made to offer the same results. Cyrix was also able to produce
its 486 for *only 4 percent of Intel's initial investment.* After the success of the
486 and the accumulation of knowledge from that effort, the company
announced plans to leverage its fast-follower skills and know-how to become a first mover. It announced plans to beat Intel to market for the next
generation chip, the Pentium.[35] The key questions are, Will Cyrix catch
up to or pass Intel? and Will Intel's success lead it to be just complacent
enough to underestimate Cyrix's aggressiveness? The dynamics of the strategic interaction between first movers and followers often reverse themselves when one player becomes complacent and the other is hungry for a
win.

At the same time that Intel is under attack by rivals such as Cyrix on
innovation in its existing family of chips, it also faces increasing pressure
from competitors who threaten to leapfrog past it by establishing a new
standard for microprocessors. Several companies that have developed fast
RISC (reduced instruction set computing) chips are fighting to depose
Intel's CISC (complex instruction set computing), which has been the
standard since the advent of personal computers. Makers of RISC-based
chips face significant obstacles in their battle with dominant Intel, including the reluctance of software writers to support the technology and the
challenge of convincing PC makers and users to adopt a different technology.[36] But many powerful industry players have joined the RISC fight, and
other less radical technological assaults on Intel have become increasingly
aggressive in 1993. For example, an alliance among Apple, IBM, and
Motorola introduced the PowerPC chip in 1993 with a direct attack on
Intel's new Pentium chip before the Pentium was even available. An ad
announcing the PowerPC chips in the *Wall Street Journal* crows, "It has the
power to blow away Pentium."[37] The key questions are, Can Intel continue
to move fast enough in developing new technology to match or exceed the
performance of competing technologies? Can it maintain the X86 family
as the industry standard? Should it be moving into RISC chips on its own,
even at the sacrifice of its existing position in the market? Former followers are now trying to seize the initiative and the market innovator could
just lose the gains it has made as the first mover and standard setter of the
industry.

Transformation and leapfrogging strategies are not mutually exclusive,
but the managerial energy put into one detracts from what a company can
put into the other. For example, if the first mover chooses the transformation strategy, it will have to divert resources from product R&D into im-

proving production and distribution systems. But at the same time, the product R&D costs are amplifying tremendously if the first mover wants to pursue future leapfrog efforts.

This pattern is most pronounced in high-tech markets such as semiconductors and audio-video equipment, but similar patterns of resource and know-how escalation are seen in other markets. Even a decidedly low-tech industry such as fast food can "hit the wall" with some new innovations. As McDonald's leapfrogged its competitors by reconceptualizing itself as not just a burger restaurant, it considered selling shrimp but realized that its demand would outstrip the entire world's shrimp catch. Moreover, at some point McDonald's will be considering new menu items that have only limited consumer demand. So even if funds are not the constraining resource, other constraints may interfere with significant leapfrog activities.

In sum, the leapfrog strategy can't be used forever, and the transformation strategy leads to more price competitive markets. Leapfrogging forces the imitator to replicate the first mover's new resource base, and transformation requires the first mover to replicate the follower's manufacturing resource base. Thus, once each resource base is replicated, neither player has an advantage in the long run. Both of these strategies, as we have seen, push the limits of the firm's resources and know-how, leaving the firm fighting a bloody price war on a crowded field akin to perfect competition. One escape from this endless cycle of price wars without competitive advantage is to expand downstream, leading us to the next countermove.

The Sixth Dynamic Strategic Interaction: Downstream Vertical Integration

If leapfrogs and transformation become too expensive or difficult for the first mover to implement, the first mover sometimes moves downstream to offer higher value to the customer and more product variety. An aluminum company, for example, might offer sheet metal and ducts, fabricated parts for equipment, and aluminum construction materials to the same customers. This gives it an advantage over companies that offer only aluminum. It might also offer aluminum pots and foil to a completely different market, consumers. Faced with strong price competition and increasingly skilled followers, such as Matsushita, in the consumer electronics market, Sony entered the software side of the entertainment business with the purchase of a motion picture giant, Columbia Pictures. We also see this vertical integration with IBM's move from being a hardware company to being a company where software is as important as hardware. And we see this move in Intel's transition from being a semiconductor maker to entering downstream markets with chips that are essentially a full computer market (combining processing and storage capabilities on one chip) to escape the chip imitators. All of these moves help the first mover to differentiate its now undifferentiated product and to expand its resource base into arenas where its imitators are not present.

Thus, forward vertical integration is similar to the strategy of leapfrogging on technology in that it develops new resources and know-how to offer new products or services. And like the leapfrogging strategy, it leads to a new cycle of competition as imitators duplicate these new resources. The typical counterresponse to this move is for the competitor to acquire or build similar downstream operations. We can see this one-upmanship with Matsushita's purchase of MCA in response to Sony's earlier acquisition of an entertainment firm. It is not clear whether either of these firms can manage such a subsidiary, given their unique cultures and competencies. But, as we can see from this example, even downstream services may be imitable by acquisition. If the acquisitions are managed well, relatively undifferentiated products result, and the firms offer a similar variety of products, making price the only means of competition again.

One problem with both the transformation and downstream vertical integration strategies is that they tie up resources that could be fruitfully committed to building the company's core business. For example, the move by Sony and Matsushita moves them away from their electronics competencies (movies are not required to build VCRs). These strategies should be used only if there are resources left after doing what is needed in the core business. Sometimes opportunities in the core business are so narrow because of competition that the company has no choice but to look elsewhere for profits. But it is a common error of many vertical integration moves to divert funds that could be productively invested in building the core business.

TIMING AND KNOW-HOW ADVANTAGES ARE NOT SUSTAINABLE

Even if the company successfully negotiates its way downstream or upstream, it experiences yet another barrier that limits the continued use of new downstream moves to create advantage. As firms move into more and more downstream activities, the complexity of the organization grows. Management finds it more and more difficult to coordinate all the activities of the diverse but interconnected subsidiaries. So it creates a top-heavy bureaucracy. Without the bureaucracy the benefits of the vertical integration are lost. But with it the firms slow down. It becomes harder to innovate. Changes in one part of the company have ripple effects to all its upstream and downstream activities. So it becomes hard to adapt.

> GM's extensive vertical integration has slowed its efforts to achieve the quality improvements that Ford has achieved and the cost reductions that Chrysler has. GM's less vertically integrated competitors have the advantage of being more nimble. They also have access to purchasing higher-quality and lower-cost components available in the marketplace.

Thus, as firms use vertical integration to escape commodity-like or perfectly competitive markets, they also create more complex, nonadaptable organizations that are easy to outmaneuver.

Thus, the dynamic strategic interactions built around creating timing and know-how advantages eventually lead the company to a price and resource competitive market. Either the follower replicates the new resource base of the first mover and becomes as good at this crucial' technology as the first mover or the first mover replicates the resource base of the follower and becomes a low-cost producer.

Either way, the cycle of leapfrogging, following and moving downstream cannot continue forever. So, neither strategy is sustainable. The first mover cannot afford to keep innovating. As the followers follow more and more quickly, the first mover cannot recapture its R&D investment and it loses its incentive to innovate. If the first mover stops innovating, the followers have no one to imitate. The cycles of innovation and imitation are replaced by a deadly battle over price, and neither side can keep its resource-based advantage forever.

The Escalation Ladder within the Timing and Know-how Arena

As they do with cost and quality competition, companies escalate up this second ladder of moves and countermoves, seeking to gain a temporary advantage at each step in the process until they reach perfect competition. As illustrated in Figure 2–11, the first mover starts the cycle by building a technological resource base to create an advantage. The company uses this resource base to move into a new market. Followers escalate the conflict by imitating the new product. The first mover escalates further by throwing up impediments to keep followers from imitating subsequent products. Followers escalate once again by overcoming the impediments and replicating the resource base of the first mover.

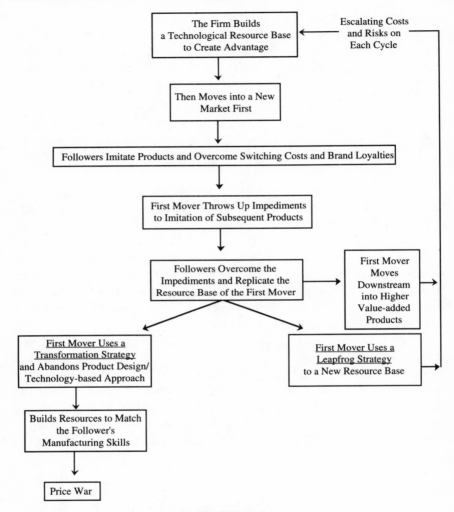

FIGURE 2–11
THE CYCLE OF TIMING/KNOW-HOW COMPETITION

At this point some first movers use a leapfrogging strategy to create a new resource base. This begins the cycle again, but with higher risks and greater costs. If the first mover does not choose to leapfrog, it can use a transformation strategy to compete with later entrants by replicating their resource base of process know-how and low-cost manufacturing methods. The transformation strategy leads to a price war, and the leapfrogging strategy eventually leads to risks and costs that are greater than the rewards. Instead of transforming itself or leapfrogging to a new product, the first mover can also use vertical integration to gain temporary advantage over competitors. But this vertical integration can also be imitated by competitors, and it creates a complex, nonadaptable organization that makes the firm vulnerable to more flexible, less integrated competitors. Ultimately, advantages that originally accrued to firms from timing and know-how are not sustainable, and the conflict escalates closer to perfect competition at each step.

Although we portray this cycle (in Figure 2–11) as sequential, it may also be parallel. Two or three resource bases may be used at the same time. Also, some companies skip steps along this ladder or end up frozen at one rung temporarily. Industries proceed up the ladder at different speeds, depending upon the aggressiveness and quirks of competitors in the industry, the technology barriers confronted, the creativity of individuals who might influence the industry, how long patents remain effective, and market conditions. Nevertheless, this escalation ladder defines the rungs in a general process that shows how one dynamic strategic interaction leads to the next. But competitors will climb up this ladder in many different ways.

HYPERCOMPETITIVE BEHAVIOR IN THE TIMING AND KNOW-HOW ARENA

We have observed how first movers and followers maneuver against each other to move ahead on the escalation ladder with new product introductions and new generations of products. We have also seen how these maneuvers speed up over time and get bolder. Hypercompetitive firms attempt to avoid or break out of perfect competition (where no one has an advantage) by (1) speeding up the ladder faster than the other players or (2) restarting the cycle by building new knowledge bases that allow new products and business methods to be used.

Hypercompetition in the Timing and Know-how Arenas of Two Industries: The Ethical Pharmaceuticals Industry and Flat-Panel Screens

As illustrated by the Hoffmann-LaRoche example at the beginning of this chapter, timing and know-how can provide a big advantage. However, dynamic maneuvering erodes these advantages. As can be seen in the following description of a half century of competition in the pharmaceutical industry (shown in Figure 2–12),[38] technological and market know-how provide only a temporary advantage. In R&D and marketing and promotions, the know-how required for success continued to evolve through innovation and competitive maneuvering. In R&D, methods for identifying new drug compounds have changed from molecular manipulation prior to World War II to soil screening and fermentation skills in the 1950s. This trial-and-error technique gave way to "rational drug design" and finally to biotechnology. Each new stage in the evolution of key competencies led to the emergence of new firms with those competencies, eventually making them obsolete and requiring the development of a new knowledge-based core competence.

Similarly, in marketing and promotion, skills have shifted from direct sales to physicians, "blockbuster" marketing, and specialized sales to different medical specialties. A new, emerging source of competence is the ability to cope with regulatory agencies, as approval processes account for an increasing portion of the cost of developing and launching a new drug.

Thus, the hypercompetitive firm is not one that allows price war to last.

FIGURE 2–12
SHIFTING KNOW-HOW IN THE R_x INDUSTRY

COMPETENCIES IN R&D

Technology	Impact and Nature	Firms/Roles
Organic Chemistry, 1870s–Present	Established by Central European dye firms through molecular manipulation, trial and error	Hoechst, Ciba-Geigy: Sustained competence in product development for over a century
Fermentation and Soil Screening, 1940s–Present	Established antibiotic firms in the United States; narrow competence not transferable to other drug classes	Lilly, Squibb: Dominant products brought industry leadership for twenty years, then began to lag
Rational Drug Design, 1970s–Present	High-cost drug development driven by advances in biochemistry	SmithKline, Merck: Able to develop drugs, required cutting edge research across classes
Biotechnology, 1980s–Present	Nonorganic approach to drug therapy	Genentech, Amgen: Specialized, cutting-edge research, knowledge and insight

FIGURE 2–12 (Cont'd.)
SHIFTING KNOW-HOW IN THE R$_x$ INDUSTRY

COMPETENCIES IN MARKETING AND PROMOTION

Skill	Impact and Nature	Firms/Roles
Direct Selling to Physicians, 1950s	Allowed for the effective marketing to gatekeepers in economic transactions	Pfizer, Lederle: Created effective differentiation of products among gatekeepers
"Blockbuster" Marketing, Early–mid 1980s	Single product focus of entire detail force and promotion; effective with narrow product line	Glaxo: Created a new way to sell; through selling, gave blockbuster potential to a chemically indifferent drug
Specialized Selling	Specialized sales forces for different therapeutic classes/medical specialities; more focus with broad product line	Merck: Specially trained and focused units in cardio, hospital, etc.
Handling Regulatory Requirements	Speeds drugs to market, expanding time available under patent for economic profits	Merck, Marion: Of limited value without competence in acquiring new drugs

Source: "Linking Competitive Advantage and Core Competence," by William Bogner and Howard Thomas. Chapter 2 of *Competence Based Competition*, edited by G.Hamel and A. Heene. © 1994 by John Wiley and Sons.

It fights by a succession of actions and the development of entirely new knowledge bases. It speeds up the escalation ladder in Figure 2–11 and restarts it frequently. But this is often an exhausting effort because imitators cannot be stopped.

The flat-panel screen industry is a good example of why hypercompetitive firms can close the innovation and knowledge gap, even when they are far behind. Flat-panel screens are turning up everywhere—on laptop computers, high definition TVs, telephones, and airplane and auto instrument panels. Nearly all of them are made in Japan. But newly hypercompetitive U.S. companies aren't giving up. Highly aggressive Motorola has committed to large-scale display manufacturing in the United States giant Texas Instruments and tiny OIS, Optical Imaging Systems, Inc., have been developing innovative flat-panel systems and components in their labs. IBM is attempting to get access to Toshiba's active-matrix technology by participating in a joint venture to make flat screens in Japan. DARPA (the Pentagon's Defense Advanced Research Projects Agency) has joined a consortium of U.S. firms (including AT&T, Xerox, OIS, and Standish Industries) to cut down Japan's lead. Moreover, the U.S. government found that Japan was dumping their screens in the United States, so there was a 62.7% tariff imposed in 1992 that has seriously hurt the Japanese flat-panel makers.

While Japan has invested almost $3 billion in factories to make advanced displays, they are using an active-matrix liquid-crystal technology where every pixel (a dot on the screen) is controlled by its own transistor. So screens require millions of transistors. Fabrication is fiendishly difficult, and these panels are limited in size to twenty inches across. They are also very costly ($1,500 for a ten-inch laptop screen).

U.S. firms (like Motorola and In Focus Systems, Inc.) are working on simpler passive-matrix screens that promise higher quality at lower cost. Texas Instruments is developing an exotic display using tiny movable mirrors. Micron Technology, Inc. (a chip maker in Idaho), is trying to make screens in which each pixel is lit by its own electron beam.

So world-class American technology is being brought to bear on the Japanese lead, and the U.S. government is helping through tariffs, defense spending, and allowing research consortia of the type mentioned above. Things are just getting started, and it is too early to say if the United States will overtake its Japanese competitors. However, U.S. electronics firms and the defense department realize they can't stay dependent on Japanese suppliers of flat screens because the screens are increasingly "selling the product."

Escalating to the Next Arena of Competition

While imitators and leapfroggers cannot be stopped, they can be forcefully kept out of certain markets by hypercompetitive firms. This is done, not by stopping them from imitating, but by limiting their ability to distribute or produce in the first mover's home turf. The first mover may let followers make and sell the product in different geographic or customer markets. As long as the followers can't get into the first mover's core market, these later entrants do not pose a threat to the first mover, and the first mover maintains a protected stronghold. Potentially competing firms can be shut out of the markets of an established firm who has walled off regions from competitive entry. This leads to the next arena of competition: the creation of entry barriers and the battle over turf, which we will discuss in the next chapter on the creation and defense of strongholds.

Management Challenges

This sketch of competitive moves and countermoves can help you analyze your current position and plan your future moves. The sequence of dynamic strategic interactions described in this chapter can also help you anticipate your competitors' next move. By seeing what's ahead, you can jump levels to speed the escalation of the cycle and catch your competitors off guard. Those who climb the ladder faster are always one step ahead of the competition, forcing the others to catch up with the new advantage created by moving up to the next step. Or you can take action to slow down the competitor's movement up the ladder if you are already ahead and don't want your competitors to jump past you. The following are some of the major issues that managers face in taking control of this cycle:

- Should your firm pursue an evolutionary or revolutionary technology strategy to meet the know-how challenges it will face in the future?
- Is it better to employ a strategy of being a first mover, a close follower, or a later follower in your industry? Why?
- How will you use timing of market entry to your advantage?
- When you enter the market, what will your competitor's response be?
- What resource base will you build up and how soon can it be replicated by your competitors? How soon can you replicate their resource base?
- What types of resources are hardest to replicate in your industry? Why?
- What intangible assets are crucial to dominating your industry? Why?
- Is it to your advantage to speed up this process of evolution of the industry? If so, how can you make it move faster?
- Can you ever really stop the process from occurring even if you have the upper hand?
- Are you leading your industry up the ladder or following? Why?
- Who and what is setting the pace of escalation in your industry? Why?

Not all industries are at the same point along this cycle. Some move through each of the rungs on the escalation ladder in Figure 2–11 quickly and others slowly. Some have potential to be frozen at one rung. Others don't. Some can be speeded up. Others can't. But most travel through these rungs over the long run. By understanding these mileposts, you can take greater charge of your direction and face fewer surprises from competitors. In Part III of this book, we will develop several techniques and strategies for dealing with these management challenges and for creating the types of temporary advantages that are available at each step of the escalation ladder in this arena of competition.

HOW FIRMS OUTMANEUVER COMPETITORS THAT HAVE BUILT STRONGHOLDS USING ENTRY BARRIERS

LIMITING COMPETITORS

When it is apparent that competitive advantage can be lost in the first two arenas—cost and quality, timing and know-how—firms resort to using the powerful impact of entry barriers. By creating hurdles for their potential competitors, established firms try to head off competitors that might engage in the price-quality and timing-know-how cycles before they enter the battlefield. Established firms build high barriers that exclude competitors and define the firm's turf for its exclusive use. This turf (or stronghold) may be bounded geographically (Japan, for instance) or by product and customer need or type (such as luxury watch consumers) or both.

Limiting competitors to a small number of firms produces several advantages:

- *Tacit cooperation among rivals* A small number of competitors makes it easier for the firms to arrive at an "oligopolistic bargain." That is, they can find a way tacitly to cooperate by signaling to each other what behavior each expects of the other. They may tacitly agree on a "focal" price that is higher than the one that would have resulted if they had competed aggressively. They may implicitly divide the market up into segments with each competitor dominating a different segment and avoiding the segments of other competitors. Or they may agree on quality and design standards that benefit their respective firms. They may even decide to restrict the industry's output quantity to create shortages that result in price increases. Occasionally such cooperative arrangements can be sustained for years if the parties have an incentive to cooperate. While sitting down over a table and agreeing to fix prices is clearly illegal, even tacit cooperation can sometimes be in the gray areas of antitrust, but it is a frequent strategy of many companies.

- *Power over buyers* A small number of competitors generates power over buyers. Customers who want the product have only a few options. They cannot shop around too much, so they must take what they can get when they can find it.
- *Power over suppliers* Similarly, a small number of competitors limits the options of suppliers. If suppliers have output to sell, they must sell it to whomever they can. Fewer options reduce the suppliers' ability to hunt around for firms who are willing to pay a higher price because of a greater need for the input.
- *Power over potential entrants and substitutes* If the barriers are high, potential entrants and makers of substitute products are forced to deal with one of the few competitors who are already established inside the walls surrounded by the barriers. U.S. firms seeking access to Japanese markets are often told to joint-venture with or license to an incumbent Japanese firm if they want any chance of selling in that market. This allows the Japanese firms access to U.S. product designs and technologies, which they can improve in their protected Japanese market. Later they can sell the improved version in the U.S. markets. The small number of competitors makes it difficult to find a more benevolent partner when shopping for a way to enter Japan.

Tacit cooperation and power over buyers, suppliers, and entrants allow firms to earn profits that would not be available if the market were more competitive. They allow firms to raise price above competitive levels, control quality below competitive levels, and remove the incentive to escalate costs by innovating and imitating each other. Thus, they slow movement up the escalation ladders discussed in the previous two chapters. Of course, as more competitors enter the industry, these advantages are reduced. Thus, entry barriers are crucial to the maintenance of limited numbers and to slowing the escalating conflicts outlined in earlier chapters.

Traditional Static Views of Strongholds and Entry-Barrier Advantages

According to traditional models, building barriers around a stronghold is an important source of competitive advantage because these barriers allow the company to earn profits in a protected market that can be used to fund price wars, R&D, and other actions in other, more competitive, markets.

Porter identifies six major barriers to entry that can be used to create a stronghold: economies of scale, product differentiation, capital requirements, switching costs, access to distribution channels, and cost disadvantages other than scale.[1]

- *Economies of scale* enjoyed by the incumbent make it difficult for a new entrant to offer competitive prices because the incumbent's higher volume reduces its costs. The entrant would have to find a way around this cost disadvantage to enter the market profitably.

  > Gallo Winery's dominant hold on the U.S. wine market, with 31 percent of the low-priced market in 1985, has given the company power with grape growers and distributors, as well as allowing Gallo to underprice competitors. Their size allowed them to launch extensive marketing campaigns and establish a distribution network in a market which previously had no central distribution. As a 1986 article in *Fortune* noted, "When it comes to business, the brothers Ernest and Julio Gallo brook neither waste nor weakness. Just ask the scores of companies, large and small, that over the past five decades have made the mistake of venturing onto their turf. . . . They are not afraid to exercise their power over grape growers, distributors, or anyone else."[2]

- *Product differentiation* involves the reputation of the incumbent for quality. An incumbent with a strong brand image or sophisticated, higher-quality product is more difficult to attack since the entrant must find a low cost way to catch up with the incumbent's image or quality.

  > Haagen-Dazs used product differentiation to capture the emerging superpremium ice cream market in the United States and later moved aggressively into European markets. It offered traditional ice cream flavors, but with a "premium" taste derived from high-quality, all-natural ingredients and 15 percent more butterfat. This high-quality image, reinforced by marketing that stressed ice cream as an "affordable luxury," helped make Haagen-Dazs "the Rolls-Royce of U.S. ice creams."[3]

- *Capital investments* needed to enter an industry sometimes make it very difficult for other firms to enter. Entrants must find a low-cost way to replicate the incumbent's investments in equipment, research, or technology.
- *Switching costs*, the one-time expenses for customers who switch to a competitor's products, can make it difficult for a firm to enter a market. If customers are locked into the products of the incumbent, the

entrant will have to find a way to lower the cost of switching or to woo them away from the incumbent with such improved value that the switching costs are trivial.

> Nintendo gained a lock on the U.S. home video game market by blanketing the market with their video game system. By 1988 Nintendo controlled an estimated 80 percent of the U.S. video game market.[4] The expense of the system and the incompatibility of Nintendo cartridges with other systems created large switching costs for consumers who wanted to switch to another system. They would not only have to buy a new system but also replace all their cartridges. Nintendo's license arrangements with some thirty software developers (including competitor Atari) also help ensure that many new games appeared on Nintendo's cartridges, reducing the incentive for customers to switch systems to gain access to new game programs and making it harder for competitors to offer such a wide variety of programs.

- *Access to distribution channels* controlled by the incumbent can be a key entry barrier. If incumbents have agreements with existing distributors that tie up distribution channels, it can be much more difficult for companies to enter. The new entrant would face the challenge of breaking into these distribution networks or establishing channels of its own.

> IBM's control of distribution channels, through its direct-sales force and large dealer network, made it difficult for many smaller companies to penetrate the market for mainframes and, later, personal computers. IBM's direct-sales force provide sales and service to major customers, ensuring a close relationship with these firms. The network of IBM dealers served smaller business and private computer buyers. The sales representatives and dealers provided technical support in addition to equipment, which was particularly valuable for early buyers who did not have computer expertise on staff. The distribution network gave Big Blue a tight grip on the market.

> Another example of the control of distribution channels is the control the major networks achieved through limited frequencies available for broadcasting. The limitation on the number of distribution channels allowed local stations and national networks to gain a strong grip on the television market.

- *Cost disadvantages other than scale* may be created by nonscale manufacturing advantages, ownership of low-cost supplies of raw materials, favorable locations, or government subsidies. All these advantages of the incumbent make it more difficult for competitors to break into the market because the entrant's costs will exceed the incumbent's costs. Thus, the entrant must find a way to lower its costs by replication or by circumventing the incumbent's cost advantages.

> The Japanese shipbuilding industry emerged as a leading player in the industry after World War II, rising in the world market from 8 percent in 1954 to nearly 50 percent in 1973. Japanese companies were aided by a number of barriers that gave them cost advantages over non-Japanese firms. The government targeted shipbuilding as a strategic industry and provided subsidies. Companies also had access to low-priced, high-quality steel. The top seven shipbuilders were integrated heavy-machine companies that could take advantage of economies of scope and synergies to increase quality and lower costs. In addition, Japanese shipbuilders were helped by an advantage in engine development and experience in high technology and design. This combination of production efficiencies, technology advantages, and government support created a substantial advantage over other companies in the industry.

- *Government policy* Although not one of Porter's original barriers, these barriers have become increasingly significant in global markets. Beyond government subsidies, countries can create direct barriers to entry to prevent foreign competitors from moving into the country. This creates strong geographic barriers. Government regulations can help strengthen the other six barriers. Government barriers have traditionally been very powerful obstacles to outside competitors.

> National telecommunications monopolies are among the most unassailable geographic strongholds. The power of these monopolies can be seen in Europe's PTT (post, telephone, and telegraph) monopolies. The PTTs have held a tenacious grip on the market despite poorer service, less technological sophistication, and higher prices than foreign competitors.

> Japan's strong entry barriers and support for its internal industries helped it rebuild after the devastation of World War II. Tight relationships between companies and government agencies and the strength of the keiretsu system make it difficult for outsiders to enter. These seemly impenetrable barriers created resentment among U.S. competitors, who felt shut out of the Japanese market while Japanese competitors moved into U.S. markets.

> The Soviet Union, with its central government and tightly controlled market, offered tremendous barriers to outsiders. Political control at the national and local level made it hard for foreign firms to break through. Shortages of supplies and infrastructures also inhibited outside development. And a commitment to communist principles, in sharp contrast to the goals of any moneymaking enterprise, tended to discourage outside investment.

Many of these barriers are derived from actions in the the first two arenas—cost-quality and timing-know-how—but the focus here is on how these barriers prevent the *movement* of companies into geographic or market strongholds. These barriers play an important role in reducing the threat of entry by potential competitors who offer similar products or even a substitute product. So long as the incumbent firms have very low costs relative to the potential entrants (with similar or substitute products), the potential entrant is less likely to attack. Even if incumbents sell at a high price, their lower cost positions them to retaliate and drive out entrants as they appear.

Useful Insights Resulting from This View of Competitive Advantage

Michael Porter, synthesizing years of work by industrial organization economists, developed his now-famous Five Forces model."[5] Based on the view that limiting competition improves profitability, he asserts there are five influences on the profitability of a firm: threat of new entrants (prevented by entry barriers), intensity of industry rivalry, threat of substitutes, bargaining power of suppliers, and bargaining power of buyers. Limiting the number of competitors improves profits by reducing the aggressiveness of the *rivalry* among competitors in the industry, the power of *buyers* over the firm, the power of *suppliers* over the firm, and the threats posed by potential *entrants* with similar or *substitute products*. Since its introduction in 1980, the Five Forces model has become a staple. Almost every consulting firm, strategic planning department, and MBA now uses this model as an analytical tool to identify how the firm can reduce the aggressiveness of rivalry, the power of buyers and suppliers, and the threat of entrants and substitutes.

THE DYNAMIC VIEW OF STRONGHOLDS: TURF BATTLES AND BREACHING ENTRY BARRIERS

Thus, entry barriers and the five forces play an important role in competitive strategy. However, as competitors have become more aware of the strategic importance of entry barriers and as the market becomes more dynamic, companies have become more creative and aggressive in circumventing entry barriers. These barriers, as we will show in examples that follow, are often more effective in creating temporary delays than permanent obstacles to progress. When an incumbent builds a wall around a region or market, its competitors then try to find ways to overcome or circumvent that entry barrier. This launches a series of dynamic strategic interactions that eventually erode all entry barriers. We will examine this process in this chapter.

Falling Barriers

Like the Berlin Wall, barriers are falling around the world and across product markets. While some barriers continue to hold back competitors, they are being overcome with increasing rapidity. Geographic barriers are under pressure from growing globalization and technological improvements. Product market barriers are also falling because of the same forces and the increasing flexibility and aggressiveness of competitors as well as growing awareness and discrimination by customers. As product cycles become shorter, scale economies and product-based experience curves become less important. Rather than shoring up their existing strongholds, companies such as 3M move aggressively into innovations with their core competencies. In addition, improved telecommunications, transportation, and other technologies have created strong global markets and eroded local fiefdoms.[6] In fact, each of the seven entry barriers we discussed can be and has been eroded. Consider a few ways to erode each of these barriers.

- *Economies of scale* By exporting from a larger plant in its home turf, the entrant can draw on its own economies of scale even if it has a small position in the incumbent's market. For example, Japanese and Taiwanese semiconductor manufacturers used economies of scale gained in domestic markets to achieve low prices when entering the U.S. market. This gave them such an advantage that U.S. companies filed dumping charges.[7] The large size often required to achieve economies of scale can also decrease the flexibility of the company, making it vulnerable to more nimble competitors.

  Although its economies of scale helped Gallo Winery become the largest wine producer in the United States, its size also inhibited its ability to respond to changes in the market. Tastes of consumers changed. Customers preferred Varietals using special or unique grapes which were more expensive. Gallo had difficulties obtaining the grapes from its suppliers. At the same time, a fitness craze and concerns about drunken driving began to dry up the market for cheap wine in favor of limited consumption of more expensive wines. *Fortune* notes that early on Gallo's name was associated by some customers with mass-produced, inexpensive table wine, making it harder for it to expand into premium wines.[8] Growers also forward-integrated to create new capacity in the market. When the market shifted, the barriers that once helped Gallo keep out competitors now tended to hold it in a less profitable segment of the market.

- *Product differentiation* In the chapters on cost and quality and timing and know-how advantages, we examined how competitors can overcome a differentiation strategy through a variety of interactions. This can be done by direct imitation or by variations that create difference or higher perceived quality.

> Ben & Jerry's successfully challenged Haagen-Dazs's differentiation barriers by creating further levels of differentiation. Ben & Jerry's matched Haagen-Dazs's premium ingredients but then upped the ante by introducing a variety of unconventional flavors. They mixed in Heath bars, Oreos, and something called Rainforest Crunch and brought out exotic flavors such as Cherry Garcia and White Russian. Ben & Jerry's also differentiated itself by its corporate philosophy of supporting social causes. This support of causes also helped the small Ben & Jerry's gain widespread publicity and compete with its deep-pocketed rival (Haagen-Dazs is owned by Pillsbury). Instead of trying merely to catch up with the incumbent, Ben & Jerry's went one or two steps farther. *Marketing News* reports that, by the end of 1991, Ben & Jerry's had snatched nearly 29 percent of the superpremium ice cream market, enough to attract the attention of market leader Haagen-Dazs (with 43 percent). In 1992 Haagen-Dazs, in an apparent attempt to match Ben & Jerry's differentiation on flavor, announced plans to branch out from traditional flavors to such goodies as Carrot Cake Passion, Cappuccino Commotion, Caramel Cone Explosion, Triple Brownie Overload, and Peanut Butter Burst.[9] The move was expected to cut into Ben & Jerry's market, eroding its own differentiation barrier.

- *Capital investments* We will examine strategies firms use to overcome capital requirements in the next chapter. For now, it is important to note that many foreign entrants are very large companies with lots of resources and sometimes even lower costs of capital, so capital often is not a problem.
- *Switching costs* The entrant can eliminate switching costs by reducing the risk of trying the new product. It can offer free samples or redesign the product to make conversion less costly for customers. For example, Pepsi recently sent free cases of Diet Pepsi to Diet Coke

drinkers. Computer software makers are also including free samples of their programs on the hard drives of new computers or packaging it with PCs or peripherals. This overcomes the cost of having to purchase the new software.[10]

> While Nintendo retains its stranglehold on video game players, companies have found ways around its grip on the more lucrative game software market. Atari, who licensed its games for sale through Nintendo, announced plans in 1988 to market its own video games that could be used on Nintendo hardware.[11] Atari also rolled out game cartridges and accessories such as joysticks and battery packs for both Nintendo and Sega systems.[12] As lawsuits raged between Nintendo and Atari, Nintendo conceded the right to several smaller companies to produce Nintendo-compatible game cartridges which bypass Nintendo's security chip, which is designed to keep out foreign cartridges.[13] Meanwhile, on the equipment side, Nintendo is under attack by innovations from Sega Enterprises, which developed a color screen for the portable video game players.[14]

- *Access to distribution channels* The new entrant sometimes acquires its own distribution network. For example, Schneider, a French electrical products firm, acquired the largest U.S. distribution network for electrical products when it bought Square D. Others piggyback on U.S. distribution networks owned by others. For example, when Kirin Beer, the largest Japanese beer company, was unable to crack the U.S. beer and wine distribution network, it tried to distribute through the network used by soda-bottling plants. Similarly, many Japanese car companies use the dealers of American cars.

> IBM's hold on computer distribution systems suffered tremendous erosion when the market shifted toward personal computers and buyers became more sophisticated. Dell Computer circumvented IBM's direct-sales force and dealer network by shifting to mail-order sales. In addition to staking out a new distribution channel, Dell also cut the high overhead of a dedicated sales force or dealer network. This helped it drive prices down far below IBM. This new distribution network provided other advantages. Dell could offer twenty-four-hour replacement and service numbers, while dealers might take weeks to obtain parts. Four years after Dell entered the market, its revenues topped $250 million while IBM was laying off workers.[15]

> The hold of the major networks on television channels has been sharply eroded by the rise of cable television. This grip on the market continues to weaken with the spreading coverage of cable and technology that will allow cable companies to crowd more channels onto their lines. A new digital-compression technology was expected to allow cable companies to supply five hundred or more channels to subscribers by early 1994.[16]

- *Cost disadvantages other than scale* The entrant can use its own cost advantages (e.g., low-cost labor) and process innovations (e.g., just-in-time inventory systems) to overcome the cost advantages of the incumbent.

  The Japanese rise in the shipbuilding industry—exploiting its non-scale cost advantages—was an inspiration to Korean shipbuilding. Korean firms duplicated Japan's success and in the process showed that the gains that could be developed through government subsidies and other national advantages could also be eroded by a competitor with the same advantages. Although Korea lacked experience, an experienced workforce, and economies of scale, its nonscale advantages allowed it to become a major player in the industry. The government targeted the industry for growth, offering special financing arrangements to shipbuilders. In addition, Korean companies had low-cost labor ($4.50 per hour compared to $18 per hour in Japan) and access to low-cost steel. Japanese and European shipbuilders, not recognizing Korea as a serious threat, shared training and technology with Korean companies. By 1983 Korea had gained 19 percent of all new shipbuilding orders.[17]

- *Government policy* If the incumbent's government is throwing up obstacles to the entrant, the entrant can turn to its own government for assistance. New technology has also allowed creative entrepreneurs to circumvent barriers. Government regulations have also been under attack from innovative overseas competitors on the one side and customer pressures for new policies on the other.

  Europe's PTTs are losing their hold on the international long-distance market to entrepreneurs with sophisticated ring-back operations. These U.S.-based companies have circumvented the European stronghold by routing calls through a toll-free number to the United States at a substantial discount to customers. European businesses call the number, and a computer dials them back, so the call technically originates in the United States, outside the PTT's control. Customer pressure is also forcing governments to open markets to keep their other industries competitive. Major companies in Europe, such as Unilever, are establishing their own communications networks and giving the contracts to U.S. firms rather than the sluggish European national monopolies. This has placed pressure on regulators, who are dismantling the national monopolies. The European Community has ordered its twelve governments to abolish the monopolies in sectors such as data transmission and electronic mail, and deregulation of voice transmission may not be far behind. Europe's post, telephone, and telegraph markets, insulated so long from competition, cannot match the quality or cost of foreign competitors.[18]

  U.S. firms have made headway in Japanese markets through aggressive marketing and alliances with Japanese companies. Two U.S. securities firms, Salomon Brothers and Morgan Stanley, have done so well on the Tokyo Exchange that they outranked all but two Japanese securities houses on pretax earnings in November 1991.[19] In what may be a response to these gains, Japanese regulators introduced a wave of new rules in 1992 on arbitrage trading that hit non-Japanese firms hardest.[20] Apple has teamed up with Japanese giants such as Sony, Sharp, and Toshiba in creating its latest line of computers and electronic organizers, gaining more than 8 percent of the Japanese computer market in 1993. Microsoft has moved into the fragmented Japanese software market with a Japanese version of Windows, taking sixty-five thousand orders in two days. Riding on the coattails of the Windows introduction, U.S. computer companies such as Compaq, IBM, and Dell are making new inroads into the NEC-dominated Japanese computer market. Meanwhile, U.S. semiconductor companies doubled their market share in Japan over the course of three years, gaining 20 percent of the market by 1993.[21] The Ford-Mazda alliance has given Ford one of the strongest footholds in the market of U.S. automakers. Meanwhile, the Big Three automakers from Detroit have placed increasing pressure on U.S. officials to push the Japanese government for policy concessions that would promote increased foreign sales within Japan. U.S.-Japan negotiations on supercomputers have resulted in a more open market for U.S. manufacturers.[22]

Aggressive and creative U.S. companies have managed to break into the markets of the former Soviet Union. Consumer goods such as Pepsi and McDonald's had a relatively easy time finding a spot in Moscow compared to complex industries such as petroleum. Yet even with the substantial political and technical challenges of oil exploration in the former Soviet Union, Chevron and other companies have made their way through this minefield, drawn by some of the most promising oil fields in the world. Chevron—surviving the collapse of the Soviet Union and a military coup—spent four years working out the agreement that eventually led to a 50–50 joint venture with a Kazakh partner.[23] Even if such countries are not overly enthusiastic about the prospect of outside partners, they often have no choice because they cannot find the expertise or capital for the project within the country.

In addition to overcoming the above entry barriers, entrants often rely on synergies with their other businesses and acquisitions to break into strongholds.

- *Synergies with existing businesses* Johnson & Johnson's Ethicon unit used synergies with its existing operations to enter into the new market for noninvasive surgical equipment (laparoscopic equipment) dominated by U.S. Surgical, according to *Business Week*.[24] U.S. Surgical, which arrived in the laparoscopy market a year and a half before J&J, had seized 85 percent of this market, expected to grow to three billion dollars by 1996.[25] This headstart gave U.S. Surgical economies of scope and scale, creating switching costs and other barriers for doctors already using its equipment. But J&J overcame these barriers by using synergies with its Hospital Products Group and suture division. In entering the market for laparoscopy, J&J unleashed its preexisting sales force of five hundred people and opened a state-of-the-art training center for surgeons. J&J, although it had only a small position in that market, could throw the weight of its preexisting distribution network (to hospital purchasing agents), research facilities, and good brand image behind the market entry. J&J also offered lower prices and high levels of customer service. By 1992 it had introduced forty-five new surgical instruments and was rapidly closing the gap with U.S. Surgical, according to *Financial World*.[26]

In what appears to be a response to J&J's entry into the laparoscopy market, U.S. Surgical used its technological skills, brand image, and marketing channels to move into the $1 billion traditional suture business with a new line of absorbable products for orthopedic surgery. Sutures had been J&J's stronghold for decades (but U.S. Surgical had already made some headway in the market with its surgical stapler). In this way U.S. Surgical appears to have responded to J&J's entry with its own counterentry into J&J's stronghold. This erodes U.S. Surgical's position in the laparoscopy market and at the same time erodes J&J's position in the suture market, merging the two marketplaces into one full line of surgical products. This illustrates some of the dynamic strategic interactions that work to undermine strongholds, as we will examine in the rest of this chapter.

Similarly, Gallo used synergies with its existing wine production, marketing, and distribution to launch its Bartles & Jaymes wine cooler. The wine cooler was launched two years after pioneer California Cooler attempted to use beer distribution and bottling to sell its cooler. Building on synergies with its wine business, Gallo became top seller in the market just eight months after launching Bartles & Jaymes.[27]

- *Acquisition* Companies often use acquisitions or alliances to overcome product/market and geographic entry barriers. Hershey Foods Corporation, which had almost no presence in European markets, entered through acquisitions. In 1991, for example, Hershey bought a German boxed-chocolate company and a 19 percent share of the largest confectionery company in Scandinavia.[28]

These examples of the erosion of entry barriers are in line with perceptions of managers. A study of 293 managers found that only a little more than half the respondents reported the "frequent" use of one or more entry barriers to keep out competitors. The main reasons for not deterring entry were the intensity of competition, product-line growth, or because deterrence strategies were too expensive.[29] When another researcher asked 137 executives in 49 different companies about the importance of Porter's barriers to entry, they indicated that only cost advantages seemed to be a significant barrier. If the entrant can meet or beat the incumbent's cost, there is little to stand in the way of entry. Even for the remaining entry barriers, different respondents weighed the barriers very differently. Thus, a given barrier is unlikely to deter all potential entrants. These perceptions held for both industrial and consumer markets.[30]

Is it just large, foreign companies that can batter down entry barriers? Innovative small companies can also maneuver around entry barriers, as we saw in the case of Ben & Jerry's above. A cross-sectional study of 247 manufacturing industries found that small firms have successfully circumvented or overcome entry barriers. Smaller companies have used strategies of product innovation and "flexible specialization" to enter and survive in markets in which they suffer severe size and cost disadvantages.[31]

This is not to imply that every potential entrant will have the ability to break down the entry barriers protecting an industry. In fact, for most potential entrants, the barriers will keep them out. However, to work, entry barriers must hold out *every* potential entrant. All it takes is just one hypercompetitive entrant anywhere in the world with the skills to breach the barriers—a likely scenario. Also, if the entry barrier is lowered even temporarily by technology shifts and other discontinuities, aggressive competitors will very likely enter through this "strategic window." These windows can open as a result of new primary demand opportunities, new competing technology, market redefinition, and distribution-channel changes.[32] Competence-destroying technological discontinuities can also permanently reshape markets through new product classes such as cement and plain-paper copying, product substitutions such as transistors for vacuum tubes, and process substitutions such as open hearth to oxygen furnaces in glassmaking. These discontinuities provide opportunities for new entrants in the market.[33]

Figure 3–1 illustrates some major technological changes in three industries, identifying whether these changes were competence destroying or enhancing (i.e., whether they obsoleted or neutralized the existing skills of the incumbent firms) and whether they were niche opening (i.e., whether

FIGURE 3–1
THE EXPLOITATION OF SIGNIFICANT TECHNOLOGICAL
DISCONTINUITIES BY NEW FIRMS IN THREE INDUSTRIES

Industry	Year	Event	Importance	Type of Disconti- nuity	LOCUS OF INNOVATION	
					New Firms	Exist- ing Firms
Cement	1872	First pro- duction of Portland cement in the United States	Discovery of proper raw materials and importation of knowledge opens new in- dustry	Niche opening	10 of 10	1 of 10
	1896	Patent for process burning powdered coal as fuel	Permits eco- nomical use of efficient rotary kilns	Compe- tence- destroying	4 of 5	1 of 5
	1909	Edison pa- tents long kiln (150 ft.)	Higher out- put with less cost	Compe- tence- enhancing	1 of 6	5 of 6
	1966	Dundee Cement installs huge kiln, far larger than any previous.	Use of pro- cess control permits oper- ation of very efficient kilns	Compe- tence- enhancing	1 of 8	7 of 8
Airlines	1924	First airline	Mail con- tracts make transport fea- sible	Niche opening	9 of 10	1 of 10
	1936	DC-3 air- plane	First large and fast enough to carry passen- gers economi- cally	Compe- tence- enhancing	0 of 4	4 of 4
	1959	First jet airplane in commer- cial use	Speed changes eco- nomics of fly- ing	Compe- tence- enhancing	0 of 4	4 of 4

(*Continued*)

FIGURE 3–1
THE EXPLOITATION OF SIGNIFICANT TECHNOLOGICAL
DISCONTINUITIES BY NEW FIRMS IN THREE INDUSTRIES (*Cont'd.*)

Industry	Year	Event	Importance	Type of Disconti- nuity	New Firms	Exist- ing Firms
					LOCUS OF INNOVATION	
	1969	Wide body jets debut	Much greater capacity and efficiency	Compe- tence- enhancing	0 of 4	4 of 4
Mini- com- puter manufac- ture	1956	Burroughs E-101	First com- puter under $50,000	Niche opening	1 of 8	7 of 8
	1965	Digital Equip- ment Corp. PDP-8	First inte- grated circuit minicomputer	Compe- tence- destroying	3 of 6	3 of 6
	1971	Data Gen- eral Super- nova SC	Semiconduc- tor memory much faster than core	Compe- tence- enhancing	0 of 7	7 of 7

Source: Michael L. Tushman and Philip Anderson, "Technological Discontinuities and Organizational Environments," *Administrative Science Quarterly* 31 (1986):439–465.

they created a new skill not previously used by any competitor). The figure indicates that new firms entered by taking advantage of competence-destroying and niche-opening technological discontinuities. Thus, incumbent firms saw their entry barriers fall, and entrants exploited these technological windows of opportunity. Leaders also watched their position erode as technological windows allowed existing firms to surpass them with enhancements.

As long as one wild-card player may try to enter the market, the market is contestable; so it is no longer a safe haven. Thus, even where we observe that entrants have not attacked yet, we can't be sure they won't enter in the future. The mere threat of their entry is enough to force firms to act like they have entered. Incumbent firms will use "limit" pricing (pricing low enough to deter entry) or make excessive advertising or R&D expenditures as additional barriers to entry. In the process they squeeze out all the profits and escalate the conflict with existing competitors to a higher level, usually moving up the escalation ladders discussed in the two earlier chapters.

This ability to erode geographic and market strongholds sets off a series of dynamic strategic interactions, described below. Even when entry barriers are no longer a source of sustainable competitive advantage, they continue to be an important source of temporary advantage. Companies construct obstacles to competitors, and competitors overcome them. These barriers can be geographic or based on industries, products, or market segments.

For the sake of simplicity, the following dynamic strategic interactions are described as related to geographic strongholds. As we will discuss at the end of the chapter, there is a similar pattern of interactions in market strongholds.

The First Dynamic Strategic Interaction: Building Barriers to Create a Stronghold

Creating strongholds to block competition has been a vital part of political and competitive strategy for centuries. The East India Trading Company held monopolies that regulated trade in the East. Royal "franchises" to portions of the New World gave individuals exclusive rights to commerce in certain territories. While today's geographic barriers are less concrete than the walls that were once used in the past, strongholds can be protected for a while by using the entry barriers discussed above, shutting out competitors from markets in ways that are challenging to overcome.

Geographic strongholds are often created to take advantage of the company's "home court" advantage. Among the factors that can contribute to a company's home court advantage are:

- *Customer familiarity,* that is, knowing the nearby local customers' needs and tastes better than distant or foreign companies.
- *Customer loyalty to a local brand,* arising from customer loyalty for home-grown or domestically produced products. We have seen this advantage in Japanese loyalty to products made in Japan or the "Made in the USA" labeling used to sell American products.
- *The low costs associated with operating over short distances,* including

(1) lower transportation costs, (2) elimination of exchange-rate fluctuations, and (3) the reduced costs of monitoring and enforcing compliance with contracts that comes from being able to see what is happening nearby.

- *Government barriers to foreign entry* created by licensing, tariffs, ownership restrictions, or regulatory requirements. Even regulatory requirements related to consumer protection and safety requirements may restrict some competitors from entering.
- *Control over domestic distribution systems*, for example, major home appliances in the United States and Japanese vertical integration and keiretsu membership in the consumer electronics and car industries in Japan.
- *Local customs*, that is, fear of outsiders, cultural abhorrence of foreigners, and nationalism.
- *Unique factor advantages* in the home country; for example, lower costs of domestic labor, capital, and key skills such as technological expertise and natural resources.
- *Dominance of domestic market share*, so entrants can't enter with full-scale advertising, manufacturing, or other operations.

These advantages are formidable, but as we shall see, they are not invincible for the resourceful competitor.

In the early stages of an industry, a stronghold can protect the company from forays from outside the geographic region or market. The company concentrates on the market within its stronghold and concedes other markets to competitors. However, once the company dominates its own stronghold, it has excess resources but nowhere else to expand at home. Managers within the firm want growth and enhanced power, shareholders want continued growth in profits and full utilization of corporate resources (e.g., via capturing global economies of scale and synergies), and everyone wants to reduce the risks of relying upon a single geographic region or market segment by becoming more diverse. We see this desire for diversification in the development of U.S. regional banks that fund real estate. These banks are seeking to become national to diversify the risks of regional business cycles. Demand in the stronghold market may also decline, as was the case for U.S. cigarette companies that are now seeking new markets overseas. Finally, sometimes firms move into another market to preempt an opponent's move into that market.

Eventually success with the first dynamic strategic interaction motivates companies to look for entry opportunities in other regions or markets. This often means entering another company's stronghold, the second dynamic strategic interaction.

The Second Dynamic Strategic Interaction: Launching Forays into a Competitor's Stronghold

LAUNCHING AN ATTACK FROM THE STRONGHOLD

The company may find that its dominance of the stronghold provides funds that it can use for expansion. At this point companies tend to make forays out of their protected strongholds and into another region.

When Honda, then a Japanese motorcycle manufacturer, decided to expand into new markets, it didn't choose to enter the low-end car market in Japan. Instead it crossed the Pacific to enter the low-end motorcycle market in the United States. It moved from its stronghold in Japanese motorcycles to a geographic market where the competitors were weakest. Honda next moved to high-end motorcycles, then to the low-end auto market in the United States. Finally, it moved into the high-end auto market in the United States before finally exporting cars through the United Kingdom into Western Europe.

Honda is a good example of one strategy for launching an assault on a new stronghold: the escalating sneak attack. At each move it created and consolidated strongholds. Its stronghold in motorcycles in Japan allowed it to break into the motorcycle market in the United States. It entered neglected segments, consolidating its new beachhead into a stronghold and then moved up, leveraging the skills, reputation, and systems used in earlier strongholds. At each step it entered neglected niches to avoid a strong retaliation by the established competitors in the stronghold. By the time the established firms recognized Honda as a challenge, it was too large to be pushed back. In each new market the intruder had already established such a solid beachhead that it could not be turned away.

Honda's example illustrates some critical success factors for forays into the strongholds of another firm:

- *Avoid or delay retaliation where possible* To ward off an all-out retaliatory strike and avoid a war of attrition (price war), the foray should be launched against an enemy that will not or cannot respond in the entered niche or in the attacker's own stronghold.
- *Use adequate resources* To achieve a quick victory by using decisive force, the attacker needs adequate resources to carry out the foray

and picks a niche small enough to dominate. To secure the beach-head, the attacker must follow up with subsequent investments and move inland quickly, once the market has demonstrated receptivity to the product being introduced.

- *Concentrate force on a single point* To avoid becoming overextended itself, the attacker needs to concentrate its efforts on one point of entry, not several products. Scattershot approaches tend to diffuse the effort, draining the attacker's resources and therefore leaving it more vulnerable to counterattack. Attackers tend to add products later on, only when the initial entry is complete and successful.

- *Attack weaknesses first* To avoid or minimize retaliation, the attack is usually launched against the incumbent's weak point, not its strength. For example, if Honda had gone right for the jugular and tried to seize GM's Cadillac market, it would have had a tough fight. But on the low end it had plenty of time to establish itself. The attacker finds places where the domestic firm has ignored market segments or is not serving them very well. Alternatively, the attacker will strike at geographic areas where the established company does not serve customers as well as it should because it has overextended itself by entering too many markets.

- *Minimize risk of failure* To avoid excessive losses and explore other opportunities, attackers withdraw to their stronghold quickly if a rapid and violent response is elicited from the incumbent firm.

- *Protect the home base* To insure that the foray does not weaken the stronghold, forays must use only the "excess" resources generated by the home base. Thus, the foray must not cost more than the cash flow after reinvesting enough to guarantee control at home. Preferably the cost should never be more than the cash flow when the home base is in a down cycle, so that hard times don't put the home base at risk.

These forays are basically guerrilla tactics, following the principles of guerrilla war outlined by Mao Tse-tung. These guerrilla tactics help to circumvent the entry barriers by making the incumbent delay use of (or less likely to use) its cost advantages from economies of scale, switching costs, and the other entry barriers.

Even if the intruding firm starts by sneaking into an unwanted part of the stronghold, large competitors in the market eventually launch a counterattack. If they are vigilant, they may see the long-term threat posed by this interloper early. If not, they may respond late. These responses are the next level of interaction.

The Third Dynamic Strategic Interaction:
The Incumbent's Short-Run Counterresponses to a Guerrilla Attack on Its Home Turf

If the entry grows, it will eventually trigger a response. Sometimes the response is more immediate and severe. Sometimes it is delayed and/or insufficient to stop the attack because of the nonthreatening nature of the entry (as noted in the section on circumventing barriers). There are several factors inside and outside firms that prevent them from being aware of and responding quickly to forays into their territories.

Among these blind spots are a company's tendency to filter and deny information about competitive threats. Many companies seem slow to reshape their view of the world to acknowledge a foray as a serious threat. Obviously, the Big Three U.S. automakers might have easily crushed the German or Japanese entrants before they had a chance to gain a significant foothold in the U.S. market. Who at GM could have predicted at that point that these two countries would have such an impact on the development of the U.S. auto market?

Successful entrants tend to aim for a segment of the market that is not only the incumbent's weak point but also its blind spot—the place that it will be least likely to recognize as a serious competitive threat. Once the incumbent company has recognized this threat, its response strategy depends on its strength at the point of attack.

CASE 1: A STRONG INCUMBENT

If the new entrant has misjudged the incumbent's strength in the segment under attack and the incumbent recognizes the threat, the incumbent may try to deliver a quick and decisive crushing blow to the upstart before the entrant can gain a beachhead. Using the advantages inherent in the entry barriers or the home court advantages listed above, incumbents may use price wars and product introductions to drive the entrant back home before it can grow into a big player that is much more difficult to compete against. However, such efforts may be costly, so many incumbents wait and see in order to gain more information about the seriousness of the attack before launching such a counterattack. The challenge is to recognize when a potential threat is a nuisance and when it is dangerous. If an incumbent were to defend itself against all attacks from competitors, it could waste substantial resources. But if it waits until the entrant emerges as a clearly defined threat, the entrant may already be too strong to be effectively defeated.

CASE 2: A WEAK INCUMBENT

If the entrant has attacked a niche where the incumbent is truly weak, the incumbent will not be able to respond and win easily. Under such circumstances, the incumbent has two choices in dealing with the new entrant in the short run:

1. *Raise new barriers and change the rules of the game* The incumbent sometimes takes advantage of its home court advantage to throw up new barriers to the entrant. These might include new tariffs and regulations that would directly or indirectly shut out the competition. For example, when Volkswagen began making inroads into the U.S. auto market, domestic firms could have pushed for strong safety regulations that would have forced the Beetle off the road. However, the U.S. government is often reluctant to do this, fearing a trade barrier war that would hurt U.S. exports more than it will help protect domestic market share.

2. *Cut and run* If the incumbent can't win the battle because it has truly been attacked in an area where it is weak, the incumbent is best off getting out of the way of the attack. If the entrant has found a weakness that cannot be overcome, the incumbent must withdraw and concede, otherwise the incumbent wastes its efforts. The incumbent may also withdraw because it decides the market is not worth fighting for. General Electric, for example, seems to have used the cut-and-run strategy in small home appliances, consumer electronics, computers, and aerospace, where it faced aggressive competitors or maturing markets.

ACCOMMODATION AND APPEASEMENT

In sum, whether the incumbent is weak or strong, the incumbent will usually offer little or no reaction to the new entry. A study of 115 new entrants in oligopolistic markets found that incumbents rarely reacted by marketing mix, changing their product lines, distribution methods, marketing expenditures, or pricing.[34] Incumbents responded aggressively to new entrants in only 9 percent of the cases during the first year after the entrant's arrival, and the reaction tended to be an increase in marketing expenditures. The second year after entry saw a higher level of reaction, but still a mild one. In the second year incumbents responded aggressively in only 17 percent of the cases. A second study also concludes that "no reaction is the most common reaction by an overwhelming margin."[35]

There are several explanations for this lack of reaction. Normally, even if the incumbent is a strong one, the incumbent's losses from fighting will be greater than the expected losses from allowing the entrant in. If the entrant is smart, it often gives signals indicating that it is not ambitious and will not seek a large market share, so the incumbent thinks the expected losses from allowing entry are small. If so, the established firm will allow the newcomer to enter, especially because many incumbents believe that their higher market share will make it more costly for them to fight a price war than for the entrant. A price cut for a firm with 80 percent share will result in greater losses than the same price cut for a firm with only 2 percent share. For companies that are focused on immediate earnings, these losses during the fight offer a powerful disincentive to battle new entrants. Thus, whether a strong or weak incumbent is attacked, entrants are frequently accommodated in the hope of appeasing them.

Thus, in the short run, a strong incumbent often waits to see if the threat is serious, and a weak incumbent either (1) concedes and allows entry or (2) puts up token resistance. This encourages the entrant to be bold, allows it to prosper in a segment of the incumbent's stronghold, adds to its resources, and often leads to further expansionary efforts. Moreover, other potential entrants recognize that this is occurring, so they also attempt to enter without fear of retaliation. By signaling only modest market share goals, they can forestall a strong reaction from the incumbent. Then, after gaining a toehold, these entrants often expand their goal. This leads directly to the next dynamic strategic interaction.

The Fourth Dynamic Strategic Interaction: The Incumbent's Delayed Reaction

If the incumbent has not already launched a full-scale defense of its turf because it decided to wait and see, it will eventually react to defend itself, especially when failure to do so will result in significant market share losses due to the increasing number and boldness of entrants. Using the advantages inherent in its home court advantages and entry barriers, the incumbent will respond, often trying to contain the entrant to its beachhead and only rarely to drive the entrant entirely out of the market. These responses may include price wars, product introductions, shoring up customer loyalty, locking in established customers, and other activities that leverage off the advantages inherent in the entry barriers listed above. However, incumbents tend to use nonprice methods first, though these don't work very well.[36] This forces the entrants to look for low-cost alternatives that will breach these barriers without creating massive losses for themselves.

The entrants usually respond to the incumbents' moves and take action to overcome the new obstacles that are thrown in their path, thereby escalating the conflict from merely trying to circumvent the barriers to trying to breach them. Thus, this dynamic strategic interaction leads directly to the next one, wherein the entrants attempt to overcome the barriers.

The Fifth Dynamic Strategic Interaction: Overcoming the Barriers

If the entrant can't circumvent the barriers with guerrilla tactics or is hit with a retaliatory response that adds new barriers, it is forced to try to breach the barriers in a way that won't exhaust its resources. When the Big Three managed to get Washington to impose import quotas and tariffs on Japanese imports, it looked like they may have at least slowed down the Japanese juggernaut. But the tariffs and the quotas tended to create more interest in (and higher prices for) Japanese cars because of the scarcity of supply. Then, when the U.S. automakers added an appeal to the U.S. public to buy American, the Japanese car companies responded to both threats by developing their own plants in the United States.

This move to overcome the U.S. firms' defensive moves saved transportation costs, increased sales, and also made it much harder for the U.S. industry to claim that jobs were being lost to Japan. When some of the Japanese car companies were contributing to employment and local economies in the United States, it helped to mute the "Buy American" movement.

Even if the entrant is not successful in breaking through the obstacles to the stronghold, some entrant somewhere will eventually have the resources in place to enter the market. Numerous examples of this were described at the beginning of the chapter. The examples show that each of the entry barriers are not solid. Holes exist, and entrants eventually find a way over or around even the most formidable barriers created by giants such as GM, IBM, Caterpillar, Xerox, Kodak, and American Express.

When this occurs, this sign of the incumbent's weakness often generates further problems. The entrant's success may attract even more competitors to the market, so the incumbent is forced to take a longer-term countermove to deter additional entrants. This leads us to the next dynamic strategic interaction: protecting the stronghold from long-term erosion.

The Sixth Dynamic Strategic Interaction: Long-Run Counterresponses to the Attack

Once the first entrant has established a solid beachhead in a geographic stronghold, other companies tend to move in, like sharks attracted to the smell of blood. If the incumbent loses the short-term and intermediate battle for the entered niche, it has to reshape itself and its strategy to maintain its long-term position in the broader stronghold.

Assuming that the incumbent has not decided to cash out of the market via harvesting, exit, or divestiture, there are two ways that established firms respond in the long run. Both are attempts to signal the incumbent's strength and to scare away other potential entrants.

- *Defensive moves—shoring up the walls* Eliminating the weakness that drew the new entrant in the first place. This may or may not be followed by returning strongly to the entered niche to recapture its market position. In any event, successful incumbents try to close the door to later entrants by eliminating the portal of entry exploited by the first entrant. GM did this by joint-venturing with Isuzu and Dae Woo to produce a small car to compete with Toyota, Nissan, and Honda. Over the longer term GM developed Saturn to fill this niche. Ford improved quality quickly to eliminate its weakness.
- *Offensive moves—teaching respect* Some incumbents fight the guerrilla attack with a guerrilla counterattack to force the entrant to back off. Such an incumbent finds the entrant's weakness in the entrant's own home territory and then launches a counterattack of the sort that was launched against it. This is not a frontal assault on the entrant's home territory. Instead it is designed to discipline the intruder and cause it to back off or devote resources and attention to defending its home markets. This sometimes leads to the entrant's withdrawal from the incumbent's stronghold, or it weakens the entrant's efforts by diverting resources back to its home market. For example, if GM had hit Honda in some niche of the U.S. motorcycle

market at the time Honda entered the small car market, GM might have been able to deal a severe blow to Honda's efforts in the U.S. auto market. At that time Honda was not a very powerful player, and it had a lot to lose at this early stage. GM, on the other hand, had little to lose in motorcycles and a lot to lose in the car market.

Note that the defensive move heats up the war on the incumbent's own turf, while the offensive move shifts the focus to the entrant's turf. The defensive option will appear more attractive if:

- The incumbent doesn't have the resources to wage total war (because the battle will escalate to two fronts if the incumbent counterattacks the entrant's home market).
- The incumbent's weakness is easily corrected. If it is not, counterattacking may be quicker and more effective than allowing the entrant to exploit the weakness for years.
- The incumbent cannot afford to lose any share in its stronghold because this market is central to the firm's strategies; if, for example, it has many economies of scope with its other product lines.
- The incumbent doesn't have the skills to enter the other player's home markets.

One key question, however, remains: Will the defensive option be enough to stop the attack? Peter Drucker once noted that playing defense can only limit a firm's losses, not improve its gains. In addition, unless executed properly by using the price-quality and timing–know-how cycles described in Chapters 1 and 2, the defensive option cedes the initiative to the opponent, allowing him to determine the rules of the game. Given the importance of maintaining their stronghold, many incumbents have no choice but to switch to the offensive. Moreover, the defensive and offensive options are not mutually exclusive, so some incumbents start with defensive moves and escalate to offensive ones if the defensive moves do not work.

Such actions can teach an entrant that its actions will not be ignored, and they demonstrate to other potential entrants that entry will not always result in withdrawal by the incumbent. Unfortunately, not all entrants get the message, and some of these counterattacks are not successful because they are poorly executed. This leads to further escalation and the next dynamic strategic interaction.

The Seventh Dynamic Strategic Interaction: Slow Learners and the Incumbent's Reactions to Entrants Who Don't Get the Message

If the last round of threats and responses doesn't cause the new entrant to retreat, the battle escalates to a higher level. With a very aggressive entrant or incumbent, the incumbent may go directly to this level without going first to the preceding dynamic strategic interaction. If the incumbent has sent a signal of its strength, either by eliminating weaknesses or launching a guerrilla counterattack, there may be several reasons why the entrant has not responded. First, the attacker may not back down because he doesn't want to get a reputation for weakness or retreating too easily. This would hurt its future attempts to enter new markets. Another reason might be that the incumbent's counterattack is not very costly to the entrant.

The battle now escalates because the entrant leaves the incumbent little choice but to escalate the war by exporting it directly to the core of the entrant's home turf. The incumbent will tend to find the opponent's weakness and mount a large-scale assault there. This is usually not the initial response of established firms, which prefer to respond by working in their relatively secure stronghold. But when all else has failed, the use of excessive force in the entrant's home base (its stronghold) can sometimes be much more effective than further tries to face the entrant down on the incumbent's home turf.

Several sequential steps are required to successfully move into the entrant's home turf. Successful counterattacks against the entrant involve

1. using the incumbent's home government to negotiate away tariff barriers, force integration of capital markets, or take other actions to make entry into the entrant's home base easier.
2. eliminating the entrant's home court advantage. This is sometimes done by buying firms or establishing joint ventures in the entrant's home country. Novell, a U.S. software firm, cracked the Japanese market by forming a partnership with six Japanese computer companies to produce a Japanese-language version of NetWare.
3. gaining access to distribution systems in the entrant's home country.
4. entering the stronghold of the entrant with sufficient force to disrupt the market and redirect the company's attention back home.

This last step is perhaps the most challenging. There are two options for launching this assault, with two different goals. Julius Caesar, in his commentaries about the battle for Gaul, notes that there are two types of warfare—wars of punishment and wars of conquest. So, too, in business. In wars of punishment, one side tries to force its opponent to back off and stop attacking. In wars of conquest, the attacker doesn't stop until it subjugates and controls the opponent's former stronghold.

OPTION 1: A WAR OF PUNISHMENT IN THE OPPONENT'S HOME BASE

This is the "scorched earth" approach of burning the city down and sowing salt in the soil, the business equivalent of the approach used in Rome's Third Carthaginian War or Sherman's march to the sea in the U.S. Civil War. The intent of this strategy is to damage the profitability of the entire industry in the opponent's stronghold and then withdraw. Once the entrant has been counterattacked at home, it is weakened and demoralized so that it cannot move as aggressively abroad. Before retreating, however, this move may escalate to global war. It could trigger a violent price war in the incumbent's stronghold as well as the entrant's because the entrant may react in the incumbent's market.

> Until November 1991 MarkAir Inc. and Alaska Airlines peacefully coexisted in the Alaskan market. Then MarkAir, after it was spurned in its attempt to sell itself to Alaska Airlines, "declared war," according to *Business Week*.[37] MarkAir moved aggressively into its rival's routes, including the prime Anchorage-Seattle route and Southern Alaskan routes where Alaska Airlines had had a monopoly according to *Business Week*. Even though MarkAir had just one-ninth the revenues of Alaska Airlines, the small carrier still had the ability to inflict serious damage. MarkAir chairman Neil Bergt retained Frank A. Lorenzo, former Texas Air chairman, as an adviser to help build resources through an initial public offering. As MarkAir moved into lucrative markets, Alaska Airlines' stock plummeted by 18 percent between January and April of 1992, *Business Week* reported. MarkAir, in addition to seeking the IPO, was selling off planes and hangars to support the costly price war. Alaska Airlines responded with what appeared to be a war of punishment by moving aggressively into routes where, *Business Week* reported, MarkAir "had once enjoyed a monopoly."[38] Alaska Airlines also opened up new routes in the far northern part of the state. Both airlines stretched their resources to sustain this war. Both were locked in a deadly battle in 1992 that would probably be won by the one with the deepest pockets, the one who backed down first, or a third party who would come in and take advantage of these two weakened rivals.[39]

For a war of punishment to succeed, the incumbent, without destroying itself, must inflict heavy losses on its opponent and force it to exit the incumbent's home market. This can sometimes be done by introducing a product with a low market share at a very low price into the entrant's home market. If the entrant has large market share in its stronghold (as it usually will), then it cannot match or beat the price without suffering large losses. This may force the opponent to react only by counterattacking the incumbent's home market. But if a price war has already been started in the incumbent's home base, the incumbent has nothing to lose by escalating in the entrant's home market. Attacking the entrant's home market with full force cannot escalate the war in the incumbent's home base any more than it already had been. That is, the incumbent would have suffered the losses from the battle in its home market anyway. Following this counterattack, if the opponent doesn't respond in its home base, it stands to lose market share. If it does, it will incur big losses, and it won't be able to pay for its attacks in the other market. Either way the opponent loses.

OPTION 2: A WAR OF CONQUEST IN THE OPPONENT'S HOME BASE

This is a fight to the finish, laying siege to the city, winner take all, as in the Trojan War. The key to success in this battle is to nullify the opponent's advantages in its stronghold by using the techniques described in Chapters 1 and 2 (moving up the escalation ladder toward the ultimate value position and imitating or leapfrogging). This is accomplished by innovation, differentiation, outflanking, and systematically capturing niche after niche in the opponent's stronghold.

Whereas the intent of the war of punishment was to discipline the competition, the intent of this approach is to move aggressively into the competitor's territory not only to discipline him but also to conquer and control his markets.

Southwest Air is engaged in what might be described as a "war of conquest." Three airlines, Braniff, Texas International, and Continental, tried to shut down Southwest Air in court in the late 1960s, claiming that the Texas market could not sustain another carrier. Southwest won the court battle and launched a guerrilla attack against its larger competitors. Rather than compete head-to-head with the hub-and-spoke systems of the larger players, Southwest undercut the prices of the other major airlines by as much as 60 percent, according to *Business Week*,[40] and outperformed its competitors. In 1990 it was the only major airline to show a profit on operations, and it achieved these results by offering more frequent flights at lower prices than competitors.[41] Southwest then moved into larger cities such as Phoenix and Chicago[42] where it successfully competed against America West (Phoenix) and Midway (Chicago).[43] Southwest has apparently moved from market to market, capturing larger and larger market share.

When an incumbent counterattacks the entrant by launching a war of conquest or a war of punishment on the entrant's home turf, it can be costly for both the incumbent and the entrant. Because of this, the two players may try to avoid such direct confrontation by maintaining a temporary standoff, which is the next dynamic strategic interaction.

The Eighth Dynamic Strategic Interaction: Unstable Standoffs

Competition across several geographic or industry strongholds sometimes leads to a standoff between multilocation firms (and conglomerates) that tends to reduce competition within both strongholds. Consider the situation illustrated in Figure 3–2.

Company 1 can prevent company 2 from expanding in the U.S. market by shifting its attention to Japan and using price competition to sting company 2 in that location. This stinging will hurt company 2 a lot. On the other hand, company 2 can apply the same strategy to keep company 1 from expanding its toehold in Japan. Thus, the two companies can discipline one another into being nonaggressive if neither has the stomach for a fight. Just the mere knowledge of the fact that each can sting (or even destroy) the other should force a stalemate. This is essentially the business equivalent to MAD, the doctrine of mutually assured destruction, which prevented the Soviet Union and the United States from starting a nuclear war during the Cold War period. Each knew the other could destroy it if it started a war, so neither escalated to a real conflict.

In business settings this type of standoff has a high probability of being broken if (1) a third competitor acts aggressively in one party's turf, (2) one of the companies develops a protected stronghold so well as to be invulnerable to a sting by the other company, (3) one of the competitors gains a substantial advantage in quality and price or timing and know-how

FIGURE 3–2
UNSTABLE STANDOFFS ACROSS GEOGRAPHIC MARKETS

	STRENGTH OF POSITION	
	U.S. Markets	**Japanese Market**
Company 1	Stronghold	Toehold
Company 2	Toehold	Stronghold

sufficient to allow it to win a war of punishment or conquest, (4) one party gains the will to endure a fight because of a change in leadership or circumstances, or (5) one party loses the will to continue a credible threat to sting or discipline the other player. (Note: Many believe the standoff between the United States and the U.S.S.R. ended because one or more of the above conditions were met. First, the United States gained the upper hand due to the declining economic power of the U.S.S.R., making it impossible for the U.S.S.R. to continue the arms race. Second, the Soviets realized that the Strategic Defense Initiative (SDI), if successful at shielding the United States from nuclear attack, would make it possible for the United States to protect its stronghold from the sting that the Soviets could deliver. Thus, the United States would be free to break the peace with impunity, forcing the Soviets to prepare for such an event. Yet because of their weak economy the Soviets didn't have the money to pay for an SDI program of their own or to build enough missiles and submarines to compensate for the U.S. advantage. So the stalemate was broken.)

Since it is frequently the case that the balance of power breaks down, especially in business, standoffs are rare. When they do occur, they are almost always broken, because each player has the incentive to try secretly to get the upper hand by finding a way to protect its own turf and then openly expand into the opponent's turf. This may result in firms' testing the resolve of their opponent and triggering the escalating battles outlined in this chapter.

BARRIERS TO ENTRY AND STRONGHOLDS ARE NOT SUSTAINABLE FOREVER

Over the long run the result of most of these turf wars will be to heat up the competition in the strongholds both of the incumbent and of the original entrant. Both strongholds are eventually eroded and destroyed as safe havens. Often the two markets merge into one larger market.

Thus, we may tend to overestimate the strength of entry barriers, and in some cases we may have even invented barriers where none ever really existed. This myth of strong entry barriers is a barrier itself, like the screen in front of the wizard in *The Wizard of Oz*. But once the belief in entry barriers is eroded, it becomes apparent that many barriers are not so formidable as they appear. Even after they have eroded, their weakness may not be apparent until someone actually challenges them. Competitors assume that a barrier stands because it is unassailable when, in fact, it may be standing because it has gone unassailed. When a competitor attacks an entry barrier, it often falls away more easily than expected. Firms that thought it impossible to fight a well-established incumbent have often learned otherwise.

The Escalation Ladder in the Stronghold Creation/Invasion Arena

In summary, the erosion of safe havens occurs because of the escalation ladder shown in Figure 3–3. Both the incumbent and the entrant initially build barriers around their strongholds. The entrant launches a foray into the incumbent's market with tactics designed to delay the incumbent's response. Initially most incumbents respond by accommodating the entrant. A few defend their turf fiercely. Eventually all incumbents respond to serious attacks by using the advantages inherent in the entry barriers that they have created. Entrants often overcome these barriers and take market share or trigger a price war in the incumbent's market. The incumbent then attacks the entrant's home market. The battle over control of both markets usually escalates, sometimes with brief periods of standoffs. Thus, both strongholds erode, and the two merge into a single marketplace.

HYPERCOMPETITIVE BEHAVIOR IN THE STRONGHOLD CREATION/INVASION ARENA

Competition does not always become bloody. Competitors sometimes learn from the signaling process to tacitly divide the turf into different territories. This allows parties to create local monopolies and make profits by avoiding direct competition. But many competitors either don't consider this or, believing they will win, draw their opponent into battle. They want their home market protected but want access to the opponent's market. This leads to escalation by forcing the incumbent in the entered market to counterattack.

As already described the two strongholds eventually merge into one, with two competitors slugging it out in a perfectly competitive market without the benefits of entry barriers between them. They use all the hypercompetitive methods based on cost-quality and timing–know-how to avoid perfect competition. The firm that can last the longest in this battle may eventually win out and create dominance over the combined

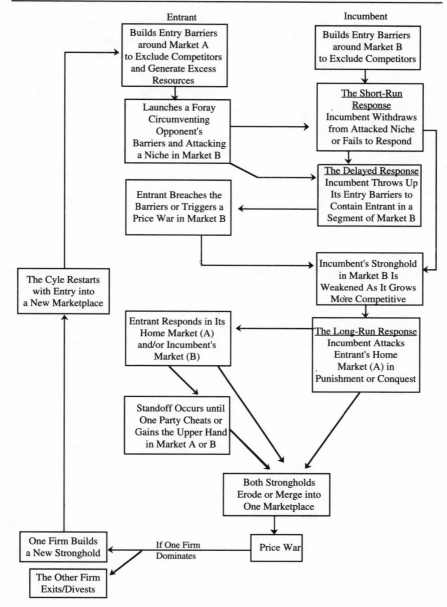

FIGURE 3–3
THE CYCLE OF TURF BATTLES AND ENTRY BARRIER COMPETITION

market. If so, the cycle in Figure 3–3 could restart, since this player would logically build entry barriers around this combined marketplace and then look for a new market to invade. As this occurs, firms move from one geographic market to another until they all merge into one. Thus, in an effort to establish dominance over one or more strongholds, firms engage in hypercompetitive behavior that includes moving up the escalation ladder in the stronghold arena faster than competitors or restarting the stronghold creation/invasion cycle in Figure 3–3 when a combined market is created.

Consider the attacks and counterattacks in the roasted coffee market that moved from city to city, escalating up to a national battle.

> Maxwell House was dominant in the East Coast market. Folger's was strong on the West Coast. After being acquired by Procter & Gamble, Folger's entered the Cleveland market to increase its eastern penetration. Maxwell countered by attacking in Folger's stronghold, lowering prices and increasing marketing expenditures in Kansas City. Maxwell also introduced a fighting brand called Horizon, which was similar to Folger's in taste and packaging. Folger's then escalated by entering Pittsburgh. Maxwell responded by entering Dallas with the reduced prices. The battle continued until the market was no longer two coastal segments but one national battleground.

Thus, the above patterns of dynamic strategic interactions explain why many industries expand beyond local boundaries to become national and then global in nature. Sometimes these cycles are slowed when the players decide to tacitly cooperate, each with its own protected stronghold. However, this only leads to a temporary respite. Cheating or the arrival of new entrants inevitably ends this period of cooperation. At each step on the ladder, firms continue to move up to the next stage because doing so provides a temporary advantage in this arena of competition based on maintaining control over turf. Failure to seize the initiative and move up cedes the advantage to the other player. Reactive firms, always lagging and responding to the unanticipated moves of competitors, are often the losers in this escalating battle.

Hypercompetition When Strongholds Are Built around Industries or Product/Market Segments

Although our discussion of the dynamic strategic interactions focused primarily on geographic strongholds, the same patterns can be found in strongholds developed around product or market segments within an industry.

Consider Federal Express. The stronghold of FedEx was in transporting intercity, priority-letter-sized documents. But with the advent of the fax machine, this stronghold was eroded. Letter-sized documents could be faxed easily from city to city in less time and at less cost. FedEx was forced to move from its stronghold into an ill-fated effort in the facsimile market called ZapMail. Later, FedEx moved into bulkier and lower-priority mail that could not be faxed or didn't need to be. This pushed it into the stronghold of UPS—intercity, nonpriority packages of up to seventy pounds—and the U.S Postal Service—intracity delivery of nonpriority packages and letters. But these attacks brought retaliatory responses by UPS and the postal service, leading to entry into FedEx's stronghold.

Rather than directly assault UPS's stronghold, FedEx might have tried to find untapped segments of the UPS market. It could, for example, have concentrated on a specialty such as shipping live animals, blood, or very large packages. But this would have meant entry of markets held by Emery and Purolator. It also could have provided special inventory management services to corporations (which indeed it does today). In any event, UPS, FedEx, and many other players are now engaged in a battle that has escalated to hypercompetitive and sometimes perfectly competitive conditions almost everywhere in the world. The battle is intense at home and abroad. In 1992, after building an expensive hub system in Europe, FedEx pulled out because of slower-than-expected market growth and intense price competition. FedEx continued to serve the region through European partners and retained its leadership in the U.S. market, but only through price wars that shaved more than 4 percent from the company's yield.[44] FedEx employs new technology and new planes to compete more aggressively on cost and quality, but many of these innovations are rapidly duplicated by aggressive competitors. Today, the priority and semipriority package and letter segments have become one integrated market served by the same players on a global basis in many different products throughout the world. Perfect competition is not far behind unless the players continue to be hypercompetitive.

Similarly, the hypercompetitive behaviors in Figure 3–3 may occur across industries. Consider the competition between BIC and Gillette.

BIC revolutionized the disposable ballpoint pen with its mass merchandising skills, but Gillette entered the market for disposable pens, overcoming entry barriers (access to distribution channels, economies of scale in advertising, product differentiation because of brand equity) by using its own considerable skills in mass merchandising. Since this was BIC's stronghold, it had to respond. So BIC counterattacked by entering Gillette's stronghold, disposable razors. Today the two industries are merged into one marketplace for small disposable personal items sold in supermarkets, drugstores, discount stores, and stationery stores. Previously each product was purchased through different distribution outlets. Gillette and BIC continue to compete, using several disposal products that were previously made by competitors in separate industries.

These two industries merged because their product characteristics resulted from similar manufacturing technology—molded plastics. Other industries have merged because of such similarities. Once deregulated, several financial services industries merged into one. Insurance, commercial and investment banking, and pension and mutual funds now all overlap into each market because they all share a similar function. They help bring people with money together with people who need money. Thus, they are middlemen for cash. With the rise of health maintenance organizations, the medical industry has seen the merger of private physicians, insurance, and hospitals. In the future several other industries will merge for a similar reason. Consumer electronics, photography, xerography, and computer terminals, among others, all rely upon visual images that can be digitized and stored electronically. When the technology develops further, these diverse industries will become one. The force that will propel them there is the same force that caused the integration of FedEx's and UPS's market segments, BIC's and Gillette's industries, and the financial services industries. That force is the force that pushes firms to escalate up the ladder described in this chapter—the desire to seek advantage at each rung of the ladder by controlling, protecting, and expanding into new safe havens.

Although we portrayed the escalation ladder (in Figure 3–3) as a sequential process, it may also occur in parallel. Firms may build strongholds in a geographic region, several different regions, a product segment, several product segments, an industry, several industries, or all of these simultaneously. The cycle may proceed differently for each stronghold of a firm. Some cycles skip steps along this ladder. Others may end up frozen at one rung temporarily. Industries proceed up the ladder at different speeds, depending upon the aggressiveness and quirks of competitors in the industry, the types of entry barriers confronted, the trade policies of governments that might influence the industry, and market conditions. Nevertheless, this escalation ladder defines the rungs in a general process that shows how one dynamic strategic interaction leads to the next. But competitors will climb up this ladder in many different ways.

The Only Remaining Barrier: Hypercompetitive Behavior

We have seen how the traditional entry barriers have been eroded or circumvented—from economies of scale, switching costs, and other barriers identified by Porter to barriers of government regulations. The strongest barrier in hypercompetitive markets may be the hypercompetitive behavior of the players. In fact, a survey of managers found that a third of the managers who chose not to take active steps to deter entry said the main reason was "existing firms compete so intensely that profit margins are cut so low that entry is extremely unlikely in any case."[45] For example, in the cola market the traditional barriers are marketing skill, bottling and distributor networks, and access to shelf space. But there are many companies that could enter the market. Beer companies such as Anheuser-Busch could take advantage of their existing bottling facilities and distribution networks. Similarly, juice manufacturers could enter the market. A baby food maker or a winemaker could also enter. They all have economies in scale in bottling and advertising, brand image, distribution, and access to shelf space. If it is not these entry barriers, what is keeping these competitors out? Perhaps more than anything else, they are deterred by the vicious hypercompetition in the market. There's no point in jumping into a snake pit. So perhaps the most significant barrier to entry is now the hypercompetitive behavior of the companies in the market. By making the industry hostile, they make it less attractive to enter.

Since the 1960s the U.S. market for large turbine generators has seemed virtually unassailable. General Electric had created strong barriers to entry in the turbine business due to cost and technology advantages. From 1948 to 1962, GE had a 15 percent cost advantage over Westinghouse and a nearly 30 percent advantage over Allis-Chalmers. Allis-Chalmers was driven out of the market in 1962, demonstrating to would-be entrants the hostility of the market. The only other major player in the market, Westinghouse, was pinned in a less attractive niche in the market.[46] This cozy relationship invited foreign entrants with low costs and advanced technology. Some entered during the 1990s by picking up pieces of Allis-Chalmers, which had been virtually driven from the market. Some entrants such as Rolls-Royce and Mitsubishi came in through joint ventures with Westinghouse,[47] and others gained a foothold in the replacement/repair market. The market is clearly heating up, and barriers that seemed impenetrable are showing their weaknesses. To paraphrase what J. Richard Stonesifer, Executive Vice-President of GE, said at a 1992 conference in New York City, power generation in the old days was GE versus Westinghouse. Now it's very different. Now there are Japanese, German, and Swiss companies. It is no longer civil. All competitors are offering high tech, high quality, and high service. These are no longer advantages. There are very few entry barriers, and companies are all competing in each other's turf. With the market expected to grow rapidly in the years ahead, competition promises to continue to be intense.[48]

Escalation to the Next Arena of Competition

We have seen how these dynamic strategic interactions eventually erode the advantages of strongholds. Once strongholds erode, markets based on product segments and geographic regions merge, and the competitors end up fighting on a global basis. The battle then shifts to who can outlast the other players in this hypercompetitive situation. This often depends on who has the deepest pockets. Since each can attack the other anywhere, the player who can launch the most attacks and sustain the most hits for the longest period of time has an advantage. This deep-pocket advantage is the focus of the next chapter.

Management Challenges

These competitive moves and countermoves can help you examine your own strongholds, analyze your current position, plan your future moves, and anticipate your competitors' responses and next actions. By looking at the sequence of dynamic strategic interactions described in this chapter, you can see what's ahead, jump levels to speed the escalation of the cycle, and catch your competitors off guard. Those who climb the ladder faster are always one step ahead of the competition, forcing others to catch up with the new advantage created by moving up to the next step on the ladder. Or you may take actions to slow down competitors if you are already ahead and don't want your competitors to jump past you. Here are some of the major issues that managers face in taking control of this cycle:

- Do you base your stronghold on geographic areas or product markets? How do your competitors define their strongholds?
- Where are your strongholds vulnerable to attack?
- What barriers do you use to protect your strongholds?
- What barriers do your competitors use to protect *their* strongholds?
- How can you hold onto your strongholds longer? How can you shore them up?
- How can you respond to an attack from outside?
- How will you make your move into another firm's stronghold? If you do, what is that firm's likely response?
- Is it to your advantage to slow down the erosion of your stronghold, or do you want to actually speed up the escalation? If you want to slow it down or speed it up, how can you make that happen?
- Are you leading your industry up the ladder or following? Why?
- Who and what are setting the pace of escalation in your industry? Why?

Not all industries are at the same point along the cycle. Some move up the rungs on the escalation ladder in Figure 3–3 quickly, and others have the potential to be frozen at one rung for years. But most travel through these points over the long run. By understanding the mileposts, you can take greater charge of your direction and face fewer surprises from competitors. In Part III of this book, we will develop several techniques and strategies for dealing with these management challenges and for creating the types of temporary advantages that are available at each step of the escalation ladder in this arena of competition.

HOW FIRMS OUTMANEUVER COMPETITORS WITH DEEP POCKETS

We have seen how companies exhaust their competitive options on cost and quality, how their advantages from timing and know-how erode, and how entry barriers are overcome. After these escalation ladders have been ascended, the industry may have merged into a large global market without barriers and fast-paced, aggressive maneuvering. Once this has occurred, firms have only one option: to compete using their deep pockets. In this environment the largest firms have certain advantages.

There is an old military adage, "All things being equal, God goes with the big battalions." A company with substantial financial and managerial resources can withstand many onslaughts and sieges by lesser companies and still come out ahead. Deep pockets give the firm powerful options in pricing and market expansion that can leave its smaller peers in the dust. Deep pockets allow a firm, for example, to sustain losses for a long period of time. Smaller competitors may simply be exhausted by the fight. Of course, deep pockets can also make competitors less aggressive and less flexible, as we will examine later in this chapter.

While deep pockets can be used to launch a low-price or predatory-price attack, they can also be used to subsidize attacks based on higher quality or service for the same price, more R&D or plant investment without increasing product price, more advertising without raising price, or expanded distribution channels or convenience without increased price. Deep pockets are usually related to size, but not always. The resources of some large firms are so tied up or stretched thin that they cannot be used against opponents. Deep pockets are more closely related to the size of the company's "slack" resources (i.e., those that are readily available for use in competition), but most large firms have a lot of slack in them.

The power of these deep pockets can be seen in Toyota's dominance of the Japanese forklift industry. Toyota used its deep pockets to build the largest service network in the industry, a huge fixed cost that few others could afford. This investment allowed it to respond anywhere in Japan within two hours. This level of service in an industry in which delays are very costly helped Toyota crush its smaller competitors.

A huge firm can derive many other advantages from its large size. For example, Sears offers discounts to its employees. This ensures that employees will buy Sears products and, with very large sales forces, assures a certain level of customer purchases. These inside sales can amount to more than the entire sales of a small or mid-sized retailer. This is a case of the rich getting richer and the deep-pocketed firm getting ever deeper pockets. Yet even Sears is facing serious troubles from smaller competitors and other deep-pocketed retailers. Deep pockets are an advantage, not a guarantee that a firm will win.

TRADITIONAL VIEWS
OF THE DEEP-POCKET ADVANTAGE

The deep-pocket advantage appears to be intuitively obvious. Common sense tells us that a larger and better-supplied firm will usually win against a smaller, weaker competitor. Its resources give it the ability to outlast the smaller firm or to win in a test of strength, such as a war of attrition.

Besides the ability to invest in assets that others can't afford (as Toyota did in forklifts) and the ability to sustain price wars longer than smaller competitors, deep pockets provide three other advantages: a wide margin for error, global or national reach, and political power. Each of these is addressed in turn in the next sections.

A Wide Margin for Error

Deep pockets offer a powerful advantage because they can be used to neutralize the effects of the strategies detailed in the preceding three chapters in the same way that a tractor-trailer operated by a driver with moderate abilities wins in a crash with a highly skilled driver in a subcompact. If a company has deep enough pockets, it can outlast its competitors even if they have a better strategy.

Deep pockets win in war as well as business. While military historians agree that the Confederacy had better generals and strategy during the American Civil War, the Union won. Its victory was largely due to a superior level of resources. More men and supplies allowed it to "win" battles simply by being willing to sacrifice more men and use up more supplies. In many battles the Union's inferior strategy was outweighed by its willingness and ability to sacrifice ten thousand men in one four-hour fight.

In business deep pockets allow firms to lose a price war or the battle for cost and quality and still develop the next level of technology or know-how and rebuild strong entry barriers. If it has deep enough pockets, it can make a strong foray into another company's territory, even when the costs are so great that they don't make sense except to prove to competitors that the firm is a force not to be trifled with. Companies use the brute force of deep pockets to overcome better skilled opponents by pursuing so many attacks and multiple strategies that competitors can prepare for them. A deep pocket eliminates the need to determine which countermove its competitor will make, because, no matter what the opponent does, it can be overwhelmed by sheer numbers. Many businesspeople say that the opponent they most hate to fight against is one who is stupid but very rich.

Thus, deep pockets give the company breathing room for errors in the other three arenas of competition. If you have deep pockets, poor quality, high costs, loss of a protected stronghold, and bad timing and know-how are not fatal mistakes (at least not in the short run). The large firm can sustain losses for long periods of time and still have the resources to catch up to or jump past competitors, neutralizing their advantage in the first three arenas.

Global or National Reach

Deep pockets also provide the ability to reach around the world or nation to tap the best talent, find the most modern equipment, purchase the latest technological advances, line up the most responsive and aggressive dealers, and search out the highest-quality suppliers in the world or nation.

Global reach also gives the firm the ability to monitor its competitors anywhere that they compete, eliminating surprises. It gives the ability to experiment in one location and transfer that knowledge elsewhere. So a firm can test a product in one place, work out many of the bugs, and then introduce it to key markets without risking its brand image for quality products. It will still have to work out local variations, but the core product and process technology can be refined in a smaller market with less room for serious damage. Smaller competitors, on the other hand, often are faced with a "bet the firm" proposition in launching new products.

Finally, global reach means the ability to move resources from place to place, so that the firm can overwhelm smaller domestic players. Once victorious, the deep pocket can then move its resources to new locations, much like a conquering invader on the march.

Political Power

Large firms with deep pockets also gain political power over the communities where they operate. Often, multinational corporations have budgets that are bigger than the countries in which they operate. Exxon, for example, is bigger than all but a few countries.

This translates into political power in several ways. Not only may closing a plant affect local jobs, but decisions of some multinationals about where to locate often affect regional economies and even U.S. foreign policy. Many believe that the alliances between U.S. oil companies and Saudi Arabia and Kuwait affected U.S. willingness to send troops to the Gulf. Moreover, U.S. military contractors intentionally locate plants in the districts of key congresspeople so as to use their influence to insure the continuance of contracts long after the military equipment is no longer needed. Even presidents succumb to the influence of military contractors, allowing fighter plane sales to Taiwan and Saudi Arabia to curry favor in key districts that might sway the Electoral College. Thus, largeness and the concomitant deep pockets allow some firms to influence governments in many locations and in ways that smaller firms cannot.

Banking on Size

When NCNB and C&S/Sovran joined forces in 1991 to create a $116 billion megabank, then the third largest in the country, the move sent shock waves through the southern banking industry. The new bank, NationsBank, was larger than the next three largest banks in the South combined. It created the greatest resource gap between the large and small banks in any region in the country.[1]

Hugh McColl, the CEO of NationsBank, who steered NCNB of North Carolina on its meteoric rise into the ranks of the largest banks in the United States, believed that a company is either growing or dying. His banking empire has grown as fast as the sixty-story office building he constructed in Charlotte, North Carolina, that has been nicknamed the Taj McColl. Under his guidance, NCNB's assets rose from $7.7 billion in 1982 to more than $100 billion when he merged with C&S/Sovran in 1991.

With its new scope of operations, NationsBank was no longer reliant upon the declining economy of North Carolina, so it was no longer overly dependent upon textiles, furniture, and tobacco farming for its survival. In addition, real estate fluctuations in Texas, linked to the decline of its oil industry, became less of a factor in the bank's success. The impact of major Florida hurricanes on real estate loan default rates was also reduced. The expanding asset base and national reach of the bank reduced the risks posed to the bank's performance by unforeseen and uncontrollable shocks. The combined operations were expected to produce annual cost savings of $450 million by 1994.[2]

In addition, the large "supercommunity" bank can leverage its assets to provide better service to its local branches and to its customers. Its greater resources allow it to offer a broader product line, produce costs savings by centralizing some functions of the bank, and make investments in scale-sensitive technology.[3] Moreover, large banks can compete longer on price. This is not just because of the effects of economies of scale, which are rather small in banking. (In fact, some research suggests that there may even be some diseconomies of scale in banking.) If large banks offer loans at lower interest rates, they can afford the lower margins in the short run without risking their survival.

Large banks also have political power. Where they invest affects the economies of cities and states, in turn affecting the fate of political leaders in those locations. Decisions concerning whether to fund an airport, a power station, or a port expansion can have serious political implications, placing the bank right in the middle of the political action. Even decisions about whether to work out a loan or force a large debtor into bankruptcy can have political implications. Closing down firms kills jobs, a hot political topic.

Shortages of resources also pose problems for smaller banks. Below a certain size, for example, banks do not have the resources they need to be profitable. Studies of small banks show that the minimum size for survival lies somewhere between fifty million and two hundred million dollars in assets.[4]

Thus, the building of a large asset base is one of the key arenas in which firms compete. Expanding resources through growth or mergers can be an important strategic tool.

Useful Insights from This View of Competitive Advantage

The main insights that this view of deep-pocket advantages has produced are in the public-policy realm, especially antitrust regulation. The government often steps in to protect small firms from large ones. Using a deep-pocket advantage has been considered anticompetitive because it is seen as driving the "little guy" out of business unfairly. When small firms offer a better product and have a better strategy, the use of brute force to crush them is seen as hurting the public interest. Among the many implications is the need for policies that prohibit predatory pricing (i.e., pricing below one's own costs) and encourage tighter scrutiny of large market-share firms seeking to expand via mergers or acquisitions.

These two government policies are designed to reduce the impact of deep pockets and are testimony to the power of deep pockets. In fact, the U.S. government has long regulated the size of banks out of fear that they would grow too powerful and endanger the survival of a democratic society.

THE DYNAMIC VIEW

This model of the deep-pocket advantage is static, however. It assumes that battles can be won or lost by tallying up the level of resources of each player at a given moment in time. But sometimes a small competitor can neutralize the advantage of the deep-pocketed company. Superior resources can sometimes actually be an obstacle to success. By relying on superior forces rather than strategic maneuverability and flexibility, the player with deep pockets sometimes loses its advantage. It is actions and maneuverability that create advantage. Through dynamic maneuvering, a relatively small company can defeat a large one and in the process become a large firm with its own deep pockets. In addition, alliances can be built to add to the resources of small players.

NationsBank's rise illustrates how deep-pocket advantages are unstable in dynamic markets. The expansion of NationsBank was driven in no small part by its intense rivalry with its crosstown competitor in Charlotte, First Union Corporation. Both NationsBank (the fifth-largest bank in the United States in 1993) and First Union Corporation (the ninth largest) started as small local banks. At that time the largest bank in their region was Wachovia Corporation—but not for long. NationsBank's Hugh McColl says, "We always thought we were competing against Wachovia until we got so much bigger and looked back."[5] Wachovia's deep pockets were no match for the aggressive maneuvering of its two smaller rivals.

Both NationsBank and First Union pursued a policy of resource escalation. First Union made thirty-five acquisitions between 1985 and 1993. NationsBank expanded into Florida in 1982. First Union followed. In fact, it was First Union's pursuit of the high-profile Southeast Bank in Miami that led

NationsBank to purchase C&S/Sovran. The two large banks have fought a fierce battle on building deep pockets as well as fighting for dominance in the other arenas of competition.

But their relatively large resources were no match for the huge threat that appeared on the horizon. While banks were battling for dominance, giants from other industries were lumbering into banking, undermining the deep-pocket advantages of the two banks. Large securities firms such as Merrill Lynch and Company entered traditional banking areas (e.g., making loans).[6] Mutual funds have siphoned off deposits. Companies as diverse as General Motors and AT&T moved into the credit card business. As Edward E. Crutchfield, chairman and CEO of First Union Corporation, commented, "We bankers are throwing snowballs [at each other] and there's someone out there with an Uzi."[7]

The competition between NationsBank and First Union shows how when one competitor builds resources, it may lead to a cycle in which competitors match or exceed ever-higher levels of resources. Wachovia saw how quickly its deep-pocket advantage over local rivals could be eroded by aggressive competitors intent on building their own positions. Then NationsBank and First Union found that even a relatively secure deep-pocket advantage in one industry is no protection from entry by giants from another industry. Deep pockets are a key part of competitive maneuvering, but like all the other traditional advantages, they do not ensure long-term sustainable advantage for companies.

As can be seen from the example of NationsBank and First Union, leveraging the deep-pocket advantage to create competitive advantage in the marketplace is a much greater challenge than it appears. Largeness is not always as sustainable as some might think. Looking at the long-term maneuvering of large and small firms may add to our understanding of deep pockets, leading us to the first dynamic strategic interaction—attempts to use deep pockets to gain advantage.

Although most of our discussions here focus on small and large companies, with the large one considered to have deep pockets, similar interactions can occur between two large rivals. The two large companies compete to gain deeper pockets than the other.

The First Dynamic Strategic Interaction: Drive 'Em Out

Although they may not admit it for reasons of antitrust law, deep-pocketed firms occasionally throw their weight around. In the first dynamic strategic interaction, the large firm uses its superior force (deep financial pockets) to drive its competitors into bankruptcy, to seize market share, and to create highly concentrated industries. By using very competitive or even predatory pricing, the deep-pocketed firm can use more force than is needed to win, thereby overwhelming the competitor. Since the true costs of a product are often hard to determine, predatory pricing can be difficult to prove. Thus, the deep-pocketed firm can drive smaller competitors out of the market and then keep the spoils for itself.

But this approach is tricky. To protect the gains in new customers that are made using this strategy, there must be barriers to firms returning to the market or entering it after the price war ends. Otherwise, the advantage the large firm gains from the costly price war will be short-lived. The deep-pocketed firm would have no time to recapture the losses from its low-price strategy if reentry is easy and swift.

> A&P found this out the hard way. It kicked off one of the most bitter and damaging price wars in the supermarket industry with its WEO campaign (Where Economy Originates) in the early 1970s.[8] Using deep pockets that it had amassed over several years, A&P started a price war that forced a few large chains into the red and drove smaller ones into bankruptcy.[9] A&P may have won the battle, but it lost the war. Its sales increased by $800 million,[10] but it posted a $51 million loss in the 1973 fiscal year,[11] and buyers became even more price sensitive. This sensitivity actually made it harder for A&P to hold onto its newfound customers. These shoppers, drawn to A&P by bargain prices, were just as easily wooed back to competitors when A&P's prices went up again and competitors cut their prices in response to A&P's reductions.

After driving back a competitor, the deep-pocketed firm needs to be able to build a wall to protect its gains, using the entry barriers discussed in Chapter 3. One way companies do this is to create switching costs for customers who are using their products or services. In industries such as retailing and consumer goods, where switching costs are generally very low, the drive 'em out strategy may be difficult to pull off successfully, as A&P apparently found out. In industries such as durable goods and heavy equipment, where the switching costs are much higher or purchase frequency is low, this strategy may be a bit more successful. Although, as we showed in Chapter 3, switching costs are not as substantial a barrier as they are thought to be. With switching costs and incentives to trade up within the company's line of products, the deep-pocketed firm can hold on to some of the stolen customers. Using deep pockets to initiate a price war can make it more difficult for companies to create switching costs. If customers come for lower prices, they are just as likely to leave for lower prices later, unless the company can offer other incentives for the customers to stay. A&P wasn't able to do this.

One of the most challenging aspects of a large company dropping prices is dealing with the fallout of public perceptions. No one likes a bully. While this approach is effective, it can be highly inflammatory. After American Airlines announced it was restructuring its fares in April 1992, rival carriers, including Continental and American West, filed suits accusing American of predatory pricing,[12] although a federal court cleared American in August 1993.[13] And a headline in *Business Week* asked, "The Airline Mess: American's Bob Crandall: Is he part of the problem? Or is he the solution?" The public may tend to side with the underdog, and the smaller player who wishes to fight back has several options. The aggressive deep-pocket firm is not immune from counterattack, as we can see in the next dynamic strategic interaction.

The Second Dynamic Strategic Interaction: Smaller Competitors Use Courts or Congress to Derail the Deep-Pocketed Firm

The biggest opponents of an aggressive firm with deep pockets, at least in the United States, are the courts and legislative bodies. As we saw in the case of American's aggressive pricing strategy, one of the first responses of its competitors was to file a suit alleging predatory pricing. This can discipline the large firm and keep it from fully using its deep pockets against smaller competitors.

A tiny manufacturer of Party Animals snack crackers, Owen Ryan and Associates, successfully fought off an alleged attempt to crush its name by Anheuser-Busch, which was concerned the cracker would be confused with the beermaker's mascot, Spuds Mackenzie, The Original Party Animal, according to *Marketing News*. The Trademark Trial and Appeals Board ruled in Ryan's favor in June 1989. When Anheuser-Busch kept up the battle, Party Animals responded by planning a public relations campaign focused on a one-day boycott of Bud Light and a slogan of "free the party animals!"[14]

The Manhattan Toy Company, with twenty-two employees, successfully fought off Gerber's Toy Division, part of the one billion dollar multinational, when Gerber allegedly copied one of the toy company's stuffed dinosaurs. The toy manufacturer went to court and gained a temporary restraining order against its deep-pocketed rival. *Success* magazine reports that Gerber pulled the dinosaur from its catalog and settled out of court.[15]

When Haagen-Dazs allegedly used its substantial clout (through parent Pillsbury) to try to squeeze Ben & Jerry's off the supermarket shelves, according to *Success* magazine, the smaller Vermont ice cream maker responded with a public relations campaign that painted Pillsbury as an oversized bully. Using the slogan "What's the Doughboy Afraid Of?" they set up an 800 number and a Ben & Jerry's Defense Fund. They encouraged callers to send letters to Pillsbury. Ben & Jerry's also filed a suit under federal anti-trust laws, which Pillsbury settled out of court.[16]

In some industries where national security is an issue, the government can sometimes provide direct subsidies or aid that gives the small firm access to deeper pockets. Governments provide protection and resources to industries that are considered vital to national interests such as defense, agriculture, aerospace, railroads, and supercomputers.

In order to balance the scales against deep-pocketed Boeing, a $29 billion company that is number one in airplane manufacturing, Airbus Industrie has received European government subsidies for over twenty years, and Mc-Donnell Douglas Corporation will most likely be receiving Taiwanese aid toward the $4 billion development costs associated with developing the next generation of planes.

If these lawsuits or government subsidies are effective, the deep-pocketed firm may be forced to back down. But large firms do not sit idly by as these small firms file lawsuits or seek government support. The deep-pocketed firms take measures to defend themselves against antitrust suits, which is the focus of the next dynamic strategic interaction.

The Third Dynamic Strategic Interaction: Large Firm Thwarts Antitrust Suit

Several large U.S. firms, such as American Airlines and IBM, have been sued but managed to escape from the antitrust vise without serious damage (except perhaps for the long-term dampening effect of the actions on corporate aggressiveness). It is to be expected that smaller competitors will file a suit against almost any aggressive move from a larger competitor. So these suits sometimes have little ground to stand on. Even when there are grounds for the suit, the large firm may try to bury the smaller firm in an avalanche of documents during the discovery process that precedes going to court. When trucks and trucks of memos arrive at the plaintiff's lawyer's office, it may take years and millions of dollars in legal fees to read, catalogue, and find the documents that incriminate the firm. This can exhaust the resources of smaller plaintiffs or at least delay the proceedings long enough for circumstances to change, allowing a favorable negotiated settlement. So large firms can sometimes successfully battle these challenges in court.

Also, government support for vital industries is just as likely to go to large competitors as to smaller ones. If the large competitor can demonstrate its ability to meet the needs of national security, it can cut off the smaller company's efforts to gain protection or support.

More interestingly, Japanese firms avoid U.S. government meddling by locating their operations outside the influence of the U.S. government and financial systems. Japanese keiretsu are not easily made susceptible to these government controls and therefore can operate much more freely than their U.S. counterparts. The United States has a hard time identifying the costs of Japanese competitors, making it difficult to prove predatory pricing in the United States. These firms may also be able to use monopolistic practices in Japan that would not be allowed under U.S. law. They not only avoid U.S. laws, but they also benefit from the support of their own government through subsidies and beneficial regulations. However, many Japanese firms have opened plants in the United States for reasons partially outlined in the previous chapter. This is making many Japanese competitors subject to U.S. laws.

> Consider De Beers, the South African diamond-mining concern that controls an estimated 85 percent of the world's gem-diamond sales through its London-based Central Selling Office. De Beers must be careful where it does business to avoid becoming subject to U.S. antitrust regulation. Since the U.S. Supreme Court in the mid-1940s dismissed a U.S. antitrust action against the company, De Beers has been very careful to do nothing that would give it a presence in the United States because it is widely seen to exercise near-cartel control over the natural diamond gemstone business.[17]

Even when antitrust suits are successful, competitors can work around them with price and quality positioning. For example, Polaroid successfully used antitrust suits to drive Kodak out of the instant-film market, but Kodak used the availability of one-hour processing to cut into Polaroid's instant market. Kodak also introduced disposable cameras to counter the convenience of instants, and Polaroid responded with a peewee camera to counter the portability of the disposables. In this case the antitrust suit did little to dampen the pace of competition.

The difficulty of carrying out the threat of antitrust action against many deep-pocketed firms means that small companies have to resort to other tactics to counter the deep-pocketed aggressor. This is the subject of the next dynamic strategic interaction.

The Fourth Dynamic Strategic Interaction: Small Firms Neutralize the Advantage of the Deep Pocket

Even without resorting to antitrust laws, the small firm has a variety of defenses against the deep-pocketed firm that is using its brute power to drive the small competitor out of business. Small firms can sometimes outmaneuver larger firms, drawing on alliances or focusing on niche markets. These resource-scarce, but nevertheless resourceful, small firms can sometimes turn the deep-pocket advantage of their larger rivals into a liability. We observed five options that were used successfully to counter the deep-pocket advantage.

OPTION 1: RESOURCE ESCALATION

Probably the most common response to an aggressive large opponent is that the smaller firm starts to develop its own deep pockets through mergers or alliances. Relaxed enforcement of antitrust rules allows for mergers with other companies in the same industry. For example, Seagram, a small player in the wine industry, bought a number of smaller wineries so it could compete with Gallo. Smaller law firms in the United Kingdom and Denmark merged to create larger companies that can compete against the large U.S. law firms.[18] These combinations can create a force that rivals that of the deep-pocketed competitor.

Besides traditional mergers with competitors in the same industry, firms build up their own deep pockets through nontraditional partnerships. There are a variety of alliances that can build the small firm's resources.

- *Alliances based on ownership of banks and other financial institutions* Sears and General Electric have both benefited from owning an investment bank, not only through the business it produces but also because having relationships with loyal bankers provides access to markets that can generate a substantial war chest in the event of a hostile takeover or a serious competitive challenge in their customer or product markets. Although both companies often use outside partners for their own banking, the potential to draw upon these alliances creates a deterrent effect for smaller competitors. It could also be a mistake to own these resources when these services could be rented whenever needed.
- *Alliance with employees and suppliers* The support of employees and suppliers provides some firms with deeper pockets than they would

otherwise be able to develop. These constituents sometimes invest in the firm and add to resources that fund efforts to counter the attack of a larger competitor. Employees and suppliers are sometimes willing to join with a firm to fight for its market since doing so is tied to their own self-interests.

- *Franchising* Some businesses, such as fast-food chains, clone themselves quickly into a larger organization through franchises. This method gives the firm the power of a much larger organization by giving it access to the funds of franchisees. Even the large soft drink and car manufacturers use franchised dealerships/distributors to extend their deep pockets.

- *Other Alliances* Alliances with other companies in the industry can draw together the scale and power to dominate an industry. For example, Matsushita successfully beat back Sony's Beta system by sharing its VHS technology with other firms. More recently, Sony has turned this strategy back against Matsushita by sharing Sony's new 8 mm camcorder technology with its competitors to increase penetration and standardization of the format. The strategy helped the 8 mm format capture at least half of the world camcorder market in 1991. Research alliances such as the U.S. Sematech consortium can help companies overcome the monumental costs of R&D for new high-tech products and fight the deep pockets of subsidized overseas competitors.[19] Sematech combined the expertise and resources of fourteen U.S. electronics companies, as well as more than half a billion dollars in federal assistance. Among its early successes was the development of a new, faster, and more precise chip-making tool that is expected to surpass Japanese technology.[20]

Another approach to building resources through alliances can be seen by looking at the structures of alliances surrounding AT&T and IBM. Although these are both deep-pocketed firms, they challenged one another with an escalating level of resources. This process of escalation led each side to establish ever-widening networks of alliances, as shown in Figure 4–1. At each stage of their development, the two giants added alliances to deepen their resources and expertise in diverse areas. Smaller firms sought the protection of joining up with each alliance. AT&T moved into computers and data networks through alliances with Lucky Gold, NCR, Star, Wang, and Sun Microsystems. IBM complemented its computing power through alliances with Intel, Rohm, Siemens, MCI Communications, and Bell Atlantic.

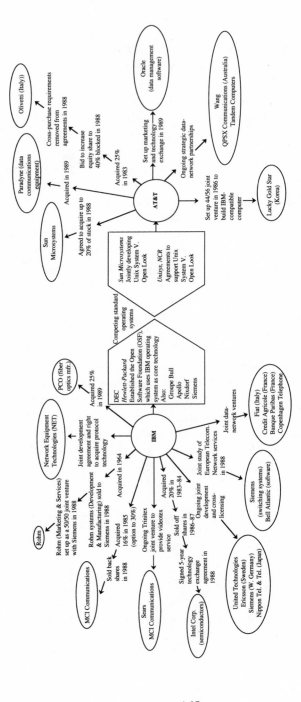

FIGURE 4-1

COMPETING GLOBAL NETWORKS: IBM AND AT&T

Source: Original chart by Braxton Associates, J.B. Quinn, and P.C. Paquette.
Taken from *Intelligent Enterprise* by J.B. Quinn (Free Press, 1992).

To fit into an alliance of the type in Figure 4–1, smaller firms often focus their resources on a smaller mission. Firms sometimes conserve their resources by focusing on being specialized on one component of the product or in one aspect of the value chain where they can be the "best in the world." This decreases the firm's vulnerability to a broad-based attack by a deep-pocketed rival and invests more resources in that component or stage of the value-added chain than the deep-pocketed firm has. Thus the deep-pocketed firm is likely to want to ally with the smaller firm to gain access to its greater expertise.

Of course, it is not always possible to escalate the depth of a firm's resources through mergers and alliances. Moreover, trying to do so can be difficult. During the 1980s, for example, many of the megabanks that were born of huge mergers stumbled, including the ill-fated merger between C&S and Sovran before the creation of NationsBank by NCNB. Statistics on bank mergers show that acquisitions are very rarely successful. They usually depress earnings, returns, and share price of the acquirer. The New York consulting firm FMCG found that on average the shares of an acquirer fall 40 percent lower than competitors' six years after the acquisition. Other studies show that bigger banks are less profitable than medium-sized ones.[21]

Besides the poorly structured deals that are entered in the rush to grow, the bigger bank faces several other obstacles. While, in theory, a larger bank can reorganize to cut costs and achieve economies of scale, it is often difficult to reorganize the resources of a sprawling organization to achieve savings. This is the lesson that C&S and Sovran learned during their merger in 1989 that preceded the merger with NCNB. *Euromoney* comments that the combined bank ended up running itself as two separate banks, making it difficult to capitalize on the synergies between the two operations.[22]

Thus, smaller firms sometimes use some of the following alternatives for dealing with deep-pocketed rivals: taking out the aggressor, swarming, cooperative strategies, and avoiding direct competition.

OPTION 2: TAKING OUT THE AGGRESSOR—DAVID BUYS GOLIATH

When a small firm can't beat its deep-pocketed opponent in the customer/product marketplace, some resort to winning in the stock market by launching a takeover. The resources of the deep-pocketed aggressor are sometimes stretched through fierce price competition in several markets, making it susceptible to a hostile takeover. When using their deep pockets to fight price wars, these aggressors are leaving money on the table by charging less than the price the market will bear for their product. They are growing for the sake of growing, often sacrificing shareholder value in pursuit of market share. This can sometimes be an excellent environment in which to successfully launch a takeover, especially if the smaller firm can gain access to the resources needed for the takeover. The smaller firm might be able to fund the takeover through junk bond financing, through bootstrapping by selling off the slack assets of the acquired deep-pocketed firm, or by entering a consortium or alliance to buy the larger firm. Although hostile takeovers have been less common in the early 1990s, this can still be a viable means for a small firm to overcome a deep-pocket advantage.

In 1988 Ames Department Stores purchased the Zayre Corporation, which more than doubled Ames' sales, according to *Business Week*. The purchase was described by one analyst as "a small company swallowing the whale."[23] The move allowed Ames to swallow a large competitor as well as to expand its geographic reach. But the risk of such moves, as Ames found, was a 56 percent debt-to-equity ratio (according to *Business Week*) that eventually led to financial troubles.[24]

While this strategy can be effective in the United States, it is nearly impossible to use in other parts of the world. In Japan, for example, as T. Boone Pickens discovered during his attempt to buy an auto-parts supplier, hostile takeovers are not a viable option, especially if the bidder is a foreigner.

Even if the takeover attempt is not successful, this still is an effective defense against an assault by a deep-pocketed opponent. By defending itself against the takeover, the large company may be so depleted that it could find its own pockets are much more shallow. It could also be so distracted that it loses its momentum in seizing market share. Nevertheless, this is not a frequently used option because smaller firms often can't muster the financial resources to launch the hostile takeover, especially since the collapse of the junk bond market.

OPTION 3: SWARMING

Even without formal mergers and alliances, small firms sometimes tacitly work together to respond to an aggressor. Under this scenario, groups of small firms attack the large aggressor simultaneously from different directions, like a swarm of killer bees attacking a cow. This forces the aggressor to respond on several different fronts, making it difficult to sustain its response. While U.S. antitrust laws prohibit explicit collusion, tacit alignments sometimes occur naturally in the course of business when firms are just independently following good strategies that only appear to complement one another. This type of "swarming" by small companies can provide a substantial sting to a large company. Sometimes laws can actually help the small "swarming" competitors by preventing action by the large company, as in the case of pay phones in the United States.

The 1984 Federal Communications Commission's breakup of the Bell System forbad the Baby Bells from manufacturing or selling pay phones, although they could install and operate them. This opened the doors to many small entrepreneurs in the private pay-phone business. These companies with high-tech phone systems have forged agreements with convenience store chains by offering higher cuts to businesses providing space for the phones. These small pay-phone companies, in alliances with retail chains leasing, owning, or operating a small number of pay phones, are stinging the Baby Bells with thousands of small bites in the pay-phone marketplace. Just five years after the FCC ruling, an estimated 175,000 of the nation's two million pay phones had been replaced by privately owned telephones.[25]

To take another example, specialty retailers and family-owned retailers who compete with large department stores, such as Sears, have successfully attacked by offering improved selection or pricing tailored to beat each department in the large stores. Each specialty retailer focuses on a narrow product segment offered by the large store. The cumulative effect of several competitors offering better selection or prices than Sears in several product areas has been to force Sears to respond across all its product lines, a considerable investment. In contrast, the smaller retailers make countering changes with more speed and less expense, given their lack of bureaucracy.

An attack by small firms against a deep-pocketed opponent can be risky. If one small firm acts before the others, the deep-pocketed firm may beat it back to "set an example" for the others. Thus, a simultaneous attack is required. Because firms cannot explicitly collude by sitting down at a table, many firms communicate through announcements and published fares or prices. This allows them to signal their intentions and tacitly coordinate their activities.

OPTION 4: COOPERATIVE STRATEGIES

Small firms sometimes try to avoid the costly competitive battles inherent in the first three options by means of sharing their profits with the deep-pocketed firm by forming joint ventures or through licensing arrangements with the deep-pocketed aggressor. The large firm may agree to distribute the small firm's products in Asia, for example, in exchange for mutual sharing of technology for use elsewhere in the world. Besides the financial benefits of a joint venture, the small firm may also be able to learn the large firm's methods of doing business, including manufacturing techniques and strategies of marketing and product design.

Joint ventures between "Davids" and "Goliaths" frequently offer the large company access to new products and technology while the small companies gain the resources needed for R&D. One such joint venture was a deal between Gilead Sciences and Glaxo, Incorporated, a subsidiary of Glaxo Holdings, the world's second-largest maker of prescription drugs. Gilead received about twenty million dollars for research while Glaxo gained an equity stake in the company and its anticancer drugs.[26]

It almost goes without saying that such a shotgun marriage is not always comfortable. These joint arrangements have sometimes proven very costly, especially in U.S. ventures with foreign firms, where many joint ventures have failed. Sometimes the larger joint venture partner doesn't deliver on its half of the bargain. The smaller firm may give the large competitor access to its markets, which could undercut the small firm's control of its own niche. The information the small firm obtains may be about old manufacturing methods rather than state-of-the-art technology and processes, and the small firm may end up a captive of the larger firm. In any event, the small firm simply ends up as part of an alliance with a deep-pocketed firm that is facing an opposing alliance composed of a second deep-pocketed firm and its numerous smaller allies. Thus, this option does not eliminate competition between deep-pocketed firms. It merely creates alliances of balanced strength to neutralize the advantage of deep pockets on the other side.

OPTION 5: AVOID COMPETING DIRECTLY WITH THE DEEP POCKET

Because deep-pocketed firms are so large, small competitors may be able to squeeze into product/market niches that large firms can't or won't enter. By finding new niches outside the primary niches of the large aggressor, small firms often avoid direct competition. Niching strategies can carve out safe places that are too small to be of much interest to the big company. Rolls Royce, for example, was able to move into the U.S. auto market at the high end of GM's market. By choosing a position that was well above the Cadillac range, it avoided attracting a strong response from the automotive giant.

Niching can be done by concentrating on a small geographic region, specializing the product, and segmenting the market by focusing on a small pocket of customers. It can be aided by the application of new manufacturing technology or through increased output flexibility.

Small companies often use technologies such as computer-aided design and flexible manufacturing to develop niches and escape from price competition with larger firms. For example, Peerless Saw Company, a small Ohio manufacturer of saw blades, was rapidly losing market share to large foreign competitors that offered mass-produced standard blades at lower prices. By developing a computerized laser system to cut its blades, Peerless could offer customized saw blades in smaller batches and still provide fast turnaround. The technology allowed Peerless to focus on the high-margin, premium market for custom blades rather than the low-margin, mass-produced standard-blade market. By creating this niche, it was able to outmaneuver the deep-pocket advantage of its competitors.[27]

The small firm's lack of bureaucracy and its more flexible cost structure (since it often avoids a lot of fixed assets and overhead) give it greater flexibility than its larger rivals. This flexibility allows smaller firms to vary their output more easily in response to changing market conditions. The large firm, on the other hand, has to maintain a fairly constant output. A study of more than three thousand firms in eighty-three industries found that output flexibility provided a significant competitive advantage for small firms, especially in volatile and capital-intensive industries.[28]

Thus, it is clear that deep pockets can be outmaneuvered by smaller firms. Small companies have numerous options to obsolete or neutralize the deep-pocketed firm's ability to use brute force.

SUMMARY: WHO WINS—BRAINS OR BRAWN?

Brawn, then, is not a replacement for brains. Even the deepest pockets can be tapped dry. They provide a margin of safety, but not absolute safety. General Motors, for example, once seemed invincible because its pockets were so deep and its markets so secure. Its large size, due to earlier successes in the marketplace, made it able to sustain individual product failures without going under. It could launch a few duds without worrying about losing the war. Because it was so big, it could take a hit in one division by subsidizing the losses from other parts of the corporation. Its size also gave it significant economies of scale and scope.

But all these tremendous resources were not adequately rallied to meet the threat of the upstart Japanese automakers. With declining market share GM's large size suddenly became its greatest liability. Its pockets became so depleted by years of losses that it finally led to the decision by ex-CEO Robert Stempel to reorganize, shuttering twenty-one plants and scaling back its workforce by seventy-four thousand people, including twenty thousand white-collar workers. Moreover, the GM board has replaced Stempel with new management, which is now under orders to turn GM around quickly or be held accountable.

On the other hand, a company such as Honda would not have been voted most likely to succeed in U.S. markets several decades ago. It was small. It had little presence or reputation and a much smaller resource base to devote to the car business. But this may have made it more aggressive and creative in using the resources it had. In the end, its product and process innovation was more valuable than deep pockets.

Similarly, NCR's rise to seize control of the automatic teller machine (ATM) market in 1987 was helped by deep-pocketed IBM's misstep in new product development. IBM introduced a flashy ATM in 1985 that could read the magnetic coding on checks and cash them on the spot. Although this was a revolutionary machine, customers were looking for incremental improvements in a lower-cost machine. NCR provided it, along with a relentless commitment to high quality, reliability, and customer service. Operating out of a single plant in Scotland, NCR rose from being the ninth-largest producer of ATMs in 1980 to surpassing market leaders IBM and Diebold in 1987.

IBM essentially gave up on the ATM business, becoming the minority partner in a joint venture with Diebold (Diebold owns 70 percent of the venture and its president is head of it). NCR's single plant continued to expand its sales.[29]

Thus, the smart move can beat the big move, and brains can beat brawn. To do so, however, requires the small firm to outmaneuver the large one by using the hypercompetitive techniques discussed in Chapters 1, 2, and 3. This, interestingly, restarts the other cycles all over again, each time pushing the conflict level even higher.

Sometimes brains can't beat brawn, and the small firm has exhausted all the options in the fourth dynamic strategic interaction—resource escalation, taking out the aggressor, swarming, cooperative strategies, and avoiding direct competition. But even in this case, deep-pocketed firms often meet a countervailing force from outside their industry that restrains their behavior. This is the next dynamic strategic interaction.

The Fifth Dynamic Strategic Interaction: The Rise of a Countervailing Power

When a deep-pocketed firm comes to dominate its industry so much that it develops excessive power over its competitors, it also develops power over suppliers and customers. Suppliers and customers may try to recapture power by building themselves up into a countervailing force. They may merge or develop consortia (such as buying cooperatives or supplier councils) that put pressure on the deep-pocketed firm.

> When CBS announced plans to begin charging its network affiliate stations for programming and marketing services it used to provide for free, the affiliates (buyers of the network's programs) acted together as a countervailing power against the powerful network. The affiliates began replacing network news programs with outside news suppliers. In response to this countervailing power of the affiliates, CBS increased the amount of time affiliates have for local news broadcasts during *CBS This Morning*.[30]

Customers sometimes integrate backwards into the deep-pocketed firm's industry. Suppliers sometimes integrate forward into the deep-pocketed firm's industry. And labor can form a countervailing force against the deep-pocketed firm.

> The Belgian company Food Lion drove prices down, mostly by offering employees substantially lower wages and fewer benefits according to *Business & Society Review*. This, in turn, forced its surrounding competitors to obtain similar labor concessions to be able to match Food Lion's prices.[31] Labor unions, however, formed a countervailing force, attacking on several fronts. Local 400 of the United Food and Commercial Workers International Union counterattacked with coordinated job actions in the United States and Belgium and filed a grievance with an international trade organization.[32]

Thus, even if the competitors don't destroy the deep-pockets advantage, the customers or suppliers will eventually try to do so.

THE DEEP-POCKETS ESCALATION LADDER: DEEP POCKETS TURNED INSIDE OUT

There is no question that deep pockets are a vital strategic weapon. But they do not last forever. As we have just seen, clever competitors can circumvent a deep-pocket advantage. Even the firm with the deepest pockets has limits to how much it can throw its weight around without self-destructing because of customer or supplier reactions.

Like the young man born into old money, the firm with substantial resources has great opportunities and a leg up on competitors. But, contrary to the old days, this resource-rich firm does not have a clear path to success. Street-smart small firms often end up outmaneuvering the deep-pocketed firm and pushing the competitive conflict up the escalation ladder shown in Figure 4–2. Thus, a deep-pockets advantage isn't sustainable forever.

Hypercompetitive Behavior in the Deep-Pockets Arena

The cycle begins when a firm with deep pockets launches an assault against its smaller competitors in an attempt to drive them out of the industry. The small firms counter by invoking antitrust laws or other forms of government intervention. If these don't work, small firms are forced to try to outmaneuver the large firm by hostile takeover, escalating their own resource bases, cooperative strategies, or avoidance through niching and other approaches. Thus, the small firms resort to the hypercompetitive techniques discussed in Chapters 1, 2, and 3. By restarting the cycles in the other arenas of competition, they continue to push large competitors toward hypercompetition in a never-ending process of escalation. Meanwhile, buyers and suppliers may develop a countervailing force that undermines the large firm's advantage. At each step of the cycle, firms move to the next step as a way to gain a temporary advantage. The result of all these interactions is the neutralization or elimination of the deep-pockets advantage and the creation of an environment of perfect competition.

Competition among food retailers has been characterized by the development of deep pockets and their subsequent erosion or circumvention. Before the 1960s most supermarkets were either single stores or small local chains. Then consolidation and the development of chains upped the ante. By the mid-1980s it cost $5 million to open a single superstore. To support these larger stores, distribution systems and warehouses had to be maintained. With the purchase of A&P by the Tengelmann Group in 1980, the

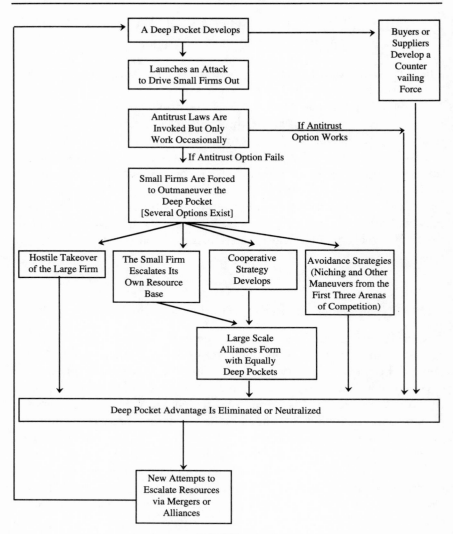

FIGURE 4–2
THE CYCLE OF COMPETITION IN THE DEEP POCKETS ARENA

most recent deep-pockets race in supermarkets began. *Chain Store Age Executive* reported in 1988 that A&P had spent over $500 million on acquisitions and that American Stores Company, which owned the Star Market, Alpha Beta, Osco Drug, and Jewel companies, attempted to purchase Lucky Stores for $2.5 billion, a move which would have made it the largest supermarket chain in America. But the purchase was blocked as anticompetitive. These and many other reorganizations of the industry, with Kroger emerging as the only supermarket chain to fight off the advances of unwanted suitors, led to an uncertain result. The large firms, after all their acquisitions and aggressive competition, are so deeply in debt that they can't be considered to have deep pockets. Smaller chains have been launching their own price wars.[34] See Figure 4–3 for an example of Kroger's apparent hypercompetitive behavior in this industry.

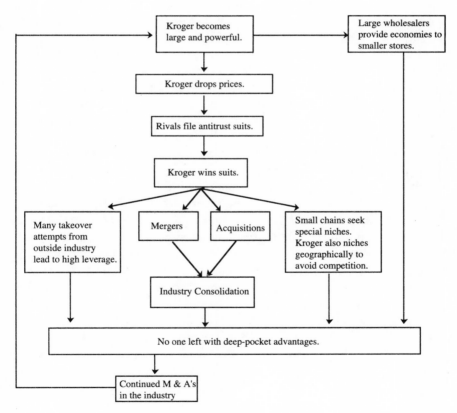

FIGURE 4–3
AN ILLUSTRATION OF HYPERCOMPETITIVE BEHAVIOR BY KROGER IN THE
GROCERY STORE INDUSTRY IN THE 1980S

CONTINUING ESCALATION

In an attempt to end this level of hypercompetition, some firms may again try to gain an even-deeper-pocket advantage. Through alliances and mergers, one firm or another will try to get the upper hand, restarting the deep-pocket cycle all over again.

We even see this in the international arena. Before World War I Germany was bigger than France, so France allied with Imperial Russia to balance the equation. In response, Germany allied with the Austro-Hungarian Empire. Britain was expected to weigh in on the French side (when Belgium was invaded), so Germany also allied with the Ottoman Empire. And so it went until a tangled web of alliances locked nations into a world war. In business too, so it goes. And hypercompetition results, with each cycle ratcheting up the conflict level to new heights.

Although we portray this cycle (in Figure 4–2) as sequential, it may also be parallel. For example, the competition for deep pockets may be thought of as occurring corporate-wide (e.g., as PepsiCo versus Coca-Cola Corporation). Or it may be thought of as occurring at the subsidiary level (e.g., at the soft drink division level in PepsiCo and Coca-Cola Corporation). This is an important distinction because, to make up for the lack of its deep pockets in soft drinks, PepsiCo has diversified outside of soft drinks to increase its size. In soft drinks Coke is much larger than Pepsi, but PepsiCo is now bigger than Coca-Cola Corporation in total size. Thus, Pepsi has neutralized the deep-pocket advantage of Coke in soft drinks by escalating its resources at the corporate-wide level, a trick that many "number twos" use to prevent the "number ones" from bullying them.

In addition, we portray this escalation ladder as a set of steps, each following the previous one. However, some companies skip steps along this ladder or end up frozen at one rung. Industries proceed up the ladder at different speeds, depending upon the aggressiveness and quirks of competitors in the industry, how long firms can stay beyond the reach of the U.S. government, and market conditions. Nevertheless, this escalation ladder defines the rungs in a general process that shows how one dynamic strategic interaction leads to the next. But competitors will climb up this ladder in many different ways, inventing new hypercompetitive ways to rush up the ladder, restart the cyle, or jump to a new arena before perfect competition is reached.

Management Challenges

This sketch of competitive moves and countermoves can help you examine your competitive position against deep-pocketed firms or your own use of deep pockets. The sequence of dynamic strategic interactions in this chapter can also help you anticipate your competitors' next move. By seeing what's ahead, you can jump levels to speed the escalation of the cycle and catch your competitors off guard. Those who climb the ladder faster are always one step ahead of the competition, forcing the others to catch up with the new advantage created by moving up to the next step on the ladder. Or you can take action to slow down the cycle if you are already ahead and don't want your competitors to jump past you. The following are some of the major issues that managers face in taking control of this cycle:

For the smaller competitor facing a deep-pocketed opponent:

- How can you neutralize the advantage of the deep pocket?
- Can antitrust laws be invoked to slow or derail the deep-pocketed firm?
- Can you build implicit or explicit alliances with other competitors or with the deep-pocketed firm itself to neutralize its advantage?
- Is the deep-pocketed firm vulnerable to a hostile takeover? Do you have access to the resources to launch one?
- Can you develop niches or exploit technology and output flexibility to avoid direct competition with the larger firm?
- If you use tacit coordination strategies (such as "swarming") are you vulnerable to antitrust actions?

For the deep-pocketed firm:

- Have you exploited all the advantages of your deep pocket (global reach, political power, room for error, pricing flexibility)? Do you have a strategy for capturing these advantages?
- Are you willing to use your deep pocket to drive competitors out of business? When? How will you capture the benefits of doing this?
- How are you vulnerable to attack by smaller competitors trying to neutralize your deep pocket?
- How can you maintain the flexibility that is often lost with greater size and bureaucracy?
- What are the dangers of your suppliers and buyers developing a countervailing force? How can this move be prevented?
- Can you form alliances with smaller competitors to benefit both you and them? Are other deep-pocketed competitors in your industry trying to do this to neutralize your deep pocket?
- Are you vulnerable to antitrust action?

For both players:

- Is it to your advantage to speed up the cycle in Figure 4–2? If you want to speed it up, how can you make that happen?
- Are you leading your industry up the ladder or following? Why?
  Who and what is setting the pace of escalation in your industry? Why?

Not all industries are at the same point along this cycle. Some move up each of the rungs on the escalation ladder shown in Figure 4–2 quickly, and others move slowly. Some have potential to be frozen at one rung. Others don't. Some can be speeded up. Others can't. But most travel through these points over the long run. By understanding these mileposts, you can take greater charge of your direction and face fewer surprises from competitors. In Part III of this book, we will develop several techniques and strategies for dealing with these management challenges and for creating the types of temporary advantages that are available at each step of the escalation ladder in this arena of competition.

CHAPTER 5

NEW ANALYTICAL TOOLS

Analyzing Competition Using the Four Arenas

Chapters 1 to 4 described how competition escalates in each of the four arenas—cost and quality, timing and know-how, strongholds, and deep pockets. Competition also moves from arena to arena as companies seek temporary advantages. This movement has been portrayed as if it follows a straightforward progression from the first arena to the second to the third to the fourth. However, it can shift back and forth among the arenas, especially for older industries. When companies reach a deadlock in one arena or when achieving the next advantage is too difficult or expensive, they shift the competition to another arena.

Two Types of Uses for the Four Arenas

This chapter develops two analytical tools based on two radically different views of how competitive escalation moves across these four arenas. The chapter introduces two approaches for using all four arenas to analyze competition and market conditions, approaches that look at dynamic strategic interaction over long periods of time. This analysis can help firms assess their competitive situation, predict competitors' moves, and identify the locus of competition; that is, which arena is the current or future battleground.

The first approach is a Four Arena analysis; it looks at the evolution of competition over time across the four arenas to identify trends and patterns of dynamic strategic interactions between competitors. The second approach is a Four Lens analysis; it looks at a single competitive move and analyzes its impact on each of the four arenas of competition.

A Four Arena analysis of competition in the soft drink industry (presented below) shows how competition in the four arenas has played out historically, how the arenas are interrelated, and how competition has intensified. This analysis offers a framework that strategists can use to anticipate strategic opportunities and likely actions of competitors in each of the arenas.

A Four Lens analysis of the computer printer industry illustrates how the impact of a single competitive action can be gauged by its effect on each of the four arenas. In one case (presented below) the introduction of the laser printer influenced competition in the cost and quality, timing and know-how, strongholds, and deep-pocket arenas. By analyzing the action through these four lenses, strategists can anticipate the moves of competitors and plan their next actions. They can also analyze the full implications of a competitor's move.

Hypercompetitive Markets Involve a Tangled Web of Complexity

The Four Arena analysis and Four Lens analysis are based on a simplification of the dynamics of competitive interactions that breaks reality into its component pieces. In reality, the arenas are not quite so distinct, the progression is not quite so clear, and the nature of dynamic strategic interaction is not so predictable or easily labeled.

The complexity of dynamic strategic interactions in the four arenas may blur the boundaries of the arenas, for example. The lines between two arenas can blur because some actions span more than one arena. Several actions may play out in different arenas at the same time. For example, building quality can be seen as playing itself out in the cost-quality, the timing–know-how, and stronghold arenas. Improving quality can be the basis for building or overcoming a "differentiation" entry barrier in the stronghold arena or the means a follower uses to compete with a first mover in the timing–know-how arena.

Another action that spans different arenas at the same time is the use of advertising. For example, a company that uses a massive advertising campaign to launch a product in opposition to a competitor's existing product may be operating in all four arenas simultaneously. The aggressor may be using its deep-pocket advantage to pay for the campaign. It may be creating entry barriers to future players by differentiating its product. It may be using the advertising to overcome the advantage of the first mover. Finally, the advertising campaign may be used to shape an image of higher perceived quality among customers.

Although thus far Part I has described competition as moving from the first through the fourth arena in succession, this is not always the case. In particular, the cost and quality arena and the timing and know-how arena present a chicken-and-egg question. The jump to the timing and know-how arena has been viewed as a way of breaking out of cost-quality competition. But before companies can compete on cost and quality, they must first introduce products or services, which come from the timing and know-how arena.

Finally, several cycles could occur simultaneously within a single arena. For example, deep pockets may be developed at a corporate level or subsidiary level. Or though two firms might be of equal size at the corporate level, one may have much larger market share in the soda business than the other. A second example based on the cost-quality arena is one in which firms compete on four or five different types of quality simultaneously.

These four arenas, therefore, are conceptual arenas. They are a way of emphasizing the strategic moves of competitors. Real competition, particularly in today's hypercompetitive environment, is much more complex. It resists being wrapped in neat packages. But it is only by breaking it down into such packages that we can understand it and begin to take charge of it.

The Four Arenas Are Actually Frameworks to Understand Market Processes

Although some aspects of competition within these four arenas are well known, the escalation ladders and cycles presented here are new concepts. The escalation ladders, the sequences of moves and countermoves, help explain the process of how competition evolves over time. These ladders are actually cycles that can be restarted by actions of the firm. At each step of the ladder, companies move up a rung to gain advantage. Competitors are then forced to react to these moves, further escalating competition. If competitors do not react, if they fall behind on the ladder, they die. In sum, the four arenas are a way to view the market process; that is, the sequences and complexities of maneuvering for position that have never been articulated explicitly before.

These four escalation ladders—cost and quality, timing and know-how, stronghold creation/invasion, and deep pockets are, therefore, a conceptual way to understand market processes that occur naturally due to the competitive instincts of rivals. Part I has shown how advantages in each of these areas are eroded by a process involving a series of moves and countermoves. It has also shown how the escalation moves up each ladder and from one arena to another as each of the traditional sources of advantage is repeatedly destroyed and recreated momentarily. Here and in subsequent parts this book will illustrate how the four arenas can be used as an analytical tool to describe a competitive maneuvering over time or to analyze a single action affecting more than one arena at the same time.

FOUR ARENA ANALYSIS OF THE SOFT DRINK INDUSTRY

To illustrate the power of viewing competition in each of these four arenas, this chapter first examines how to use the four arenas to analyze the strategic maneuvering of competitors in a single industry: soft drinks. This first approach—which will be called a Four Arena analysis—is a study of the progression of a single industry by looking at its progress through each of four arenas over a very long period of time. A second approach—a Four Lens analysis—examines the impact of a single event in an industry (the introduction of laser printers, for example) and considers its impact on each of the four arenas. This second approach will be discussed in the latter half of this chapter.

The Four Arena analysis, presented below, has been focused on the development and escalation of competition in the soft drink industry. This analysis is intended to

- show how the four arenas and escalation ladders discussed in Chapters 1 to 4 can be used to increase your understanding of the dynamic strategic interactions between competitors
- help predict future actions of competitors
- identify which competitor has seized the initiative in each of the arenas and determine why
- identify the arenas that have remained dormant for years but that might be reopened
- point out opportunities for restarting or jumping arenas that have not been used recently
- identify the battleground of the future, by showing where the interactions have not yet reached the top of the escalation ladders
- open the reader's mind to seeing the rise and fall of different competitive advantages as part of a dynamic market process
- illustrate how a market becomes more and more hypercompetitive as rivals seek to outmaneuver each other in new and more aggressive ways

Consider the long and winding evolution of the dynamic rivalry between Coke and Pepsi through the frame of these four arenas, as summarized in Figure 5–1.[1]

FIGURE 5–1
HISTORY OF THE SOFT DRINK INDUSTRY IN EACH OF THE FOUR ARENAS

ERA	Cost/Quality	Timing/ Know-how	Strongholds	Deep Pockets
King Coke 1886–1930	Coke dominates quality in mind of U.S. consumers.	Coke protects its secret formula.	Coke develops U.S. geographic strongholds through bottler network and fountain sales.	Coke builds profits and uses deep pockets to challenge other colas in court.
Poor Pepsi 1893–1930	Pepsi begins as small brand; Coke and Pepsi hurt by fluctuations in sugar prices during WWI in 1920.	Pepsi develops own formula, sweeter than Coke's.	Pepsi develops parallel network of bottlers. Coke unconcerned.	Pepsi fails to build deep pockets, moving in and out of bankruptcy. Sugar crisis sends Pepsi belly-up; Coke profits continue up.
Pepsi's Price War 1930–1940	Pepsi cuts price of 12 oz. bottle to 5 cents, seen as bargain, gains share.	Coke doesn't respond to new formula or packaging.	Coke introduces vending machines and coolers to control distribution channels and gain economies of scale in advertising in the U.S. (1932).	Lower price boosts Pepsi earnings to more than $4 million, with 313 bottlers by 1938.
				Pepsi seen as serious contender. Coke files suit (1938) to ban Pepsi from using "Cola." Suit dropped.
The War Years/Global Expansion 1940–1950	Pepsi's price inches up; uses ads to boost image of quality; earnings drop 70 percent (1946).		Coke launches Coca-Cola Export Corp.; in 1930 already has 64 bottlers in 28 countries. Pepsi	Coke uses political power to push law limiting sugar supplies during war. Pepsi responds by buying Cuban

(continued)

FIGURE 5–1 (Cont'd.)
HISTORY OF THE SOFT DRINK INDUSTRY IN EACH OF THE FOUR ARENAS

ERA	Cost/Quality	Timing/ Know-how	Strongholds	Deep Pockets
The War Years/Global Expansion 1940–1950 (*cont'd.*)			opens first foreign plant in Montreal (1934).	sugar plantation (1943).
			Coke rides on the coattails of World War II, building plants to supply troops with soda; leads diplomatic efforts into Latin America.	Winegrowers in France fight "Coca-Colonialism" in court. Coke uses muscle to overcome this resistance.
Pepsi's Comeback 1950–1960	Pepsi successfully focuses its ads on reaching the expanding middle-class market.	Pepsi introduces first 24-oz. bottle for family consumption. Coke belatedly introduces 10-, 12-, 26-oz. bottles.	Pepsi uses cofranchise with Schweppes to enter England and expand product line.	Pepsi's profits up 15 percent. Complacent Coke's profits drop 8 percent (1954).
			Pepsi expands vending machines.	Pepsi ad budget boosted from $14 to $30 million (1955–1959).
			Pepsi foreign plants grow from 67 to 237; Coke still ahead with 647.	
Product Proliferation 1960–1970		New product battle begins. *Coke*: Sprite, Tab, Fresca. *Pepsi*: Patio, Diet Pepsi, Mountain Dew.	Pepsi uses political connections; Khrushchev tries Pepsi, Russian market open.	Cash-poor Pepsi merges with Frito-Lay to build resources.

FIGURE 5–1 (Cont'd.)

HISTORY OF THE SOFT DRINK INDUSTRY IN EACH OF THE FOUR ARENAS

ERA	Cost/Quality	Timing/ Know-how	Strongholds	Deep Pockets
Product Proliferation 1960–1970 (*cont'd.*)		Flip-top can introduced		
Hypercompetition 1970–1990	The Pepsi Challenge (based on blind taste tests) attacks on quality (1974).	Product proliferation accelerates: diet, caffeine-free, juice flavors, sports drinks.	Coke's U.S. stronghold is invaded. 7-Up attacks colas head-on with the Uncola. Niche players enter.	Pepsi adds restaurants; Coke enters entertainment (1982).
	Pepsi's sweetness viewed as a better taste.		Pepsi gains share in U.S. cola market through youth segment.	
	Coke, on the ropes, begins discounting, driving prices down.			
	Coke tries New Coke to leapfrog quality and recapture the initiative.	New Coke a disaster. Coke Classic revived.		
		Pepsi rolls out 3-liter bottle in 1984; four-month lead over Coke.		
Overall Comments on Each Arena	Pepsi kept the initiative in this arena.	Initially RC and 7-Up seized the initiative in this arena.	Coke kept the initiative in this arena for most of the century.	Coke kept the deep pocket advantage and used it well through most of the century.

(*continued*)

FIGURE 5–1 (Cont'd.)
HISTORY OF THE SOFT DRINK INDUSTRY IN EACH OF THE FOUR ARENAS

ERA	Cost/Quality	Timing/ Know-how	Strongholds	Deep Pockets
Overall Comments on Each Arena (cont'd.)	Quality is now essentially equal in the cola market.	Later Pepsi was more aggressive.	Pepsi is catching up by expanding in most geographic areas.	Pepsi is now larger on a corporatewide basis through the use of mergers and diversification in fast food and snacks.
	Price competition continues in the cola market.	Now both Coke and Pepsi are aggressively inventing new soft drinks.	This area is where the action will be in the future.	
		New tastes are now focusing on smaller and smaller niches.	The battle for emerging and growth markets around the world will determine the long-run winner.	

Hypercompetition: The Real Thing

Coke and Pepsi have been competitors for nearly a century. But it has only been in recent decades that the competition has escalated to what journalists and authors have labeled "the cola wars."

In the first seventy years of the industry, aggressive dynamic strategic interactions were infrequent. Perhaps the most aggressive move was Pepsi's halving the price of its twelve-ounce bottle in 1933 to offer twice as much soda as Coke for the same price. Even so, it took Coke more than twenty years to introduce a twelve-ounce bottle. Competition was much less intense.

But the 1960s ushered in a new wave of aggressive product proliferation and price competition. After sticking to Coke and Pepsi for virtually all of their histories, suddenly the two soft drink giants began a series of new product introductions, with competition focused on the timing of the introductions and the know-how associated with developing new tastes. Coke and Pepsi entered the lemon-lime market in the 1960s with Coke's Sprite (1961) and Pepsi's Mountain Dew. Royal Crown's development of diet cola in 1962 launched the diet war, stimulating the introduction of Tab (1963), Diet Pepsi (1964), and Diet Coke (1983). During the 1970s and 1980s this process had accelerated to the point where Coke and Pepsi alone introduced more than thirty-four new products. If Seven-Up, Dr Pepper, and Royal Crown are included in the count, the major soft drink makers launched nearly one hundred new products in those two decades.

Advertising spending has soared in the 1980s and 1990s. At the same time, competition has driven prices lower and lower. As an indication of the intensity of this competition, the inflation-adjusted price of a case of soda has dropped from $6.19 in 1965 to $3.99 in 1988.[2]

These wars and their increasing intensity illustrate the escalation of competition in each of the four arenas. This industry also shows the complexity of the dynamic strategic interactions between the two players and the interrelation between the different arenas. Interestingly, the progression of competition has moved across the four arenas in the same orderly progression as presented in Chapters 1 to 4. But now that the industry is more mature, the locus of competition will probably focus on the stronghold arena in the future. The ebbs and flows of battle are illustrated in each of the four arenas below. The initiative in each arena has shifted back and forth between Coke and Pepsi for decades in ways that are becoming increasingly aggressive over time.

Analysis of Arena 1: Cost-Quality

Coca-Cola began its life in 1886, quickly becoming the king of the cola market. Pepsi, which appeared in 1893, was one of many young upstarts, most of which fell by the wayside. Pepsi's sweeter taste, then viewed as a disadvantage, left Pepsi outmaneuvered by Coke. (See Figure 5–2.)

In 1933, Pepsi-Cola was struggling to stave off bankruptcy. Then it dropped the price of its ten-cent, twelve-ounce bottle to the same nickel price as Coca-Cola's 6.5-ounce bottle, making it a better value. (See Figure 5–3.) At that time cola was cola, so more soda meant a better value. Pepsi advertised "twice as much for a nickel," and the company came back from the brink. A survey showed that its advertising jingle was better known in the United States than "The Star-Spangled Banner."[3] Coke couldn't counter this move without changing its bottle design or its nickel

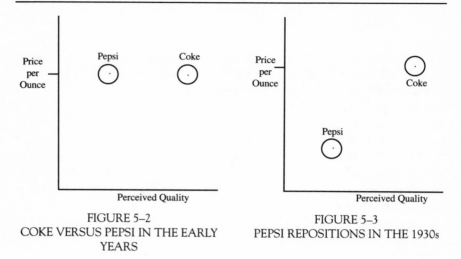

FIGURE 5–2
COKE VERSUS PEPSI IN THE EARLY
YEARS

FIGURE 5–3
PEPSI REPOSITIONS IN THE 1930s

soft drink machines. Its strength was turned against it. Pepsi rushed past Royal Crown and Dr. Pepper to become the number-two player in the industry.

Pepsi kept its price advantage through the 1960s and 1970s, when Pepsi-Cola charged its bottlers 20 percent less than Coca-Cola for its concentrate. In the early 1970s Pepsi changed the rules of competition by raising its price to equal Coke's, giving Pepsi a war chest to fuel its aggressive advertising campaigns that attacked Coke on quality. (See Figure 5–4.)

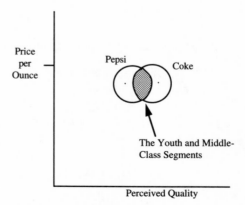

FIGURE 5–4
PEPSI BEGINS THE ASSAULT ON
COCA-COLA BY HITTING NICHES
WITHIN COKE'S POSITION

With rising ingredient costs, Pepsi no longer could offer twice as much soda for the same price.

The battle had clearly shifted away from price to quality. It was addressed through advertising that associated youth with Pepsi ("the choice of a new generation"). Later, through the Pepsi Challenge, a blind taste test that proved soda drinkers preferred Pepsi to Coke, Pepsi began a clear campaign to outmaneuver Coke's entire position because consumer tastes had changed, preferring Pepsi's sweeter formula. Coke countered with an ad campaign touting its position as "the real thing," implying that as it was the originator of the cola industry, no other player was as good as the original. (See Figure 5–5.)

As both colas' perceived quality caught up with each other, the deeper-pocketed and lower-cost Coca-Cola initiated a fierce price war. Coca-Cola made price cuts in selective markets where Pepsi was weak in the 1970s. Under Coca-Cola CEO Roberto Goizueta, price promotion reached new levels of intensity, and Pepsi responded with its own discounts. At the end of 1980, an estimated half of Coke and Pepsi in food stores was sold at a discount.[4]

As Coke and Pepsi wrestled their way up the price-quality escalation ladder, other companies moved into the low end of the cola market. These included Royal Crown and generic and store-brand colas, which had a lower perceived quality and a correspondingly low price. However, this low-end niche was outmaneuvered as the two industry leaders forced their prices down to the point of ultimate value. (See Figure 5–6.)

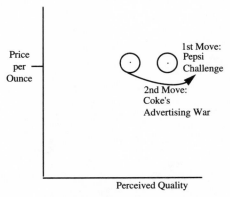

FIGURE 5–5
MANEUVERING FOR THE
HIGH-QUALITY POSITION IN THE
COLA MARKET

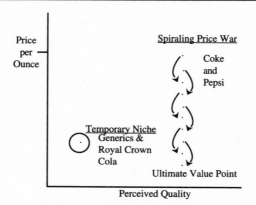

FIGURE 5–6
LOW-END ENTRANTS SURVIVE UNTIL
THE POINT OF ULTIMATE VALUE WAS
REACHED

In a desperate move to reestablish dominance and break out of the price spiral shown in Figure 5–6, Coke reformulated its product, introducing New Coke. The intent was to create a major quality jump that would capture many Pepsi drinkers (who preferred sweetness) while keeping Coke's loyal customers. (See Figure 5–7.) However, the market rejected the new formula, forcing Coke to return to Classic Coke and locking Coke and Pepsi into a continuous battle over the ultimate-value position.

In order to avoid this endless warfare and to restart the cycle in the price-quality arena, the major players in the cola market have tried to take

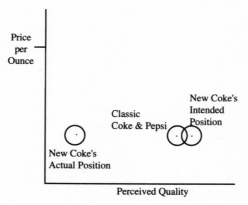

FIGURE 5–7
NEW COKE'S FAILED ATTEMPT TO
OUTMANEUVER PEPSI

advantage of changing perceptions of quality that are creating emerging niches. When Coca-Cola was first developed, the fact that it allegedly contained caffeine, cocaine, and sugar was seen as a positive product characteristic. Then cocaine went out of style and had to be removed. Finally, caffeine went out of style, and caffeine-free colas were developed. Sugar also has gone out of style. As consumers have become increasingly diet conscious, sugar-free versions of the colas have formed an important part of the market.

Each shift in the definition of quality provided an opportunity to renew the battle on a new playing field and to restart the escalation ladder in this arena. But now the players have replicated each other's moves, leaving little room to maneuver in the saturated cola market where competitors battle over fractions of a percent. So price competition continued, and the firms are stuck at a point of ultimate value due to cutthroat discounting and inability to improve quality any further. Price and quality continue to be central factors in competition, but they are becoming less and less powerful as the perceived quality and the cost structures of the two rivals converge on the ultimate-value point. Despite their large market share, the two colas retain a precarious hold on the industry, as variety-seeking consumers become anxious to try new beverages. The locus of competitive initiative in the industry has now moved to the next arena, where new noncola formulas are developed, tested, and imitated.

Analysis of Arena 2: Timing-Know-how

In the soft drink industry, perhaps the most basic and important know-how is the knowledge of how to invent a formula with a taste customers like and to package that formula in a way customers want. These skills involve a mixture of industrial design, chemistry, and cooking knowledge that is as much an art form as it is a science.

However, this type of know-how is hard to protect in the soft drink industry. The "Merchandise 7X" recipe for Coca-Cola was strictly guarded. It was never written down. The labels were scratched off the bottles of ingredients, and the formula was mixed in back rooms by a handful of senior executives in the old days.

But Pepsi, entering second, found a way around this know-how hurdle. The know-how in this industry was much more easily duplicated than might be expected. Pepsi simply developed its own formula (in a new-sized bottle) that was not the same as Coke's. In fact, because Pepsi's new formula was about 9 percent sweeter than Coke's, it actually had an advantage in blind taste tests, later allowing Pepsi to develop the Pepsi Challenge.

Perhaps because of its belief in the strength of its formula and its strong reputation, Coca-Cola fiercely resisted new product or packaging introductions until the mid-1950s. It held onto its single product in a single-sized bottle. It wasn't until 1955, against the protests of its bottlers, that it finally introduced larger bottles to counter Pepsi's packaging initiative.

In the meantime competitors seized the initiative by developing new know-how and being first to market with new formulas. One of the most significant innovations in the industry was the development of diet sodas. This innovation initially came from neither Coke nor Pepsi. It provides an example of a first mover advantage that was unable to be sustained. Royal Crown introduced its Diet Rite Cola in the early 1960s, three years before Coke or Pepsi rolled out diet products. Royal Crown's market share in diet colas initially equaled or exceeded Coca-Cola's.[5] But with the introduction of diet soft drinks by Pepsi and Coke, that position was eroded. By the end of 1983, Diet Coke had become the largest selling diet soft drink.[6] Royal Crown also was the first to launch a decaffeinated diet cola in 1980, but again it was counterattacked by offerings from Coca-Cola and Pepsi.[7]

Sweeteners used in diet sodas shifted from saccharine to aspartame, and each innovation in sweeteners provided a temporary advantage until it was copied. When Pepsi introduced aspartame (sold under the Nutrasweet brand name) into its diet soft drinks in 1984, it had only a six-week lead over Diet Coke. Pepsi used this lead to aggressively promote Diet Pepsi. Coca-Cola countered with a national campaign claiming that it also had 100 percent aspartame (but didn't say that it was available in only certain packages and markets). Pepsi then responded with point-of-purchase displays stressing that it contained Nutrasweet in all its markets and package sizes. But this was a short-lived advantage because Diet Coke eventually added aspartame in all its markets.

Another entrant into the battle was Seven-Up, which positioned itself as a caffeine-free alternative to colas. Sales went up 15 percent in the first year of the campaign. Seven-Up was not in direct competition with the colas, but by positioning itself as the "uncola," it challenged them to a fight. Fight they did. Less than six months after the launch of the no-caffeine campaign, Pepsi introduced its Pepsi Free. Coke and other makers were quick to follow. Both Coca-Cola and Pepsi introduced lemon-lime soft drinks (Sprite and Slice) to compete directly with Seven-Up.

Coke could no longer take decades to follow in product or bottling innovations and turned to innovations of its own. These innovations were not always successful. Pepsi's relentless comparisons of its cola to Coke eventually drove Coca-Cola into creating a major product reformulation. Unfortunately New Coke was a dismal failure. The new product was met with disapproval by loyal Coke drinkers, but Coca-Cola couldn't abandon the new group of customers who liked New Coke. This led to the relaunch of the original Coke as Coke Classic, forcing Coca-Cola to offer two similar sodas with similar names in an already crowded market.

By the 1980s new flavors proliferated at an alarming rate. Coke introduced Cherry Coke. Pepsi introduced Cherry Pepsi. Coca-Cola introduced Minute Maid Orange soda and Pepsi expanded its Slice line to include Mandarin Orange Slice. The speed at which Coke and Pepsi responded to each other increased until neither could gain any real advantage. Moreover, as the number of new tastes increased, each new product focused on narrower and narrower niches while making bottling more expensive due to the need for more complex bottling operations and order/delivery systems. Ultimately, maneuvering in the know-how–timing arena reached a point of diminishing returns.

Soft drink companies also competed on packaging know-how and distribution skills. Glass bottles have been replaced by tin cans, aluminum, and plastic bottles. Product innovations by one competitor have been copied by others, but they often provide a temporary advantage. In the 1950s Pepsi introduced the first twenty-four-ounce bottle for family consumption. Seven-Up came up with the liter bottle. After the introduction of the two-liter bottle, Pepsi rolled out a three-liter bottle in 1984. It took Coca-Cola only four months to obtain supplies of bottles to copy the innovation.[8] In 1960 only two container sizes were offered. By 1975 consumers had a choice of ten sizes, from 6.5 ounces to two liters. Cans, which accounted for just 4 percent of all sales in 1960, rose to 35 percent in 1975.[9]

But this growth of product and packaging variety also may have led to some product cannibalization. After Coke introduced its Diet Coke, sales of its diet soft drink Tab fell from 4.0 percent of the market (by volume) in 1982 to 1.6 percent in just two years.[10] The market share for Coke also fell during the same period. This suggests that some of the gains of Diet Coke were made at the expense of existing products.

Each taste and packaging innovation in the soft drink industry is now quickly copied by competitors, despite patents or attempts to keep formulas secret. Because the barriers to imitation are very low, it is hard to sustain a product advantage for long before it is eroded by competitors. Since Royal Crown's three-year lead in entering the diet cola market, there have been few opportunities for first movers to gain long leads in launching new products or packages.

One of the latest product battlefields between Coke and Pepsi (and the rest of the world) has been the sports-drink industry. Gatorade, which reigned over the $800 million U.S. market, suddenly found itself under attack, the *Wall Street Journal* reported. In 1992 Pepsi moved into supermarkets with a carbonated beverage called All Sport, using blind taste tests against Gatorade similar to its earlier Pepsi Challenge. Coca-Cola, a "lap or so" behind Pepsi according to the *Journal*, rolled out tests for its new PowerAde.[11]

With both Pepsi and Coke carrying very similar full lines of products and imitation time getting shorter and shorter, gaining advantage based on know-how and timing has become almost impossible. So opportunities for gaining advantage in the soft drink market have shifted to the third arena—creating and controlling strongholds by using entry barriers and then battling for turf in the strongholds of others.

Analysis of Arena 3: Strongholds

In soft drinks the key to creating and controlling a geographic stronghold is distribution. Extensive penetration and exclusive control over territories give a firm a safe haven that others cannot enter easily. If all the retail outlets in an area are already satisfied by one of the competitors, then entry by a rival is difficult to pull off. Building an expensive distribution network into an already saturated area is less attractive than moving to a virgin territory.

THE BATTLE FOR CONTROL OF THE U.S. TURF

Early on, both Coke and Pepsi granted bottling franchises based on geographic regions. The franchises were granted in perpetuity and often passed down within families. The franchisees were given exclusive rights to market the company's soft drinks in the territory but had to agree not to sell products of direct competitors.

In the early 1900s Coca-Cola pushed to make its cola available everywhere, "within the arm's reach of desire." The penetration of Pepsi's early network of franchisees was much less extensive, perhaps because Pepsi was losing in the price-quality arena (as shown in Figure 5–2). In addition, Coke's head start in the lucrative fountain market gave Coke a dominant position in distribution through theaters, drugstores, restaurants, and other nongrocery vendors.

Despite building elaborate entry barriers based on distribution channels and production facilities around the country and despite Coke's advertising economies of scale resulting from its dominance in North America, Coke's U.S. stronghold was vulnerable to entry by the guerrilla methods discussed in Chapter 3.

The network of geographic franchises left the franchisees room to bottle noncola soft drinks from companies that were not in direct competition with Coca-Cola or Pepsi-Cola. So Seven-Up, a leader in the lemon-lime market, could piggyback on Coke's bottling system. Coke introduced Sprite as one means to block Seven-Up's access to Coke's bottlers and fountain distributors. Finally, when Seven-Up took on the colas, positioning itself as the "uncola," it became a more direct competitor and aggressively attacked Coca-Cola's Sprite to lure bottlers and fountain outlets away. Coca-Cola responded with a lawsuit against Seven-Up to try to shore up its turf barrier.

Seven-Up, as a noncola product, did overcome the entry barriers that kept colas out of the picture. Seven-Up used its access to Coke and Pepsi franchisees to achieve national distribution. Unlike Coke and Pepsi, Seven-Up did not initially distribute through fountain sales. But after entering fountain sales in the 1960s and aggressively pursuing fast-food chains, it brought its product into nine out of ten chains.

Another intense guerrilla battle was fought over the demographic turf of the youth market. Pepsi went after this market aggressively with its "taste of a new generation" campaign. It used rock stars such as Michael Jackson and actors such as Michael J. Fox in its endorsements. Coke's emphasis on tradition ("the real thing") gave it a natural appeal to older drinkers. But the fast-growing youth market could not be ignored. Coke rolled out its own endorsements from rock stars to counter the Pepsi offensive.

Pepsi also breached Coke's seemingly impregnable entry barriers around the fountain market. Pepsi made inroads into Coke's fountain stronghold by acquiring several fast-food chains, like Taco Bell and Pizza Hut. However, Coke responded by forcing its way into competitor fast-food chains, like Wendy's, that had previously carried Pepsi products, and Burger King. Pepsi lost these accounts as Coke attacked with the argument that PepsiCo was a major competitor of these fast-food chains.

Another attack designed to weaken Coke's control over its U.S. stronghold occurred in the 1970s. Regulators at the Federal Trade Commission took action to try to weaken the exclusive territorial agreements of Coke's and Pepsi's franchise networks, which it charged were anticompetitive. But a ruling by an administrative law judge went in favor of Coke and Pepsi.[12] The intervention may have been unnecessary. Supermarket warehouses and beer distributors offer alternative distributions systems that allow competitors to circumvent the franchise networks. Even with the franchise networks of Coke and Pepsi, entry barriers in the industry are actually quite weak, as evidenced by the more than five hundred carbonated beverages introduced in 1988 and 1989. There are also geographic and product niches where small players can enter and grow through access to bottlers and distributors. New entrants now have access to an array of companies that can produce concentrate, bottle the soda, and distribute it to stores, restaurants, or warehouses. R. J. Corr Naturals, Incorporated, introduced a natural soda with a twelve hundred dollar investment in 1978 and had built a ten million dollar business a decade later.[13] While Coke and Pepsi have not lost their dominance of the U.S. market, their margins are eroding and their market share is in jeopardy for the first time in decades.

Of course, not all entry attempts are successful. Seven-Up's launch of a caffeine-free cola, Like, in 1982 proved the difficulties of overcoming barriers to entry into the cola market. Despite a twelve million dollar advertising budget, Like gained only 0.3 percent of the market in its first year. Court rulings that it was a cola shut it out of the Coke and Pepsi distribution channels that had helped make Seven-Up a national brand. It couldn't achieve economies of scale, distribution, or market share, and it folded.

Despite this successful defense against Seven-Up in the cola segment, Coca-Cola and Pepsi found that even this part of the market is not impregnable. Although Seven-Up could not compete directly against the colas with a new product, it could reposition its existing product as an uncola. In addition to challenging the colas, Seven-Up's "uncola" campaign was also aimed at the sixteen- to twenty-four-year-old group of customers.

With Coke and Pepsi each sparring for access to the other's markets (through attacking the youth segment and with new flavors positioned against the colas) and with easy entry for niching concepts, entry barriers are falling. Moreover, the demand for colas is declining in the 1990s so that barriers around the cola segment are becoming less important for keeping and gaining market share in the soft drink industry. The juice, cola, uncola, all-natural, and perhaps even wine cooler markets are merging. Established manufacturers face threats from other beverage makers, such as juice maker VeryFine, which jumped into competition with soft drinks by positioning its advertising against soft drinks such as Pepsi. Turf in the soft drink industry has become very difficult to defend, as any manufacturing company with a bottling system and a distribution network can continue to use its synergies to capture market share from the traditional soft drinks, carbonated beverages.

In response to the numerous attacks on Coke's and Pepsi's turf, Coke and Pepsi have used synergies from their soft drink distribution network to expand the boundaries of their U.S. turf into sports drinks. Coke's and Pepsi's networks of vending machines and distribution lines give them an advantage in their attack on long-time market leader Gatorade. Even so, Gatorade's recognition and hold on the fountain market make it a tough competitor to unseat. Their success will depend on Pepsi's and Coke's willingness to use their deep pockets to overcome Gatorade's resistance, a topic covered below.

With the increasing difficulty of excluding competitors from the U.S. turf, the ability to seize the initiative in soft drinks has now shifted to a new territory—international markets.

THE BATTLE FOR TURF IN INTERNATIONAL MARKETS

In the 1960s and 1970s growth in the soft drink industry outside the United States was greater than growth in domestic markets. Coke achieved dominance in European and Asian markets by following U.S. troops in World War II. Responding to a request by General Eisenhower that Coke be available to troops anywhere in the world for a nickel, Coca-Cola built bottling plants in Europe and Asia, satisfying the needs of servicemen while building the structures for its future growth. In 1959 Coke built 30 new foreign bottling plants, bringing its total to 647. By 1960 Pepsi had driven its total up to 237 plants in 37 countries (from only 67 plants in 23 countries a decade earlier).[14]

Pepsi followed diplomats into the Soviet Union and China, staking out its claim in those territories. With the help of Richard Nixon, Khrushchev took a highly publicized sip of Pepsi in Moscow in 1959, opening the Soviet market. But by mid-1972 Rumania was the only Eastern European country without a Coke plant.[15] In 1972, through shrewd diplomacy, Pepsi built the first bottling plant in the U.S.S.R., in partnership with the Soviet government. Still, Coca-Cola dominated overseas markets. By 1980 international sales accounted for 62 percent of Coke's soft drink volume while amounting to only 20 percent of Pepsi's.

In the future, dominance and growth will be determined by who controls the near-term growth markets in newly industrializing nations and long-term growth markets in high-population-growth nations. Coke's and Pepsi's aggressive competition in the United States may distract attention away from these growth markets. However, the future will focus on the geographic turfs that have not yet reached hypercompetitive conditions.

Winning these battles over U.S. and international markets will in part be determined by who has the deeper pockets. With the price-quality, timing–know-how and stronghold arenas all but lost in the United States, the dominance of the U.S. market will be determined by who can throw the most resources into the battle. Moreover, the aggressiveness of expansion into foreign growth markets will also be influenced by the level of each competitor's resource base. This brings us to the assessment of the four arenas.

Analysis of Arena 4: Deep Pockets

As noted above, deep pockets will be as important in the future as they were in the past when Coca-Cola initially used its resources to drive out other competitors such as Bola-Cola and a host of other pretenders. It used its deep pockets in court to defend its name at every turn. It had the resources to advertise heavily. Early on, it was spending very heavily on advertising, with a fifteen million dollar ad budget in 1939.

But the deep pockets were not always an advantage. Coke had used its deep pockets to invest a lot of money into promoting its bottle design and into building its distribution system. The distinctive design of the Coke bottle was used in advertising and became almost synonymous with the drink itself. Its nickel soft drink vending machines increased the accessibility of Coke. But, as we saw, these advantages became disadvantages when Pepsi-Cola cut its price to a nickel, offering twice as much soda for the same price as Coke. Because of its size Coca-Cola would have faced high costs in moving to a new bottle (both in the physical production of new bottles and the name recognition) or changing its prices (because of the need to replace or retool its vending machines). Pepsi used Coke's inflexibility (which arose from use of its deep pockets) to its own advantage in introducing a larger bottle for the same price.

Deep pockets are, nevertheless, becoming crucial to survival in the soft drink industry. The industry has become increasingly concentrated in the hands of major players. By 1988 Coca-Cola and Pepsi held more than 71 percent of the soft drink market, up from 64 percent just six years earlier.[16] Both Pepsi and Coke used their deep pockets to purchase bottlers at an increasing pace in the 1970s and 1980s and have moved into other industries.

In January 1986 PepsiCo announced its plans to purchase Seven-Up, but the Federal Trade Commission intervened on antitrust grounds. Pepsi was permitted to acquire Seven-Up operations in Canada. Coca-Cola, following Pepsi's lead, announced plans to purchase the Dr Pepper Company a month after Pepsi's announcement. But when Pepsi's bid for Seven-Up was shot down, Coke backed off its plans to acquire Dr Pepper.[17]

Both Coke and Pepsi increased their ownership of bottling plants through vertical integration. In 1986 Pepsi bought up several franchises so that it owned 32 percent of its bottlers. Coke also increased its ownership of its bottlers from 11 percent to 38 percent in the same year.[18] Coke was working to consolidate its bottlers into a deep-pocketed player that it could spin off to the public, while Pepsi was hoping to own its distribution networks so that it could consolidate control, capture distribution synergies, and offer new services to its customers. Either way, each player needed deep pockets to carry out its distribution strategy.

Some smaller competitors worked around the deep-pocketed players through attacking regional markets. Dr Pepper, for example, was a strong regional producer in the Southwest. Smaller firms also used resource escalation and countervailing power by piggybacking on existing bottling networks. Before the 1960s, however, Dr Pepper was considered a cola, so Coke and Pepsi franchisees were barred from carrying it. The resources of Coke and Pepsi—their franchises of bottlers across the country—allowed them to shut out Dr Pepper's growth. But the little guy often has the courts on his side. Dr Pepper prevailed in 1962 when a U.S. court ruled that it was not a cola, opening access to Coke and Pepsi bottlers.

A more far-reaching attack on the franchise system held by the two deep-pocket players was action against the system by the Federal Trade Commission in 1972. The FTC alleged that the system kept soft drink prices artificially high and prevented price competition between brands. But the industry, particularly the franchisees, successfully fought this attack.[19] As it turned out, with the government's intervention price wars would become common due to the dynamics of strategic interaction that played themselves out in the three arenas discussed above.

To overcome Coca-Cola's overall size advantage in the soft drink industry, Pepsi branched out, diversifying into fast food and snacks. It used the deep pockets from its soda business to move into other areas and used these areas to further build its soft drink empire. For example, as restaurant fountain sales continued to increase, Pepsi's ownership of Pizza Hut and Taco Bell gave it an assured channel for selling its products.

Countervailing power has also developed, as bottlers develop the capacity to manufacture syrup. These bottlers can also sell off their excess capacity to smaller noncola brands in strategic alliances with syrup makers. This makes it very easy for a small player to enter the market. Instead of building its own syrup-making know-how, the bottling companies can now rely on partnerships with syrup manufacturers.

Entering the 1990s, the size advantage of Coke over Pepsi has been virtually eliminated. Not only are these two biggest players in the soft drink industry on a more equal resource footing, their size is not always an advantage against the many new small players entering the soft drink market. While deep pockets are no longer the advantage they were when Coke crushed Bola-Cola out of the business, they will be important if used to win the battles being fought in the stronghold arena.

Hypercompetition in the Soft Drink Industry

One might also expect that, with such high concentration of power in the industry, the major players would be docile and congenial. The "conventional antitrust paradigm (structure-conduct-performance) would predict . . . that the carbonated soft drink industry would not be competitive . . . [that is, in an industry where] price increases outstripped costs, there was little price discounting, no new product development occurred, production inefficiencies abounded, and demand was stagnant or falling. This same paradigm would predict that PepsiCo and Coca-Cola would perceive their mutual interest to be served by nonaggressive, nonthreatening behavior, particularly toward one another. But this conventional wisdom does not hold up here."[20] There is intense competition, real prices have continued to fall, and many new varieties of soft drinks have been introduced.

Why is competition so intense when there are so few players? First, soft drinks are not only competing with other soft drinks but also with other beverages such as coffee and juices. The industry is also open to entry and expansion by fringe players, as has occurred regionally and nationally over the years. None of these new entrants have gained significant national share, but their existence and potential for success forces the major players to be extremely competitive to prevent new players from gaining a foothold. Overall, the intense competition is driven, at least in part, by a culture of rivalry between Coke and Pepsi and "the tenuous nature of their hold on a substantial number of consumers."[21]

The intense competition—hypercompetition—in the soft drink industry continues to keep all players moving quickly from advantage to advantage and trying to seize the initiative in each of the four arenas. This example also points out the declining need for legal intervention to keep an industry competitive. At least in this case, an intense and aggressive marketplace protects consumers far better than laws against collusion or "anti-competitive" behavior. This issue will be explored in more detail in the conclusion to the book.

Coke and Pepsi are now in a fiercely competitive market. They are forced to continue to introduce new products to meet demands of customers. But these products are imitated quickly, and their success often comes at the expense of sales of existing products. When Coke introduced Diet Coke, the new soft drink grew quickly, but Tab and regular Coke suffered corresponding losses in market share. The competition has also left the shelves full of diverse caffeinated and caffeine-free, diet and non-diet, classic and nonclassic colas. So both players have broad, comparable lines.

Both companies (especially Pepsi) continue to succeed by moving from advantage to advantage more rapidly, shifting between the arenas to keep ahead of their opponents.

A Series of Temporary Advantages

PLAYING OFFENSE: PEPSI SEIZES THE INITIATIVE

Pepsi's rise in the cola wars from a bit player to the industry leader was accomplished by seizing the initiative in two arenas—cost and quality and timing and know-how—through a series of temporary advantages. Each advantage moved it a little farther forward. Coke, because it thought that its dominant position and resources suggested that it should defend its stronghold, was often slow to respond to these initiatives by Pepsi, giving the upstart time to gain a strong foothold. As Figure 5–8 indicates, Pepsi's advantages have become increasingly short-lived as competition heats up. Over time, Pepsi has sought to create a series of advantages that sustain and build its long-term position.

PLAYING DEFENSE: COKE TRIES TO PROTECT ITS DOMINANCE

Coca-Cola, on the other hand, maintained the initiative in the remaining two arenas—strongholds and deep pockets—at least at first. It defended its turf and created new strongholds by throwing up entry barriers, such as introducing Sprite to keep Seven-Up out of its distribution network and expanding into new international geographic territories. These barriers

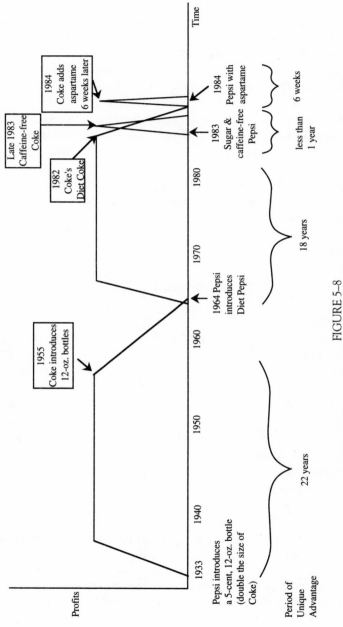

FIGURE 5–8

PEPSI SEIZES THE INITIATIVE AND COKE RESPONDS: SHRINKING CYCLES OF ADVANTAGES

(A Few Representative Examples)

were not completely successful, however. Coke eventually lost share to Pepsi's assault on the youth market and held the lead in resources only until Pepsi's success in the other arenas, along with mergers and acquisitions, tended to even the field. Although it may seem that Coca-Cola's domination of the industry rested on one steady foundation (i.e., its secret cola formula), it in fact has defended its position through a series of advantages used to reseize the initiative or neutralize the series of temporary advantages created by Pepsi (as illustrated in Figure 5–8). Even though Coke had few product innovations in its early history, it developed new distribution channels and advertising messages that protected its position. If Coca-Cola had continued to sell its product through pharmacies, the company would now be little more than a footnote in history. Instead it changed distribution channels, packaging, and advertising. The advantage that Coke had in the 1920s is very different from the advantages it had in 1950, 1960, 1970, and 1980.

A METAPHOR FOR AMERICAN LOSSES
TO AGGRESSIVE FOREIGN COMPETITORS

While Pepsi used a largely offensive strategy, Coca-Cola (as the market leader) used a more defensive approach, responding to first moves by Pepsi or other players. This defensive posture caused trouble when Coke, under the constant pressure of Pepsi's attacks in the first two arenas, tried its boldest effort to respond to the threat. Coke issued New Coke to imitate Pepsi's sweeter taste because consumer tastes were shifting to sweeter sodas. This move, which Coca-Cola thought would seize the initiative against its competitor, actually ended up losing it. While it was a good idea to neutralize Pepsi's advantage, this move failed in part because it was an admission that Coke lost the Pepsi Challenge. Instead of seizing the initiative, it clearly signaled both the loss of the initiative to Pepsi's superior taste and Coke's poor position, as illustrated in Figure 5–7.

Coke's defensive strategy is similar to the way many large, dominant American firms compete with aggressive foreign firms. IBM and General Motors, for example, both lost the initiative in the first two arenas (cost-quality and timing–know-how). Both saw foreign competitors with equal or better quality enter with lower-cost products. Both lost the edge in introducing new products and, even though both had superior technological know-how in their labs, they failed to apply it to their products and product process as fast as their more nimble competitors did. Instead, both firms tried to use their deep pockets and distribution barriers to hold onto their strongholds for as long as they could.

Over the long haul, winners play offense in all four arenas, because only by staying one step ahead of their competitors do they continue to maintain the initiative.

IF ONLY COKE HAD DONE A FOUR ARENA ANALYSIS

If Coke had done a Four Arena analysis, it would have realized that

1. Pepsi had the initiative in the price-quality arena, despite Coke's lower costs (which it was not using to lower price earlier on)
2. Pepsi—and especially the smaller players—had the initiative in the timing–know-how arena, where Coke was introducing products mainly to defend against inroads made by competitors
3. sustaining strongholds through the use of entry barriers is not going to win the game over the long haul, because entry barriers can be breached
4. if Coke loses in the first three arenas, its deep pocket would eventually be neutralized

These realizations might have radically altered Coke's behavior. By the time Coke finally attempted to seize the initiative with New Coke, it didn't know how to disrupt the marketplace. Disruption takes practice and knowledge of how to do it. The New 7-S's, discussed in Parts II and III, are designed to provide guidance for managing disruptions.

FOUR LENS ANALYSIS

In addition to its use in analyzing the dynamics of strategic interaction between rivals over long periods of time, as in the case of the soft drink industry, the four arena framework can also be used by a company to analyze and interpret a single action by a competitor. By examining the impact of this event on each of the arenas, companies can develop a more detailed view of the strategic implications of a competitor's moves. It can also identify a fuller set of possible responses involving all of the arenas.

To examine how this analysis works, consider the introduction of the commercial laser printer as viewed by the manufacturer of dot matrix printers. Hewlett-Packard introduced the first laser printer for the mass market in 1984 (the Laser Jet) with a price tag of $3,750. The new printers slowly gained share from dot matrix printers as prices fell, but dot matrix printers still held half the printer market in 1992.

Through the Cost-Quality Lens

The introduction of the laser printer, from the perspective of a dot matrix producer, tended to drive up the quality of products in the industry and put even the best dot matrix printers in the low-cost, low-quality position. Unless they wanted to remain at this low position and watch the laser printer makers continue to drive down prices, dot matrix producers had a choice of either reducing costs or increasing quality. They, in fact, did both.

Laser printers first entered the cost-quality arena at what would appear to be the differentiator's position. They defined the high end of the price-quality spectrum, offering much higher quality (higher resolution, lower noise, faster printouts) but for a higher price. Both ends of the market began moving toward higher levels of value. Laser printers, which started with high quality, worked to drive prices down, shaving them by more than half in less than a decade. Manufacturers of dot matrix printers moved in the other direction. Starting with lower costs, they worked to increase quality—speed of the printers (up to four pages per minute), resolution, and quietness. At the low end, prices of dot matrix printers have been driven down to about $300 for a twenty-four-pin dot matrix or under $200 for some models compared to the $1,000 to $1,500 price tag for laser printers (although some have now cracked the $1,000 ceiling). Although there are still differences in price and quality between dot matrix printers and laser printers, the gap is closing and both are moving toward ultimate value. As a 1991 article speculated, prices below $1,000 may mean the end of the domination of dot matrix printers.[22]

Through the Timing–Know-How Lens

The technological advance of inexpensive laser printing created several advantages for its manufacturers. They could offer customers a higher-resolution printout and many options such as scalable fonts and paper trays. This placed even the most advanced dot matrix printer at a technological disadvantage and led to a series of innovations in the dot matrix market.

Epson America combated the laser printer by trying to incorporate advanced know-how into its dot matrix units, where it is the market leader. In early 1992 it continued to introduce new scalable fonts for dot matrix printers to enable them to compete more directly with low-end laser printers.

Epson also imitated HP by moving into laser technology along with forty other manufacturers. Compaq introduced a new printer with a multi-tray paper mechanism that can draw in different-sized sheets to gain an advantage over Hewlett-Packard. Innovations in color printing have also been used to give companies a technology advantage.

Through the Stronghold Lens

Some dot matrix printer companies sold their products directly to retailers or customers. Others sold them to OEMs (original equipment manufacturers) that made computers. The OEMs either put their own name on these printers or sold the printers with the brand name still on them as part of a bundled system containing the computer and peripheral equipment. Some dot matrix printer manufacturers built strong, long-lasting relationships with high-volume OEMs, relationships that were both lucrative and low risk since the large OEMs guaranteed large sales. Once established in such an arrangement, printer companies fought to defend their relationships with the OEMs, considering them the cornerstone of their business. To protect their core markets, printer companies tried to establish barriers to entry, thereby creating strongholds in the OEM market. Epson was particularly successful at this.

The introduction of laser printers undermined the OEM-based strongholds of dot matrix producers. Unless competitors such as Epson could introduce their own laser printers or comparable high-quality printers, they might lose any advantages they had in bundling the printer with computers. They could also lose their access to OEMs.

Initially, dot matrix printer manufacturers were confident that the technology would hold its share of the market because of the high cost for laser printers (over $3,000) compared with that for dot matrix printers. But shifts in both users and uses of computers (from data processing to increasingly high quality text processing) broadened the market for more expensive, high-quality outputs provided by the laser printer. Further, new graphics programs added to the demand for quality outputs.

With a new set of users and new user demands, customer loyalty to the old dot matrix brands was weaker, making it easier for new competitors to enter the OEM supply business. As customers became increasingly informed about computers and peripherals, differences between laser and dot matrix printers could be emphasized by OEMs, and new players had a better chance of success with OEMs seeking to satisfy their customers.

Some OEMs even entered the printer market. HP's easy entry into the printer market and that of the many companies that followed it there are an indication of how few barriers to market entry really existed there. Even the laser printer segment was vulnerable to attack. With aggressive competition in price and quality, timing and know-how, and new entrants, *PC World* reports that Hewlett-Packard's share of the laser printer market fell from 60 to 46 percent in 1991.[23] HP still dominated the market for fifteen- to thirty-page-per-minute laser printers, and none of the other competitors in the industry held more than 10 percent of the market. Its first arrival in the market and continuous innovation gave HP a powerful hold, but the market is wide open to entry by computer companies and other office-equipment manufacturers in the United States and abroad. These companies used their existing strongholds in these areas to develop their markets for printers. Compaq, for example, could sell its new laser printer through its existing computer sales network by bundling computers and printers.

Through the Deep-Pockets Lens

OEMs like Hewlett-Packard had deep pockets that could be used to threaten the manufacturers of dot matrix printers. Competitors responded by using several strategies. They have used niching—producing printers just for Apple computers rather than going head-to-head with Hewlett-Packard on IBM compatibles. They have drawn on deep pockets from other businesses to finance their entry into the market—for example, Apple and Compaq have used their deep pockets to take on HP in price wars over printers. Companies have also formed alliances to overcome deep-pocket advantages of HP. For example, Apple and Adobe allied to produce a printer with a better "language" for producing graphics than HP's proprietary printer language.

Implications of the Four Lens Analysis

It is clear that the entry of laser printers had a major impact on dot matrix printers. But when the laser printers were introduced, the implications of the move were not clear, and no framework existed for analyzing those implications.

The Four Lens analysis provided above illustrates that it would be easy to ignore some of the options available to the dot matrix manufacturers. The four lenses suggest that the dot matrix companies must do an analysis of

1. how to position dot matrix printers in the price-quality arena given the expected trajectory of matrix printers on price and quality.
2. the types of know-how that a dot matrix printer might need. The alternatives are to acquire laser technology or other know-how to improve the speed, quality, and cost of dot matrix printers.
3. how to protect strongholds like the OEM-supplier segment of the market.
4. the need to build deep pockets through alliances.

Would the entry of laser printers trigger all of these? Perhaps the more savvy companies might have known all of these intuitively. But the Four Lens analysis provides a formal framework that ensures that no stone will be left unturned.

CREATING NEW ADVANTAGES BY USING THE NEW ANALYTICAL TOOLS

Using the Four Arena and Four Lens analysis methods, companies can determine challenges and opportunities in each of the arenas for creating temporary advantage. Once the competitive terrain is mapped out using the tools introduced above, hypercompetitive companies determine where they need to create their next advantages. They can use their knowledge of competitors' typical dynamic strategic interaction to ask, What strategies are effective in building these advantages? How can they move to create advantage, disrupt the status quo in the industry, and sustain this momentum through a series of temporary advantages? What will the competitor do in response? What is it not likely to do? In other words, what does it take to succeed in hypercompetition? The answers to these questions provide guidance for deciding upon the arena that the firm should focus on in the future.

Part II will examine this issue and provide a more detailed look at hypercompetitive markets. Part III will introduce a series of approaches that companies have used to succeed in hypercompetitive markets, approaches that this book has labeled the New 7-S's.

Management Challenges

The Four Arena and Four Lens analyses described above can be applied to viewing your industry or to analyzing a specific competitive move, from either your own perspective or that of your competitors.

- Analyze the evolution of competition through a Four Arena analysis. What are the major trends in the development of competition? Which arenas has your company been strong in and which have been dominated by your competitors? Where are the primary future opportunities for gaining advantage? How can you seize these temporary advantages before your competitors?
- Analyze a specific competitive action by a competitor in each of the four arenas, as described in the Four Lens analysis above. How does the move affect cost and quality? Timing and know-how? Strongholds? Deep pockets? What are your potential responses in each of the arenas?
- Choose an arena on which to focus. The choice can be made by using the following criteria. For each arena, ask whether it is
  - hyperactive—lots of maneuvering in the last five years
  - erratic—characterized by big movements sporadically
  - evolutionary—slow, continuous movement
  - temporarily dormant—inactive for a definite interval
  - arrested—no changes occurring and none foreseen

In arenas that are dormant or arrested, the company should act to speed up competition because these arenas offer the biggest opportunities for surprise. In very active arenas the company should work to seize the initiative or shift attention elsewhere.

IMPLICATIONS OF UNSUSTAINABLE ADVANTAGE

NEW CONCEPTS OF COMPETITION AND COMPETITIVE STRATEGY

CHAPTER 6

THE NATURE OF HYPERCOMPETITION

What It Is And Why It Happens

This business is intensely, vigorously, bitterly, savagely competitive.
> —ROBERT CRANDALL, CEO, American Airlines
> (quoted in *Business Week*, July 6, 1992)

Major sustainable competitive advantages are almost nonexistent in the field of financial services.
> —WARREN BUFFETT (quoted in *Harvard Business Review*, Sept.-Oct. 1986)

I don't believe in friendly competition. I want to put them out of business.
> —MITCHELL LEIBOVITZ, CEO of auto parts retailer Pep Boys
> (quoted in *Fortune*, Feb. 22, 1993)

Declare business war. *This* is the enemy.
> —Statement over a photo of Northern Telecom CEO Paul Stern on posters at an AT&T plant in Denver (from *Newsweek*, Dec. 28, 1992)

The dynamic escalation of competition in the four arenas described in the preceding chapters is an indication of a faster and more aggressive competitive environment. This chapter examines the characteristics of this environment of hypercompetition and the strategic approaches companies use to deal with it successfully. These approaches have been labeled the New 7-S's both to organize them in a useful framework and to emphasize their distinction from the concept of "fit" implied by the traditional McKinsey 7-S framework.

This chapter examines the characteristics of hypercompetition and how it relates to traditional views of competition in the four arenas. The chapter discusses why this isn't perfect competition. It also examines why lack of awareness of this competitive environment has led to decline and failures by once-successful companies.

Chapter 7 addresses the question, How do companies deal with hypercompetition? It outlines strategies that are dynamic rather than static. It focuses on taking the offensive. The chapter then describes the seven key factors that we have observed as crucial to the success of companies in this environment. These New 7-S's help companies to position themselves to build a series of advantages and to seize the initiative in any of the four arenas or in multiple arenas simultaneously.

WHAT IS HYPERCOMPETITION?

The four arenas and escalation ladders that were discussed in Part I define the bases of competition. Cost and quality, timing and know-how, strongholds, and deep pockets—these have not changed for decades. Companies continue to move up these ladders and, upon reaching the top, restart competition in them or jump to dormant arenas that have not been the locus of rivalry in the past.

In traditional competition, however, this movement up the ladders occurs over long periods of time. The time it took for companies to move from one rung to the next could often be measured in decades or even longer. The time between these jumps or disruptions was thus long enough that the environment appeared relatively stable. Movement up the ladders was sometimes slow enough to be imperceptible, giving the impression that it was possible to sustain advantage.

Companies worked to sustain their position by staying at one rung of the ladder for years. IBM's strength in mainframes, for example, was an advantage it tried to sustain as long as possible. It tried to protect this market for good reason. Even in 1992 mainframes accounted for 42 percent of IBM's revenues and 60 percent of its profits.[1] But technology and aggressive competitors have escalated competition in spite of IBM's focus. And by clinging to mainframes, IBM has not made a strong showing in the growing personal computer market and is still catching up on workstations.[2] As a Hewlett-Packard executive commented on the difficulty of undercutting current advantages to build new ones, "You almost have to kill your children."[3]

When competition was not escalating so rapidly, companies could tailor their organization around the environment. Then they could look at "internal fit" within the corporation, to ensure that all parts of the company worked together smoothly toward clearly defined goals that remained stable for years. This tended to create a rigid structure and strategy that was appropriate for a relatively stable environment.

In this context, huge changes in strategy, such as Pilkington's development of float glass technology, were seen as discontinuities. In response, the players would renew themselves with significant but rare structural reorganizations and strategic reorientations. They would then once again begin seeking sustainable advantage at this new level of competition.

As the process of movement up the escalation ladders has accelerated, however, the stable periods between disruptions have become shorter. Now, instead of stable periods punctuated by disruptions, the environment is one of disruptions punctuated by rare stable periods. Sustainable advantages have been shown for what they were all along—temporary; and they are becoming more temporary every day. This is an environment that we have called hypercompetition.

This difference between traditional competition, used when the environment stayed stable for years, and hypercompetition is illustrated in Figure 6–1. As shown in the first box of each row of the figure, the strategies needed to succeed in traditional stable environments are very different from those needed to succeed in hypercompetition.

In the old days of stable environments, companies created fairly rigid strategies designed to fit the long-term conditions of the environment. The goal of the company's strategy was to sustain its strategic advantages by working to slow the movement up the four escalation ladders described in Part I. In other words, the company did not disrupt the status quo of the industry and tried to prevent competitors from doing so. Its goal was to sustain its own advantage and establish competitive equilibrium wherein the less dominant firms accepted their secondary status because they were given the opportunity to survive by a leading firm that avoided competing too aggressively. The nonleaders accepted a permanent secondary status in exchange for leniency from the leader. Under this view, competition either stayed on one rung of the escalation ladder or moved up very slowly. It would never move quickly or reach the top of the ladder.

In hypercompetitive environments this equilibrium is impossible to sustain. Here, successful companies rely on a different combination of strategies and actions to achieve the goal of temporary advantage and to destroy the advantages of competitors through constantly disrupting the equilibrium of the market. Companies in hypercompetitive environments succeed or fail based on their ability to manage the process of moving up the escalation ladders, jumping from advantage to advantage. When companies realize that their advantages are not sustainable, they consistently

FIGURE 6–1
TRADITIONAL VERSUS HYPERCOMPETITIVE BEHAVIORS

Type of Competition	Strategies	Actions	Goals	Methods for Avoiding Perfect Competition
Traditional Competition in Stable Environments	• Internal fit • Rigid, stable strategy • Make commitments (irreversible investments) that are hard to change so others know to avoid your turf	• Slow movement up escalation ladders • Find markets or segments that no one else is competing in	• Sustain advantage of player who is ahead • Establish stable "equilibrium" among the players, letting the players who are behind make money and survive	• Firms never reach top of escalation ladder in each arena • Even if all players reach a state of competitive parity (i.e., all reach the same rung on an escalation ladder), the parties tacitly cooperate to raise prices or reduce competition
Hypercompetition in Rapidly Changing Environments	• Frequently shifting strategies based on the New 7-S's	• Fast, aggressive movement up the ladders	• Temporary advantage • Constant disruption of the status quo among the players • Once ahead, crush the competitors who are behind	• Firms shift arenas rapidly and go quickly past top of escalation ladders in each arena to restart hypercompetition

seek out new advantages, driving competition up the escalation ladders and contributing to hypercompetition.

Hypercompetition may be viewed, therefore, as just a faster version of traditional competition. But that is like saying that a hurricane is a faster version of a strong wind. The acceleration of the cycles up the escalation ladders has created an entirely different environment, one in which being behind often results in bankruptcy and success depends on a new set of strategies. Strategies for surviving in a hurricane are very different from those that are useful in a strong wind.

It is important to note that if one competitor in an industry acts aggressively by moving up the escalation ladders quickly, the others must follow. In this environment failure to keep up is not met with leniency. The leader continues to move up faster and faster, taking no prisoners. Moreover, the nonleaders are not satisfied with being number two, even if the leader is lenient and doesn't try to crush them. All it takes is just one hypercompetitive firm to force the shift from traditional competition to hypercompetition. Even a small firm that enters an industry can sometimes drive the entire industry up the ladder. This hypercompetitive firm forces other companies to ante up or be left behind.

Sometimes even the presence of *potential* aggressive competitors (i.e., ones that *might* enter the market) can force the players in a market to behave hypercompetitively. As noted in the earlier discussion of the battle between Coca-Cola and PepsiCo (see Part I, Chapter 5), even though the two giants control three quarters of the soft drink industry, they still behave very competitively—in part because of a tradition and culture of rivalry but also because of competition from other beverages and the potential for entrance by beer makers, winemakers, or consumer goods companies. Any large firm with a bottling/distribution network is a threat that forces Pepsi and Coke to stay on their toes.

This cycle of aggressive competitive maneuvering is being fueled by changes in the environment. Consider the changes in technology. Hypercompetitive behavior by computer companies has driven a succession of new products and rapid innovations. These innovations, in turn, have increased the speed of competition by easing communication and increasing flexibility with new forms of information-processing technology. These changes in the environment have made it possible to increase the speed and aggressiveness of competition in many industries. In summary:

- *Hypercompetition* is an environment characterized by intense and rapid competitive moves, in which competitors must move quickly to build advantages and erode the advantages of their rivals. This speeds up the dynamic strategic interactions among competitors.

- *Hypercompetitive behavior* is the process of continuously generating new competitive advantages and destroying, obsoleting, or neutralizing the opponent's competitive advantage, thereby creating disequilibrium, destroying perfect competition, and disrupting the status quo of the marketplace. This is done by moving up the escalation ladders faster than competitors, restarting the cycles, or jumping to new arenas.
- *Perfect competition*, in contrast, is a situation in which no competitor has an advantage in any of the four arenas. Despite the common belief that this is an end point, this is a transitional and unstable point of competition as we'll see below.

Note the irony in these different views of competition. There is no opportunity to compete (in the sense of hypercompetition) in a perfectly competitive market. Perfect competition, by definition, excludes hypercompetitive behavior.

THE EXTENT OF HYPERCOMPETITION

Hypercompetition Is Widespread

As illustrated by the quotes at the opening of this chapter, there is growing evidence of intensifying competition in a wide range of industries. Hypercompetition is not limited to high-tech industries such as computers, but has left its mark on more mundane operations, such as diapers and auto parts. It is not just limited to aggressive Japanese competitors. As noted above, the once-monopolist AT&T has plastered the image of Northern Telecom's CEO on a poster in a Denver plant, with the declaration, "Declare business war. *This* is the enemy." This approach to competition is every bit as aggressive as Honda's declaration of war against Yamaha ("We will crush, squash, slaughter Yamaha!") Even once complacent old U.S. companies have converted to tigers to compete in this environment.

This intense competitive environment is not just in the United States; it is worldwide. In Europe, for example, there are fierce price and product wars in automobiles, computers, consumer electronics, retailing, and other industries.[4]

There are few industries in the United States and other parts of the world that have escaped hypercompetition. Consider the following examples:

- *Consumer products* Customers expect higher quality and lower prices, putting the squeeze on profits. New products are a necessity, even if they are costly to launch and may cut into existing brands. Retailers are also more demanding as this product proliferation places strains on shelf space and distribution.
- *Aerospace* Cuts in defense budgets driven by geopolitical changes have reshaped the industry, which is now faced with converting resources from government contracts to consumer market. Former Soviet states are also selling top-of-the-line defense equipment at cutthroat prices to generate hard currency for their struggling governments.
- *Public utilities* Once insulated from competition by regulatory protection, they now face new competition. Independent power producers, for example, are now allowed to enter the market.
- *High technology* Rapid changes in technology and consumer demands have created pressures on companies to move faster not only on product innovation but also on serving the needs of customers.
- *Telecommunications* New technology, changing regulations, increased product lines, and globalization are driving intense competition in this industry. With deregulation many new rivals have gained a foothold in all sectors of this industry, creating intense competition.
- *Automotive manufacturing* Foreign competitors have driven up levels of quality while holding down costs. An influx of new competitors has filled the market with options. Declining customer loyalty has also heightened competition. American manufacturers are making big efforts to become competitive again.
- *Financial services* Global markets for financial services and shifting U.S. regulations are heating up competition. New entrants into consumer credit markets (such as AT&T and GM) have created greater pressures at the same time that a wave of failures and consolidations has demonstrated the fierce nature of competition in this environment.

Perhaps one might expect intense competition in fields such as financial services or telecommunications, but even industries as prosaic as cat foods and children's toys provide examples of hypercompetitive behavior:

Competition over the $880 million canned cat-food market has heated up into what one magazine dubbed a "cat fight."[5] Although the overall size of the market has remained relatively stable, it has attracted new entrants lured by the growth of gourmet-style cat foods, which have high profit margins. There is a proliferation of new packaging, new flavors, and new segments such as diet cat foods and foods for certain life stages (kittenhood, for example). Companies are aggressively expanding into Europe and other foreign markets. Meanwhile, at the low end of the market, Ralston Purina slashed prices on its Purina 100 discount-priced cat food in 1989. Although the brand is only marginally profitable, *Marketing & Media* described Purina's strategy, as to "deplete rivals' war chests so that they will stay out of categories Purina is strong in." Approximately one third of all cat food was bought on sale in 1988.

The $9 billion U.S. toy industry is also wound tight. In addition to major companies such as Hasbro, Incorporated, and Mattel, Incorporated, there are hundreds of smaller competitors. The lure of creating a new hit toy has drawn a steady stream of competitors to the industry. Low entry costs—as little as $25,000 to break into the stuffed toy business, for example—ensure that there will be many new entrants into the industry. Successes such as Pictionary, Trivial Pursuit, and Cabbage Patch Dolls came from entrepreneurial inventors. Because of the short lifespan of most toys, companies have to be constantly launching new products. Even if a product lasts for more than one season, it is almost certain to be copied by other companies.[6]

While there are some industries that are less aggressive, it has become increasingly difficult to find industries that are not in hypercompetition. Those that do not currently face aggressive competitors still have to deal with the *threat* of aggressive competitors, and this is enough to force them to act hypercompetitively. But is this increasing aggressiveness a temporary adjustment or fad before the level of competition returns to the lower, more stable environment of yesteryear?

A Passing Phase?

While acknowledging the intensity of competition in current markets, some observers have seen hypercompetitive environments as a passing stage in the evolution of industries. A study of hostile environments, for example, concluded that "hostility does eventually end" even though it often takes five or ten years or more.[7] The study contends that industries become less hostile through the consolidation of players or the growth in customer demand.

It is often argued that increasing consolidation makes collusion more likely and decreases hypercompetition. However, Part I, Chapter 5, has shown the continuing intensity of competition between Coca-Cola and Pepsi, despite their dominance in the soft drink market. As long as one player acts hypercompetitively, the others must follow suit. As demonstrated in Part I, the advantage always goes to the player who is one step ahead on the escalation ladders, so companies have an incentive to break any collusive arrangement that might be developed. And hypercompetitive behavior is still rewarded, even among a small number of players. As players gain deeper pockets and have more at stake in the market, they often will compete more aggressively. In addition, new aggressive global competitors are emerging from Asia and will soon do so from the rest of the Third World. In an effort to gain share, they are likely to use their low labor costs and other advantages created by their location to disrupt the status quo of the industry. If the players do not remain aggressive, they will be subject to moves from new competitors from the outside, especially as entry barriers fall, as we discussed in Chapter 3 of Part I.

Similarly, demand growth, while it is a welcome sight in any environment, will not in and of itself bring an end to hypercompetitive behavior. Again, the soft drink industry illustrates this point. Even where demand growth had skyrocketed, the competition remained intense. Growth offers a new market for competitors to battle over and may also invite new competitors into the market. Also, hypercompetitive rivals may develop new ways of meeting the growing demand. The growth of demand therefore does not offer an easy escape from hypercompetition.

A culture of hypercompetition is setting in. One characteristic of the older, more genteel competition in the stable markets of yesteryear was that it involved trust. In these environments a stable equilibrium among the players was sought. Once reached, the dominant player had to be trusted to be lenient. The dominant player restrained itself from aggressiveness, allowing the secondary firms some room for survival as long as they also behaved cooperatively. But once trust is lost, it is very hard to recapture, especially in global markets where xenophobia makes foreign competitors suspect. Moreover, cultural differences between nations make some competitors more aggressive than others. They can be perceived as untrustworthy, not because they aren't willing to live up to their agreements, but because they are not willing to accept the equilibrium solution.

Hypercompetition is, therefore, here to stay. Competitive actions designed to escape hypercompetition by moving aggressively up the escalation ladders tend only to drive it forward. So companies will have to learn to live with hypercompetition. The methods by which they can do so are outlined in Chapter 7 and then described in more detail in Part III.

Perfect Competition Is Just a Pause in the Hypercompetitive Action

How is hypercompetition different from perfect competition? The economic state described as perfect competition is also portrayed as a very aggressive and challenging competitive environment, but it is quite different from the concept of hypercompetition described here. Perfect competition is viewed as a point at which no competitor has an advantage over the other. The players compete aggressively, squeezed by price competition until margins fall to zero.

In perfect competition no player has an advantage over any other player. In hypercompetition, by contrast, players gain advantages that are rapidly eroded. But instead of remaining in a position of no advantage, companies actively create new advantages. In the model of the four arenas of competition in Part I, points of perfect competition would be temporary and unstable. These points appear when no competitor has an advantage in any arena or when companies have reached the top of the four escalation ladders at the same time. They have competed away advantages in cost and quality, timing and know-how, strongholds protected by entry barriers, and deep pockets.

Perfect competition is the hope of some economists and the fear of many corporations. It is the hope of economists because it appears to serve customers best by providing value through low prices and high quality. Unfortunately, this is static thinking. Over a long period of time, a lack of profits may actually mean that companies could not sustain future innovations to launch the next generation of products, so customers could ultimately be deprived of more advanced products in exchange for short-term lower prices.

Perfect competition is the fear of corporations because it is a state in which it is almost impossible to survive. In perfect competition, supply exactly equals demand and prices fall to marginal costs. There are no strongholds because entry is easy. Competitors have nearly equal resources and know-how. The field is level. Because there is no advantage, there are no winners. And without winners, there are few, if any, profits. A large number of players fight over a fixed pie, so no one wins.

This is a very hostile environment. In *Competitive Strategy*, Michael Porter discusses some of the industry conditions that lead to more intense competitive rivalry and greater risks. "The greater the number of competitors, the more equal their relative power, the more standardized their products, the higher their fixed costs and other conditions that tempt them to try to fill capacity, and the slower the industry's growth, the greater is the likelihood that there will be repeated efforts by firms to pursue their own self interests. . . . Broadly speaking, both offensive and defensive moves are more risky if these conditions favor intense rivalry."[8]

Because perfect competition is so hostile, corporations will not allow it to persist. They will restart the cycles of competition in each of the four arenas, shift the locus of competition to a new arena, or invent entirely new competitive weapons and arenas. As long as there is a way to win, as there always is, corporations have an incentive to find it. Perfect competition is more of a fiction than a reality since firms will use hypercompetitive behavior to avoid it. Thus, perfect competition is not the steady-state equilibrium that some would like it to be, and it makes little sense for antitrust laws to try to force firms toward an equilibrium that they cannot accept or thrive in.

WHY HYPERCOMPETITION PERSISTS

The Negative Consequences of Hypercompetition

Although hypercompetition is not a dead end, as perfect competition is, it is such an intense competitive environment that companies might be expected to avoid it as much as they avoid perfect competition. Hypercompetition forces companies to go through the agonizing process of reinventing themselves, developing new advantages, undermining the advantages of their competitors, and increasing the intensity of competition. This is a costly process compared with the more genteel competition of old days.

Consider consumer electronics, where manufacturers were experiencing a surge in sales in the fall of 1992 but found it a mixed blessing. The demand surge was a result of a price war in color televisions, where prices have dropped from $799 to as little as $399 for a twenty-seven-inch set. More sales did not translate into higher profits. As an electronics industry spokesman noted, "It's profitless prosperity."[9] Similarly, we saw how Coca-Cola and PepsiCo have increased their sales of soft drinks at the same time their margins have continued to shrink.

Intense competition in price and quality leads to price wars. Intense competition on timing and know-how leads to shorter product cycles. Intense competition on strongholds leads to rapid entry into new markets. Intense competition on deep pockets leads to shifts in resources through acquisitions, alliances, and other approaches. None of these developments is particularly beneficial from the corporation's perspective, except perhaps in the short-term. The companies locked in this competition are forced to develop new advantages (for example, moving into stereo television or HDTV in the consumer electronics market) to restart competition in a new arena or at a higher level on the escalation ladder.

Other results of hypercompetitive behavior can be perverse for many markets. As quality improves, replacement demand starts to decline. People drive their cars longer, and the used-car market begins to compete with the new-car market. Disposable razors destroy the market for blades and cartridges. Fluoride treatments by dentists cut down on the number of cavities that need to be filled. Cable television offers so much variety that the networks can't afford to make as many new shows. Consequently, fewer shows will be available for syndication on cable in the future.

In order to fund their hypercompetitive use of high quality-low cost goods, many Japanese industries have cooperated to charge Japanese consumers higher prices at home. Moreover, while some Japanese firms try to ensure full employment and security, their employees work longer hours and experience more job-related stress than American workers. Thus they cannot achieve the same standard of living unless they reduce the productivity of their workers.

Drivers of Hypercompetition

With these negative effects, why does hypercompetition persist? Why would any company want hypercompetition? Why don't firms return to the older, more genteel methods of the past? And if no one wants it, why does it happen?

Traditionally, some companies have sought to escape this intense competition by implicit collusion or developing sustainable advantages. Competitors would implicitly agree not to upset the status quo. For example, competitors may allow one player to be the price leader and follow that company's lead in pricing because the price leader never uses its deep pockets to crush the higher-priced followers. Or competitors may tacitly divide up the market, each taking one geographic or customer segment and not attacking the other's stronghold. This is done even though such tacit collusion may often be in the gray areas of antitrust. This environment was relatively stable for many years.

Sustainable advantages mean that the field is uneven but competitors have no way of reshaping the field. The company with the advantage can charge higher prices and enjoy higher profits. The company can avoid direct and aggressive competition with other players because they cannot match its advantage. This also leads to a relatively stable environment in which the company with the advantage retains its leadership.

Neither advantages nor collusion are very effective in holding competition in check. Part I showed how sustainable advantages are eroding more rapidly. Collusion is also a less viable alternative. Not only do U.S. laws prohibit explicit collusion, but even tacit collusion is now difficult or impossible to maintain in an environment of aggressive competition. New entrants, particularly foreign competitors, who are not part of the collusive structure of the market can shatter it. Or competitors may choose to break this agreement to make a play for market share.

The evolution of global markets and technology has contributed to this erosion of trust. When primary competitors were next-door neighbors, it was much easier to act on friendly terms and tacitly collude. If Pillsbury took share from General Mills, for example, it would be replacing one U.S. job with another U.S. job. If one moved aggressively, they both would suffer, because layoffs would hurt local property values or put relatives out of work. But now Pillsbury is owned by a multinational firm, and the stability of the system has been upset. Similarly, when the Big Three in Detroit ruled the U.S. auto market, they lived in a state of relative peace and prosperity until foreign competitors started shaking things up. The battle now is over jobs and over which nations have a high standard of living and which don't. The stakes are much higher. With today's more fluid global markets, there is less incentive to dampen the aggressive impulses of firms. Some governments even encourage hypercompetitiveness by their corporations as a way to increase their nation's wealth.

This leads competitors into a "prisoners' dilemma." Both sides would be better off if they cooperated, but neither side can trust the other to sustain the agreement. If a player is first to violate a tacit agreement to avoid escalation up the ladders, that player would be better off than if it waits for its competitor to move first. So both sides have an incentive to compete aggressively if they lack trust of each other. They both pursue their own best interests—doing worse than if they had cooperated—and moving into hypercompetition.

Recently there has been an increase in cooperation through strategic alliances and other partnerships. Although in some areas these can limit the aggressiveness of competition, in most cases alliances merely circumscribe the turf in which competition will take place. For example, if companies cooperate on developing new technology, they will compete on the applications of that technology. This competition will be just as intense. Or to take another example, two domestic companies may team up to compete in international markets or two global companies may team up to compete against other companies or groups of companies. Here the partners have agreed not to compete with one another but to face off against their rivals. This competition can be just as intense as a market in which none of the players is aligned.

Another reason why companies move into hypercompetition despite its negative effects is that these effects are not immediately apparent. The negative effects may initially be hard to see because competition escalates one step at a time, each one leading to more intense competition. While each step seems logical, if not inevitable, the net result is a competitive environment that none of the competitors would consciously choose. Companies pursue temporary advantages because they can make money for a short period before having to move on to the next advantage. At each new level in the escalation of competition, the costs of playing become higher and the opportunities for profits decline. But companies don't see the long-run effect. They see only the next incremental move. Thus the competitors slide down a slippery slope into hypercompetition, not realizing where they are headed in the long run.

Hypercompetition is also encouraged by market forces that benefit from it. Consumers usually win because competitive escalation in the first three arenas improves quality, prices, innovation, product variety, and choice of vendors to do business with. Also, competitors whose primary goals are to build market share or increase employment rather than generate profits, are willing to sacrifice short-term profits to gain dominance in their industries. The entry into automobile and electronics markets by Japanese firms is an example.

Hypercompetition is also encouraged by those whose ideological view of competition is based on competition as a Darwinian struggle that leads to survival of the fittest. Although U.S. strategy has focused on collusion and developing unique advantages to slow competition, true capitalism in its purest form is based on a free-market ideology that extols the virtues of aggressive competition. Many competitors have made millions by acting in a hypercompetitive manner. This view that intense competition is a way of rewarding the best and the brightest or weeding out the weaker competitors has tended to spur support for hypercompetitive behavior from conservatives.

This escalation into hypercompetition is in some ways similar to an arms race between two countries. Even though the players do not want it to escalate, no one knows how to stop it. The conflict tends to build, even though it would be in the interests of both players to operate in a more stable environment.

THE NATURE OF COMPETITION HAS CHANGED IN A FUNDAMENTAL WAY

Some Fundamental Shifts in the Realm of Economic Competition: The New Paradoxes

The shift to hypercompetition is so fundamental that it turns some of the intuitive principles of competition on their heads. Success in a hypercompetitive market is based on the following paradoxes, indicating the need for a new approach to strategy:

1. *Firms must destroy their competitive advantages to gain advantage.* Many companies have delayed launching new products because of fear of cannibalizing their existing lines. IBM's hesitation in entering the personal computer market and Coke's reluctance to use its brand name on a diet soda both led to missed opportunities and falling behind on the escalation ladders. These decisions were based on the ideas that the mainframe market would continue to be a source of advantage and that Coke's advantage in the cola market wouldn't erode. Of course, these assumptions proved to be faulty. Since every advantage eventually is outmaneuvered, companies are forced to destroy their own competitive advantages to create new ones. The challenge is for companies to get the most out of their existing advantages before destroying them to create new ones.

2. *Entry barriers only work if others respect them.* Entry barriers aren't entry barriers unless the players perceive them as such. Many players who want to overcome them can. So firms can deter competitors from entering their markets only if the competitors do not want to enter the market, in which case the entry barrier wasn't really a barrier at all.

3. *A logical approach is to be unpredictable and irrational.* To compete effectively, companies take a tough stance and demonstrate an irrationality that scares competitors away because of fear that the hypercompetitive firm will go all out. Too much consistency and logical thinking can make the firm predictable. So the company must at least appear to be irrational. Yet if the company is too irrational, it can be costly in the short run or spark a strong preemptive strike by a competitor to eliminate a wild card. So companies have to appear tough and irrational without being crazy.

4. *Traditional long-term planning does not prepare for the long term.* Long-term planning that is based on *sustaining* an advantage is ultimately shortsighted. As we observed in Part I, advantages are eroding more

quickly, so true long-term strategy depends on obsoleting the company's own advantages and undermining those of its competitors. Long-term success depends not on a static, long-term strategy but rather on a dynamic strategy that allows for a series of short-term advantages.

5. *Attacking competitors' weaknesses can be a mistake.* Traditional approaches such as SWOT analysis (strengths, weaknesses, opportunities, threats) may not work in a hypercompetitive environment. Using the company's strengths against an opponent's weaknesses may work once or twice, but not over several dynamic strategic interactions. This approach becomes predictable, and over a period of interactions, the competitor may practice enough to develop its weakness into a strength. For example, if a tennis player consistently serves to his opponent's weak backhand, the opponent will eventually be forced to strengthen his backhand. Now the first player faces a tougher opponent, with a strong forehand and strong backhand.

6. *Companies have to compete to win, but competing makes winning more difficult.* Companies have no choice but to move the level of competition up the escalation ladder or be left behind. Yet each move up the escalation ladder raises the stakes of the game and makes winning more difficult. Advantages become increasingly difficult to sustain.

Because of the difficulty of recognizing these paradoxes, companies often make mistakes by pursuing a strategy of sustaining advantage in an environment in which every advantage is eroded.

THE CONSEQUENCES OF COMPETING
WITH TRADITIONAL STRATEGIES
IN A HYPERCOMPETITIVE WORLD

There is growing evidence that companies are at a loss as to how to deal with hypercompetition. There have been recent waves of mergers followed by waves of divestitures. The failure of effective management strategy has led to the dominance of financial strategies, measuring success by quarterly profits because the strategies that lead to *long-term* success are so difficult to identify. And as the conclusion to the book will examine, countries may also be responding ineffectively to this competitive environment. National policies and antitrust regulations, designed to encourage perfect competition or eliminate "unfair" practices that are hypercompetitive in nature, may be counterproductive and unnecessary in today's environment.

Companies make strategic mistakes in responding to hostile environments, including errors due to setting goals for high profits that lead to failure to protect market share.[10] Some companies expect to always earn high profits, and when competitors cut into their returns they exit. But industries with high returns inevitably attract new entrants, and this leads to lower margins. So seeking high returns through high prices rather than cutting costs will lead to the very competition most companies want to avoid. Many once high-profit industries that have attracted competitors—including airlines, calculators, and copiers—have become "tomorrow's sick businesses."[11]

As margins are squeezed by intense competition, companies then make the mistake of believing that they can move to a smaller niche where they can enjoy larger margins in a smaller market. But these higher margins draw entrants into this niche. We saw this when Honda and other Japanese firms entered the U.S. motorcycle market, and European motorcycle companies abandoned the low end of the market to migrate upscale to larger bikes. It was not long before the Japanese cycle makers followed the Europeans into this market. This type of strategic retreat will result in no less than the gradual liquidation of the entire U.S. economy as more and more industries become hypercompetitive.

This focus on profit maximization leads to a related common mistake in hypercompetitive environments. Companies are so intent on maximizing their profits that they keep their price above their costs and fail to protect market share. If they don't aggressively lower costs and price, this process allows low-priced competitors to make inroads into the market. When these competitors have gained sufficient share, prices are driven down anyway.

When incumbents are forced to drop prices, they then make additional mistakes by not keeping up on features and benefits demanded by customers, including product features and quality. In addition, companies try to squeeze additional concessions out of their suppliers or sales force. All of these strategies undermine the company's competitive position, driving away customers and destroying sales or supply channels. This failure then leads to internal consolidation, as well as mergers of the inefficient firms, as companies seek to cut overhead. This move is designed to reduce margin pressure, but because it merely shifts the capacity of the industry, it does little to relieve the pressure imposed by more efficient hypercompetitive rivals.

One concept that underlies mistakes in hypercompetitive markets is the belief that hostile markets are temporary and will eventually become benign. This can lead to a wait-and-see attitude, whereas successful companies actively work to build new advantages and destroy the advantages of their competitors.

Some of the strategies above can delay the inevitable for a while, but they are not enough. Effective firms become hypercompetitive, shifting to use of a series of short-term advantages to stay ahead. The doomed stick to what worked during the earlier period of genteel competition and discover that they have been outmaneuvered.

Lost Advantages

Success is just as likely, and perhaps more likely, to breed failure as it is to lead to further success. Successful companies often try to sustain the advantages that led to their success, becoming fat and lazy, and making themselves susceptible to attack by smaller rivals. Like Coca-Cola, many companies are distracted from their own progress by competitors' moves. These companies, instead of pursuing their next advantage, try to hold on to their old advantages for too long or merely respond to competitors' actions. These tactics often prove damaging or deadly in hypercompetitive markets.

Many of the firms held up as examples of "excellent" companies in Tom Peters and Robert Waterman's 1982 book *In Search of Excellence* were losing ground just a few years later as many markets shifted into hypercompetition. Whether or not the key characteristics of the excellent companies identified by Peters and Waterman are in fact key ingredients for success (and some of them may be of questionable value in today's hypercompetitive world), the companies cited were characterized by very successful performance. Yet these successful and respected firms hit trouble spots.

The strategic mistakes made by these and other companies point to some of the weaknesses and blind spots of current strategic approaches in today's competitive environment. They also illustrate the need for the strategic approaches embodied in the New 7-S's, which are proposed and discussed in the remainder of this book. Consider some of the weaknesses that caused these companies to stumble:

- *Losing touch with customers* Hewlett-Packard's traditional focus on entrepreneurship and decentralization became difficult to manage as it grew bigger. In the early 1980s, it faced troubles in the markets for super-minicomputers, engineering workstations, and personal computers. *Business Week* commented in 1984 about HP's decline, "To regain its stride, HP is being forced to abandon attributes of excellence for which it was praised. Its technology-driven, engineering-oriented culture, in which decentralization and innovation were a religion and entrepreneurs were gods, is giving way to a marketing culture and growing centralization."[12] At this point, it appeared that Hewlett-Packard had lost its ability to satisfy customers better than its competitors did in markets such as personal computers, according to *Business Week*. As will be discussed in Part III, HP may have lost sight of the first of the New 7-S's—superior stakeholder satisfaction.

- *Lack of strategic soothsaying* What may be one of the fatal flaws in Peters and Waterman's eight characteristics of excellent firms is the one that urges companies to "stick to the knitting." A study of the fourteen "excellent" companies that fell behind found that almost all lacked the ability to adapt to change. They focused on sticking to their past rather than envisioning a new future. They "were inept in adapting to fundamental changes in their markets. Their experiences show that strict adherence to the eight commandments—which do not emphasize reacting to broad economic and business trends—may actually hurt a company."[13] This points to the need for mechanisms to understand and anticipate strategic changes in the marketplace—the second of the New 7-S's, strategic soothsaying.

- *Lack of speed* Texas Instruments was slowed by a complicated management structure and a financial orientation. *Business Week* reports that TI's home computer launch was a failure, contributing to a $660 million operating loss and write down in 1982 and its first corporate loss in 1983. *Business Week* comments that the problems were due, at least in part, to an "overly complex management system—including matrix management and numbers-dominated strategic planning— that tended to smother entrepreneurship. TI's confusing reporting structures, for instance, delayed the design and production of key new products like large-scale computer memory chips."[14] It failed to develop the characteristics and structures that allow it to position itself for the third of the New 7-S's, one that is key for success in hypercompetition—speed.

- *Lack of surprise* Levi Strauss and Company's great strength was its production. It focused on pumping out a high volume of jeans with high product quality. Year after year, Levi Strauss did the predictable thing. It made standard blue jeans, and it did so for decades. But the predictable Levi Strauss lost its footing in the early 1980s when competitors outmaneuvered it. New and fashionable apparel arrived on the scene. Marketing became more important than production. Once it lost its spot in the fashion market, Levi's also lost the opportunity to take advantage of the market for other sportswear. Its earnings declined for three years beginning in 1980, and then after stabilizing for one year, earnings fell by 72 percent in 1984 according to *Business Week*.[15] Because it lacked creativity and flexibility, Levi's became too predictable. It failed to use the fourth of the New 7-S's, surprise.

- *Inability to shift the rules* Sears, Roebuck and Company built its business as a pioneer of catalog sales to rural families, shifting the rules from traditional retailing or traveling peddlers. But after 107 years, Sears discontinued the catalog because other competitors had shifted the rules for selling to rural areas, both through the introduction of Wal-Mart stores and the fast pace of change in mail-order marketing to upscale families. Sears kept its approach essentially the same (not even accepting phone orders until very late in the game) and fell victim to the inevitable changes of competitors because it did not launch any attack to shift the rules back to those that favored Sears. It failed to use the fifth of the New 7-S's, actions that shift the rules of competition.

- *Failure to use signaling effectively and falling victim to simultaneous and sequential strategic thrusts* With the rise of the personal computer and networked systems, the computer market in the 1980s offered many new opportunities for initiative, but Digital Equipment Corporation failed to seize these opportunities. As founder and president Kenneth Olsen commented in a 1984 *Business Week* article, the PC and work station markets are "the kind of high-growth business we are trying to get out of."[16] This may have signaled to competitors that they would not face serious opposition from DEC if they moved into these new markets. Instead of warning them away, DEC's signal actually invited companies to come in. It didn't read the signals of its competitors or use signaling to outwit them. It was an open book.

DEC not only signaled that it would stay put, but an even more dangerous mistake may have been that it actually didn't pursue these new markets aggressively. Instead, it fell victim to attacks on all sides by other competitors. DEC's top-heavy management structure reportedly slowed the release of new products, according to *Business Week*.[17] The company, sticking to its knitting, looked to the past while other players launched several simultaneous or sequential attacks, outmaneuvering mainframe and minicomputers with not just one product but several—personal computers, microcomputers, and superminis. DEC was stunned and forced to become reactive. While these other competitors attacked on different fronts with these simultaneous and sequential strategic thrusts, DEC continued to focus on a single approach to the market, minicomputers. It did so even as its core market was eroded by competitors' innovations. DEC's slow and predictable strategy worked well from 1977 to 1982, when DEC posted "spectacular" annual earnings growth, according to *Business Week*.[18] But in the hypercompetitive environment of the late 1980s, its profit margins plummeted. DEC failed to use the sixth and seventh of the New 7-S's, signals and simultaneous and sequential strategic thrusts.

THE ONLY ENDURING ADVANTAGE

As the stories of these companies illustrate, none of the traditional advantages of the four arenas offers an enduring way to win. Levi's experience shows that high quality is not an enduring advantage (first arena), because quality shifted from product quality to fashionability. Hewlett-Packard's case shows that its know-how (second arena) was not enough if it could not use it to meet the changing needs of customers. DEC's performance indicates that strongholds (third arena) are not a sustained advantage when innovators created new products that eroded its traditional stronghold. Texas Instruments' case indicates that even deep pockets (fourth arena), developed over twenty years of financial success, could be eroded by top-heavy management and lack of understanding or attention to changes in the marketplace.

All advantages erode. As competitors copy an advantage, it is no longer an advantage. It is a cost of doing business. For example, automatic teller machines do not provide a competitive advantage to banks because almost all banks offer them. Now banks need to have them to stay competitive, and they need to find new sources of competitive advantage.

As Henry Ford commented in his autobiography, "Businessmen go down with their businesses because they like the old way so well they cannot bring themselves to change . . . seldom does the cobbler take up with a new-fangled way of soling shoes, and seldom does the artisan willingly take up with new methods in his trade."[19]

The New 7-S's are concerned with this very issue. In hypercompetitive environments, in which change is increasingly important, the New 7-S's are concerned with destroying the status quo, disrupting what has been done in the past, and creating a new and different future.

The only enduring advantage results from the ability to generate new advantages in the four arenas. While no cost or quality advantage is sustainable, the *skill of generating* new cost and quality advantages is sustainable. What are the key factors that contribute to this skill in moving from advantage to advantage, in seizing and maintaining the initiative in an arena or across the four arenas? These issues will be explored in greater detail in Chapter 7, which examines how to compete in an environment of hypercompetition and introduces the purpose of and the relationship among the New 7-S's for competing in these environments.

Management Challenges

- What characteristics of hypercompetitive behavior are apparent in your industry? Do the paradoxes apply to your industry?
- How has your industry evolved? Which advantages have been lost during this evolution and which advantages have replaced them? Is the pace and aggressiveness of competitive moves and countermoves accelerating?
- Are you making any of the mistakes outlined in the chapter above? If so, what assumptions do you need to change?
- Can you identify points of perfect competition?
- What forces are slowing down the escalation of competition?
- What forces are speeding up competition in your industry? Can you control them?

CHAPTER 7

LIVING WITH HYPERCOMPETITION

The New 7-S's

Paraphrasing George Bernard Shaw, while the reasonable person adapts himself to the world, the unreasonable one persists in trying to adapt the world to himself. Thus, all progress depends upon the unreasonable person. In hypercompetition the reasonable strategies that focus on sustaining advantages do not lead to progress. Companies make progress in hypercompetition by the unreasonable approach of actively disrupting advantages of others to adapt the world to themselves. These strategies are embodied in the New 7-S's.

Shoveling Sand Against the Tide

Such concepts of strategy as strategic fit and strategic planning are focused on sustaining advantages. They are often concerned with slowing down the escalation of competition in each of the four arenas described in Part I. If all advantages erode rapidly in hypercompetition, then these attempts to maintain the status quo are about as effective as shoveling sand against the tide.

Strategy, as it is widely practiced in American firms, involves establishing goals, then tactics, and then finding the resources to carry them out. Strategy is the "determination of the basic long-term goals and objectives of an enterprise, and the adoption of courses of action and the allocation of resources necessary for carrying out these goals."[1] "Traditional theory suggests that management is a tightly structured, systematic, linear mental activity. Managers presumably formulate goals with painstaking precision, then undertake carefully prescribed actions. In reality, however . . . managers never have enough information to make perfectly reasoned decisions."[2]

Managers are realizing that these current strategic approaches are inadequate. Managers do not have the luxury of such a painstaking planning process when environments are highly dynamic. By the time a formal plan is agreed to and subsequently implemented, competitive conditions have changed. Moreover, the formal plan is based on assumptions such as these:

- fundamental, deeply held values and beliefs
- the ability to sustain the uniqueness of assets
- the goal of sustained dominance over geographic or product markets
- enduring policies
- the ability to create a five- or ten-year plan that sequences steps to victory

All of these assumptions are static in nature. In hypercompetitive environments, competitive conditions change and rivals outmaneuver other players based on the inflexibilities that are created by the very assumptions that are fundamental to formal plans and strategic planning processes. But what approaches to strategies are effective in achieving a series of temporary advantages? How do companies successfully compete in hypercompetitive environments? And if sustaining advantage is not the goal of strategy, what is the goal of strategy?

The Need for a Dynamic Theory

The inability of such strategic approaches to deal with or explain dynamic strategic interactions in hypercompetitive markets has been widely recognized. Most of past strategy has focused on success at a given point in time, rather than what Porter calls "the longitudinal problem" or "the conditions that allow firms to achieve and sustain favorable competitive positions over time."[3] He points out that game theory, models of commitment, and resource-based models all fall short of describing the complexity, uncertainty, and change of the current business environment.

Others, recognizing the weaknesses of current strategic thinking, have called for abandoning conventional formal plans and planning processes in favor of less rigorous planning—what has been called variously "strategic opportunism,"[4] "hustle as strategy,"[5] or "confidence as strategy."[6] These approaches stress flexibility and change, rather than permanence, sustainability, and commitment to a single course of action. They suggest that "strategic intent, a will to win, appears to be a far more significant catalyst for success than concepts such as 'strategic fit.'"[7] This will to win is an intent to seize the initiative by escalating up the ladders in all four arenas, never looking back and never stopping. This type of aggressive behavior results in a continual and unrelenting pounding for those who are left behind trying to achieve fit among all their internal functions, people, processes, and skills. Fit diverts attention away from the dynamics by focusing the firm on creating a logical consistency among organizational characteristics that takes years to accomplish and, once completed, takes years to undo.

Thus, recent experience leads to one conclusion: Current views of strategy are inadequate to deal with the competitive environment. Given that traditional approaches to strategic planning may no longer be appropriate, some have suggested that strategy should be dismissed altogether. As one writer comments, "Strategy is good luck rationalized in hindsight."[8] This puts companies in the position of flying blind through the turbulence of hypercompetition with a rabbit's foot. Not surprisingly, some companies who have seen current strategic approaches as a distraction have chosen this course. On the other hand, companies that rely on serendipity may find profits in the short-term but are often saddled with confusion within the organization and uncertainty in dealings with the world. They fail to develop "strategic intent" and usually are undermined by a more strategic thinking competitor.

The formal approaches to strategic planning are more appropriate for environments of traditional, slower and less aggressive competition. As noted in Chapter 6, these environments are characterized by long periods of stability between disruptions. These periods call for more of an emphasis on carefully considered thought and deliberate action. Hypercompetitive environments, on the other hand, draw more upon the *instant reaction and reflexes* of the company. It is the difference between a rigidly planned and carefully orchestrated invasion, as practiced by the German military in World War I and World War II, and attacks based on the doctrine of flexible response, as practiced by the U.S. military in the 1990s. Strategy in the current environment is more a process of fine-tuning reflexes and searching out or creating temporary opportunities than it is a product of long and deliberate planning of specific actions in product markets.

Disrupting the Status Quo

Traditional models of strategy look at ways to sustain advantage or sustain the status quo in markets. Once a company has established an advantage, strategy seeks to sustain that advantage and protect it with entry barriers. Thus, traditionally, strategy was concerned with dampening competition and protecting the status quo.

The U.S. government has countered this view of strategy with antitrust regulations designed to create the stable equilibrium of perfect competition in which no competitor has a significant advantage. Leading U.S. companies have, however, traditionally sought to freeze the competition at a point of imperfect competition—namely, when they have an advantage that nonleaders will accept because the leader has not used that advantage to annihilate them.

The goal of a dynamic approach to strategy, in contrast, is to disrupt the status quo of the industry. Nonleading companies can then find advantage in this disruption and create disruption that leads to advantage. Leaders are, therefore, forced to disrupt the new status quo if they wish to maintain their past dominance, and an endless cycle of hypercompetitive behavior is triggered.

Obviously a company whose competitor has a stronger advantage in the given market would be interested in disrupting the status quo. When Pepsi began building its position in the cola market, it clearly wanted to act aggressively to undermine the advantages of Coca-Cola. Such underdogs have little to lose and much to gain from shaking up the market.

But in an environment in which no advantage is sustainable for long, forward-thinking companies realize they need to create disruption even when they have an existing advantage. They realize that *control of the evolution of competition in the market is more important than earning current profits*. They disrupt the status quo, even if it means eroding their own advantages, because they realize that if they do not erode their own advantages, competitors will. If a company with an advantage waits for a competitor to disrupt the status quo, the company that is ahead will not only lose its current advantage but lose its leading position in directing the movement of competition in the market. Thus, Microsoft introduces NT software, even though it will disrupt its current dominance of operating systems with MS-DOS.

As discussed in the preceding chapter, the resources expended to sustain an advantage can detract from the company's ability to build new advantages. With a limited pool of resources, the company must choose whether to try to sustain the past or build the advantages of the future. Only one of these paths will lead to future success.

Beyond Strategic Fit

Key to the concept of sustainability was the concept of fit. The old 7-S framework, for example, is concerned with sustaining advantage by creating fit between the structures and processes of the organization. Traditional theory says that companies should be concerned with both internal fit (i.e., matching structure and processes so that they are logically consistent) and environmental fit (i.e., matching structure and processes to cope with the demands of the external environment). Advantage is said to be created if a firm focuses all its parts on one consistent goal and purpose that the external environment is willing to pay for. This may work well in fairly stable environments. But when the environment is one of increasing uncertainty and rapid change, the concept of internal fit becomes more problematic. Environmental uncertainty, for example, requires more delegation of authority and organizational differentiation and specialization. Internal fit increases the need for coordination, counteracting the need for delegation, differentiation, and specialization.

Although contingency theory contends that organizations should achieve fit with the environment as well as synergies between internal processes and structures, these two goals can sometimes be incompatible, particularly in environments of rapid change. A recent study of ninety-seven companies indicated that "the alignment among structural and process variables needed for good environmental fit seems sometimes to violate the dictates of internal consistency."[9] The study found three reasons for this incompatibility. An uncertain external environment calls for creative adaptation rather than the more rigid structure found in a company with strong internal fit. Loose coupling of structures and activities within the organization and with the firm's environment also allows for greater ability to adapt to changes in the environment. Finally, a focus on internal fit tends to lead to tunnel vision, in which managers often ignore changes in the external environment.

Clearly the environment has a more powerful role than ever to play in the evolution and success of the firm. The movement through the escalation ladders and the more frequent use of hypercompetitive actions demands a switch from an internal to an external focus. For example, a few decades ago Coca-Cola rarely if ever acknowledged that it had competitors—either in its advertising or its boardroom. But now it has no choice but to watch competitors like a hawk and to pay strict attention to the changes in the external environment.

The old 7-S framework, with its focus on internal fit, is less useful in hypercompetitive environments. The New 7-S's, described below, are not concerned about internal fit, nor are they designed to create fit with today's external environment. Instead of merely adapting to changes in the environment, they allow the companies to reshape the environment through their actions. They are designed to provide a more flexible structure for corporate decision making and actions. The focus is on structuring the future rather than adapting to the present.

The Perils of Commitment

It has been suggested that commitment, the tendency of an organization to make investments in irreversible courses of action and to persist with a certain strategy, is a key component in competitive success.[10] This is consistent with the traditional view of formal strategic plans, which were appropriate for stable markets. But commitment is much less fruitful in unstable, uncertain environments. Commitments are so rigid and consistent that they become easily understood, overcome, or imitated by competitors. In hypercompetitive markets flexibility allows companies to seize opportunities as they present themselves and to create new opportunities.

The New 7-S's, because they are focused on disrupting the status quo, lead to unpredictable actions that often seem to lack any commitment other than the commitment to win. The vision proposed by the New 7-S's is not a vision carved in tablets in the lobby of the corporate headquarters. It is, paradoxically, a vision that looks farther forward by looking more closely at short-term market conditions, the dynamic strategic interactions among rivals. Under the New 7-S's, resources are not fixed resources for carrying out one vision that lasts for decades. The New 7-S's stress flexible resources, such as capabilities for speed and surprise, which can be deployed in countless ways to carry out visions that last for short periods of time. Actions are not formulaic generic strategies but rather a diverse and unpredictable array of options that keep competitors guessing and allow for last-minute shifts in strategy when appropriate. The only long-term vision under the New 7-S's is to create the continual, enduring ability to manage the escalation ladders by executing superior dynamic strategic actions.

A BROADER DEFINITITION OF STRATEGY: MANAGING THE ESCALATION LADDERS

Hypercompetition demands a broader approach to strategy. The focus on disruption and the creation of a series of temporary advantages demand a strategic theory with the breadth to support a long series of actions and interactions and to do so with the flexibility to accommodate shifts in direction.

In hypercompetition the ability to manage one's dynamic strategic interactions requires (1) the ability to envision the next series of disruptions in the market, which results in a superior level of stakeholder satisfactions, (2) some general capabilities that allow the company to carry out any market-envisioned disruptions with greater impact, no matter which type of disruption has been envisioned, and (3) specific tactics that are used to deliver the disruptions to the market with greater effectiveness. Thus, hypercompetitive firms must compete to get better on all three levels if they are to win in hypercompetitive markets. Over the long run, winners are those who are best able to manage the dynamic strategic interactions and win each one one at a time. The ability to win each interaction can be used again and again, providing a long-term advantage to those who are good at envisioning potential disruptions, creating capabilities to carry them out, and using tactics to deliver them.

Many strategic plans—no matter how long-term they purport to be—focus only on the last level of competition and tactics. Most five-year plans are a list of actions launching new product or market positions. They may include defensive moves to protect or sustain the firm's core product or market position. This focus on actions without adequate vision or capabilities necessary for disruption leaves most firms without the long-term ability or understanding necessary for managing the escalation ladders.

Hypercompetition demands a broader view of strategy. From our consideration of the four arenas, we can see that strategy must be both dynamic (to cope with each strategic interaction) and long-term (to cope with movement on the overall escalation ladders). It has to address each of the dynamic strategic interactions by companies and responses by competitors and still look to the long-run trajectory of these interactions as they move up or across the escalation ladders. Success in hypercompetition depends on managing the escalation ladders with the vision, capabilities, and tactics to overwhelm competitors engaged in a war made up of many battles and skirmishes for the hearts and minds of customers. The war is won not by a single enduring advantage but rather a series of temporary advantages. Strategy must extend beyond planning for the present configuration of the firm and the industry to planning for a continuous evolution of advantages, which are won and lost over time.

This long-term and flexible aspect of strategy is concerned with core competencies and capabilities. While these issues have been explored in recent literature, they have yet to be organized into a strategic framework. It is not enough to know that competencies and capabilities are important. Strategic theory also has to focus on how they are created and destroyed and why. Moreover, strategic theory must give us some guidance as to which competencies and capabilities are crucial. These broader goals of strategic theory are addressed by the New 7-S's, introduced below and presented in more detail in Part III.

Forging Fads into Frameworks

How do companies create disruption to compete effectively in hyper-competition? The business magazines and management journals are filled with strategy after strategy, each of which seems to offer the elusive goal of success in the intense and fast-paced competitive environment of the future. Some of the fads sweeping across the popular press include organizational reengineering, outsourcing to create virtual corporations, increasing speed and engaging in time-based competition, building flexibility, creating learning organizations, building on core competencies, entrepreneurship, alliances, empowerment, developing self-managed teams, and many other approaches.

Are these just fads or do they offer the keys to the strategy of the future? Which ones are snake oil and which are effective medicines? How do they fit together, and what is their goal? Certainly each of these approaches and techniques has been effective in certain instances. So each of these new business techniques can't be ignored.

But looking at them independently only shows a part of the picture. For example, a company that outsources at a time when all its competitors are vertically integrated may be very effective at creating disruption. A company that shifts to a quality maneuver when its competitors are focusing on price can catch them off guard, but this does not mean that a quality move will always be best. The best move is the one that creates disruption.

As discussed in Part I, disruption of the status quo takes the form of moving up to the next rung on the escalation ladders in the four arenas of competition, restarting the cycles in the arenas, or switching the locus of competition to a new, previously dormant arena of competition. In each case the disruption neutralizes, destroys, obsoletes, sidesteps, or otherwise makes irrelevant the competitive advantage of the opponent.

The recognition that disruption is the key to strategic success leads to the question of what characteristics and approaches enhance an organization's ability to create effective disruptions. All market disruptions are not equal in effect, and many are more difficult to execute than others. Examination of the demands of hypercompetition and companies that have competed effectively identifies a series of interrelated capabilities and approaches that enhance an organization's ability to create effective disruption. These are the New 7-S's.

The best companies already practice some or many of the New 7-S's. Many of them have turned up on the pages of business magazines in recent years. Qualities such as stakeholder satisfaction or speed are not new inventions. But as in the early days of describing any new environment, these qualities have been diluted with the clutter of many other fads. They have not been organized into a coherent system nor been focused toward a specific goal.

Until now, capabilities such as speed or surprise actually seemed at odds with traditional strategic theory. Speed and surprise tend to work against sustaining traditional advantages, which involve a slow and steady commitment to a long-term strategy or course of action. Theory has not kept up with the pages of the business press. It has moved in many different directions. It has focused on sustaining, when the environment had turned toward disruption.

The New 7-S's provide a framework for organizing and tying together what appears to be just a list of faddish capabilities and approaches presented in isolation in the business press. The New 7-S framework provides a means of analyzing and developing strategy, as will be examined in the next chapter. Most of all, it recognizes how each of these New 7-S's contribute to the goal of disruption.

THE NEW 7-S's

My studies of successful and unsuccessful companies in hypercompetitive environments reveal seven key elements of a dynamic approach to strategy that encompass the three factors for effective delivery of a series of market disruptions: vision, capabilities, and tactics. The New 7-S framework is based on a strategy of finding and building temporary advantages through market disruption rather than sustaining advantage and perpetuating an equilibrium. It is designed to sustain the momentum through a series of initiatives rather than structure the firm to achieve internal fit or fit with today's external environment, as if today's external conditions will persist for a long period of time.

The New 7-S's are

- superior stakeholder satisfaction
- strategic soothsaying
- positioning for speed
- positioning for surprise
- shifting the rules of the game

- signaling strategic intent
- simultaneous and sequential strategic thrusts

Because of the nature of the hypercompetitive environment, the New 7-S's are not presented as a series of generic strategies or a recipe for success. Instead these are key approaches that can be used to carry the firm in many different directions. They are focused on disrupting the status quo through a series of temporary advantages rather than maintaining equilibrium by sustaining advantages. The exact strategic actions formulated under this system will depend on many variables within the industry and the firm. Many types of strategic initiatives can be carried out using the New 7-S's, and there are many variations.

As shown in Figure 7–1, the New 7-S's address all three factors for effective delivery of a series of market disruptions, providing increased emphasis on the first two levels (vision and capabilities) and more creative approaches to the last level (tactics) than many firms currently use. As discussed below, the New 7-S's contribute to each of these three factors for effective competitive strategy.

FIGURE 7–1

Three Critical Factors for Delivery of a Series of Disruptions	The New 7-S's
Vision for Disruption	• Envisioning disruptions that create Superior Stakeholder Satisfaction • Using Strategic Soothsaying as a means of seeing and creating opportunities for disruption
General Capabilities for Executing Disruptions	• Building the capability for Speed into the organization so the disruptions are executed better • Creating the capability to Surprise opponents so that the disruptions are more powerful
Product/Market Tactics Used to Deliver the Disruptions	• Selecting actions that Shift the Rules used by competitors in their dynamic strategic interactions • Using Signals to influence future dynamic strategic interactions • Executing Simultaneous and Sequential Strategic Thrusts as a means of molding the flow of the dynamic strategic interactions that will occur.

Vision for Disruption: The First Two S's

Successful firms learn how to disrupt the status quo and move up the escalation ladders, restart the cycles, or jump to a previously dormant arena of competition. To do so, they must be able to identify potential disruptions.

Key to their choice of a disruption is the realization that not all disruptions are good. The disruptions that work are those that involve the first S—the creation of a temporary ability to serve the customer better than competitors can. Numerous new methods have been adopted in recent times, which will be itemized later, in Part III.

To create this type of disruption, successful firms prioritize customers as the most important stakeholder. This implies that employees and investors are prioritized less highly. Thus, to create successful disruptions, the firm must find a way to satisfy employees and investors even though their interests have been subordinated to customers. Methods for achieving the correct prioritization without dissatisfying the subordinated stakeholders are also discussed in Chapter 8.

Disruptions that satisfy current customer needs are not enough. Constantly improving customer satisfaction is now so standard that firms that once led the pack on customer satisfaction now find themselves without any lead at all. Thus, the key to achieving real advantage from customer satisfaction is to

- identify customer needs that even the customer cannot articulate for him/herself
- find new, previously unserved customers to serve
- create customer needs that never existed before
- predict changes in customer needs before they happen

To do this, firms are now engaging in the second S, strategic soothsaying. This allows firms to see and create *future* needs that they can serve better than any competitor does, even if only temporarily. The ability to see and create these future needs depends upon the firm's ability to predict future trends, to control the development of key technologies and other know-how that will shape the future, and to create self-fulfilling prophecies. Methods for doing these are discussed in chapter 8.

The first two S's of the New 7-S's provide a vision for how to disrupt the status quo and create new advantages. The first S, superior stakeholder satisfaction, addresses the key source of advantage: being able to satisfy customers better than competitors. By understanding the needs of customers and the employee and investor relations required to meet those needs, the company can better serve existing needs and identify new needs. The second S, strategic soothsaying, is concerned with understanding the future evolution of markets and technology that will proactively create new opportunities to serve existing or new customers. This also contributes to the firm's vision of where the next advantage will be discovered and where the company should focus its disruption.

Capabilities for Disruption: The Next Two S's

To act on this vision, companies need two key capabilities: speed and surprise. These are the third and fourth S's, respectively. As in fencing, speed and surprise are key factors in gaining an advantage before competitors can and in delaying competitor reactions to the new advantage.

If two companies recognize the opportunity to create a new advantage at the same time, the company that can create the advantage faster will win. Because success depends on the creation of series of temporary advantages, a company's ability to move quickly from one advantage to the next is crucial. Speed allows companies to maneuver to disrupt the status quo, erode the advantage of competitors, and create new advantages before competitors are able to preempt these moves.

If a competitor is unaware of the opportunity to create a new advantage, surprise can maintain that lack of awareness. While this is not a source of sustainable advantage (once the competitor recognizes the advantage, it can usually move quickly to duplicate it), surprise allows the company to create the advantage and to extend the period in which the advantage is unique. Surprise also allows companies to act to undermine competitor advantages before the competitors can take defensive actions.

Capabilities for speed and surprise are therefore key elements for successfully disrupting the status quo and creating temporary advantages. These capabilities are flexible in that they can be deployed across a wide range of specific actions.

Tactics for Disruption: The Last Three S's

The final three S's—shifting the rules of the game, signaling, and simultaneous and sequential strategic thrusts—are concerned with the tactics used in delivering a company's disruptions, especially tactics that influence the flow of future dynamic strategic interactions. These three S's follow the vision developed by the first two S's and use the potential for speed and surprise from the third and fourth S's.

In contrast to static approaches to strategy, these final three S's are concerned with a dynamic process of actions and interactions. Most planning is concerned with the company's next move to gain advantage. It usually analyzes potential competitive responses but doesn't shape those responses to its advantage.

The view presented here is a set of tactics designed to disrupt the status quo and create temporary advantage. Tactics such as actions that shift the rules of competition create a sudden and discontinuous move in the industry, reshaping the competitive playing field and confusing the opponent. Signaling delays or dampens the competitor's actions to create advantage, throws the competitor off balance, or creates surprise. Competitive thrusts in this environment are rapid—either a sequence of moves or a set of simultaneous actions—to upset the equilibrium of the industry, disrupt the status quo, and open opportunities for new advantage. As an example of a set of simultaneous thrusts, a company might feint a move in one direction and then move forcefully in another direction, creating surprise and temporary advantage from the misdirection of the opponent. One can think of sequential thrusts as being akin to the sequence of plays used in a football game. One team may run the ball several times until the defense is conditioned to expect a run play. Then the offense switches to the long bomb at a time that should call for a run. The sequence of actions create surprise and temporary advantage, since once the play is used, the defense will watch out for the long bomb in future plays.

These three tactics reflect the increasing speed and intensity of hypercompetition. Although these actions sometime push companies into the gray areas of antitrust because the behaviors could be construed as exclusionary or anticompetitive actions, companies are increasingly seeing them as necessary for competitive survival. The tactics used by companies are becoming increasingly aggressive and quick. To survive and flourish in a world in which advantages are rapidly eroded requires a different approach to tactics. If, as proposed here, these tactics are necessary for survival, this raises significant questions about current U.S. views of antitrust and competition. Some of these questions will be examined in the conclusion to the book.

Figure 7–2 illustrates how the New 7-S's work together to develop a vision, capabilities, and tactics for disruption. As discussed below, the goal of the New 7-S's is to create disruption by identifying new advantages, moving to seize the initiative through tactics, and sustaining the momentum by creating a series of temporary advantages.

In hypercompetition it is not enough to build a static set of competencies. Good resources are not enough. They must be used effectively. Military strategist Carl von Clausewitz noted that military leaders often make the mistake of focusing only on building forces. As a commentator on Clausewitz noted, "Early writers have concerned themselves almost exclusively with the enormous problems of raising, arming, equipping, moving and maintaining armed forces in the field—an approach which Clausewitz dismissed as being as relevant to fighting as the skills of the swordmaker to the art of fencing. None of this, he insisted, was significant for the actual conduct of war, and the inability of all previous writers to formulate an adequate theory had been due to their failure to distinguish between the *maintenance* of armed forces and their *use*."[11]

This is precisely why successful firms pay attention to tactics as well as capabilities and vision in an environment of traditional competition and to competencies in an environment of hypercompetition. In slower and

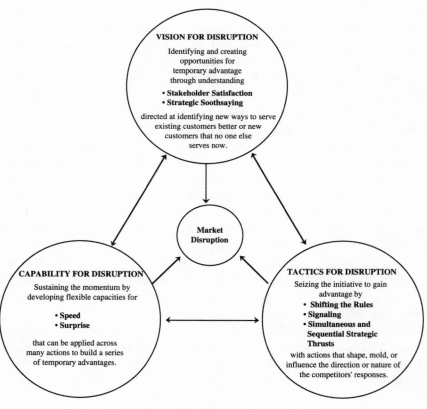

FIGURE 7–2
DISRUPTION AND THE NEW 7-S's

less aggressive competitive environments, companies could concentrate primarily on making great swords. In hypercompetition, they have been forced to concentrate much more on the skills of fencing. It is these dynamic skills that are the most significant competencies of the firm.

Recent emphasis in the strategy literature has focused on building core competencies, knowledge, and other unique intangible assets to great advantage. The "sword-making" aspect of building unique intangible assets is only part of corporate strategy, just as it is only part of military strategy. Assets, whether tangible or intangible, are not sufficient in and of themselves to succeed in an environment of hypercompetitive rivals constantly trying to outmaneuver one another. To say that Honda succeeded because of its competence in building small engines is only part of understanding its success. Many other companies had similar competencies and capabilities but did not make the same progress as Honda because they did not use them to build a series of advantages. Yamaha, for example, had small engine skills but did not become a major player in the auto market. The key to success for Honda was how it was able to deploy those competencies to seize the initiative in each of the four arenas. Success came from its ability to parlay its knowledge into new products, moving from success in motorcycles to an advantage in the auto market and using its success there to gain an advantage in the lawn mower market. Success was due to its ability to outmaneuver competitors in each of the four arenas of competition, using unexpected actions that shifted its focus from market to market skillfully. That shift upset the status quo in the U.S. auto market and the equilibrium of the players in all of its markets.

These were not random shifts. They resulted from Honda's ability to use its competencies to better satisfy customers. This is the skill of "fencing"— to use the company's competencies to better serve customers. This is the source of advantage and of new advantages. Thus, a company's success depends equally upon its swords and its fencing skills, and the New 7-S's are intended to guide firms towards making the right swords, learning how to fence, and pointing them in the right direction.

GOALS OF THE NEW 7-S's

While the traditional 7-S's are concerned with capitalizing on creating a static strategic fit among internal aspects of the organization, the New 7-S's are concerned with four key goals that are based on understanding dynamic strategic interactions over long periods of time. These four goals are

1. *Disrupting the status quo*   Competitors disrupt the status quo of competition by initiating the next dynamic strategic interaction to move competition up the escalation ladders in Part I, restart the cycles, or jump to a new arena. These moves end the old pattern of competitive interaction between rivals. This requires speed and surprise; otherwise, the company's competitors simply change at the same rate.
2. *Creating temporary advantage*   Disruption creates temporary advantages. These advantages are based on better knowledge of customers, technology, and the future. They are derived from customer orientation and employee empowerment throughout the entire organization. These advantages are short-lived, eroded by fierce competition.
3. *Seizing the initiative*   By moving aggressively in each arena, acting to create a new advantage or undermine a competitor's old advantage, the company seizes the initiative. This throws the opponent off balance and puts it at a disadvantage for a while. The opponent is forced to play catch-up, reacting rather than shaping the future with its own actions to seize the initiative. The initiator is proactive, while competitors are forced to be reactive.
4. *Sustaining the momentum*   Several actions in a row to seize the initiative create momentum. The company continues to develop new advantages and doesn't wait for competitors to undermine them before launching the next initiative. For example, while U.S. manufacturers are doing remedial work in quality improvement, Japanese manufacturers are now building key advantages in flexibility. This succession of actions sustains the momentum. This is the only source of sustainable competitive advantage in hypercompetitive environments.

Disrupting the Status Quo

The New 7-S's disrupt the status quo by identifying new opportunities to serve the customer, moving with speed and surprise, signaling, shifting the rules, and attacking through sequential and simultaneous thrusts. The purpose is to change a firm's position on the escalation ladders by moving up to the next rung of the ladder, restarting the cycles, or jumping to a new arena of competition.

Seizing the Initiative

A key focus of the New 7-S's is to seize the initiative—"to capture control of the strategic behavior in the industries in which [the firm] competes"[12] and move the industry forward in such a way that the company using them makes the opponent reactive and demoralized. The New 7-S's are concerned with creating a new and different future, altering or limiting the dynamic strategic interactions available to competitors.

The approaches needed to seize the initiative depend on the position of the firm and industry. For example, companies in the rapid growth stage of a product or service gain initiative by moving rapidly into the largest and fastest-growing segments, filling market space as quickly as possible and keeping out competitors with entry barriers as much as possible.

In the next stage, the "gradual build" stage when growth begins to slow, initiative is gained through control of the next generation of product introduction, anticipating competitive moves, and preemption of key second-stage and international segments, identifying emerging bases of industry leadership, sacrifice of full coverage, and ability to clearly identify when points of negative marginal return are reached in each position.

As competitors move through the dynamic strategic interactions of each of the four arenas, they have opportunities to move to seize the initiative by moving to the next rung of the escalation ladder or delaying competitors from moving ahead. As Kenichi Ohmae said, "In business as on the battlefield, the object of strategy is to bring about conditions most favorable to one's own side, judging precisely the right moment to attack or withdraw and always assessing the limits of compromise."[13]

The New 7-S's are most directly concerned with seizing the initiative. New advantages are identified through understanding stakeholders and the environment. By positioning for speed and surprise and using signals, actions that shift the rules of competition, and simultaneous and sequential thrusts, the company can move quickly and stealthily to seize the initiative away from the competitors.

By controlling, delaying, or influencing the competitor's movement up the escalation ladders, the company seizes the initiative. By continuing to control this movement, the firm sustains the momentum.

Sustaining the Momentum: Punch/Counterpunch Planning

Sustaining the momentum requires an approach to long-range planning that is quite different from the typical five-year plan. It demands, instead, "punch-counterpunch planning." This is more like the type of strategy that a boxer uses in the ring to "plan" a boxing match. It is not a sequence of planned actions so much as it is a set of guidelines for exploring the opponent's weaknesses, testing out one's own punches, and moving from one opportunity to land a punch to the next. Companies traditionally operate more like the sumo wrestler, building up fixed strengths that limit flexibility. Commitment is deemed as critical to success. They move against opponents and rely on superior resources—financial (fourth arena) or know-how (second arena)—to literally crush the competitor. The strategy is straightforward. May the heaviest wrestler win.

Boxers, on the other hand, evolve their strategy in the ring. They work to develop speed and surprise. They hone their reflexes and understanding of the prerequisites for success. They develop a knowledge of their competitors. They do not plan out a sequence of punches, but they plan to use a combination of punches when the opportunity presents itself, anticipating the reactions of their competitors and following up. The boxer throws a left, blocks a right from his opponent, and then delivers a stunning blow. The combination is planned, but at the same time it is flexible and may never be used if the opportunity for use never appears. And a big part of the planning that goes into the fight is the training before the boxer steps into the ring. The skill and agility the boxer brings to the fight is a flexible resource base that can be used in many different ways.

This punch-and-counterpunch planning is reflected most clearly in the final three S's of the New 7-S's. By shifting the rules of the game, companies force their competitors to respond. Signaling by one company causes competitors to make missteps or to react too late or ineffectively to the company's actions. Simultaneous and sequential thrusts are a sequence of punches that companies use to draw out the opponent and direct the flow of actions and reactions so it works to the company's advantage.

One serious challenge that companies face in sustaining a series of initiatives is "initiative fatigue."[14] In launching a rapid series of initiatives, companies burn out because of a variety of problems. Among the reasons for failure are the lack of clear overall purpose, unclear management commitment, and unclear responsibility for the initiative. Initiatives also fail because of poor communication and rumors, lack of training, improper performance systems to measure implementation, and unclear success criteria. These common sources of failure indicate that seizing the initiative is difficult, and sustaining the momentum through a series of initiatives is even more challenging.

THE SOURCE OF PROFITS

While neoclassical microeconomic theory and industrial organization theory suggest that companies earn profits by gaining a unique advantage and avoiding perfect competition,[15] the Austrian school of economics identifies a different source of profits.[16] Profits, under this view of economics, are derived from "entrepreneurial discovery." Entrepreneurial discovery is the result of a dynamic process of "creative destruction," or disequilibrium.[17] In other words, entrepreneurial discovery creates profits by finding new ways to better serve customers. It is in essence the disruption of the status quo that the New 7-S's are designed to pursue.

According to the Austrian school's view, all advantages are short-lived. This suggests that "empirically modeling business performance to find systematic strategies (regularities) that firms can implement to earn supranormal returns, as is widely done in strategy research, will be largely unsuccessful."[18] Today's cause of high performance will not work tomorrow, making it difficult to find generic or sustainable strategies that are associated with high performance. Only entrepreneurial discovery of new opportunities and creative destruction of opponents' advantages create profits.

Exploring the New 7-S's

Part III examines each of the New 7-S's in greater detail. Its chapters look at how companies build and develop each S and how each S impacts the competitive success of the firm. Part III also explores how companies use these New 7-S's to control and direct competitive escalation in the four arenas described in Part I. The implication of these approaches for the future of competition, regulation, and public policy is explored in greater detail in the conclusion and appendix to the book.

Management Challenges

Applying a dynamic view of strategy to your business requires taking a fresh look at your industry and your own firm. Managers can use this new standard to measure their current position and future plans, to shape dynamic strategies. As we move through the discussion of the New 7-S's, we will raise questions for managers about each of them. Here we consider the broad view of hypercompetition and how it has affected your industry.

- Are you focusing on static fit or dynamic maneuvering?
- Have you identified the next advantage that must be seized to move ahead in your industry? What is your vision for disrupting the marketplace?
- Are you or your competitors most likely to seize this advantage?
- Who currently has the initiative in the industry (who is leading the way)? How will you maintain the momentum if you have the initiative now?

- What are the weaknesses of your current approach to strategic planning and your current conceptualization of what a strategy is? Does it help you identify dynamic advantages and seize the initiative?
- Does your strategy encompass any or all of the New 7-S's? Which ones might be useful to add to your current strategy?
- Do you believe that the profits that come from avoiding perfect competition come through tacit collusion or through entrepreneurial discovery of new opportunities and creative destruction of competitors' advantages?
- Do you and your competitors focus most of your strategic effort on tactics, vision, or capabilities? Which is most important to success in your industry? Why? Will this change? Why?

PART III

DISRUPTING MARKETS AND SEIZING THE INITIATIVE THROUGH THE NEW 7-S's

CHAPTER 8

USING THE NEW 7-S's
TO CREATE DISRUPTION

As described in Part II, the strategic goal of sustaining advantage no longer makes sense in an environment in which every traditional advantage erodes. The object of strategy in hypercompetition is disruption of markets to create temporary advantages. Either companies must disrupt themselves to respond to disruption in their markets, or they need to proactively disrupt their markets, and their competitors. Either form of disruption creates a window of opportunity in which hypercompetitive firms can gain a temporary advantage.

This chapter examines each of the New 7-S's in greater detail and describes how each contributes to the goal of disruption. As briefly discussed in the preceding chapter, the New 7-S's work together in a strategic triangle. The first two S's (superior stakeholder satisfaction and strategic soothsaying) shape the vision for disruption, the second two (speed and surprise) provide capabilities for disruption, and the final three (shifting the rules of competition, signaling strategic intent, and simultaneous and sequential strategic thrusts) offer tactics for disruption. This triangle is illustrated in Figure 8–1.

Triangulation and the Formation of Strategy

As indicated, this is not a linear process that begins with vision and ends with tactics. Instead, it is a continuous process in which vision contributes to capabilities, which contribute to tactics. Tactics in turn contribute to vision and capabilities. As will be discussed below, strategy is developed by a process of triangulation that copes with and creates market disruptions over and over again.

257

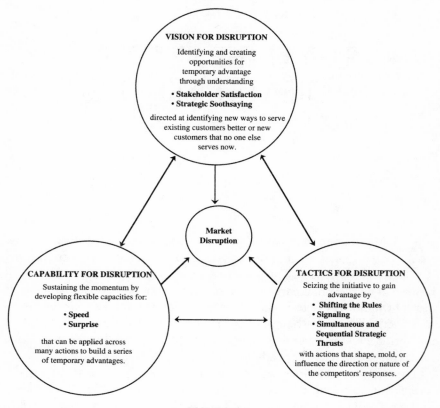

FIGURE 8–1
DISRUPTION AND THE NEW 7-S's

TWO FORMS OF DISRUPTION

Hypercompetitive firms are concerned with two forms of disruption—the one that comes from the outside into the firm and the one that comes from the inside out. In the former case, a change in the external environment occurs—brought on by competitors or the environment itself—and the firm must disrupt itself to respond to that change. In the latter case, the company moves in a preemptive strike to actively disrupt the environment and its competitors. It disrupts itself to disrupt the environment.

Both cases are examined below. Many hypercompetitive firms exhibit a combination of both forms of disruption. In the example of E. & J. Gallo Winery, for example, it experienced disruption from the outside from shifting tastes, demographics, and legal/social mores concerning alcohol consumption. It also created market disruption through its product development, marketing, and manufacturing strategies. The examples from Gallo Winery used below focus primarily on the outside forms of disruption and how Gallo overcame them, but Gallo created its share of market disruption as well.

In the competition between Komatsu and Caterpillar, Komatsu appears to have deliberately disrupted its larger competitor. This aggressive stance helped Komatsu seize the initiative until Caterpillar responded with its own attack to disrupt Komatsu.

Fast-flowing Wine: Disruptions in the Wine Industry

Gallo Wines is one of the largest and most successful wineries in the world, with annual sales of over one billion dollars and 28 percent of the U.S. wine market.[1] Gallo accounts for one out of every three bottles of wine made in America.[2] At the time it was founded in 1933, Gallo was one of hundreds of small wineries that entered the market after the fall of Prohibition. While many of these small companies, and even some of the giants of that time, have since disappeared, Gallo has grown to dominate the industry.[3] It is said jokingly that Gallo spills more wine than its competitors make. It has achieved this degree of dominance by disrupting its competitors and responding quickly to disruptions in its markets.

Gallo built its dominance over the wine market by building large-scale modern plants that were more like chemical processing plants at a time when its competitors treated wine making as an art form done in small batches. Gallo installed a mass-market and widespread distribution system that generated volume and captured economies of scale in an industry that thought small was better.

Gallo's approach put into place a cycle, shown in Figure 8–2, that gobbled up more and more of the marketplace by constantly improving quality and lowering costs for low-end wines. Gallo moved from "street" wines (like Thunderbird) to jug wines to table wines over the decades. This cycle was sustained and expanded for many years until it was disrupted by external events that no longer allowed it to operate as effectively.

Gallo survived a severe disruption in the demographics and drinking habits of the American population in the mid- to late 1980s. It built its strong market for jug and table wine as the baby boom was growing up. Then that market was disrupted by the aging of the boomers. As their incomes rose and heavy drinking fell out of favor, the demand for inexpensive jug and table wines was replaced by a rush for high-quality varietal and other premium wines. Gallo was able to reshape itself to respond to this external disruption by disrupting its internal operations and approach to business to meet the changes of the market, first selling wine coolers

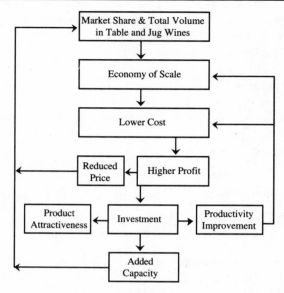

FIGURE 8–2
THE "SUSTAINABLE" CYCLE
CREATED BY GALLO WINERY'S LOW-COST
PRODUCER STRATEGY
Based on William C. Waddell, *The Outline of Strategy* (Oxford, Ohio:
The Planning Forum, 1986), p. 55.

and later selling varietals that required entirely different production, marketing, and product-development skills compared to those for jug and table wines. Through this pattern of disruption, Gallo continued to be a dominant player in the wine market, no matter what shape that market took.

As discussed in more detail below, Gallo used many of the New 7-S's in creating and responding to disruption.

Skinning the Cat: Disruption in the Earth-moving Equipment Industry

In 1981 Caterpillar was the world's largest manufacturer of earth-moving equipment, with sales close to nine billion dollars.[4] Caterpillar controlled more than 50 percent of the world market for earth moving equipment. In just a few decades Komatsu had moved from being one of a multitude of small players to becoming the dominant company in Japan but still held only 16 percent of the 1981 world market. By 1984 Komatsu's share of the world market had grown to 25 percent, and Caterpillar had dropped to 43 percent according to a Harvard Business School case study.[5]

Caterpillar had built its strengths upon a cycle of sustainable advantages, including its dependable quality, strong service and support, high global volume, which gave it economies of scale and lower costs, and high investments in R&D, which led to a full line of quality products. These quality products commanded a premium price, giving Caterpillar high margins that allowed the company to build a strong and loyal dealer network. This seemed to be an unstoppable perpetual-motion machine, as illustrated in Figure 8–3, which gobbled up more and more market share over time.

Komatsu set out to disrupt this perpetual-motion machine. It's in-house slogan was Maru-C, which meant "encircle Caterpillar."[6] Komatsu took Caterpillar's cycle of advantages apart piece by piece, disrupting the flow of the cycle in Figure 8–3 and shattering Cat's advantages. Komatsu moved aggressively through the four arenas of competition, constantly moving to disrupt Caterpillar or maneuver around Caterpillar's strategic strengths, as shown in Figure 8–4.

Komatsu rolled out one product after another into the world market, boosting quality up to or above Caterpillar's standards and undercutting Cat's prices. Komatsu focused on driving up quality first and then moved to drive down costs (competing in arena 1) on existing products in Caterpillar's line. It started out gaining know-how through alliances with other U.S. firms, but then moved beyond Caterpillar's existing line into aggressive development of new technology (arena 2). This gave it the power to expand into the geographic territory in Asia, Europe, and even Cat's home turf of America. Komatsu also expanded its distribution channels from direct sales to dealers and then to regional centers (arena 3), especially in countries where Cat

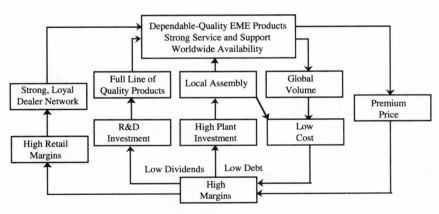

FIGURE 8–3
CAT'S STRATEGY—SUSTAINING A PERPETUAL MOTION MACHINE

Based on research by Christopher Bartlett
Key: EME = Earth Moving Equipment

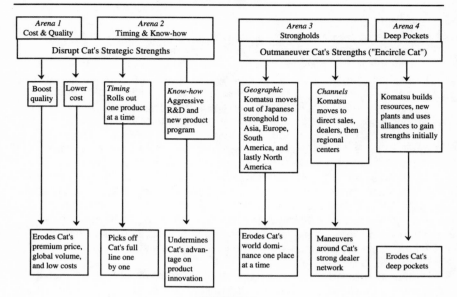

FIGURE 8–4
KOMATSU: A STRATEGY OF DISRUPTION TO DERAIL
"THE PERPETUAL MOTION MACHINE"
Based on research by Chris Bartlett

was not as strong as it was in the United States. Finally, it competed on resources, using its newly developed deep pockets for building overseas assembly plants, and entered into joint ventures to further expand its resources (arena 4).

In its rise to power, Komatsu used a series of actions that disrupted Caterpillar. However, Komatsu was also hit by external disruptions and Caterpillar's disruptive responses.

Komatsu's rise was slowed by an external disruption. In 1984 the Japanese juggernaut held 10 percent of the U.S. market and was poised to seize 20 percent of the market with plans to open a $21 million plant in Tennessee, according to a Harvard Business School case study. Then came an environmental disruption: In the last half of 1985, the dollar fell more than 20 percent against the yen. Komatsu, with most of its production based in Japan, announced price increases of 5 to 10 percent. Suddenly Caterpillar, which had been struggling to match Komatsu's prices, was the low-cost producer. In an interview in *Financial Times* a Komatsu executive made overtures of reconciliation with its arch rival.[7]

Caterpillar could have responded by raising its prices and accommodating Komatsu. But when the yen fell again, it would be likely that Komatsu would not sustain its policy of reconciliation. Instead, Caterpillar seized the opportunity and held its price down, driving Komatsu back to 5 percent of the U.S. market and hurting it overseas.

If not for the shift in the value of the yen, Komatsu might have had an even more significant effect on Caterpillar's U.S. market share. Komatsu used many of the New 7-S's to disrupt Caterpillar, as will be discussed in more detail below.

Thus, Gallo and Komatsu used the New 7-S's to respond to disruption from their competitors or other sources in their environments. They also used the New 7-S's to actively disrupt their markets and their competitors.

The remainder of this chapter is dedicated to examining how the New 7-S's can be used to create effective disruptions that seize the initiative for the disruptors. In particular, the next section looks at the criteria for envisioning a disruption that will create temporary advantage. Thereafter, the chapter looks at the resources, capabilities, and tactics needed to deliver the disruption with the greatest effect.

A VISION FOR DISRUPTION

A vision for disruption comes from being able to identify ways to satisfy customers better than competitors at a given point in time and over and over again. The battle for the market is the battle for the hearts and minds of customers. This is accomplished by satisfying current customers in existing markets, finding new ways to satisfy current customers, and finding new markets. One part of this vision is superior stakeholder satisfaction— to satisfy customers, employees, and then shareholders, in that order. The other part is strategic soothsaying—to understand emerging technologies and trends and to identify ways to shape the future through creating self-fulfilling prophecies.

S-1: Superior Stakeholder Satisfaction

The first priority of hypercompetitive firms is superior stakeholder satisfaction. Disruption is a result of finding new ways to satisfy existing customers or better satisfying new customers by entering new markets. The prioritiza-

FIGURE 8–5

Static Priorities	Dynamic Priorities
1. Shareholders	1. Customers
2. Top Managers	2. Workers
3. Workers	3. Shareholders
4. Customers	4. Top Managers

tion of stakeholders in less hostile, static environments was usually share-holders first, employees second, and customers last. In recent years hypercompetitive firms have turned this prioritization on its head, as indicated by Figure 8–5.

While the concept of putting the concerns of the customer above the concerns of shareholders has certainly gained widespread attention in recent years, the cause of this shift in priorities and its implications have not been so clearly examined. The erosion of sustainable advantage has also shaken up the priorities of the corporation. Creating disruption by serving customers better and developing a series of temporary advantages has demanded a different view of customers, employees, and shareholders

In static environments, where companies had sustainable advantages, customers were there largely to serve the company, and the company existed to maximize shareholder wealth, as indicated in Figure 8–5. Companies created advantages, such as barriers to entry, that meant they could, within limits, dictate to their customers what products or services would be available. Certainly, when Henry Ford told his customers they could have any color automobile they liked as long as it was black, customers had little choice. The forces that limited access to the market by competitors—and created sustainable advantage—tended to dampen the need for achieving high levels of customer satisfaction. No company could completely ignore its customers, but many could place the concerns of their customers below those of shareholders. In the extreme case of a monopoly or near monopoly, customers had so little power in the market that they often had to be rescued by government antitrust action from the clutches of the corporate giants seeking to exploit their monopoly power. As will be examined in the conclusion, the need for this protection is rapidly declining in hypercompetition.

In dynamic environments the company is largely there to serve the customers. With intense competition and fewer or weaker advantages such as barriers to entry, customers vote with their feet. Companies can only keep their market share as long as they can keep customers highly satisfied. Even giants such as IBM or Sears, with their massive market power, live or die at the whim of their customers. The decline of brand loyalty in recent years is just one indication of this phenomenon.

A survey of shoppers found that brand loyalty declined from 45 percent in 1988 to 37 percent in 1992. Faced with declining brand loyalty, Philip Morris was forced to slash prices on its well-known, best-selling Marlboro cigarette brand under pressure from private-label brands. Frito-Lay cut prices by as much as 15 percent as it began to lose market share to lesser brands and private labels. Gerber dropped prices on its baby food under intense competition from private labels and less well known brands.[8]

In static environments employees are cogs in the wheels of the organization. They are held by strong incentives for career growth and stable employment. The same entry barriers and other advantages that allow the company to hold onto customers also help the company to keep its employees.

In dynamic environments employees are the frontline troops in achieving customer satisfaction and understanding future opportunities for disruption. The company that can motivate and empower its workers can ensure that it will continue to be in touch with changing customer tastes and have the ability to satisfy them. The uncertainty of markets and a greater reliance on knowledge workers demands greater flexibility and investment in the workforce. This is ironically occurring at a time when concepts such as "job for life" are increasingly difficult to maintain. Workers are no longer replaceable gears in a machine that produces sustainable competitive advantage. They are, instead, an important part of developing temporary advantages and shifting to new ones.

In static environments the company usually exists to maximize shareholder wealth. But companies that have put their shareholders first in hypercompetitive environments have found that they have often lost market share and money over the long run. When a company sets a goal of generating profits for shareholders by exploiting its sustainable advantage, it frequently ends up milking the advantage for profits without adequate reinvestment designed to create the next advantage needed to seize the initiative. So, in the long run, stockholder value plummets. One has only to look at the dramatic plunge taken by IBM's stock to realize that sustaining its distribution and brand-name advantages was not a high-profit strategy in hypercompetitive markets. IBM, in essence, milked its dominance in the mainframe computer industry without paying adequate attention to the future and the creation of new advantages. Shareholders that demand high returns in a short period of time, rather than realize that returns result from customer satisfaction and employee satisfaction, find that they serve neither their customers nor their shareholders well.

The current belief is that investors have two choices. They can either milk what they know, milking as much out of current advantages as possible before they erode, or reap what they sow, investing tons of up-front capital to build a new advantage and then reaping the return once this sustainable advantage can be harvested. The former results in the negative consequences stated above, while the latter option requires very patient capital.

There has been a great deal of debate about whether U.S. firms are forced to milk what they know due to the pressure of stockholders and hostile raiders. Many have argued that the reap-what-you-sow approach positions firms better for long-run advantages. However, in hypercompetition even the reap-what-you-sow approach is not appealing. With advantages eroding quickly, firms don't have the time to wait for the harvest of their investments. Competitors move quickly to destroy the advantage that is sown, leaving firms with this supposedly better "long-term" perspective in the dust.

In contrast, the most successful hypercompetitive firms offer a third approach to investment, which might be called pay as you go. Investors fund a series of temporary advantages that provide a steady return because as one fades, another moves into its place. This ensures a steady payback, unlike the increasingly risky strategy of reaping what you sow, which often ends up throwing seeds on infertile soil and rarely returns as much as is invested because of the short window in which the advantage is unchallenged. But this third approach also allows investors to make a long-term commitment through a series of short-term investments and payoffs. This avoids the opportunistic milk-what-you-know approach, which often leaves the company drained dry and unable to continue to produce returns. As investments are increasingly concentrated in the hands of institutional investors looking for profits and without the patience needed for the reap-what-you-sow approach, this third investment strategy is becoming even more essential to success in hypercompetitive markets.

Gallo built its market by being closely in tune with the needs of customers. Because it is a closely held family firm, it didn't have to worry about answering to shareholders and could move freely to reinvest profits into increasing customer satisfaction, often using the reap-what-you-sow method. It set the standards for wine making in the United States, gaining advantages in cost and quality that were used to provide higher customer satisfaction in the table wine segment. When the definition of quality shifted from good-tasting table wines to prestige wines with snob appeal in the 1980s, Gallo responded with a fad product (wine coolers) and a longer-term move to up-scale varietals. Its very popular Thunderbird was developed after marketers saw retailers selling lemon juice to mix with port wine, so Gallo recognized the need and created a premixed version of the fortified wine. Its varietals and wine coolers were designed to capture the new customer tastes caused by the origin of the baby boomer generation. The wine cooler strategy, using this fad product to fill capacity in the main plant while batch-production processes were developed for varietals, was an example of finding a series of temporary advantages that constituted a pay-as-you-go approach.

Komatsu sought to improve its position against Caterpillar by improving the value it offered to customers. It did so by utilizing its main asset, its people. Cat had a history of tumultuous labor negotiations with its unions that led to a 204-day strike in 1983—one of the largest against any U.S. firm.[9] Komatsu, in contrast, had a strongly stated corporate policy of striving for the monetary and professional satisfaction of its employees.[10] Between 1976 and 1981, labor productivity increased at an estimated annual compound rate of 15 percent at Komatsu compared to just over 11 percent at Caterpillar.[11]

These two examples illustrate the power of building superior shareholder satisfaction. Using employees and innovative investment strategies can place customers first without hurting performance for stockholders.

Superior stakeholder satisfaction creates disruption by eroding customer loyalty to competitors' brands, as can be seen in the cases of both Komatsu and Gallo. Both of these companies were once insignificant players, but a consistent focus on developing new products and providing better customer satisfaction made them giants in their industries. In turn, this pool of customers and the resources they provided built both loyalty and resources for each company's next initiative.

Losing market share to a competitor that builds its market share by satisfying customers better creates a powerful force for disruption. The loser realizes that it cannot continue in the same direction that had made it strong in the past. It cannot continue to work to sustain its advantage. It is forced to follow the initiating company to this new level of customer satisfaction or to find a new way of satisfying customers better.

Along the way, a competitor that has not placed a high value on its workers faces a disadvantage in achieving these higher levels of customer satisfaction. It is then forced to shift its view of workers and restructure its relationships with them. In the United States the Total Quality Management movement and the emergence of such innovations as self-managed teams are a recognition of the need to change the company's view of its employees.

S-2: Strategic Soothsaying

To develop a series of temporary advantages, companies need to do more than satisfy customers today. They need to gain "future share."[12] Strategic soothsaying is envisioning new customer needs before they can articulate them for themselves and then creating that future. Soothsaying requires that the company have the ability to do more than predict future trends. They must influence them by controlling the development of key technologies and other know-how that will shape the future. Soothsaying also involves a passive reading of the technological and competitive environment ahead, so that firms can react to disruptions from outside the firms. But soothsaying also involves the creation of self-fulfilling prophecies by actively influencing and shaping future events. By continuously engaging in strategic soothsaying, companies envision and create a series of ways to proactively disrupt the market and achieve superior customer satisfaction. They also take advantage of external disruptions beyond their control by conceptualizing them as opportunities, not threats.

In static environments, where companies are working to sustain their current advantages, long-range planning is used to project the present advantage into the future. Long-range-planning models call for companies to build upon their strengths rather than undermine their current strengths by shifting to new ones. When the external environment was relatively stable, it demanded only modest course corrections. The requirements for seizing future share of the market are not radically different from those needed to sustain current market share. Long-range planning, as it is currently practiced in many U.S. firms, has become a projection of the organization's past strengths rather than an active engagement in identifying or creating opportunities in the future environment. This view of the future is focused on *sustaining* the past rather than *disrupting* it. Companies look at the challenges of sustaining their current strengths despite the changes of future markets rather than looking at how to change the organization to take advantage of opportunities in the future.

In dynamic environments, in which every advantage erodes, the requirements to seize future share are very different from the qualities that were needed to gain current share. The key to successfully moving from temporary advantage to temporary advantage is to identify opportunities for disrupting the present and creating new advantages in the future. Long-range planning involves, not a projection of the strengths of the past, but a vision for stringing together a series of temporary advantages. This vision is the result of strategic soothsaying.

Customer satisfaction in hypercompetition is not a static goal. The requirements for creating customer satisfaction continue to evolve as companies search for new and better ways of achieving ever-higher levels of customer satisfaction. Advances in technology often offer new opportunities for satisfying customers. At the same time, customer satisfaction itself is a moving target because customer tastes and demographics change.

The hypercompetitive firm looks for ways to gain not only current market share by satisfying current customers but also future share of the market by developing a view of the future customers or the future requirements of customer satisfaction. The hypercompetitive firm disrupts competitors by being the first to find new ways to achieve customer satisfaction through engaging in strategic soothsaying. This is actively examining the future for emerging opportunities to create disruption.

The Sears catalog is an example of a business that lost sight of future share. It grew into a giant by creating its catalog business, being the first to identify the catalog as an effective means of reaching rural buyers. But it tried to sustain this initiative when the market changed. Sprawling malls were at the doorstep of virtually the entire U.S. population. Busy, two-career families had a different view of catalogs. Those that were sharply focused, with twenty-four-hour ordering numbers that made it easy to shop at odd hours, continued to build share. But Sears, which plodded along with its old catalog, found that what once had been an advantage was now an albatross. It ultimately shut down its catalog business. It had seized current share but lost its ability to seize future share because it stopped using strategic soothsaying.

Gallo built its company by realizing the potential market for table wines in the United States and actively working to create that market (as a self-fulfilling prophecy). As college students of the baby boom became yuppies, tastes shifted from the inexpensive jug wines to the more upscale varietals. In recognition of this change, Gallo built an oak aging cellar with a three-million-gallon capacity, planted vineyards with new varieties of grapes, and worked to dramatically reshape its image.[13]

Once Komatsu had gained a foothold in existing markets for earth-moving equipment, it continued a process of understanding its customers and creating new products to satisfy their needs. Its 1979 F and F program (future and frontiers) charted an array of new products and new businesses that took advantage of current competencies. Through this program all employees were asked to examine the needs of society and the know-how of the corporation to develop new products or business ideas. It produced thirty-five hundred suggestions, many of which became new growth areas to counter the stagnation of the world construction industry.[14]

Strategic soothsaying disrupts the market by identifying ways that existing views of the market can be broken or identifying opportunities for the firm to break existing paradigms. This disruption of the current hold of competitors on the market forces them to move, either to follow into these new areas or to find a new way of satisfying customers.

By using strategic soothsaying, hypercompetitive firms understand emerging shifts in the market better than competitors. This understanding creates the opportunity for the soothsaying firm to respond to and shape the future evolution of the market. This ability to take an active role in reshaping the market disrupts the competitor, caught off guard by the changes, that may be expecting to sustain a current advantage, only to see it slip away.

As hypercompetitive firms use their vision of the future to move into new areas, competitors are forced to either respond or die. Competitors with a less highly developed view of the future will be at a disadvantage when such a shift in the rules of competition occurs. These competitors will not only have to respond to the reality of the shift but also have to quickly reshape their mind-set and view of the market. This psychological disruption is often as debilitating as the physical disruption that results from shifting the rules.

CAPABILITIES FOR DISRUPTION

To capitalize on the advantages identified through the first two S's, hypercompetitive firms develop capabilities for speed and surprise. Speed and surprise are capabilities that can be used in many ways.

Fixed capabilities, such as investments in plants and other resources, tend to commit a company to a certain course of action. In static views of competition, this clear commitment to a certain course or to sustaining a certain advantage tends to warn away competitors from attacking that advantage. It makes it clear that they will have little chance of success.

In a dynamic environment, on the other hand, a commitment does not necessarily warn competitors away from an advantage. Because advantages can be eroded, a strong commitment merely gives away the company's hand and makes it easier for competitors to disrupt it. The predictability of commitments also makes it harder for the company to surprise and disrupt its competitors.

In hypercompetition companies develop flexible capabilities that enhance their actions but do not give away their strategic position. Capabilities for speed and surprise are deployed in a variety of different ways.

Therefore, if a competitor knows a company has capabilities for speed and surprise, it does not necessarily know how the company will use those capabilities, making it unpredictable and, hence, more threatening. This flexibility and unpredictability create disruption and force an opponent to act differently as a result of the potential threatening posture of its competitors.

S-3: Capabilities for Speed

In static environments, where advantages eroded more slowly, speed was concerned with increasing the efficiency of current processes. Speed was viewed as a way to strengthen existing advantages by making current organizational processes move more quickly. The innovations of Frederick Taylor and the Scientific Management School, for example, increased the efficiency and productivity of manufacturing companies many times over. The pace of organizational and strategic change, however, was not of great concern, and companies tended to move very slowly in shifting their direction because they were focused on sustaining their current advantages rather than disrupting them.

Because of this focus in static environments on speeding existing operations, the conventional wisdom was that companies had to sacrifice quality or flexibility to achieve greater speed. If a machine runs at a faster rate, the quality will usually go down. If service is delivered more quickly, it will be more standardized and less courteous. So to speed operations, companies increased their focus. Producing a narrow range of products or services allowed firms to speed delivery to customers. Speed was concerned with the speed of operations rather than the speed of organizational and strategic change.

In dynamic environments, in contrast, companies are focused on speeding up their ability to move and to change. All advantages are temporary, so the clock is always ticking. Because they must move quickly from advantage to advantage, organizations need to develop the capacity to turn on a dime. They need to be able to move in new directions and pursue new opportunities before their competitors. Companies reengineer their organizations to increase quality and flexibility while achieving higher levels of speed in current operations and greater speed in taking advantage of new opportunities.

To achieve speed, companies reorganize their organizational structure, processes, and individual behaviors. Rigid and slow hierarchical structures are replaced with flatter, team-oriented structures that allow for rapid decisions and actions. Processes within the company are streamlined or reengineered, and excessive work is forced out. Individual behaviors and the culture of the organization are being changed to create a more involved workforce and facilitate teamwork. All these approaches contribute to the company's capabilities for speed.

> Hypercompetition is often unforgiving to the slow-moving company. As Monsanto's patent for aspartame was about to expire in December 1992, *Business Week* reported that competitors were lining up to move in on the market with lower-priced versions of the sweetener. More troubling, however, was that the company's next generation of sweeteners appeared to be years away from a rollout, according to *Business Week*. Meanwhile, competitors such as Johnson & Johnson and Coke were preparing to launch new sweeteners of their own that could seize the market away from Monsanto.[15]

> Gallo's shift from screw-top wines to high-class varietals was a rapid transformation. In a period of a few years, the company was able to transform its operations and reputation from a high-production, low-quality factory to a premium-quality winery (without abandoning its high-production capabilities). Its ability to quickly build a large cask winery, to change its advertising and marketing, and to shift its grape growing allowed it to move quickly. In Gallo's case, this speed resulted, in part, from the central control of the winery by the Gallo brothers.

> Komatsu's ability to roll out a series of new products continued to chip away at Caterpillar's market and then keep going to outpace Cat in technological development. Komatsu made a rapid and aggressive push overseas to move quickly into new markets. The company's "management by policy" system allowed it to set broad policies of innovation to get staff to work together to achieve common goals. It also instituted a system of feedback loops, known as the PDCA system (plan, do, check, act) to provide consistent and rapid midcourse corrections. Caterpillar's more rigid organizational structure, constrained by its contract with its unions, slowed its progress.

Speed creates disruption by preempting competitors. Even if two competing companies are able to recognize an opportunity at the same time through the first two S's, the one that has the capability to act quickly will be the one that is able to seize the initiative and disrupt the other competitor. Speed allows companies to be the first mover if this is to their advantage, forcing competitors to be reactors.

By moving quickly, the company also disrupts competitors by giving them less time to find out about the move or prepare to respond to it. This extends the time it takes for competitors to duplicate or undermine the advantage and also increases the shock of the move. In this way speed works to enhance surprise.

S-4: Capabilities for Surprise

In static environments consistency and commitment are the keys to success because they help the company sustain its current advantages. Conventional wisdom says that companies, like athletes, only become excellent by concentrating on and practicing an activity over and over. Companies are encouraged to "stick to their knitting" and develop strategic fit. Consistency and commitment make it virtually impossible to create surprise. The company's actions and strategies are visible and unchanging.

In dynamic environments, in which the focus is not on sustaining but on disrupting the status quo, consistency and commitment undermine the company's ability to move from temporary advantage to temporary advantage. A constant course decreases flexibility, gives away the firm's position to competitors, and leaves it open to be outmaneuvered. Hypercompetitive companies recognize that the skills developed by an athlete in one activity can be applied to others, so they invest in generalizable resources. Not only does this give the company more flexibility, this approach also increases the firm's ability to surprise competitors. In dynamic environments companies use surprise to delay, confuse, or outmaneuver their competitors. Surprise results from disrupting the status quo, and when companies build new temporary advantages, the new advantages that create the most surprise also create the most advantage.

Because surprise is, by definition, unpredictable, it is something that usually can't be planned for explicitly. Instead, companies *develop capabilities* for being able to create and carry out surprises that will move them in unpredictable directions. These capabilities for surprise result from stealth, flexibility, and creativity.

The capability for stealth is an important way of keeping competitors guessing about the company's next move. At the same time that surprise has become increasingly important, the growth of public information and burgeoning of industry analysts has made it harder to keep secrets by stealth. Even closely held private companies, such as Gallo, have been the subjects of magazine stories and books. So while companies still use stealth, most depend more heavily on flexibility and innovation.

Companies achieve flexibility in a variety of ways. A flexible cost structure within a firm allows it to shift resources quickly. Companies also actively develop and manage flexible knowledge bases and core competencies that can be applied in various ways. For example, Honda's abilities in small engines could be applied to motorcycles, cars, snowblowers, and a wide range of other products, and its competitors still don't know which product it will be applying this competency to next.[16]

Finally, hypercompetitive firms work to surprise themselves. Through a commitment to innovation, companies create opportunities to come up with creative new technologies and products that shake it up internally and shake up its external markets. For example, 3-M's Post-its were as much a surprise to the internal organization as they were to the marketplace. But they were a result of the company's commitment to allowing its employees the time to exercise their creativity.

Gallo's tight-lipped policies helped to shield its strategies and moves from competitors, but a public court case in which the two founders' younger brother sued for an interest in the business opened much of the company's operations to public scrutiny. E. & J. Gallo Winery also created surprise through its commitment to innovation, developing new technology to process wine and new varieties of grapes. Its flexibility has also surprised competitors. For example, California Cooler introduced the first wine cooler in 1981, but Gallo had the flexibility to move aggressively into the market with its Bartles & Jaymes coolers. *The New York Times* reported in 1987 that Gallo's B & J had gained a quarter of the market while California's share fell to 16 percent.[17]

Komatsu used its competencies in flexible new ways and encouraged innovation through its F and F (future and frontiers) program. This led to products such as arc-welding robots, underwater-excavation equipment, and new silicon materials, as well as new uses for solar energy.[18]

Surprise creates disruption by catching the competitor off guard through an unexpected action. Because the competitor is never sure of where the next volley is coming from, it is in a constant state of disruption, even when its unpredictable opponent is not acting on its opportunities for surprise. The capacity for surprise forces competitors to sustain a higher level of vigilance and creates the uncertainty that throws opponents off guard.

Surprise, therefore, disrupts the competitor's ability to successfully defend against an attack because the competitor cannot plan for the attack. It also gives the surprising company a longer window for its temporary advantage before the competitor recovers from the surprise and successfully mounts a counteroffensive.

TACTICS FOR DISRUPTION

The final three S's are concerned with tactics for delivering disruptions—shifting the rules of competition, signaling strategic intent, and simultaneous and sequential strategic thrusts. The vision for disruption and capabilities for disruption help shape the tactics that will be used. And if a firm is good at specific tactics, the company may shape its vision and capability around these tactics.

Tactics in static environments are focused on sustaining existing advantages. They are concerned with holding the course and warding off attacks on a stronghold. Thus, in stable environments controls are important to prevent strategic drift, and signals are keys to deterring opponents.

Tactics in hypercompetition are faster, more flexible, and less predictable because they are used to create disruption. Tactics in hypercompetition are not based on five-year plans and the creation of fixed, inflexible plants. They are more like tactics used in boxing, in which the competitor trains his reflexes and plans combinations of moves but thinks fast and changes direction quickly in the ring. In this way the tactics themselves are constantly feeding back information so the company can adjust its vision and strengthen its capabilities based on reactions of opponents.

S-5: Shifting the Rules of Competition

Companies shift the rules of competition in hypercompetitive markets to disrupt competitors. Every industry is guided by conventional wisdom and unwritten rules of behavior. By attacking and overturning these rules, companies shatter the current advantages of their competitors and create the opportunity to build their own temporary advantages. Canon's creation of the disposable cartridge for its personal copiers, which allowed customers to self-service their machines, defied the conventional wisdom that copier companies would need a huge service force to maintain personal copiers. Dell's shift of computer sales from retailers to mail-order sales defied conventional wisdom that customers wanted and needed personal attention to buy and install a computer. Like the fall of communism in the former Soviet Union, this shift in rules creates a significant disruption for competitors and allows the initiating firm to seize the initiative.

In a static environment the rules of competition are rules that endure. The rules of competition ensure that companies do not overstep their bounds and trigger extreme retaliation. These rules of competition allow companies to sustain their advantages. The static firm lives by rules, such as IBM's belief that competition in computers would center on mainframes or the Swiss watchmakers' belief that watches would be based on mechanical movements in spite of the successes of quartz watches. These companies held on to to their old rules of competition until they were slapped in the face by the paradigm-shifting force of hypercompetition.

Hypercompetitive firms realize that the rules of competition are like the emperor's new clothes—they are only there if everyone sees them and pretends to go along with the rules. The rules of competition are self-perpetuating, as long as no one challenges them. For example, as discussed in Part I, if all companies believe that there are barriers to entry, then these barriers become a reality because no one challenges them. It takes only one company to challenge the existing rules, to point out that the emperor is truly naked, and the system crumbles. This is a dramatic form of disruption.

> When Gillette introduced its Sensor razor, forcing up quality and using Super Bowl advertising, it violated all the rules that guided the market for disposable razors. But the company successfully redefined the rules of competition and then seized a major share of this reshaped market.

In a dynamic environment, in which companies are focused on gaining temporary advantages, they look for ways to disrupt the existing rules of competition—especially if the status quo benefits their competitors more than themselves. The most successful hypercompetitive firms even challenge these existing rules when they work to their own benefit. These companies know that if they don't challenge these rules, their competitors will. The rules cannot be protected, so the best situation is to be the first to see the opportunity to shift the rules and then to act upon that opportunity. Thus, Intel is working on the next generation of chip even before the current one reaches market.

Hypercompetitive firms realize that a shift in the external rules of competition begins first with a shift in the internal mind-set of the organization. They develop cultures that encourage iconoclasts and revolutionaries. They encourage the creativity that leads to surprise. As noted in S-2 above, they actively look to the future not just to react to trends but to create opportunities for shifting the rules of competition and disrupting the status quo.

> As noted earlier, Gallo first rose to power by shifting the rules of competition in the wine industry. At a time when most small wineries left their marketing to distributors, Gallo built a powerful marketing organization that worked directly with retailers. This organization paid attention to details down to the placement of the product on the shelf. On the production side Gallo shifted the rules by abandoning the small-batch production of most small wine makers in favor of the high-tech, high-volume production of undated wine in huge stainless steel vats. Wine making shifted from an artist's cellar to a chemical production plant. Then when tastes shifted, Gallo again shifted the

rules back to the old oak-barreled aging process of the vintage and varietal wines.

Komatsu shifted the rules of competition by shifting away from using service and dealer networks. It was also able to boost its quality and cut its costs below Caterpillar, eroding Cat's brand loyalty. In the 1960s Komatsu, with little know-how needed to be a world-class competitor, was a sitting duck for Caterpillar's impending entry into Japanese markets. Komatsu shifted the rules of competition by forging alliances with Bucyrus-Erie and International Harvester. These alliances gave Komatsu access to the technology it needed to compete against Caterpillar in Japan. Komatsu used these alliances to build its own technological know-how until it outgrew them in the 1980s.[19]

Shifting the rules of competition creates disruption by shattering the existing beliefs and paradigms in the industry. The depth of competitors' investment in the current paradigm determines the level of disruption that can be created by the move. A company that has based its entire structure and strategy on the assumption that current rules will be sustained will find itself severely disrupted by a shift in the rules. A company that is itself actively looking to shift the rules will be less disrupted by a shift in the rules caused by competitors. A shift in the rules of competition creates internal disruption, as well, by forcing the organization to change its mental models of competition.

The competitor is forced to shift its own direction in response to the shift in the rules. If it fails to follow this shift in the rules, it is faced with the loss of market share. If it does follow, it might still lose market share through slowness and costs associated with changes and catch-ups because it will have to reorganize its planning and thinking. The best response to a shift in the rules is another shift in the rules that turns the table to disrupt the disrupter.

S-6: Signaling Strategic Intent

In static environments signals (verbal statements or symbolic actions) are designed to reinforce the company's strategic advantages. These signals show the company's commitment to a specific course of action. The more commitment they involve, the more credible they are. They clearly show the direction the company is headed and warn competitors away from that position. They tend to lock the company into a specific course of action and provide little flexibility. This loss of flexibility is not a major concern, however, because the company is plodding on a course that will allow it to sustain its current advantages and deter others from attacking its strongholds.

Signals in static environments are also used to generate tacit collusion. For example, a company announces its intent to concede certain markets to a competitor rather than fight for them. Or a company signals a price increase, allowing time to see whether competitors are willing to match the increase. After the decline of the dollar against the yen in 1985, for example, Komatsu seemed to signal its willingness to de-escalate competition. In a 1985 interview in *The Financial Times*, Komatsu president Soji Nogawa said, "What is important is to have enough share so we can exist and cooperate in this market. If we take a combative attitude, it will be very difficult to survive. We have no intention of taking on Caterpillar and fighting them like an enemy until one of us falls."[20]

Hypercompetitive firms use signaling to show their strategic intent to win, but not their specific actions.[21] They clearly state that they will defend a certain market against all comers, or they describe their vision for a shift in a technology market. Their commitment to win is credible because they have a history of moving aggressively against competitors that challenge them. This reputation for fierceness makes their threats meaningful, even without a strong and visible commitment to a specific course of action. Signals in hypercompetition, therefore, do not require a specific commitment of inflexible resources to be credible, offering the signaling company greater flexibility for future moves. Competitors are kept guessing about the actual moves that will be made.

In an environment in which there is a constant flow of information, hypercompetitive firms use their signals to create uncertainty or make implied threats against their competitors. For example, the announcement of so-called vaporware by IBM and, later, by Microsoft is widely seen as an attempt to forestall moves by competitors and encourage customers to wait for their product rather than buy competing products that make it to the market sooner. This creates uncertainty for the competitor and disrupts its plans for launching the new software. Without having to have a successful, working product in hand, IBM and Microsoft were able to compete on signals alone.

Gallo has clearly signaled its intent to dominate the wine market, as can be gathered from the title of a 1986 *Fortune* article on the E. & J. Gallo Winery, "How Gallo Crushes the Competition," and description of the Gallos' "desperate will to dominate."[22] The relentless pursuit of markets by Ernest Gallo is legendary, as are the exploits of Gallo salesmen, who have a hefty sales manual outlining tactics for success. According to the *Fortune* article, the sales representatives reportedly have even oiled the bottles of competitors to make dust stick to them or turned their caps on tighter to make customers angry. While the company denies any official policy so aggressive or extreme, the stories reinforce the company's reputation for fierceness and toughness. The Gallos have a reputation for being tough on growers, tough on retailers, and tough on competitors. While they have clearly signaled their intent to win, the Gallos have maintained an official silence about the nuts and bolts of their strategy.

Komatsu's internal battle cry, Encircle Caterpillar, was reflected in aggressive external signals of its intent to move into Cat's market, such as the announcement of plans to build a $21 million plant in Tennessee and projections that it would seize 20 percent of the U.S. market. Yet the specifics of its actions were left undefined. There are many ways to encircle Caterpillar, so a pledge to encircle it gives away little information about the company's detailed plans of attack.

Hypercompetitive signaling creates disruption by unsettling the opponent with a clear statement of an intent to win, not an intent to cooperate on price. The attack is even more unsettling because the details of it are uncertain. The competitor knows that it will be attacked, but not how or where. Even when the signal conveys more detailed information, the recipient cannot be sure if it is a signal of real intent or a feint. As considered above, signals such as vaporware can disrupt the plans of competitors—sometimes winning the war before a single shot has been fired.

A company that is using signals aggressively also forces its opponents to more carefully analyze all the information flowing from the firm. Once it finds questionable information, it may have to question all the data it obtains. This creates further disruption because it has trouble conducting an accurate analysis of its competitors.

S-7: Simultaneous and Sequential Strategic Thrusts

In hypercompetition steady and linear actions (such as being a low-cost producer or differentiator) are too predictable. Hypercompetitive firms use more dynamic and less predictable strategies. These strategies are distinguished by their use of two or more strategic thrusts at the same time (simultaneous thrusts), a planned series of strategic thrusts against a competitor (sequential thrusts), or a combination of both.

In static environments strategy moves on a steady course of sustaining the company's advantage. It moves in a single direction, like the old style of formal military engagement. The troops moved in the direction that they wanted to travel and clashed at the border. The company's strategic thrusts moved it toward its goal of sustaining its advantage. Strategy is a steady-as-she-goes process. The organization has its marching orders, and it follows them, running over anyone in its path.

In hypercompetition, where success depends on stringing together a series of temporary advantages and disrupting competitors, companies plan to zigzag through a series of thrusts against competitors, or they hit the competitor from several different directions at once. These approaches leave the competitor harassed or stunned, in other words, disrupted.

Against a competitor moving in a predictable, linear direction, the hypercompetitive firm can attack from the side or harass from several different fronts until the competitor is forced to respond. Thus, the static approach to strategy, even in the hands of a more powerful competitor, is often no match for the guerrilla tactics of hypercompetitive firms.

Like experienced chess players, hypercompetitive firms play out a series of moves and countermoves in their heads before making the first move. By the time competitors have reacted to the first move, the initiator is moving on to the next. Or the competitor's response may lead it down a blind alley or dead end while the initiator moves on to a second powerful strategic thrust. This involves a much more aggressive, fast-paced exchange of maneuvers, and it is a less chivalrous view of competition, as will be discussed in the conclusion to the book.

As mentioned above, Komatsu used a series of sequential thrusts to gradually erode Caterpillar's hold on the market. It introduced, first, a limited product line of crawler-tractors and crawler-loaders in the United States in 1970. It used this single product to gain a foothold by pricing its equipment 30 to 40 percent below Cat. Then Komatsu slowly upgraded pieces of its line to face Cat and added them one at a time, until Caterpillar was facing a full-line of Komatsu products on its home turf. Komatsu also used simultaneous thrusts against Caterpillar, moving in several geographic markets and innovating in several different product areas at once. These actions disrupted Caterpillar's hold on the market.

When faced with the taste and demographic shifts of the 1980s, Gallo Wineries faced off against its largest competitor (Seagrams) with a series of simultaneous moves. These included introducing wine coolers (which Seagrams responded to with its own wine cooler targeted to a different segment). It also included a major advertising campaign to help reposition its unaged, mass-produced wines into a midprice range. Finally, Gallo also entered the varietal market. So Seagrams was hit from several directions at the same time, forcing it into a catch-up mode.

Simultaneous and sequential strategic thrusts create disruption because many companies respond only to the first thrust of a series or expect a thrust from one direction rather than multiple thrusts. This is especially true when these thrusts are used against a competitor that expects a single, consistent approach to strategy.

Even against competitors that realize that companies will use simultaneous and sequential strategic thrusts, these tactics create disruption. Only the initiating company knows the exact series of thrusts it has planned or how it plans to use simultaneous thrusts. When the company makes its first move in the series of sequential thrusts, its competitor has no way of knowing what the next thrust will be and where the series of thrusts will lead. It can only guess, and this is what creates uncertainty and disruption.

HOW THE NEW 7-S's WORK TOGETHER TO CREATE DISRUPTION

This chapter has described how each of the New 7-S's contributes to the disruption of competitors. It has described how the strategies of sustaining advantage used in static environments have been replaced by strategies of disruption in hypercompetition. The "three circles" diagram (see Figure 8–1) suggests how the New 7-S's work together toward the goal of disruption by contributing to vision, capabilities, and tactics. But actually all the New 7-S's are related to one another, though there are sometimes tradeoffs among them, as will be considered in the next chapter.

The relationship among the three circles in Figure 8–1 is not a linear relationship. Companies don't necessarily move from vision to capabilities to tactics. It is much more fluid. The tactics contribute to the company's vision of customer satisfaction and suggest opportunities through strategic soothsaying. Capabilities for speed and surprise contribute to the success of tactics, but practicing the tactics helps to build capabilities for speed and surprise.

The formulation of strategy is not a linear process. It is a process of triangulation. Just as ships can navigate through the alignment of three points on the deck and shoreline, so companies use these three circles as guides in setting the course of their strategy and making constant corrections to that course. New disruptions are invented every day. The New 7-S's destroy the advantage of opponents by creating and recreating new temporary advantages for their users.

The Point of Disruption: Seizing the Initiative

THE WILL TO DOMINATE

Disruption is not an end in itself. There is no great virtue in churning the marketplace for its own sake. Disruption is only useful if it destroys the advantage of an opponent and moves the firm up the escalation ladders faster than anyone else. In hypercompetition the rule is to disrupt or be disrupted. This is not a matter of macho destructiveness, but rather an issue of survival. As discussed in Part I, companies have no choice but to move from temporary advantage to temporary advantage or be routed out of their secure position by their competitors. It is change or be changed.

The point of disruption is not to create trouble. It is to create opportunity. Companies disrupt the market so they can seize the initiative from their competitors. The company that is disrupting, providing that it serves customers' needs, will seize the initiative from its opponent, force the opponent into a reactive mode, and ultimately exhaust the opponent's ability to resist or reseize the initiative. In sum, hypercompetitive firms have the will to dominate their competitors, and they do so by using the New 7-S's to seize the initiative away from them.

A RADICAL DEPARTURE FROM THE PAST

The New 7-S's may seem obvious. After all, they are a framework for understanding why current management fads have appeared. What is new, however, is that these fads are actually pieces of a larger system designed to create disruption and cope with the dynamism and uncertainty of hypercompetition. Thus, the New 7-S's are more than a list of seven fads. They are part of a new theory about temporary advantage. They encompass cutting edge practices that managers and the popular press have developed by intuition. The New 7-S's place these fads in the context of a larger theory—the theory of hypercompetition.

Moreover, the New 7-S's are a radical departure from the past. Traditional views of strategy, based on sustaining advantage and protecting turf with entry barriers, are about defending what a firm has gained control over. Whether a geographic region or a unique advantage, the traditional view says defend it and make it persist. Traditionalists say to use clear, consistent, long-term strategies. They also suggest that firms should stake out turf by using inflexible commitments (like investing in plants with specific assets or developing brand images that are difficult to change) so that a firm can deter competitors and reduce rivalry by differentiating itself from competitors.

While these traditional methods are still useful in some circumstances, the view of strategic behavior and purpose in hypercompetition is quite different. The New 7-S's stress flexibility, change, inconsistency, unpredictability, and seizing the offensive. The New 7-S's are about empowering managers to be proactive and to seize the initiative with innovation, change, and aggressive movement into new markets, new products, new business and manufacturing methods, and new paradigms about the nature of competitive interaction between rivals.

COOPERATIVE STRATEGIES AND PERPETUAL DISADVANTAGE

Before hypercompetitive firms were engaged in competitive maneuvers, it was possible to find cooperative arrangements that worked to everyone's benefit. Traditional views suggested that profits were created by reducing rivalry. For example, profits are said to be generated when rivalry is reduced via

- *barriers to entry* that keep down the number of competitors in an industry, making it easier to encourage and manage cooperative behavior among competitors
- *segmentation* of the market into niches by using generic strategies that focus firms on the high-end, the low-end, or specialized niches, allowing the firms to avoid direct competition with each other
- *use of signals* to tacitly agree to raise prices, divide up a market into undisputed territory, or restrict output, essentially creating an informal cartel
- *formation of strategic alliances* that co-opt competitors into being less aggressive
- *retreating to safe, non-price-sensitive, hard-to-replicate niches* (e.g., high technology industries and luxury items), where price competition is not a major competitive dimension

However, Part I demonstrated that these are not stable solutions, especially if a hypercompetitive foreign firm enters the market. Part I also showed how all of the traditional competitive advantages evaporate quickly. Moreover, Part II showed that it was impossible to avoid the deterioration of unstable cooperative arrangements into hypercompetitive rivalry.

Hypercompetitive firms, many of whom are seeking dominance, force others to follow them up the escalation ladders in each of the four arenas of competition. In the process, the leading firm generates profits while the laggards lose out.

So the New 7-S's are not about winning by cooperating or avoiding competition. They are about winning by competing harder than others. Of course, some firms would prefer to cooperate and allow every one of its competitors to survive and prosper, but this is becoming less and less possible in a world where nations are now fighting economic battles instead of military ones.

Not surprisingly, the traditional compete-by-not-competing approach has left many American firms noncompetitive in a world of global multinationals that subscribe to the winning-by-competing-hard philosophy. Any use of the old cooperative rules is doomed in a world of aggressive competitors using the New 7-S's. Like sheep exposed to a wolf among the flock, the meek do not inherit the earth. If one steps back for a moment, it may even seem ridiculous to believe that competing by not competing is a way to become competitive. It can only slow a firm's movement up the escalation ladders and force it into perpetual disadvantage.

COMPETING BY COMPETING HARDER

When firms adopt the New 7-S's, they learn to compete by competing harder. They disrupt by creatively destroying competitors' advantages, making them obsolete, or neutralizing their effectiveness by generating new advantages. However, this aggressiveness can be uncomfortable for many managers. The implicit goal is the defeat of competitors, which, if done improperly, could constitute a violation of U.S. antitrust laws (a subject of the conclusion to this book).

It is possible, however, to win by competing harder and to do so legally and ethically. After all, the consumer benefits from such activity, and the nation benefits from the jobs that are created (or saved) by hypercompetitive firms.

Thus, the New 7-S's are a radical departure from old views of how to win. They are about offensive, aggressive, noncooperative behaviors. While the fads encompassed by the New 7-S's are well-known, the change in underlying goals that these fads imply were not obvious until now. The theory of hypercompetition makes it clear that firms win by outmaneuvering competitors, not by trying to cooperate in a way that freezes the players into fixed positions. The latter cannot be sustained for very long in a dynamic, uncertain environment, especially if one firm or potential entrant intends to win by competing hard. This is the core insight that a dynamic view of strategy provides and a static view does not.

The New 7-S's are the difference between winning by defeating an opponent versus winning by not playing. In today's world, firms who don't play the game can't win.

Using the New 7-S's to Win

The process of analyzing how to use the New 7-S's to seize the initiative will be the focus of the next chapter. As discussed above, each of the New 7-S's contributes to disruption. But the choice of S's to seize the initiative is determined by the strategic context of the organization. Which of the S's is stressed in any given competitive situation will depend on the situation of the company and its competitors. The following chapter examines techniques for using the New 7-S framework to analyze companies and competitors and to determine which of the New 7-S's are needed to seize the initiative in a given competitive situation.

Management Challenges

The New 7-S's represent a radical departure from traditional approaches to winning, which are based on reducing or avoiding rivalry with opponents. They present a serious challenge to the ideology of many managers who don't believe you can make money by competing aggressively. So resistance may be a problem that advocates of the New 7-S's must overcome.

- Do your managers believe that they can make profits using the aggressive New 7-S's? Or do they favor reducing or avoiding rivalry (i.e., cooperative approaches) over aggressive approaches?
- Do you have a choice but to compete to dominate? Is there an opponent who won't cooperate? Are the cooperative approaches to winning sustainable? Do the cooperative approaches reduce your competitiveness in worldwide markets, especially against foreign competitors who do not share the cooperative ideology?
- How can the status quo of your marketplace be disrupted? How can you use the New 7-S's to do so?
- If you don't disrupt the market, will a competitor do so, forcing you to play catch-up?

- What is your vision for creating the next disruption? Does it involve moving up to the next rung on an escalation ladder, restarting the cycle in one of the four arenas of competition, or switching the locus of competition to a new or previously dominant arena of competition? What temporary advantage are you creating with your disruption?
- What tactics are you prepared to use? What repertoire of tactics have you used in the past? Does it include signals, actions that shift the rules of competition, and simultaneous or sequential strategic thrusts? Are you using them to signal cooperation or to confuse and overwhelm competitors?
- How can you add new capabilities and tactics for disruption to your repertoire?
- Have you seized the initiative from the competitor by destroying, neutralizing, sidestepping, or obsoleting the competitor's competitive advantage? If not, has the competitor used the New 7-S's to do these to you?

CHAPTER 9

APPLYING THE NEW 7-S's:

New Analytical Tools to Seize the Initiative

Successful hypercompetitive companies use a combination of the New 7-S's to seize the initiative in their markets. They move the competition forward, up escalation ladders, or restart competition in the four arenas described in Part I. Or they move the competition to another arena. Using a dynamic strategy, these companies constantly move forward from temporary advantage to temporary advantage. They disrupt the status quo of the industry, establish a new status quo, and then go on to disrupt it as they move from rung to rung on the escalation ladders. By driving constantly forward, they sustain their momentum and force competitors to follow behind them. (This is not necessarily the same as being a first mover in product or service introductions, but rather a pacesetter for movements within each arena of competition.)

The New 7-S's offer valuable tools for analyzing competitive strengths and developing competitive strategy. Through a New 7-S analysis, companies analyze their strengths and weaknesses in the New 7-S's to find new opportunities in their competitive environments. Companies determine how they can use the New 7-S's to develop new skills and in which of the four arenas to apply these skills at a particular point in time. Intel serves to illustrate this type of analysis. A broader, more dynamic analysis is also described below, which is used to examine the complex evolution of competition in an industry over time to determine emerging strategic opportunities. The watch and camera industries are used to illustrate the shifts over time in how the New 7-S's are used in an industry.

The dynamic strategic planning model, described below, offers an alternative to static five-year plans, which do not prepare companies for a series of competitive maneuvers to seize the initiative in hypercompetitive environments. In developing long-range plans, companies also analyze their strengths and weaknesses in each of the four arenas of competition and how they can bolster their positions in each arena through the New 7-S's. Because tradeoffs must be made among the New 7-S's, companies often have to choose which to emphasize at any given point in time.

The goal of this analysis is to determine how the company can seize the initiative in the market by using the New 7-S's. When a company seizes the initiative, competitors lose the initiative. The repeated loss of initiative over time ultimately leads companies into a spiral of decline. While the hypercompetitive firm builds success upon success, its opponent is forced into a similar cycle of internal disruption and defeat.

The New 7-S's separate companies that seize the initiative from those that are sliding down a spiral of decline. With every temporary advantage eroding, the only sustainable advantage in hypercompetitive markets is the knowledge of how to use the New 7-S's, because they provide the skill to successfully manage the firm's dynamic strategic interactions. Because of their built-in inflexibility and the tradeoffs in this dynamic system, companies continually shift and improve their use of the New 7-S's. Companies use the New 7-S's to build a continuous series of temporary advantages. It is this series of advantages, this constant seizing of the initiative, that is the true source of sustained advantage.

A NEW 7-S ANALYSIS OF INTEL'S SECRET TO SUCCESS: THE NEW 7-S'S INSIDE

The New 7-S's can be used to assess competitors, especially to identify their strengths, weaknesses, and use of these factors in the four arenas of competition. Intel Corporation provides an illustration of how a hyper-competitive company uses the New 7-S's to seize the initiative over and over again. It has drawn upon most, if not all, of the New 7-S's in maintaining its leadership in chip making despite (or even because of) fierce assault by competitors. It has moved from advantage to advantage, keeping one step ahead of competitors in not only its product innovation but also other aspects of its strategy.

Although this example is of a high-technology industry, hypercompetition extends across many industries, as noted in Part II. The intensity of competition and the highly visible nature of high-technology companies make them an easier subject for analysis. It is not to imply that hyper-competition is limited only to high-technology industries.

S-1: Superior Stakeholder Satisfaction

Before the Pentium chip, Intel rarely asked customers what they wanted, but now they have instituted a process of concurrent engineering to get customers (and internal manufacturing) involved as early as possible. Before designing the Pentium, Intel designers visited every major customer and major software houses to ask them what they wanted in a chip. Intel has also provided early software simulations of its new chips to computer makers, allowing them to get a jump on designing their new machines, and produced software compilers to help software companies use the new chip.

CEO Andrew Grove holds regular meetings with employees from all parts of the organization to brainstorm about the future, competitive challenges, and customer needs. Employees are motivated and empowered to serve customers' priorities above their own. Employees have a right to demand AR—"action required"—of any executive. Over the years Intel has also worked to avoid layoffs through asking staff to put in overtime or cut back on hours.

S-2: Strategic Soothsaying

Intel CEO Grove has quipped that the company bets millions on science fiction.[1] As pressure builds from clonemakers and rival systems, engineers are brought together to consider the emerging technological capabilities and the performance needed to keep ahead of competitors. Intel has also expanded into other areas such as supercomputers, flash memories, video chips, and networking boards. Its sales in these areas are climbing at an average rate of 68 percent per year.[2] It has gained 85 percent of the emerging market for flash memory chips and practically owns one third of the market for massively parallel computers. This experience provides knowledge that Intel can then apply to standard chips, adding features such as video.

S-3: Speed

Intel used to bring out one or two new chips each year and a new microprocessor family every three or four years. In 1992 it drove out nearly thirty new variations on its 486 chip and introduced the next generation of chip, the Pentium. To stay ahead of clonemakers, Intel plans to create new families of chips every year or two throughout the 1990s.[3] Instead of waiting until the current generation of chip is rolled out before working on the next one, Intel now develops several generations of chips at once. It is already working on obsoleting its chips before they have even hit the market. Intel has created design-automation software that allows it to add two or three times the transistors to each new chip design with no increase in development time. It also has achieved a breakthrough in modeling systems that promises to cut the four-year product-development cycle by six months. The new Quickturn system will allow Intel to perform engineering tests up to thirty thousand times faster.

S-4: Surprise

Intel's multiple capabilities—with strengths in microprocessors, other chips, flash memories, personal computers, and supercomputers—keep competitors guessing about its next move. Since its early days, it has often pursued a strategy of simultaneously pursuing alternative technology, and it currently has its own versions of the competing RISC-based chip (Reduced Instruction-Set Computing) although it continues to defend its stronghold of CISC (Complex Instruction-Set Computing), which offers more software. Not wanting to compete with its customers, Intel hasn't entered the personal computer market under its own name, but it has developed the capabilities to do so as the only supplier to computer manufacturers with a brand name—so competitors never know when it might decide to enter the PC market.

Intel has used advances in modeling and design of new chips to surprise competitors. Its new modeling system gave it a strategic victory over a competing RISC-based chip. At a technology forum in November 1991, an Intel executive demonstrated a working model of the Pentium chip, using a link to the model, before an actual chip was ready. In what may have been a response to Intel's signal, six months later Compaq Computer Corporation canceled plans to launch a RISC-based personal computer.[4] And it is still unclear whether new research efforts in RISC chips will surprise Intel.

Intel also maintains a flexible workforce, shifting employees to different projects and keeping operations lean. Despite its continued growth in revenues, Intel cut its number of employees between 1984 and 1992 to maintain flexibility.

S-5: Shifting the Rules

Intel's move into new areas such as supercomputers, interactive digital video, and flash memory has helped shift the rules of competition. Flash memory provides an alternative to the standard memory market, where Intel lost out to Japanese competitors. Intel is adding ancillary products, such as networking circuit boards and graphic chips, that make it easier for computer makers to add these features. It has also designed a personal computer with workstation power, the Panther, which it is licensing to computer makers. This shifts the rules by creating a machine that Intel is not marketing itself. The purpose of the design is to take full advantage of Intel's Pentium chip.

S-6: Signaling

Grove has signaled Intel's intent to fight the clonemakers "with everything we've got."[5] It has also stated a vision of making the company the center of all computing, from palmtops to supercomputers. Its precise strategy for doing this is less visible. Although it has clearly revealed that it has 686 and 786 chips in the works, what these chips will be able to do is still open to speculation. As discussed, Intel used signaling to shift the rules of competition by transforming computer chips from a hidden commodity to a marketing asset through its Intel Inside campaign. By making the chip visible and using branding in marketing PCs, it made major gains in its battle against the clones. But the brand is only as powerful as the computer chip behind it.

S-7: Simultaneous and Sequential Strategic Thrusts

Intel has used a variety of simultaneous and sequential strategic thrusts to seize the initiative. In the late 1970s, struggling with its 8086 microprocessor chip, Intel launched an all-out assault—code-named Operation Crush—against Motorola and other competitors. Intel set up war rooms to work toward making the 8086 the industry standard. It was this effort to simultaneously attack several segments of the market that helped lead to IBM's decision to adapt the 8088 as the center of IBM's personal computer.[6] Intel rode the wave of the PC's growth to dominance in the microprocessor industry.

Intel also participated in both the memory and microprocessor markets at various points in time. In a way, Intel's retreat from the memory chip market and return with flash memory might be seen as a sequential set of moves akin to a strategic retreat followed by regrouping and counterattack. It has used multiple exploratory attacks to develop a variety of know-how and technology capabilities and gauge competitor and customer reactions (for example, its simultaneous development of RISC and CISC technology). It has also explored promising markets (such as video and massively parallel computing) and moved into those with the highest potential for growth. It has built its businesses by using a sequential strategy, moving from memory chips to microprocessors, to boards, to building personal computers (although not marketing them).

Assessing Strengths and Weaknesses by Using the New 7-S's

The above analysis has shown that Intel is good at using all of the New 7-S's for moving from advantage to advantage. Although it is the market leader, it still views itself as "under attack."[7] And it is. A misstep in this hypercompetitive minefield can prove fatal. But by building temporary advantage upon temporary advantage, Intel has seized the initiative again and again. In contrast to this cycle of gathering momentum, a firm that loses the initiative faces a cycle of competitive decline and a downward spiral, as will be discussed later in this chapter.

Normally a company will not be good at all the New 7-S's, so the New 7-S's can best be used as a guide for building new strengths and plugging glaring weaknesses. It can also be a basis for identifying where to attack competitors (their weaknesses) and what to avoid (their strength in the New 7-S's).

Analyzing the Four Arenas by Using the New 7-S's

Unlike many chip makers that have gone into decline, Intel has used the New 7-S's to seize the initiative in the four arenas of competition. The New 7-S analysis is also designed to evaluate the relative strengths and weaknesses of competitors in using the New 7-S's in each arena of competition, as well as in each of the New 7-S's per se. Companies can analyze which of the New 7-S's they are using and which are being used by their competitors in each arena. Companies then are able to see where they need to concentrate on building their strengths or where their competitors are particularly vulnerable to attack in each arena. For example, a competitor that has not developed the capability for speed could be less able to respond to a rapid attack or competitive move in the know-how–timing arena.

THE COST AND QUALITY ARENA

Intel's added attention to customers (S-1)—drawing them into the design process and assisting software developers—has added a service component to its definition of quality. Intel has rapidly achieved increases in product quality through speed (S-3) and strategic soothsaying (S-2) to identify new product attributes desired by users. It has also used its speed to roll out products quickly and then drive down the price before competitors. Its Intel Inside campaign shifted the rules of competition (S-5) to emphasize chip quality and brand image among purchasers of personal computers.

Intel is vulnerable to a competitor that can provide better service to customers (S-1) and identify emerging customer needs (S-2) in the fast-paced environment of high technology. Because definitions of quality constantly shift with technology, Intel must stay ahead at each shift. The technological strengths of each new innovation are quickly copied, driving prices down, so a competitor with a process innovation that reduces costs (surprise, S-4) could seize the initiative by increasing its profits or offering a lower-priced chip.

THE TIMING AND KNOW-HOW ARENA

Intel has used its capabilities for speed (S-3) to move from new technology to new technology, working on the next generation of chips before the previous generation has hit production. This has kept rivals constantly behind Intel. But competitors are becoming ever faster. Intel's position of being innovation leader and the first mover in the microprocessor chip market is an expensive and risky one. Intel's windows for gaining returns on its massive R&D investment are increasingly shorter, and it depends more on speed (S-3) and surprise (S-4) to quickly gain an advantage over competitors and to remain unpredictable. It has sought to define the future of the industry through strategic soothsaying (S-2) and gaining know-how and capabilities in new areas such as video that can later be used to enhance its microprocessor chips. By signaling (S-6) that it has plans for new technological breakthroughs in chips throughout the 1990s, Intel encourages customers to wait for its next chip rather than adopt those of its competitors.

Intel, with its rapid and steady development of each new family of chips, could be blindsided by an innovation that comes from left field. If a competitor is better at reading emerging customer needs (S-1) and technological advances (S-2), it could come up with a product that Intel hasn't imagined. Because Intel is skilled at assessing the future and keeps a sharp eye on new technological breakthroughs, the competitor would have to come up with a breakthrough that is not publicly known. This would require stealth and innovation to create surprise (S-4). The competitor might also shift the rules (S-5) by applying know-how from another industry. For example, increasing consolidation of television, CDs, telephones, and computers could provide opportunities that Intel may not recognize with its primary focus on the computing industry. Similarly, a shift in the standards of computing—such as the rise of RISC-based chips—would provide an opportunity for a strong competitor to Intel to emerge. But Intel, which already has its own RISC chips, would be expected to quickly and forcefully respond to such a threat.

THE STRONGHOLDS ARENA

Intel lost its stronghold in the computer memory chip market to the Japanese in the 1980s, who used surprise (S-4) by coming from overseas and achieving higher customer satisfaction (S-1) coupled with lower costs. Intel has come back in this market by shifting the rules (S-5) to flash memory. Intel also gained another significant stronghold when IBM adopted Intel's microprocessor as the heart of its PC in 1980. From its loss of the memory chip market, Intel realized that it had to work hard to sustain this new stronghold in microprocessors. But it overestimated the strength of the entry barriers that it created in microprocessors.

Intel's apparent attempt to shore up its stronghold in microprocessor chips by cutting back on licensing its chip technology to other manufacturers may have been a mistake. Intel had granted twelve licenses for its 16 bit chip, but only one for the more powerful 386 chip (to IBM—to manufacture half of the chips in its own computers).[8] It overestimated the strength of its technology-based entry barriers. By trying to hold onto the manufacturing itself and creating barriers for others, Intel may have brought on itself (or at least speeded up) the competition of clonemakers who reverse-engineered Intel technology. These clonemakers used speed (S-3), to rush chips out quickly after Intel's release, and surprise (S-4), by attacking Intel when it thought it was protected by patents, and shifted the rules (S-5) by using reverse engineering to copy Intel's chips rather than original R&D to create the next generation of chips.

Realizing that the technological and legal barriers to imitators are much weaker than it originally thought, Intel is now relying on speed (S-3) and signaling (S-6) to counter the efforts of the imitators. As CEO Grove has commented, "We will guard our intellectual property like a hawk, but ultimately, speed is the only weapon we have."[9]

Intel remains vulnerable to a shift in the rules of competition (S-5), for example, a new platform that supersedes the PC or doesn't operate on standard chips. Just as the advent of the PC created Intel's stronghold, this new system could further undermine it and create a temporary advantage for another company. Companies with capabilities in both the computer and microprocessor chip industries could create the new machine that would undermine Intel, and at the same time, they could manufacture the competing chip to take advantage of this new opportunity.

THE DEEP-POCKETS ARENA

Intel built up deep pockets during its early years with memory chips and the 8086 processor. But its resources have risen and fallen with changes in the competitive landscape. Intel is well aware that each new wave of technology is a bet-the-firm decision in which it could completely lose its deep pockets.

Intel has thrown its deep pockets behind every one of the New 7-S's. It has increased customer satisfaction (S-1) by rapidly developing chips and keeping its hands in new technology (S-2), boosted speed (S-3), and increased surprise (S-4) through innovation. It has shifted the rules (S-5) through its leadership in developing each new generation of chips. Intel also has used its deep pockets to send strong signals (S-6) to competitors about its intent to win. In 1992, *Business Week* reported that Intel plowed about $800 million into R&D, on revenues of about $4.8 billion.[10] Its deep pockets have allowed it to pursue several simultaneous markets and innovations and plot a series of sequential attacks (S-7).

Clonemakers have already turned Intel's resource advantage against it by shifting the rules (S-5) through reverse-engineering its chips for a fraction of the cost of the original R&D. Former partners such as AMD have used the courts to gain access to licenses[11] and surprise (S-4) Intel. Alliances among major companies such as Apple and IBM have also shifted the rules of competition (S-5) by creating new competitors with deep pockets to counterbalance Intel's stranglehold over the PC market.

The Outputs of This "Static" New 7-S's Analysis

As illustrated above, the New 7-S's can be used to analyze a particular company's use of the New 7-S's. Such analysis offers insights into current strengths and weaknesses in the opponent and opportunities in the industry. But even this type of analysis is too static for hypercompetitive environments—companies do not operate in a vacuum, and conditions change over time. An analysis of how several competitors have used the New 7-S's over time provides a more dynamic examination of the changes industries undergo and the reversal of fortunes of individual firms within the industry.

DYNAMIC 7-S ANALYSIS:
ANALYZING HOW COMPETITORS SEIZE
THE INITIATIVE FROM EACH OTHER

Even if the company is good at using the New 7-S's, competitors can still seize the initiative, as indicated by the above discussion of the four arenas. Competitors have taken advantage of vulnerabilities of Intel in each of the arenas. They have also used their own strengths in certain S's or changed the way the S's are used.

If a company is concentrating on only a few S's, competitors often shift the competition to other S's that are not the current focus of competition. For example, if a company is focusing primarily on increasing speed (S-3), its competitor could seize the initiative by focusing on customer service (S-1).

Even if a company such as Intel is using all the New 7-S's, competitors still have the opportunity to shift the way some or all of the New 7-S's are used. Because the company's skill in using the New 7-S's is *relative* to the skill of its competitors, a company that is good at using them against one competitor may be less skillful against a new competitor. For example, Ford was relatively strong in achieving superior stakeholder satisfaction (S-1) when competing for customers against only GM and Chrysler, but it fell behind when Honda and Toyota came along and raised the stakes.

Because skill in the New 7-S's is relative and competitors create shifts in emphasis among the various S's, the use of the New 7-S's is a dynamic process. This dynamic view is the focus of the second analytical tool presented here, Dynamic 7-S analysis. In addition to the competitor analysis described above, the New 7-S's are useful for evaluating the stages of evolution of an industry to identify future opportunities. As indicated by the two examples below—in cameras and watches—this dynamic process often leads to a pendulum swing in how the New 7-S's are used.

Companies that recognize this swing can take advantage of opportunities to push the industry in the opposite direction from the one in which it is traveling. Companies that do not understand these dynamic swings concentrate on sustaining their current advantage and keeping the pendulum moving in the same direction. They ride high during the swing of the pendulum that favors them. Then they are shocked by a sudden reversal of fortune as the pendulum swings in the opposite direction. The hypercompetitive firm, on the other hand, anticipates these shifts in direction and actually works to encourage and take advantage of them.

Consider two examples of how this dynamic analysis is applied to the camera and watch industries.

Dynamic 7-S Analysis of the Camera Industry

ROUND ONE: KODAK VS. POLAROID

The first stage of competition was between Polaroid and Kodak over instamatic cameras. Kodak invented the market for amateur photography as the world's first integrated photographic firm. Because it controlled both film manufacturing and development, it had a lock on the U.S. market that could not be shaken by either foreign or domestic competitors. Kodak kept one step ahead of competitors in film quality, using inexpensive cameras as a way to sell more film and using the New 7-S's to its advantage over Polaroid (see Figure 9–1).

Polaroid's development of instant photography gave it an advantage in technological know-how that allowed it to grow by an average annual compounded rate of 25 percent from 1947 to 1979.[12] It continued to fuel its growth by extending its basic innovation of instant photography with enhancements such as instant color photography and the SX-70 system. Still, Kodak controlled an estimated 85 percent of the camera market in 1976.[13]

In 1976 Kodak declared war on Polaroid. It announced that it would introduce its own instant camera. The two companies competed head-to-head on instant photography. But the greatest gains were made in twenty-four-hour film processing, which eroded the advantage of instant photography. Despite losing its right to make and sell instant cameras in a court battle with Polaroid, Kodak's superior film quality and increased ease of snapping a good photo captured many more amateurs than instant film. So Kodak won the battle against Polaroid for market share.

As a sidelight Polaroid moved into the motion picture business. In 1977 Polaroid introduced its instant motion picture camera to compete with Kodak's Super-8 movie cameras. The Polavision system produced a film that could be viewed two minutes after it was shot. Its drawbacks were that it did not have sound and was limited to two minutes and forty seconds. Polaroid dropped the product in 1980, after it was run over by advancing videotape technology that offered instant films with greater length and sound.

FIGURE 9–1

DYNAMIC 7-S ANALYSIS: KODAK VERSUS POLAROID

S-1 Stakeholder Satisfaction	Kodak created a series of camera and film innovations that satisfied customers. Polaroid improved the speed of film processing, but Kodak undermined this customer advantage through its own instant cameras and 24-hour film processing.
S-2 Strategic Soothsaying	Both companies used demographic and technological shifts to define new opportunities and refine their products. But Kodak was able to match or exceed Polaroid's read on the market.
S-3 Speed	As the companies competed head-to-head, both increased the speed of new product innovations coming to market. When Kodak introduced its instant camera, it could not gear up fast enough to meet demand and had to throttle back.
S-4 Surprise	Kodak's entry into the instant market, although widely rumored, came as a surprise and put Polaroid on the defensive.
S-5 Shifting the Rules	Polaroid initially shifted the rules of competition from film quality to speed of processing. Kodak shifted the competition back to camera and film quality (quality of photograph). This also set it up for its next round of competition with Canon.
S-6 Signaling	Both sides used product announcements to signal their intent, including Polaroid's entrance into film production and Kodak's announcements of capacity expansion.
S-7 Simultaneous and Sequential Strategic Thrusts	Both companies have moved against each other in several directions at once. In particular, Kodak, by extending its dominance of the traditional film and camera markets to enter instant photography, allowed itself several options for future growth. Kodak and Polaroid relied on a sequence of instant camera models and consistently upgrading film quality.

ROUND TWO: CANON VS. KODAK

Kodak's relative strengths against Polaroid were not strong enough to hold out against Japanese competitors. Kodak was successfully attacked by Canon and other companies in the growing 35 mm autofocus market. Canon used the New 7-S's to create advantage over Kodak (see Figure 9–2). The 35 mm camera was once used only by the most sophisticated amateur photographers. But Japanese R&D investments created advances in technology that made the 35 mm camera as convenient to use as Kodak's instamatics, giving amateurs the advantage of higher-quality 35 mm film. Prices of these cameras also came down to the amateur's range. Kodak tried to defend its instamatic product by offering more processing. More competitors, such as Minolta and Olympus, entered the 35 mm market. By 1989, in the first few years after their introduction, these "point

FIGURE 9–2
DYNAMIC 7-S ANALYSIS: CANON VERSUS KODAK

S-1 Stakeholder Satisfaction	Kodak's continuous innovation that boosted quality and cut prices was undermined by the superior photographic quality of Canon's 35 mm, without losing the convenience of point-and-shoot or easy loading.
S-2 Strategic Soothsaying	Kodak failed to see the importance of technology in transforming 35 mm market from a complex camera for skilled operators to a simple, inexpensive camera for everyone.
S-3 Speed	Canon's rapid introduction of new products kept it one step ahead of Kodak.
S-4 Surprise	Since Canon had not been a major player in the camera industry before introducing autofocus 35 mm cameras, it was able to blindside Kodak, which was more focused on its competition with Polaroid. Canon's creativity and flexibility added to its surprise.
S-5 Shifting the Rules	Canon shifted the rules by eliminating the tradeoff between convenience of loading and shooting and the quality of final photo.
S-6 Signaling	Both sides have used signals to demonstrate their intent to dominate the markets.
S-7 Simultaneous and Sequential Strategic Thrusts	Canon's moves in several different industries (copiers, cameras, etc.) made it less predictable. It built its strategy on a series of related moves, using its optics and electronics technology from photocopiers in its move to the camera market. Canon's move, in conjunction with rising competition by film manufacturers (such as Fuji) and film processors, meant that Kodak was hit from several different directions simultaneously.

and shoot" cameras captured nearly 40 percent of the world camera market,[14] and by the early 1980s 35 mm had grown to more than 50 percent of the amateur market.[15] Kodak attempted to change the rules of the game by entering the disk market, but this has turned out to be rather unsuccessful to date.

Kodak lost this round of competition as Canon and others seized the initiative with 35 mm cameras. Kodak continued to retain the instamatic market and dominated film manufacturing and production. But a big chunk of the camera market was carved out by the 35 mm camera companies.

ROUND THREE: SONY VS. KODAK

The next level of competition is focusing on digital photography—images that can be stored on magnetic disks or CDs and edited on personal computers. Here Sony used the New 7-S's (see Figure 9–3) and seized the initiative early on, but the battle for this new market is still far from over. In the fall of 1981, Sony announced the Mavica, an all-electronic camera for recording still pictures on a magnetic disk. The images could be viewed instantly on a television. The initial price was $650 for the camera, $220 for the playback unit, and approximately $1,000 for a printer. This was far above the price of a standard film-based camera, even with the savings on film developing. The quality of the image on a television screen was much lower than that of a print, but Sony knew that high-definition television eventually would dramatically alter the quality of the image to make it competitive with that of 35 mm or instant photography.[16]

In response to the digital-camera threat, Kodak implemented a $1 billion push into digital images in the late 1980s and 1990s but ultimately decided to aggressively market only a $400 digital storage system. The Photo CD stores up to one hundred 35 mm film negatives on a compact disc. Customers still use traditional film and receive prints, but they can also have the prints transferred to a CD that can play on their televisions. This allows Kodak to continue to benefit from its current advantages in film, paper, and chemicals while beginning to build a market for digital images. But has the company, as a 1993 article in *Business Week* suggests, "decided that boosting today's bottom line is more important than a distant threat" from digital photography?[17] Has it tried to shore up its current advantages at the expense of aggressively pursuing future advantages in this emerging market?

Although its major push is the Photo CD, Kodak, along with Sony and other competitors, has continued to develop capabilities and launch digital photography products. Kodak's DCS 200, priced at between $8,500 and $10,000, is attached to a Nikon camera body and provides high-resolution digital images.[18] Sony has also continued to upgrade its Mavica to create the ProMavica MVC-7000, priced at about $7,500 and up.[19] The high prices and sophistication of these cameras limit the market, but they could be the forerunners of a large future market for amateur digital equipment. Although Sony was first out of the box with the Mavica and initially may have seized the advantage, the ultimate winner in this contest is still far from certain.

In sum, this dynamic analysis of the New 7-S's shows how each of them shifts over time. At one moment Kodak had the advantage by doing each

FIGURE 9–3
DYNAMIC 7-S ANALYSIS: SONY VERSUS KODAK

S-1 Stakeholder Satisfaction	Sony knew that even with the advances of instant film and 35 mm cameras, customers still faced challenges in developing and storing prints that digital technology could resolve, once it overcame its own weaknesses. It also offered customers a means of editing photos.
S-2 Strategic Soothsaying	Sony saw the convergence of electronic cameras with high-definition television as revolutionizing how photos are stored and viewed.
S-3 Speed	Sony's rapid production and production innovations allowed it to arrive first to market. It launched a high-priced version to gain experience rather than wait for one with broad commercial appeal.
S-4 Surprise	Sony's Mavica was its first still camera, moving into Kodak's industry from the outside. It used its flexibility and innovation to make this move.
S-5 Shifting the Rules	Sony shifted the rules of competition from chemical expertise (Kodak's strength) to electronic expertise (its strength). It also shifted product quality concern back to speed and ease of developing and viewing photos.
S-6 Signaling	Through product announcements and the early launch, Sony signaled its intent to be a strong player in this emerging digital photography market.
S-7 Simultaneous and Sequential Strategic Thrusts	Attacking with still and motion photography simultaneously, Sony struck at several of Kodak's key products with electronic rivals. Sony also used a sequence of actions to build the capabilities and resources it needed to succeed in still photography.

of the New 7-S's well. Then, despite doing the 7-S's well, Kodak lost its advantage to 35 mm's and, perhaps, the electronic cameras of the future to competitors, using the New 7S's to destroy the advantage created by Kodak.

This analysis illustrates what must be done by Kodak to survive in the future against the 35 mm and electronic cameras. To reseize the initiative, Kodak will have to do each of the New 7-S's better than their competitors, disrupting the market by finding ways to serve customers better than (or in new ways compared to) the electronic and 35 mm cameras have done. Kodak's disposable camera (made from cardboard) is one example of how Kodak is reseizing the initiative.

Dynamic 7-S Analysis of the Watch Industry

The Swiss had gained and sustained the initiative in the watch industry through a commitment to high-quality watches. In 1969 one of every two watches was Swiss-made, almost all of them with mechanical movements.[20] Until the 1970s, perhaps the most significant technological innovation was the hairspring in 1675. In the early 1970s Swiss watchmakers took a one-two punch from two innovations—quartz watches and digital electronic watches—that transformed the industry.

ROUND ONE: SEIKO (QUARTZ) VS. SWISS WATCHMAKERS

Many of the leading Swiss watchmakers were so busy trying to sustain their existing advantage in mechanical watches that they did not move on to the next temporary advantage in the market. They lost the initiative in these new markets and their dominant position in watchmaking to Japanese and U.S. competitors, allowing these competitors to seize the opportunity to gain dominant positions in the market. Swiss watchmakers later regained the initiative by moving watches into the fashion industry with Swatch watches.

The quartz watch shifted the rules of competition. Seiko introduced the electronic quartz watch in 1969, and only one major Swiss watchmaker, Longines-Wittnauer, followed closely with its own watch. By using the New 7-S's, Japanese manufacturers such as Seiko (see Figure 9–4) and Casio seized this opportunity in the timing and know-how arena, shifting the rules of competition from mechanical watches to quartz watches. Their aggressive move into the medium-priced market gave Japanese manufacturers 35 percent of world sales in the medium-priced market by

FIGURE 9–4
DYNAMIC 7-S ANALYSIS: SEIKO VERSUS SWISS WATCHMAKERS

S-1 Stakeholder Satisfaction	Most Swiss watchmakers were convinced that customers wanted mechanical, handcrafted watches rather than highly accurate timepieces. Seiko and other quartz watchmakers understood that customers were more concerned about accurate time than internal works.
S-2 Strategic Soothsaying	Swiss watchmakers had the technology to move into quartz but not the vision to see that the future of watchmaking would be in quartz watches. But Seiko recognized quartz as the future of watchmaking and saw an opportunity to seize the initiative.
S-3 Speed	The heavy investment and traditions of the Swiss made most of them slow to respond, even when it was clear quartz watches were a threat.
S-4 Surprise	The innovativeness of Seiko and other quartz watch manufacturers caught the Swiss watchmakers by surprise. Also, they didn't expect their competition to come from Japan.
S-5 Shifting the Rules	The rules of competition shifted from handcrafted, mechanical watchmaking to high-tech, mass-produced quartz watches.
S-6 Signaling	Seiko and other companies signaled their intent to move aggressively into the markets held by the Swiss.
S-7 Simultaneous and Sequential Strategic Thrusts	With the advent of quartz watches and nearly simultaneous introduction of digital watches, Swiss makers were hit by competition from two directions that may have further slowed their response.

the beginning of the 1980s and cost the Swiss industry forty-five thousand jobs.[21] Quartz watches won dominance in the market. By 1988 five of every six timepieces produced worldwide were quartz watches.[22]

ROUND TWO: PULSAR (DIGITAL) WATCHES VS. THE SWISS WATCHMAKERS

Then came solid-state digitals. In 1970 U.S watchmaker Hamilton Watch Company unveiled a solid-state electronic watch with digital readouts, under the brand name Pulsar. Its first digital watch went on sale in 1972 for $2,100 with a red LED display. LEDs were later replaced by LCDs, and growth of the digital market continued. Pulsar used the New 7-S's to seize the initiative from the Swiss watchmakers (see Figure 9–5). Sales of the space-age watches continued to climb through the 1970s and by the end of the 1970s, nearly one in four watches sold worldwide was a digital.[23]

Then the initiative shifted again. An influx of inexpensive digital watches from hundreds of manufacturers in Hong Kong made the city the world's largest-volume exporter of watches, with nearly 50 million watches by 1978. It led to what the president of the Hong Kong Watch Manufacturers Association called a time of "vicious competition."[24] This influx of inexpensive watches also killed sales of high-end digitals. Hamilton sold its Pulsar operations. Digitals dropped into the low-end of the watch market, with multifunctional watches, clocks on pens, and calculators.

FIGURE 9–5
DYNAMIC 7-S ANALYSIS:
PULSAR (DIGITAL WATCHES) VERSUS SWISS WATCHMAKERS

S-1 Stakeholder Satisfaction	Swiss makers failed to see that customers were willing to give up the traditional watchface for the high-tech image of accuracy conveyed by the digital face.
S-2 Strategic Soothsaying	In an era of moonwalks, the digital readout became a powerful and attractive image for consumers. Pulsar realized this and saw its future in watches. It failed to see that entry from Hong Kong at the low end as well as shifts in tastes away from high technology would force this innovation down to the lower-priced watches.
S-3 Speed	The rapid introduction of new technology such as LCDs and multifunction watches kept Pulsar ahead. The rapid development of the low-priced Hong Kong market rapidly destroyed the market.
S-4 Surprise	Pulsar's digital watch surprised Swiss competitors because it employed electronic rather than mechanical technology and opened the market to high-tech companies with no history in watchmaking.
S-5 Shifting the Rules	The rules shifted from mechanical to digital watch displays. This opened new opportunities for using digital watches (e.g., on calculators) but made the digital watch so ubiquitous that it finally lost its hold on the middle and high-end market.
S-6 Signaling	Pulsar's launch of its new digital watch with a high price tag signaled it wanted direct competition with high-end Swiss watches.
S-7 Simultaneous and Sequential Strategic Thrusts	As noted above, the nearly simultaneous development of quartz and digital technologies hit Swiss watchmakers from both sides. Sequential developments in both fields kept it from catching up until the introduction of Swatch.

Digitals also had sacrificed fashion and design for high-tech image. This opened up opportunities that the Swiss were now positioned to use to seize the initiative to shift competition back to quartz analogs (traditional faces with quartz works).

ROUND THREE: SWATCH (SWISS) VS. TIMEX

In 1983 it was the Swiss watchmakers' turn to use the New 7-S's (see Figure 9–6). They seized the initiative in the medium-priced market through Swatch watches. Swatch, created by the Société Suisse de Microéléctronique et d'Horlogerie (SMH), recognized that watches are a combination of timepieces and fashion accessories—and emphasized the latter. When these inexpensive ($35–$75) watches, using plastic and mechanized production, were introduced, they were derided by some as the last

FIGURE 9–6
DYNAMIC 7-S ANALYSIS: SWATCH VERSUS TIMEX

S-1 Stakeholder Satisfaction	Swatch redefined quality as a design variety, low cost, and excitement rather than Timex's reliability.
S-2 Strategic Soothsaying	Swatch seized the opportunity for increasing emphasis on fashion and defined fashion trends in the watch industry.
S-3 Speed	Swatch process innovations allowed frequent new product changes.
S-4 Surprise	Swatch's wide range of new products and constant creativity made the company extremely unpredictable, making it hard for competitors to keep up.
S-5 Shifting the Rules	Swatch shifted watch quality from timekeeping to fashion. It shifted distribution from jewelers to department stores, where it went head-to-head with Timex and squeezed Timex out of some stores.
S-6 Signaling	Swatch used product announcements and publicized shifts into new markets such as phones to emphasize its strategic intent and aggressiveness but to keep competitors guessing about its true intentions.
S-7 Simultaneous and Sequential Strategic Thrusts	Moving in several directions at once, Swatch-maker SMH has attacked through innovations at the high end (Omega) and low end at the same time. It has used a sequential strategy of building strength in watches and then applying its know-how and resources to other products—even automobiles. It has also moved in so many different directions in its product line that it has been impossible for Timex to react or keep up.

gasp of the Swiss watchmaking industry. They were a far cry from the meticulously crafted timepieces for which the Swiss were famous. But they were a great success.

By shifting the emphasis from the quality of the timepiece to the innovation of the design, Swatch was able to seize a large share of the medium-priced and low-end watch market. It made design innovation the central focus of watchmaking—with such models as the transparent Swatch, fruit-scented Swatch, and oversized "pop" Swatches on elastic bands. Sales of Swatch watches broke all records as the largest and fastest-selling timepiece, with annual sales topping seventeen million units in 1991.[25] Even though some designs have failed, the sheer pace of product and design innovation has assured steady growth of the Swatch market. Swatch's ability to quickly and cheaply roll out new varieties of watches was gained through a process innovation that cut the number of parts in the watches and through fully automated assembly. SMH carried this emphasis on innovation into its higher-end Omega watches and RockWatches (in a granite case).

Swatch is now applying the same principle of fashion and variety to such industries as telephones, pagers, fax machines, and automobiles (in a joint venture with Volkswagen). The car, which will be powered by an electric or electric-gasoline motor, rethinks automobile design in the same way Swatch shifted the rules of watchmaking.

U.S. watchmaker Timex has pursued a slow and steady strategy that mimics its "Takes a Licking but Keeps on Ticking slogan. It took a licking from Swatch. It has rapidly followed trends in the watch industry, including the development of quartz and digital watches. It held a strong position in the low-end of the market until it was blindsided by the success of Swatch watches. Timex was cut out of many department stores during the rise of design and status in the 1980s. Timex had to develop new capabilities in design flexibility and product diversity, setting up professional design studios in France and the United States. But it never abandoned its emphasis on low-priced reliability. It has moved most of its production overseas to take advantage of lower labor costs.

ROUND FOUR: THE SHIFT BACK TO VALUE

An emerging shift in consumer taste from fashion back to value (Timex's strength) may shift the rules back into Timex's favor. Through its competition with Swatch, Timex has built new capabilities in design and product innovation. By playing against this weakness in Timex, Swatch has helped Timex develop it into a strength. This, coupled with its traditional image of reliability and value, have made it a strong competitor in the value-conscious 1990s.

As an indication of its reviving fortunes, Timex was welcomed back to Bloomingdale's and other department stores in 1989. Its innovative ring watch became Bloomingdale's hottest-selling item in that year.[26] Although a shift in demographics has aided Timex in the short run, its long-term success may rest on its own ability to identify the next temporary advantage and seize the initiative in the market. If it doesn't, its slow-and-steady strategy may be undermined by a more aggressive competitor (the next Swatch).

Swatch's diverse strengths put it in a strong position to seize the initiative again, but its weakness is that it could be blinded by success and fail to identify and create the next temporary advantage in the industry. Its emphasis on product variety has already lost some of its steam in the value-conscious nineties, but its capabilities for speed and surprise could be deployed in other ways than creating design variety.

ROLEX: EXCEPTION OR THE NEXT VICTIM OF HYPERCOMPETITION?

At the extreme other end of the market, Rolex has sustained what is an apparently stable advantage with its high-priced, limited-edition watches. After establishing a reputation with such innovations as automatic winding and the oyster casing, Rolex watches have changed very little since 1933. But the company has significantly improved its production technology.[27] The Swiss-based company makes about 500,000 watches per year, far less than the demand. Rolex has continued to emphasize its exclusive image, through famous Rolex wearers such as Ian Fleming's James Bond character and real-life heros such as politicians and athletes.

Rolex has found a way to survive in hypercompetition without being hypercompetitive by staking out the luxury portion of the market. To do so, Rolex has used some of the New 7-S's to create its image and position (see Figure 9–7). Its sales have climbed by 20 percent annually over the past twenty-five years.[28] It has circumscribed its own market by offering a limited-edition item. This may have limited growth, but it sustains a strong demand. But Rolex has also begun to face increasing competition at the high end of the market from a variety of Japanese and Swiss competitors, some of whom have entered at the middle of the market and moved up.

Rolex, with little speed or surprise, is vulnerable to attack by an aggressive competitor. In the same way that BMW and Mercedes were successfully attacked by Lexus, Infiniti, and Acura, Rolex's high-end market

FIGURE 9–7
DYNAMIC 7-S ANALYSIS: ROLEX'S VULNERABILITY TO FUTURE MOVES

S-1 Stakeholder Satisfaction	Emphasized high quality and reputation
S-2 Strategic Soothsaying	N/A
S-3 Speed	N/A
S-4 Surprise	N/A
S-5 Shifting the Rules	Ostensibly working to sustain the rules rather than shift them, but introducing incremental process innovations that reduce costs while maintaining product quality.
S-6 Signaling	Tight-lipped company has a policy of not making public pronouncements. Its lack of signaling is a strong "signal" about its reputation for being above the fray of competition in the watch industry.
S-7 Simultaneous and Sequential Strategic Thrusts	N/A

could be eroded by companies that can offer equal or superior value for a lower price. A competitor could also shift the rules of competition in the high end to turn Rolex's investments in its current advantage against it. Perhaps the lower ends of the market offer more opportunities as watch sales have grown worldwide, but if this growth tapers off, competitors may be more interested in putting resources into attacking the entrenched high-end position of Rolex.

The watch industry illustrates the dynamic nature of the New 7-S's, with firms seizing the initiative by improving their use of each of the New 7-S's compared to the historical patterns of competitors. This industry (especially Rolex) also points out the vulnerabilities created by failing to use the New 7-S's while attempting to sustain old advantages.

Reversals of Fortune: Pendulum Swings in the Use of the New 7-S's

As discussed above, industries go through a dynamic evolution in which competitors who are skilled at using the New 7-S's find themselves at a sudden disadvantage. Kodak was dominant in the use of the New 7-S's in its competition with Polaroid, but when Canon came, Kodak's fortunes were reversed.

Overall, the analysis of many industries reveals similar patterns of reversals. Often these reversals develop into a pendulum swing in which the industry moves back and forth between two or more key competitive factors.

In the camera industry the pendulum swings between photo quality and speed and ease of processing (see Figure 9–8). Kodak dominated in quality and speed of processing until Polaroid offered much faster and easier film processing. Kodak temporarily won the first round by offering its own instant photography and through the advent of twenty-four-hour processing services. Next, the focus shifted back to photo quality. Canon's introduction of the 35 mm autofocus camera offered a higher level of film quality. The emerging digital photography field again shifted the competition back to speed and ease of processing by allowing photographers to view photos instantly on their televisions. Sony's Mavica camera offered this ease of processing at a significant sacrifice in photo quality. The next key factor in this competition appears to be the increase in resolution quality of digital photos. This increased resolution will allow Sony and others to gain the lead in quality again. Speed and ease of processing may someday become

FIGURE 9–8
REVERSALS OF FORTUNE IN THE CAMERA INDUSTRY

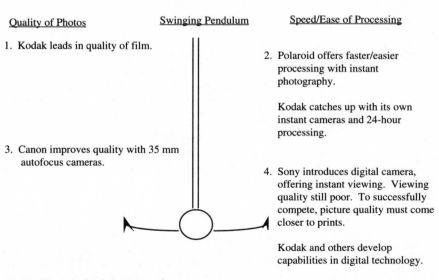

Quality of Photos   Swinging Pendulum   Speed/Ease of Processing

1. Kodak leads in quality of film.

2. Polaroid offers faster/easier processing with instant photography.

 Kodak catches up with its own instant cameras and 24-hour processing.

3. Canon improves quality with 35 mm autofocus cameras.

4. Sony introduces digital camera, offering instant viewing. Viewing quality still poor. To successfully compete, picture quality must come closer to prints.

 Kodak and others develop capabilities in digital technology.

5. Next Round: Digital photography with higher resolution viewing than even prints or slides and ability to enhance photos through computer manipulation

the next swing of the pendulum, but it is unclear when and how this will occur.

Similarly, the watch industry has shifted back and forth between accuracy and fashion. The Swiss mechanical watch established the highest standards of accuracy until the quartz watch successfully challenged it. Seiko and other leaders in quartz watchmaking won that round. Digital watches, which also used quartz crystals, challenged the Swiss watches on fashion as it became fashionable to wear the high-tech watches. As interest in high-tech fashion was replaced by flair, Swatch capitalized on this new trend. Swatch used it to attack Timex and other companies that had few skills in leading-edge fashion design. The next dramatic shift might be another breakthrough in accuracy. In the meantime companies continue to compete on changing fashion trends.

This swinging pendulum and reversal of fortunes usually catch companies unprepared. Swiss watchmakers were riding high while the pendulum was swinging in the direction of mechanical watches. They stumbled badly when it shifted to quartz. Their quartz competitors were unprepared for the success of Swatch, and the fortunes of the Swiss reversed again.

NEW TOOLS FOR DYNAMIC STRATEGIC PLANNING BASED ON THE NEW 7-S'S

As discussed in Part II, approaches to long-term strategic planning that are designed to sustain advantage actually are a poor preparation for long-term success. At best, they prepare companies to win one round of competition. Traditional five-year and ten-year planning models that emphasize sustained advantage and planned sequences of milestones and budgets are usually too inflexible to meet the dynamic challenges facing companies in hypercompetitive environments. They play out one scenario for the future rather than allow the company to develop a dynamic and flexible strategy to meet or even create several possible scenarios.

A Three-Level Dynamic Strategic Planning Model Using the New 7-S's

In contrast, the New 7-S's offer an approach to strategic planning that is more flexible and dynamic. The three groupings of the New 7-S's described in the preceding chapter are used to consider three levels of a new form of planning:

- *Planning a vision for disruption:*
  S-1 Superior stakeholder satisfaction
  S-2 Strategic soothsaying
- *Resource planning (building capabilities):*
  S-3 Capabilities for speed
  S-4 Capabilities for surprise
- *Tactics: Punch-Counterpunch Planning:*
  S-5 Shifting the rules of competition
  S-6 Signaling
  S-7 Simultaneous and sequential strategic thrusts

As indicated by Figure 9–9, this strategy development is not a linear process. Traditional long-range planning usually moves from developing a

FIGURE 9–9
DISRUPTION AND THE NEW 7-S's

vision to building resources to carry out that vision to developing specific plans for actions. This new dynamic planning model engages in these three steps simultaneously and continuously. The vision is constantly being sharpened. Capabilities for speed and surprise are constantly being developed, and a series of tactics is selected, adjusted, and readjusted to meet emerging opportunities or threats and to proactively create new futures for the firm. As resources come into place, new opportunities and visions appear. New tactics become possible. As new tactics are used, the firm builds its speed and surprise capabilities by practicing tactics that involve speed and surprise.

All three levels of the new dynamic planning model in Figure 9–9 must be focused on disruption. The New 7-S analysis for assessing competitors (illustrated by the Intel example above) has taught us that at each moment in time, the hypercompetitive firm is better than its opponents at each and every one of the New 7-S's. The Dynamic 7-S analysis (illustrated by the watch and camera examples above) has taught us that

- the New 7-S's have a theme or overall vision to them, such as improving the quality of amateur photos
- over time, firms disrupt the market by shifting to a new theme, such as ease of developing film
- these swings in theme can take the form of a swinging pendulum (e.g., in cameras, where the movement went back and forth between ease of development and photo quality) or a continuous series of redefinitions of accuracy and fashion (e.g., the watch industry)

Thus, in the short run the New 7-S analysis can be used to determine what types of vision, resources, and tactics are needed to win, given the nature of competition as it currently exists in an industry (e.g., the Intel example above). More important, the Dynamic 7-S analysis can be used to track the historical movement and shifts in the vision, resources, and tactics that have been used to revolutionize the industry periodically (e.g., the watch and camera examples above).

VISION FOR DISRUPTION: S-1 AND S-2

The vision for the company's next move is shaped through the first two S's. Superior stakeholder satisfaction (S-1) and strategic soothsaying (S-2) provide insights into the existing and emerging needs of customers and into new ways of meeting those needs better than any other competitor.

They provide the basis for developing a theme for all of the New 7-S's that disrupt the marketplace either within the current methods of competing or by inventing new methods of competing.

The Matrix in Figure 9–10 offers a useful way of analyzing the types of disruption that can be pursued by a hypercompetitive firm. It is based on selecting new or existing markets to serve and new or existing methods for serving them, as shown in Figure 9–10. By identifying which of the four squares to compete in, the company defines its next move or series of moves. Companies can jump from disruptions in one quadrant to disruptions in others, as demonstrated by the beer industry example below.

As can be seen from Figure 9–10, there are four types of disruption that can be envisioned by using the first two of the New 7-S's. Each seizes the initiative in a different way. Hypercompetitive firms stay one step ahead of their competitors by undertaking a series of disruptions that sometimes jump from box to box in Figure 9–10.

For example, the competition in the "beer wars" between Miller and Anheuser-Busch illustrates how different visions for disruption might be created through the use of the Matrix in Figure 9–10. Miller used an understanding of the customer and strategic soothsaying to shift from one quadrant to the next. As shown in Figure 9–11, in 1970 most of the beer makers were serving the same customer without much change or improvement in their methods, other than through continuously increasing economies of scale in production. Miller disrupted the market by positioning its beer as the champagne of beers, creating a premium niche in the beer mar-

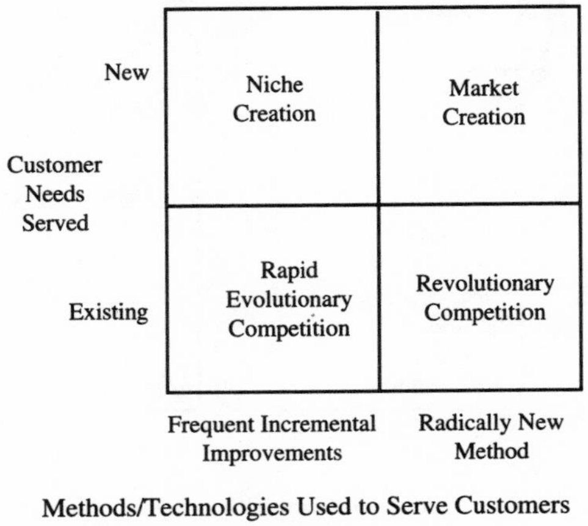

FIGURE 9–10
FOUR VISIONS OF HOW TO DISRUPT
MARKETS

ket. It then created new distribution channels and methods for selling this beer, using a national advertising campaign and other entirely new methods of serving the customer. Then Miller built on these methods to move into an entirely new market with a new brewing method when it introduced light beer and discovered that it could be positioned for women. It also moved again to serve existing customers through incremental improvements by introducing the new seven-ounce bottle. In this way Miller has disrupted the beer market by shifting its focus back and forth between existing and new customers and existing and new methods. Each new disruption was designed to seize the initiative for Miller. The sequencing was designed to maintain the momentum for Miller. (Figure 9–11 illustrates these shifts.) Unfortunately Miller lost the initiative to Anheuser-Busch, which counterattacked with many disruptions that were executed better than those used by Miller Beer. Anheuser-Busch, in particular, was gaining share due to a series of modest plant modernizations and new brewing techniques designed to serve the male beer drinker.

A similar mapping can be done for many other industries. In watches

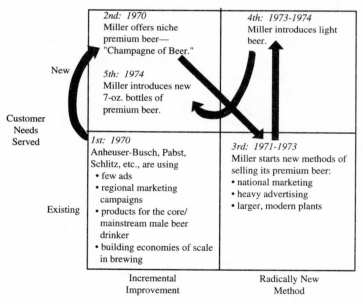

FIGURE 9–11
A SERIES OF DISRUPTIONS IN THE BEER INDUSTRY DURING
THE EARLY 1970s

(as discussed above) the vision of disruption shifted from disruptions that involved radical new methods based on quartz and digital technologies to disruptions that involved the use of fashion to capture an entirely new type of buyer.

RESOURCE PLANNING: S-3 AND S-4

At the same time that companies are defining which customers to serve and how to serve them, they also look at their capabilities for carrying out that vision in the future. By building capabilities for speed (S-3) and surprise (S-4), they are prepared for a variety of different actions. In contrast to most resource planning, which tends to commit the company to a specific action, developing capabilities for speed and surprise still leaves the company with great flexibility. Even if competitors are aware of the company's capacity for speed and surprise, they will not know how the company intends to use these capabilities. Competitors also may not be able to quickly duplicate these capabilities.

By assessing its strength in speed and surprise in comparison to its competitors, companies gain a better understanding of where their capabilities need to be strengthened. They must actively monitor whether they have the speed to carry out their vision for disrupting the market time and time again. Comparing such key indicators as product introductions or variety, speed of response to competitors' moves, creativity in design, and flexibility, companies gain a better picture of their relative strengths.

If the company has a relative weakness in capabilities for either speed or surprise, it then can identify ways to strengthen those weaknesses so it can move at least as quickly and stealthily as competitors. A key part of this analysis is identifying the process or structures of the company that tend to make it slower than competitors or give it less stealth. Then the company can focus on ways to shore up these weak points or turn them to its advantage. The key is active monitoring of the capabilities and proactive creation of these capabilities through investments, human resource practices, and related approaches.

PUNCH-COUNTERPUNCH PLANNING: S-5, S-6, S-7

Companies plan a series of actions to take advantage of opportunities for seizing the initiative identified through the development of a vision. They plan for their moves and their competitors' reactions, a series of punches and counterpunches. These tactics draw upon the capabilities above, and involve shifting the rules of competition (S-5), signaling (S-6), and simultaneous and sequential strategic thrusts (S-7).

Using speed and surprise, companies analyze the competitive environment to identify the action that would be most difficult for the opponent to foresee and most difficult for it to defend against. On the other hand, companies also avoid attacking areas where the opponent is on guard.

Companies confuse or influence their competitors through signaling (S-6). The signal is often the first punch of a series of competitive maneuvers that disrupt an opponent and create temporary advantage.

Punch-counterpunch planning offers flexibility at each stage of competition. Using simultaneous and sequential strategic thrusts, companies give themselves a variety of routes they can take at any given step in the process. By analyzing the company's vision for disruption, as described above, the company checks and adjusts its actions in pursuit of that vision.

Successful companies also emphasize deterring the opponent rather than appeasing it. Both appeasement and attempts to crush the opponent are very dangerous. Appeasement is dangerous because aggressive competitors will rarely roll over and play dead. The competitor may rise up more powerful than before. Violent aggression is also risky because it usually provokes a strong defense or aggressive response from the attacked competitor.

Companies also determine how much time and resources they are willing to devote to the actions. For example, attacking an opponent that will fight to the bitter end will require a strong and sustained desire to win on the part of the attacking firm. In analyzing potential actions, successful companies plan to use only as much force as is necessary. Otherwise it might find it is exhausted and open to counterattack.

Punch-counterpunch planning does not really result in a plan in the traditional sense of the word. Firms don't plan out each move and countermove because, as the old military maxim goes, no plan lasts longer than contact with the enemy.

Punch-counterpunch planning is more like the preparation of a boxer before a title match. The boxer works on his repertoire of moves, stamina, and reflexes. He is building the instinct and ability to use his tactical moves instantly and with surprise. Based on the opponent's repertoire of moves, he may even develop a game plan like Explore the competitor's actions in the first two rounds, use the right for the next two rounds, and then go for the knockout using a combo in the fifth round. However, he never knows the exact sequence of moves that will be used until the match is in play.

Using the New 7-S's in an Expanded Four Arena Analysis

Once these three parts are in place—vision, resources, and tactics—then companies use the Four Arena analysis of Part I to analyze their relative strengths and weaknesses in the four arenas. This tool can be extended by examining how the New 7-S's enhance and build strength in each of the four arenas.

While all the New 7-S's are important in seizing the initiative in each of the arenas, some are more important in certain arenas. Figure 9–12 contains an illustration of a hypothetical Four Arena analysis based on identifying which of the New 7-S's is critical to winning. The critical success factors in each arena may vary from industry to industry. However, the principle remains the same.

Thus, if a company uses a Four Arena Analysis and decides to move in one of the four arenas, it can then develop the necessary New 7-S's to seize the initiative in that arena. At the same time, companies look at the strengths of their competitors in the New 7-S's to determine opportunities in each arena. Among the ways companies use the New 7-S's to seize the initiative are

FIGURE 9–12
A HYPOTHETICAL EXPANDED FOUR-ARENA ANALYSIS

If the Firm Needs to Improve Its Competitive Position in Arena	Key Success Factors Are	The Most Critical New 7-S's Are
Cost/Quality	• Understanding customer needs • Cost reduction	• S-1 Stakeholder Satisfaction • S-3 Speed
Know-how/Timing	• Becoming fast at market penetration • Building new know-how and innovation	• S-3 Speed • S-4 Surprise • S-2 Soothsaying
Stronghold Creation/ Invasion	• Deterrence • Aggression	• S-6 Signals • S-7 Strategic Thrusts
Deep Pockets	• Use of brute force • Thwarting or outmaneuvering big opponents	• S-7 Strategic Thrusts • S-5 Shifting the Rules of Competition

1. to speed ahead of competitors and stay one or two rungs ahead on the escalation ladders described in Part I.
2. to restart the cycle of competition. For example, a company shifts the rules to create a new quality dimension in the first arena (cost-quality).
3. to run two cycles simultaneously in the same arena. For example, the company might redefine quality differently at the high end versus the low end of the market.
4. to jump to a new arena, as described in Part I. Using surprise, for example, the company could roll out a product or process innovation or attack a competitor's stronghold.
5. to jump back to an old arena where competition has been ignored or has died down. After moving into competition on technological know-how, a company may drive the competition back to cost and quality.

A careful examination of the New 7-S's will indicate which of these are doable and which of the New 7-S's are necessary to carry each of these out.

Tradeoff Analysis: Selecting among the New 7-S's

One final analysis can be done using the New 7-S's. In choosing which to concentrate on, companies are forced to make tradeoffs among them. This makes it difficult for companies to do all seven equally well. Companies choose among the seven to confront different challenges and opportunities that present themselves.

Thus, it is possible to analyze a competitor (or one's own company) to see what types of tradeoffs have been made. Once these are identified, the weakness of the competitor (or one's own company) is apparent. Furthermore, the tradeoff means that the competitor can't plug the weakness without giving up something else. Thus, it is possible to identify weakness, which, if attacked, forces the competition to be slow to respond or to give up some other strength in order to respond. Either way the competitor loses.

Among the tradeoffs implied by the New 7-S's are the following:

- *Tradeoffs at the expense of stakeholder satisfaction (S-1)* can be undermined by speed (S-3), as companies may sacrifice product or service quality to gain speed or push employees to work harder and faster. Speeding products to market with little testing could also reduce customer satisfaction. Similarly surprise (S-4), shifting the rules (S-5), signaling (S-6), and simultaneous and sequential strategic thrusts (S-7) also have the potential to confuse customers, employees, and shareholders as well as competitors.

- *Tradeoffs at the expense of future orientation/soothsaying* Strategic soothsaying (S-2) can be hurt by speed (S-3), which often leaves little time for reflecting on what lies ahead, and surprise (S-4), which is sudden and unpredictable enough to make prognostication irrelevant or impossible. Shifting the rules (S-5) often reshapes competition in a way that unpredictably changes future opportunities so that soothsaying becomes difficult. To the extent that competitor reactions are not anticipated, simultaneous and sequential strategic thrusts (S-7) sometimes make soothsaying more difficult.

- *Tradeoffs at the expense of speed* Speed (S-3) can be eroded through the slowness of decision making in an inverted organization such as the ones used to increase stakeholder satisfaction (S-1). Also, strategic alliances used to shift the rules (S-5) sometimes reduce speed because of negotiations. Shifting the rules of competition (S-5) may require a tradeoff with speed. It can temporarily reduce speed (S-3), for example, because of the confusion and time it takes to regroup and retool to create the new rules. Simultaneous and sequential strategic thrusts (S-7) can reduce speed (S-3) because they require more effort than single thrusts.

- *Tradeoffs at the expense of surprise* The flexibility and stealth of surprise (S-4) can be eroded by strategies to increase capabilities for speed. For example, just-in-time systems could decrease the company's flexibility while increasing speed. Alliances to shift the rules sometimes also decrease surprise because the alliances are usually public. Signaling can also reduce the element of surprise because it often involves revealing the strategic intent of the company. Sequential thrusts can reduce surprise (S-4) by committing the company to a clear set of actions.

These tradeoffs mean that firms can't always do all of the New 7-S's equally well, even if they are above a reasonable threshold on each one of them. Thus, a competitor can do a tradeoff analysis to identify the maneuvers it can do through use of the S's that the opponent can't do well because the opponent can't respond without depleting its strength in one of the other S's. Other firms will creatively switch between the New 7-S's to shift the rules of competition, sometimes focusing on the opponent's weaker S's, sometimes using several in concert.

Moreover, firms have limited resources, so they can't acquire all seven of the New S's at once. They must prioritize them and make tradeoffs. Thus, it will be rare that a firm is equally good at all of the New 7-S's. This will create opportunities for a new type of hypercompetitive behavior whereby firms use the resource investments tradeoff made by a competitor to determine which of the New 7-S's should be invested in first. Finally, truly hypercompetitive firms, like Intel, will find ways to eliminate the tradeoffs. Tradeoffs exist only if firms believe that tradeoffs are necessities and stop looking for ways to do both alternatives. After all, it was once said that firms could not achieve low cost and high quality at the same time. Now it is not just a reality but a necessity for survival in many industries.

LOSS OF THE INITIATIVE
AND DOWNWARD SPIRALS OF DECLINE

The Downward Spiral

With the new analytical tools discussed above, hypercompetitive firms can use the New 7-S's to seize the initiative. When a company using the New 7-S's seizes the initiative, its competitor suffers a parallel loss of the initiative. Just as repeatedly seizing the initiative leads to a cycle of momentum, repeated loss of the initiative can lead to a spiral of decline. Studies of corporate failures have identified these deepening spirals in advance of the bankruptcy of a firm.[29]

As Intel CEO Grove noted in a magazine article, "There is at least one point in the history of any company when you have to change dramatically to rise to the next performance level. Miss the moment, and you start to decline."[30] Grove has probably understated the challenge by saying companies reach this point *at least* once. In hypercompetition companies *constantly* face such challenges and critical moments. And if they miss these opportunities, they usually begin a downward spiral of decline. Figure 9–13 illustrates how use of the New 7-S's can drive an opponent into paralysis and competitive surrender.

Disruption of the status quo causes performance declines that shock and confuse competitors, who often deny the real problem by dismissing the threat as temporary or "unfair." As the shock and confusion deepen, top managers leave for numerous voluntary and involuntary reasons, creating a vicious circle of the type shown in Figure 9–14. As more team members leave, the information-processing capability of the team is disrupted, and the team develops holes that stakeholders (such as security analysts) point out as deficiencies. So stockholders get worried. These problems exacerbate the firm's performance problems, continually generating further disruption of the top team.

Figure 9–15 illustrates how this downward spiral of decline also involves strategic errors that follow several phases. The original disadvan-

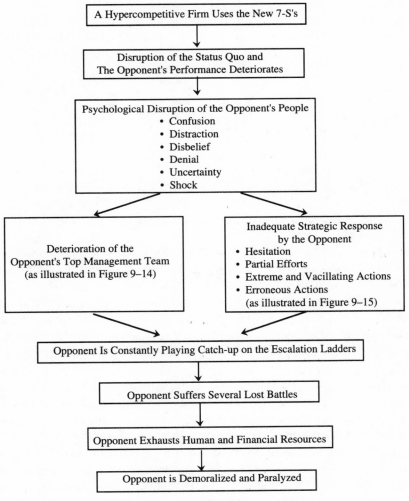

FIGURE 9–13
HOW USING THE NEW 7-S's CAN CAUSE THE OPPONENT
TO LOSE THE INITIATIVE

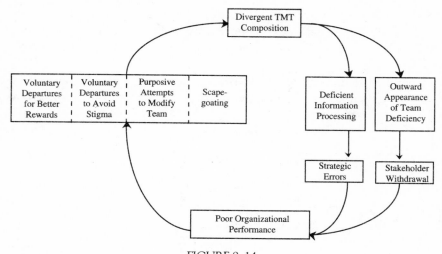

FIGURE 9–14
THE "VICIOUS CYCLE" OF TOP TEAM DETERIORATION
AND POOR PERFORMANCE

Source: Reprinted by permission. From "Top Team Deterioration as Part of the Downward Spiral of Large Corporate Bankruptcies," by Donald Hambrick and Richard D'Aveni, *Management Science* 18, no. 10, p. 1447. © 1992, The Institute of Management Sciences, 290 Westminster Street, Providence, RI 02903.

tage, or loss of the initiative, leads to impairment and then a marginal existence. If the company has sufficient working capital and a buoyant environment, it can survive this marginal existence. But the company often experiences cycles of desperate strategic extremism and vacillation as it struggles to find a way out of this malaise. But rather than using a clearly defined strategy based on the New 7-S's, the company is often so disrupted that it grasps at straws, a process leading to further internal turmoil.

If the company cannot revitalize itself by using the New 7-S's, it slips from a state of marginal existence into a death struggle. Here it faces the conflicts created by its own vacillation on strategy. It also must cope with internal pressures created by a sharp decline in performance. Top managers often turn over rapidly as the company and its shareholders struggle to break the cycle. For some companies this is enough to lead them to failure. Others are hit with a sudden environmental decline or aggressive action by a competitor, which becomes the straw that breaks the camel's back and leads to the ultimate failure of such firms.

With its loss of initiative, a company becomes a perpetual competitive laggard in each of the arenas of competition. As shown in Figure 9–13, it

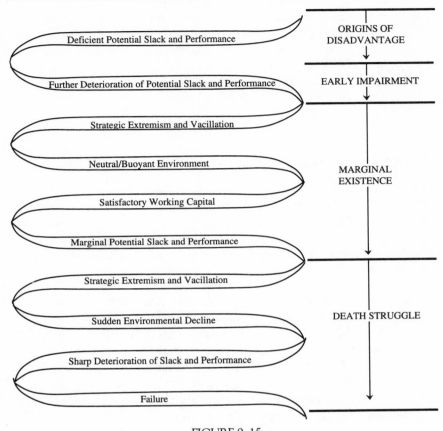

FIGURE 9–15
ORGANIZATIONAL DECLINE AS A DOWNWARD SPIRAL IN PHASES
Source: Donald Hambrick and Richard D'Aveni, "Large Corporate Failures in Downward Spirals," *Administrative Science Quarterly* 33(1988): 14.

may try to play catch-up, to learn the new rules of the game and play as well as its attacker. But the attacker is always a step ahead of its competitor. As the competitor loses more and more battles, a sense of demoralization and malaise sets in. This affects the minds of employees and corporate leaders—the places where the knowledge-based advantage resides. The company and its employees begin to accept failure as inevitable or deserved. This leads to further decline, and unless action is taken to counteract this cycle, it results in retreat or exit by the attacked firm.

This disruption and decline is the ultimate goal of hypercompetitive behavior. This decline may mean the complete failure (bankruptcy) of the opponent, but it more likely means that the opponent will exit the market or leave an opening for the firm to be preempted on the next dynamic strategic interaction. It is important to note, however, that driving one competitor into decline in no way eliminates the pressure to remain hypercompetitive. Other competitors may rise rapidly to take its place, and the first (vanquished) competitor may linger for a long time, causing trouble.

THREE POSSIBLE PATTERNS ASSOCIATED WITH LOSS OF THE INITIATIVE

As was just noted above, not every company ceases to exist as a result of this spiral of decline. Some of them, because of their own characteristics or their environment, linger on in varying states of disarray. They are damaged as aggressive competitors but not completely vanquished. There are three primary patterns of decline that are associated with loss of the initiative:

- *Slow decline* Like a cancer, the disruption and loss of the initiative slowly takes its toll on the company. This is a more likely response to strategic thrusts that don't appear to be a serious threat. The decline and resulting psychological disruption of the loss of initiative slowly takes its toll on the company. It may divest itself of some of its once-strong businesses as decline slowly sweeps across it. This is also more likely in what seems to be a relatively benign environment (like a growth market), one which later turns out to be an illusion, having been captured by more hypercompetitive firms.
- *Sudden collapse* Like a stroke victim, the weakened company takes a dramatic turn for the worse. It then exits from the market or goes out of business suddenly. This is a more common response for smaller competitors or the victims of sudden and very aggressive hyper-competitive attacks. This reaction can also result when a financially weak firm is hit with a dramatic downturn in the business environment, causing permanent loss of initiative.
- *Lingering* Like a victim in a coma, the company has long since lost the initiative and acts as if it is now brain dead, even though it is still alive. Large companies with massive resources often have the ability to linger for long periods after their competitive abilities are weakened or disabled. Some of these lingering companies, however, manage to snap out of the coma and regain their position as aggressive competitors. Others eventually slip off into death.

Breaking the Spiral of Decline by Using the New 7-S's

GM's Saturn project is a good example of an attempt to use the New 7-S's to break out of decline and regain the initiative. Satisfying customers (S-1) is the unequivocal goal at Saturn, and the entire organization has been designed around fulfilling that goal. It looked to emerging trends (S-2) in design, process, and customer demands. It used flexible manufacturing and unusual marketing methods to increase surprise (S-4). Saturn uses just-in-time delivery and sophisticated information-processing methods to increase speed (S-3). Saturn has surprised (S-4) its foreign competitors by creating a U.S.-made car that competes head-to-head on quality and reliability with foreign cars. It has shifted the rules of competition through establishing sales operations that use a fixed-price, no-haggling approach. It has used this shift in the rules as a selling point in its "a different kind of car, a different kind of company" advertising. This advertising and other signals have helped to discipline competitors by clearly going after buyers of Japanese cars. This initiative has been simultaneous with other GM projects to revitalize Buick, Cadillac, and Olds.

While Saturn has been very successful, the challenge now is how to transfer this newfound knowledge to the rest of the company. In contrast to Saturn, General Motors is a huge sleeping giant trying to transform itself into a hypercompetitive firm. Just as it is easier to establish an entrepreneurial start-up than it is to transform an existing firm into an innovative company, General Motors faced an easier task in starting up Saturn than in turning its entire organization into a Saturn-like company. But small victories can provide the insights and inspiration for further success. Perhaps the key benefit of the Saturn project for General Motors is that it has demonstrated the value of approaches such as those embodied in the New 7-S's, and it has done so much more forcefully than looking at an outside company could have. This has created a level of internal constructive disruption that could help General Motors transform itself into the world-class hypercompetitor that it once was.

The psychological dimension of this combat cannot be overemphasized. Small victories that can reverse the demoralization of the company can lead to much greater successes. For example, Motorola broke into the Japanese market with a small pocket pager. Although it was not a great victory, measured by scale, it was a major triumph for morale, and it destroyed the myth that the Japanese market could not be cracked. Motorola built on that success to become one of the most powerful U.S. competitors in Japanese markets and one of the most skillful players in the

New 7-S's. Similarly, Ford and Chrysler are now discovering that they can outpace Japanese quality standards and win with the Team Taurus and LH car/cab forward projects.

The Battle for the Mind of the Organization

Why do managers of large companies like IBM and Sears allow the downward spiral to persist when they could revitalize themselves by using the New 7-S's? The key resource, is not strength of numbers or power, but rather morale, willpower, and knowledge. The battle is for the mind of the company. Reseizing the image is fundamentally rooted in the will, morale, and knowledge of how to manage the company's dynamic strategic interactions with competitors. American corporations don't lack power or natural and human resources to win. They lack the will to fight (due to being forced into malaise by hypercompetitive opponents) and the knowledge of how the game is played today.

This lack of will and knowledge can be compared with the revitalization of the U.S. military. Consider recent changes in military strategy and morale. In World War II the goal was to establish a beachhead and take the field by superior numbers or weapons. The United States tried to do this in Vietnam, but the strategy was foiled by intense guerrilla fighting. The United States Army was demoralized and even vilified as a result of its loss in Vietnam. When the United States entered the Persian Gulf War with Iraq, on the other hand, American strategy focused on disrupting command and control centers, attacking communications, and finding ways to surprise or reduce the responsiveness of the enemy. The United States broke the cycle of demoralization within the military by practicing this new approach through a series of small successes in Grenada and Panama that rebuilt morale and added to the military's knowledge of how to win a modern war.

In the same way, large and sluggish U.S. firms such as General Motors and IBM were caught off guard by the unconventional strategies of foreign competitors. Suddenly the U.S. giants faced smaller competitors that created problems that could not be solved by throwing money at them. These challenges required a rethinking of how the business was organized. These once-dominant U.S. firms found themselves losing ground in the 1980s. This led to psychological disruption and loss of initiative, which they are working on regaining today. Because of their huge size, many of these firms persisted despite the beating they took in the marketplace. They were able to live long enough to rethink their strategies and change their directions, adopting many of the approaches outlined in the New 7-S's.

SUSTAINING THE UNSUSTAINABLE BY USING THE NEW 7-S's

Ultimately, knowledge of how to use the New 7-S's to disrupt the status quo and seize the initiative with a series of unsustainable advantages may be the only source of advantage that is sustained over time. Through using the New 7-S's to establish a series of temporary advantages, companies build a sustained advantage.

This advantage does not ignore the short-term advantages based on price, quality, know-how, timing, entry barriers, deep pockets, or any of the other traditional sources of competitive advantage. These sources remain powerful competitive forces and important arenas of competition for temporary advantage. But they are not sustainable. The dynamic process of moving from one short-term advantage to another has become more important than the company's position at any given point in time. Merely entering a market first is no assurance of advantage. It is the ability to enter, counter the moves of competitors, revitalize the market, exit, and move into a new market that keeps the company out in front.

While temporary advantage will still be achieved by racing up the escalation ladders in each arena of competition, true advantage will be sustained only by using the New 7-S's to (1) stay ahead of the competition on each ladder, (2) restart the cycles within each arena, or (3) jump to a new arena that was previously not the main focus of attention in the industry.

This new competitive advantage is based on a knowledge of how to manage dynamic strategic interactions. It is based on understanding the new rules of the game—the New 7-S's—and on the willingness to use them. This knowledge and understanding may be more sustainable than any other source of competitive advantage. It is not eroded by shifts in resources or opportunities in the four traditional arenas of competition. The skillful use of the 7-S's, in and of itself, may be the most powerful form of sustainable competitive advantage that companies have today, provided that they recognize the need to use the New 7-S's to disrupt the status quo and to move, as the pendulum swings, to creatively reconfigure the New 7-S's (as was illustrated for the watch and camera industries).

Will Advantages from Using the New 7-S's Eventually Erode?

Like all know-how, knowledge of how to use the New 7-S's might eventually be expected to erode as it becomes widely assimilated. As knowledge of these approaches becomes increasingly widespread and all competitors begin using them—this is already taking place—one might expect that any advantage would be neutralized. In particular, this erosion may be seen in the temporary advantages of a customer focus. As customer focus (a central part of S-1) has been driven through U.S. organizations by the Total Quality movement and other forces, it has become less of an advantage and more of a requisite to succeed in business.

While the impact of the New 7-S's may be diminished somewhat by their widespread adoption, there are several factors that promise to continue to make them a source of advantage even after they are widely used. First, the New 7-S's have some inherent flexibility so that different companies using the New 7-S's can take very different strategies. Unlike the three major generic strategies, the use of simultaneous and sequential strategic thrusts (S-7) presents a wide range of options and variations. There are many other thrusts that can be designed for specific opportunities as there are thousands of ways to skin a cat, making it difficult for firms to exactly replicate a competitor's use of the New 7-S's.

Second, the New 7-S's are dynamic. Companies use them in different ways over time. Stakeholder satisfaction changes, competitive opportunities change, sources of temporary advantage change. The New 7-S's and their goals of creating disruption and seizing the initiative remain constant, but the methods companies use to achieve these goals constantly change. In this way, even if all competitors in an industry are using the New 7-S's, their moves will continue to be unpredictable. After all, Kodak outmaneuvered Polaroid by using the New 7-S's only to find itself outmaneuvered by Canon using *its* New 7-S's. At both times the principles of the New 7-S's remained the same, even though their execution differed.

Third, companies usually cannot use all of the New 7-S's at once because of inherent tradeoffs among the S's. Companies perform a balancing act in weighing these tradeoffs. This adds to the unpredictability of competitive moves, because companies can move in any of the four arenas or use any of the New 7-S's in developing their next strategic move, and the tradeoffs may make it difficult to respond.

As more competitors focus on disrupting the status quo and seizing the initiative, this intent may become fairly predictable. Companies will know that their competitors will be actively working on their next competitive move. But this intent does little to reveal the actual strategies of competitors. All it does is make it clear that the company will *not* pursue one strategy, namely, sustaining its current advantage. This leaves every action other than that one open.

The one certain impact is that as the New 7-S's become more widespread, competition will become more aggressive. Instead of having one or two competitors seeking to disrupt the status quo, every competitor will be looking for the next source of temporary advantage. With this further intensification of hypercompetition, one might expect an increased interest in alliances and other forms of cooperation to dampen the intensity of competition (as has already been seen). Ultimately, however, the only way out of this dilemma is for companies to become more aggressive in seizing the initiative. Cooperative attempts to end this cycle of aggression will be seen as either (1) illegal (collusive antitrust violations) or (2) futile, since it is like shoveling sand against the tide. Leading firms will be wary of cooperative efforts that ask them to be less aggressive and give up their temporary advantage. Lagging firms with the fire in their bellies to be number one will not be satisfied with their permanent status as second-class citizens. So the New 7-S's will be used more aggressively and more frequently in the future world of hypercompetition.

While the New 7-S's will continue to be important, especially with the intensifying competition of the future, there may be even newer S's that emerge as key to competitive success. Hypercompetitive companies will continue to monitor and define these new strategic approaches in new attempts to provide temporary advantages and sustain momentum with a series of successful short-term advantages.

Management Challenges

The tools outlined in this chapter provide managers with methods of analyzing their own strengths and weaknesses and those of competitors. They also help managers identify strategies for seizing the initiative in the industry. Among the issues managers should consider are the following:

- What are your company's strengths and weaknesses in each of the New 7-S's?
- How do these strengths and weaknesses compare with those of competitors?
- What opportunities do you have to use your strengths in the New 7-S's to seize the initiative?
- Which of the four arenas offers the greatest promise for seizing the initiative? Which of the New 7-S's do you need to develop to seize the initiative in that arena?

- What are the tradeoffs you must make between the various New 7-S's? What tradeoffs have your competitors made?
- Which company in your market has the initiative now? In which area? Why? How can you gain or regain the initiative?
- Which companies are in a spiral of decline? How can you take advantage of this situation? How can you ensure that they do not come back to seize the initiative?
- Which competitors currently not in your industry are poised to enter? How do their strengths and weaknesses in the New 7-S's compare with your own?
- Can you see a pendulum swinging back and forth in your industry with respect to the theme underlying the New 7-S's (e.g., the camera industry)? Or do you expect a sequence of radical shifts (e.g., the watch industry)? What will the next swing look like?
- What is your current theme for the New 7-S's? How will competitors attack this theme with a new theme for *their* New 7-S's?

PART IV

THE RISE OF A NEW AMERICAN IDEOLOGY

HYPERCOMPETITIVE VALUES FOR A HYPERCOMPETITIVE AGE

CHAPTER 10

CAN COMPANIES COOPERATE THEIR WAY OUT OF HYPERCOMPETITION?

Using the New 7-S's to build a series of temporary advantages is a challenging route to corporate success. Falling behind on one rung of any of the escalation ladders, losing one dynamic strategic interaction, can erode much of the strength of the company. Success depends upon moving constantly forward to seek new temporary advantages. Hypercompetition is a demanding and unforgiving environment. This has led managers to ask, Isn't there some refuge from these harsh realities of hypercompetition?

Some have proposed cooperation as an antidote to hypercompetition. There has been a renewed interest in strategic alliances and cooperative manufacturing and even distribution agreements. Some managers believe that if companies can cooperate through alliances, they can dampen the aggressiveness of competition and all work together to maximize value for customers.

Giving Peace a Chance: A Dangerous Illusion

While this view may be appealing to a generation that grew up going to peace rallies and listening to arms talks, it appears to be a dangerous illusion in hypercompetitive environments. There are some hypercompetitive uses of cooperation, as discussed below. But companies cannot cooperate their way out of hypercompetition. In an environment in which every advantage rapidly erodes, cooperative agreements are inherently unsustainable. Cooperation usually leads to more intense levels of competition.

IBM found out about the competitive outcomes of cooperation during the development of the personal computer. In 1981 IBM chose Intel to make the microchip for its personal computer and Microsoft to make its software. Just a little over a decade later, IBM is on a long slide, while both Intel and Microsoft are among the most profitable and powerful companies in their industries. With the shifting terrain of the computing industry, both Microsoft and Intel have now become competitors with IBM. Both companies used the cooperative agreement to build their resources and strength. As soon as the cooperative agreement stood in the way of developing the next advantage for each company, they each turned around and captured all the value that their former partner once produced.

The push for increased cooperation is not a new direction. It is a return to the past, when companies tried to limit competition to sustain their advantages. As discussed throughout this book, slowing one's movement up the escalation ladders is not the desired strategy in hypercompetition. There is room for pacts and treaties in hypercompetition, but these are not an end to competition. As discussed below, they are, instead, part of the escalation of conflict.

TWO COMPETING AMERICAN APPROACHES TO STRATEGY

There are two competing American approaches to competitive strategy. On the one hand is the collusion-based approach. According to this view, companies sustain advantages by using entry barriers and building explicit or implicit agreements with competitors. On the other hand is all-out war. Under this view, companies sustain their leadership through a dynamic movement from one temporary advantage to the next.

A Tradition of Avoiding Competition

Cooperation has traditionally been the model of choice. Companies have avoided aggressive head-to-head competition by using cooperative strategies to limit competition or divide up the market into safe, uncontested segments. These traditional strategies are designed to build sustainable monopolies or friendly, stable oligopolies. Their goal is to reduce competition and avoid head-to-head competition to win. Companies have used entry barriers to keep out competitors in an industry, thereby reducing the level of competition in the market. They have used differentiation and focus strategies to carve up the market among competitors rather than face off in direct competition. Similarly, firms have sought first-mover strategies to move into untapped, uncontested markets.

Under this traditional view of strategy, very aggressive strategies, such as predatory pricing practices, were shunned as head-to-head confrontations that caused price wars that hurt the whole industry. Other tactics, such as disrupting the market frequently with major innovations, were also discouraged. Oligopolists found it difficult to maintain stable agreements in which players would live and let live. Disruptions destroyed the status quo and changed the power balance in the industry. Some win and some lose when there is a disruption in the equilibrium sought by strategies designed to stabilize markets.

A New Reality

Hypercompetition has invalidated the basic assumptions of sustainable monopolies and stable oligopolistic markets that have formed the foundation of collusion-based strategies. Today markets are in fact dynamic, and managing the highly dynamic process is of greater strategic importance than creating a static equilibrium that is sustainable for years. The traditional view of good strategy assumed that advantages would be sustainable, so that monopolies would perpetuate themselves for years without government intervention. It also assumed static markets, so that cooperative oligopolistic agreements would remain in effect for long periods of time without disruption or dissolution.

Cooperation Is Contestable

Cooperation might work in an environment in which there are strong entry barriers because they limit competition to a small number of competitors, making it easier to agree to be nice to each other. But, as discussed in Part I Chapter 3, entry barriers are often an illusion, and most markets are contestable. That is, if the current competitors in a market are agreeing to cooperate, there will almost always be an outsider ready to contest the market. It will move in and capture opportunities to create new advantages and profits. If the competition does not come from a domestic firm, there will inevitably be a company from a developing country that has the low labor costs, incentives, government support, and resources to compete aggressively. Or competitors may move in from an adjacent industry (for example, the move by telecommunications companies into computing). Cooperating companies may also cheat on the agreement or drop out of it (as discussed in Part II). So even when markets are not under direct attack, all players must anticipate a potential entrant (because it is likely) and stay hypercompetitive.

It would be as if all entrants in a race agreed to run in a pack to prevent the uncomfortable situation in which some win and others lose. Everyone wins as long as all travel at the same speed. If one faster competitor enters the race, however, all the cooperating runners lose. To make the point even more strongly, business races do not have the same rules as a marathon. Bystanders cannot enter a marathon with only ten miles left to run. In business, sprinters can jump in at any time, so business races are quite a contest of will and skill. By maintaining an intensely competitive race, runners are forced to stretch themselves and to get out in front of the pack. This process guarantees that they have greater long-term chances of success in global races such as when they go to the Olympics. So too in business.

AN OLD TRADITION RETURNS—WITH A TWIST

The current drive to return to cooperation may be the last gasp of diehard adherents of sustainable advantage and traditional collusion-based strategy. If they cannot cooperate tacitly, they attempt to cooperate openly. If they cannot sustain their advantages by ordinary means, they try to do so by the extraordinary means of neutralizing the competition that is eroding advantages. This is quite often the lazy way out, which appeals to unimaginative managers who do not see ways to move on to new advantages. Rather than continue to improve their products and services, rather than continually develop new advantages in each of the four arenas, they are trying to freeze everyone in place. This cannot succeed when hypercompetitors simply refuse to go along with the traditional rules of the game.

Cooperation Escalates Conflict

The current view of alliances is that they can be win-win situations. Rather than fight over a limited pie, both competitors work together to increase the size of the pie, and everyone does better. But even if the two competitors manage to increase the size of the market, they will eventually end up fighting for bigger shares of this larger market. As Plato said, "Only the dead have seen the last of war."

While there are uses for cooperation in hypercompetition, as discussed below, cooperation should not be seen as a panacea for the very real challenges of intense competition. Instead it is merely a pause in the action, leading to more intense levels of competition. Ultimately, because of the dynamic nature of markets in hypercompetition, cooperation does not lead to a dampening of competition for two reasons.

First, when one group of competitors forms an alliance to compete more effectively, another group of competitors may then form its own alliance. Each move tends to up the ante, leading to more intense levels of competition. For example, Toyota and Nissan responded to the Big Three's consortium to develop a battery for the electric car of the future by talking about their own joint effort. Cooperative strategies actually can contribute to more intense competition. The alliance of France, England, and the Soviet Union only escalated the conflict with Germany, Italy, and Japan during the 1930s to a world war. It works the same way in business.

Second, as Michael Porter comments, "Alliances carry substantial costs in strategic and organizational terms. . . . Today's partners also often become tomorrow's competitors, especially partners with more robust competitive advantages or that are more dynamic. Japanese firms have demonstrated this in countless industries." He notes that alliances are often "a response to uncertainty, and provide comfort that the firm is taking action."[1]

Kenichi Ohmae, urging managers to overcome their fear of global alliances in an article in *Harvard Business Review*, compares alliances to marriages.[2] But alliances are not a long-term commitment. Competitors are not linked until death do them part but are actually engaged in a fight to the death. Alliances are formed when they are mutually beneficial and are dissolved at will, usually leaving one partner at a disadvantage and creating confusion and disruption. Like the fate of many modern married couples, however, business alliances have to deal with the market disruption that results from the dissolution of the alliance.

As long as there are hypercompetitive firms in the market, cooperation will lead to more intense competition. Hypercompetitors will take advantage of industries with less aggressive players the way wolves attack sheep. There are a variety of ways that hypercompetitive firms use cooperative agreements to advance their positions and move to higher levels of competition.

The Hypercompetitive Use of Cooperation

While cooperation is not an effective antidote to hypercompetition, it can be an effective part of aggressive hypercompetitive strategies. There are several ways companies use cooperation effectively in hypercompetition:

To gang up against other groups Companies cooperate with two or three other players to work against other large companies or alliances. In effect, they may form an ad hoc keiretsu or larger conglomerate to match the resources or know-how of their competitors. As discussed in Chapter 4, this is one way small companies overcome large firms with a deep-pocket advantage. For example, Japanese keiretsu combine the forces of diverse firms to compete in global markets.

To limit the domain of competition Companies often cooperate in one area and compete in another. For example, they may cooperate on price by signaling and through other methods of establishing a stable price in the industry. Then they may compete on quality or on know-how, using the profits gained by avoiding price competition. Or as can be seen from Sematech and other recent R&D consortia in the United States, companies may agree to work together on developing know-how and then compete on manufacturing products, using that know-how. Companies also use cooperation to limit the geographic domain of competition. For example, some groups of Japanese companies have agreed to cooperate at home to fund competitive actions abroad.

To build resources Companies frequently use cooperative agreements to gain needed resources and expertise that they do not have in-house. Companies need to carefully measure the costs and benefits of such arrangements. It is rare that a cooperative agreement doesn't favor one side slightly over the other. In this case, one partner gains a disproportionate benefit from the arrangement, and this tilts competition in its favor. In retrospect, Intel and Microsoft gained far more than IBM from the arrangement to produce personal computers.

To buy time Companies sometimes cooperate with other companies to throw them off guard. A weak competitor will cooperate with a stronger one to keep from being killed or to build up sufficient resources for an attack. When Komatsu was weak due to the strong yen in the late 1980s, it offered Caterpillar a chance to raise prices and end the price wars it had triggered, hoping that Caterpillar would become a less fierce competitor.

To gain access This is the Trojan Horse strategy of riding into a market through an alliance with a foreign competitor and then competing aggressively against the competitor. The company that accepts the Trojan Horse often regrets the move later.

To learn In addition to gaining access to markets, cooperation is also used to gain access to knowledge. The partner joins with a competitor to gain an understanding of its unique processes or approaches. For example, the General Motors–Toyota NUMMI venture ostensibly offered GM insights into Japanese production techniques and offered Toyota insights on American markets and workforce.

These hypercompetitive uses of cooperation result in increased levels of competition. In each of these instances, cooperation is a strategy used to gain a temporary advantage over a competitor or to create an even greater challenge or threat to another alliance.

Divorce American Style

In most cases, one partner in these transactions is very often losing ground as its opponent gains ground. One partner is providing its future competitor with time to build its resources, resources to use in future competitive interactions, or its access to markets. In a dynamic market cooperative agreements are only sustained as long as they provide a temporary advantage to at least one of the companies.

In sum, cooperation is no longer a strategy that creates an oligopolistic bargain or tacit collusion. The old tradition of cooperation now has a new wrinkle. It is not used for earning excessive dividends or paying excessive wages to unionized workers seeking a piece of the action. It is used for conflict escalation because cooperation has several hypercompetitive purposes. It cannot be used to dampen competitive rivalry because the only effective strategy in hypercompetitive environments is one of dynamic, aggressive movement up the escalation ladders.

As described in the following chapter, U.S. antitrust policies—which were designed to counter the collusive strategies of companies—also need to be realigned to acknowledge the new realities of hypercompetition. Because hypercompetition has made collusion obsolete, the antitrust laws are protecting against an evil that does not exist. Hypercompetitive markets destroy sluggish colluders and force them to change their ways or die. Certainly the steel and automobile companies have learned these lessons. While more aggressive anticollusion, antitrust enforcement might have helped these industries in the 1970s, the market has taken care of the problem by itself. The steel and car companies had to adapt to more aggressive competitive methods. The old oligopolies are as dead as the ideology that it is best to compete by not competing.

A New American Ideology: Compete To Win

Traditional, collusion-based strategy no longer holds in a dynamic environment. It does not lead to stability. Instead it invites entry by more aggressive competitors or it leads to higher levels of competition by pitting hypercompetitive alliances against each other.

In a dynamic, competitive race there will be winners and losers. This is not a win-win situation for everyone. It is, however, a win-win situation for consumers, who benefit from the intense competition, and for the dynamic, hypercompetitive firms that dominate the pack. By trying to slow down the race, managers have only assured that their firms will be the losers. Our current view of competition is outdated. In a vain attempt to slow down competition, these collusive approaches and competition avoidance are undermining the source of true competitive success in hypercompetitive environments. American firms can no longer compete by limiting competition as they did in the past. They must face up to competing by using the New 7-S's.

Competing harder sounds scary. There are obvious casualties to business warfare. Witness the steel towns and automobile towns that have become ghost towns in the face of global competition. But a variety of tacitly collusive arrangements with competitors did more to create this problem than to prevent it. Only cooperative agreements that are used for hypercompetitive purposes (such as to create a market disruption based on the New 7-S's) are effective in today's hypercompetitive environments.

In hypercompetition companies cannot afford to cling to the ideologies of the past. They cannot cooperate their way out of hypercompetition. They cannot apply static strategic approaches that seek sustained advantages and stable conditions to dynamic markets. They must meet competitive challenges head-on and compete to win. This, of course, does not mean fighting endlessly fruitless price wars. It does mean staying price competitive and using the dynamic strategic interactions (discussed in Chapters 1 to 4) and the New 7-S's to disrupt markets by jumping up to higher and higher rungs on the escalation ladders. It may sound like something Yogi Berra would say, but surprisingly, the American tradition of competing by avoiding competition makes it news to say that firms only win by winning.

Management Challenges

- Are you operating under the assumption that you can build sustainable advantages?
- What other assumptions underlying your current approach to competitive strategy have been invalidated by hypercompetition?
- How can you change your strategic thinking to acknowledge the realities of hypercompetition?
- How can you develop this perspective across the organization to get the whole organization to adopt a new view or concept of what strategy and "fair" competition are?
- How are you benefiting from your use of cooperation with other firms? Are you using cooperation in hypercompetitive markets in one of the ways described above?
- Are the benefits worth the costs and other risks?
- How are your partners and competitors using cooperation in hypercompetitive ways?

CHAPTER 11

CONCLUSION:

A Call To Arms

This book has described a fundamental shift in strategy in hyper-competition. The goal of strategy has shifted from *sustaining* advantages to *disrupting* advantages. Competition advances through a series of dynamic strategic interactions in four arenas: cost and quality, timing and know-how, strongholds, and deep pockets. In this dynamic environment a company's *movement* and its *relative* position in any of the four arenas are critically important. The only source of truly sustainable advantage is the company's ability to manage its dynamic strategic interactions with competitors through frequent movements that maintain a relative position of strength in each of the four arenas. Ironically, to sustain dominance, companies must seek a series of unsustainable advantages.

Some companies have tried to resist the intensity of competition by clinging tenaciously to their current advantages. These companies have watched their advantages eroded and their positions undermined despite their best efforts. Other companies have tried to slow competition through cooperative strategies, but ultimately these strategies have led to more intense competition as groups of competitors join with one another or new players pick off companies lulled into complacency by cooperative arrangements. In an environment in which every advantage erodes, both clinging to past advantages and trying to slow change are ultimately ineffective. The most effective companies in hypercompetition actively work to disrupt the status quo and undermine current advantages, moving from temporary advantage to temporary advantage.

Companies enhance their ability to disrupt the status quo and seize the initiative through the New 7-S's. Just as companies shaped themselves to sustain advantages by using McKinsey's old 7-S framework, they prepare for hypercompetition through using the New 7-S's. The New 7-S's define a vision for market disruption by creating a series of actions that generate superior stakeholder satisfaction, and they carry that vision into the future through strategic soothsaying. The New 7-S's build flexible capabilities of speed and surprise to facilitate the creation of disruption. Finally, the New 7-S's suggest using tactics that shift the rules of competition, signal strategic intent to dominate, and confuse or overwhelm competitors through simultaneous and sequential strategic thrusts that disrupt competitors and seize the initiative away from them.

A NEW IDEOLOGY OF COMPETITION

Markets were never really static; they just moved to higher levels of competition so slowly that they appeared to be static. But today markets are driven by the forces of global information processing and technological competitions that have transformed relatively low-intensity static environments to high-intensity dynamic hypercompetition overnight. These forces create opportunities to unseat the established leaders. This has reshaped the competitive options of all companies.

Secure Fortresses

In the old view of markets, companies focused on building monopolies in a specific market or market segment, limiting competition in those segments, and making excess profits by using their monopoly power to raise price, as illustrated by Figure 11–1. If new entrants occasionally shouldered their way into the market, competitors formed oligopolies that essentially limited competition by tacitly colluding to be less competitive. Either way, companies sought to build secure and sustainable fortresses they could defend against competitors without actively fighting. Antitrust laws tried to counter this approach by herding companies toward perfect competition, where excess profits and competitive advantages are nonexistent. A "fair," or "level," playing field was forced upon the players, and the market was frozen in a state where no one dominated. At least, that was the theoretical plan.

The Disruptive and the Dead

Today the fortresses of the past have crumbled, and the knights who once defended them are left exposed on the open fields of combat. Monopolies are virtually nonexistent. Even where they were once protected by government regulations, they have been dismantled through policies of deregulation and privatization in response to competitive pressures. Oligopolies are also very hard to sustain. They last only as long as all competitors play

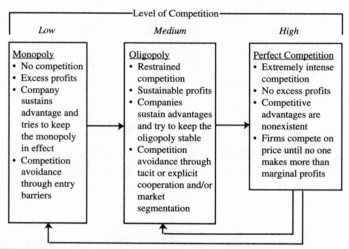

FIRMS SEEK TO MOVE AWAY FROM PERFECT COMPETITION TO GENERATE
PROFITS. PROGRESSION TOWARD PERFECT COMPETITION IS SO SLOW
THAT EACH STAGE APPEARS TO BE A STABLE, STEADY STATE

FIGURE 11–1
TRADITIONAL TYPES OF COMPETITION
IN A STABLE WORLD

by the same rules. If one player steps out of the bargain or a new one enters the market, all bets are off. In today's markets perfect competition often develops because firms hold on to their old advantages until their competitors have imitated them, resulting in bankruptcy or long-term poor performance.

In the current environment companies no longer have the option of sustaining monopolies or oligopolies. They now have two choices: to disrupt or to be dead. As shown in Figure 11–2, they can choose between perfect competition or hypercompetition. Hypercompetition does not offer the excessive profits of monopolies, nor does it offer the sustained profits of oligopolies. But it does provide intermittent profits through temporary advantages. Stringing together these advantages is the best strategy for long-term success in an environment that would otherwise offer few opportunities for using old strategies designed to create and defend monopolies or oligopolies. In other words, companies have little choice but to enter hypercompetition because it is superior to the state of perfect competition that would result if firms were left to imitate each other and reach a state of stable equilibrium. Disrupting that equilibrium by using the New 7-S's is essential to break out of it.

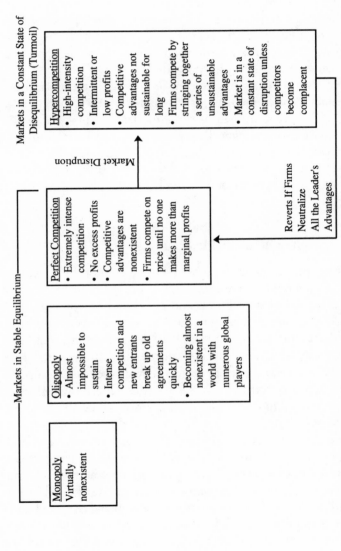

Markets in a Constant State of
Disequilibrium (Turmoil)

Hypercompetition
- High-intensity competition
- Intermittent or low profits
- Competitive advantages not sustainable for long
- Firms compete by stringing together a series of unsustainable advantages
- Market is in a constant state of disruption unless competitors become complacent

Markets in Stable Equilibrium

Market Disruption

Perfect Competition
- Extremely intense competition
- No excess profits
- Competitive advantages are nonexistent
- Firms compete on price until no one makes more than marginal profits

Reverts If Firms Neutralize All the Leader's Advantages

Oligopoly
- Almost impossible to sustain
- Intense competition and new entrants break up old agreements quickly
- Becoming almost nonexistent in a world with numerous global players

Monopoly
Virtually nonexistent

COMPANIES WOULD PREFER TO MOVE OUT OF PERFECT COMPETITION TO STABLE MONOPOLIES AND OLIGOPOLIES, BUT THESE PATHS ARE BLOCKED. THEY ARE FORCED TO MOVE INTO HYPERCOMPETITION BY CONSTANTLY DISRUPTING THE BALANCE AND STABILITY OF PERFECTLY COMPETITIVE MARKETS.

FIGURE 11–2
NEW REALITIES OF COMPETITION DRIVEN BY CHANGES IN THE TECHNOLOGICAL, GLOBAL, AND INFORMATION PROCESSING ENVIRONMENTS

The Danger of Short-Term Profit Orientations

Traditionally, oligopolistic and monopolistic strategies are preferred to hypercompetition by American business. These corporations seek the greater short-run profits provided by seeking oligopoly and monopoly. However, over the long run, profits and market position require a longer-term view of what happens when firms are trying to compete by avoiding competition. The aggressive firms eat their lunch, leaving devastation and starvation where once short-run profits prevailed.

The United States has been criticized for its short-run profit orientation, and researchers have blamed the problem on the stock market and government policy. The real problem is the American ideology of maximizing profits *by avoiding competition*. Instead firms should be maximizing their hypercompetitiveness to protect their relative strategic positions in their markets by racing up the escalation ladders faster than competitors do and by heating up the competition to even higher levels.

The End of a Chivalrous Age

The rise of hypercompetition and the subsequent erosion of the fortresses of monopolies and oligopolies have brought an abrupt end to the age of chivalry. The gentility of tacit collusion and avoiding head-on competition is gone. The days in which it was uncouth to destroy a competitor are gone. Similarly, the usefulness of antitrust laws designed to protect "fair play" by pitting equally weighted players against each other is gone. The world of strategy has moved away from an ideology where "fair" competition was supposed to be like fixing wrestling matches between wrestlers of equal weight. It has moved to a new view where winners take all and combatants of unequal weight use any tactic available to them.

This shift in the definition of competition has been relatively rapid and was largely unexpected. It is no wonder that both managers and regulators have been slow to acknowledge this new vision of what competition is and should be. Companies can no longer compete according to the old ideology of fair play and chivalry. They are increasingly realizing the need for a new ideology of hypercompetition. The most aggressive firms have already given up the traditional ideology that guided strategy and policy in a chivalrous age. They realize that they are not fighting on the contained fields of combat of relatively tranquil and insulated domestic markets. They are in the midst of the head-to-head, fight-to-the death, global business war. They are now adopting a new ideology more appropriate to the hyper-

FIGURE 11–3
CONTRASTING IDEOLOGIES OF THE PAST AND FUTURE

The Traditional American Ideology	Hypercompetition in a Global Market
• Fair play and chivalry (e.g., don't use predatory and exclusionary practices)	• Winner takes all and "all is fair in love and hypercompetition."
• Domestic tranquility	• Global business war
• Strong antitrust	• Relax antitrust to build national champions
• Not Darwinism, so protect the small company	• Darwinistic survival of the fittest
• Can't use aggressive metaphors	• Use of new metaphors to motivate seizing the initiative and aggressive action
• The goal of antitrust is static efficiency and fair play.	• The goal of antitrust is dynamic efficiency and meritocracy.
• The concept of strategy as it is practiced today by many firms (e.g., long-range plans, sustainable advantage, use of generic strategies and barriers to entry)	• New concept of strategy (based on the New 7-S's and escalation ladders)
• Profits are bad and should be punished because they result from monopolistic practices.	• Profits are rewards for behaviors that create jobs in the United States and satisfy customers better than anyone else in the world.
• America is assumed to be eternally prosperous with plentiful high-paying jobs in the United States.	• America is losing jobs to low-labor-cost locations overseas, so corporate America must protect U.S. jobs even at the expense of profits.

competitive environment of all-out war, as summarized in Figure 11–3. As Ernesto Martens, CEO of Vitro (one of North America's largest firms) said, "You could actually feel it sweep through the company, this realization that the world was becoming a different place."[1]

Hypercompetitive Exhortations to Battle

Cooperation and chivalry are not the model for the future of competition, even though cooperation and fair play have been the American tradition. The new model is Honda's battle cry of *Yamaha o tsubusu!* ("Annihilate, destroy, and crush Yamaha!") during the H-Y War or Komatsu's motto *Maru C* ("Encircle Caterpillar").

The signs of a more aggressive approach to competition can already be seen and heard across the United States. Employees in an AT&T factory are exhorted to "declare business war" against Northern Telecom.[2] United Parcel Service, in its intense competition with Federal Express and others, asserts in its television advertising, "The arms race may be over, but the package race is just heating up." Edward E. Crutchfield, chairman and CEO of First Union Corporation, comments on the shifting financial service industry. "We bankers are throwing snowballs [at each other] and there's someone out there with an Uzi."[3] Robert Lutz, president of Chrysler, declares, "The war isn't over but we've definitely landed on the beaches."[4]

There is a new intensity of competition. There is a new recognition of the demands of hypercompetition. There is a growing realization that chivalry is dead.

Kill or Be Killed

This new aggressiveness of competition is perceived by some as a ruthless drive to dominate. An industry analyst described the strategy of Intel as "a scorch, burn and plunder strategy with one aim: Kill off competitors. If you think Grove is determined to control the future of computing hardware, you're absolutely right."[5]

But Intel CEO Andrew Grove doesn't see himself as a ruthless and powerful Visigoth preparing to sweep through the countryside. He is fighting for survival. As he commented in a 1993 article, "The history of high-tech industries is filled with the cadavers of companies that lived for a while and are no longer around. I drive up and down this peninsula and see the buildings of companies that are now on their third owner. The previous owners are gone. I have daily reminders of the mortality rate when you live in the fast lane."[6]

In this environment it is kill or be killed. The aggressiveness of hypercompetition demands a new ideology. The business environment today is as untamed as the Wild West. Entry barriers and deep pockets are leveled. The rich and poor are equally in danger as they ride through the sagebrush. It takes a new breed of rugged and fearless competitor to survive. And it takes a new ideology of competition.

This recognition of the need for a new ideology is by no means universal. But as those fighting by the old rules of chivalry take a beating in world markets, it is becoming harder to avoid acknowledging the reality of hypercompetition. Still, it is not clear that U.S. managers and policymakers understand the full depth of the changes in the current competitive environment. Such a recognition is vital to the future competitiveness of the nation.

HYPERCOMPETITIVE NATIONS

In hypercompetition the advantages of nations are just as unsustainable as the advantages of companies. The past success of U.S. companies in world markets is no guarantee of their future success, as the rise of strong competitors from Europe and Asia has demonstrated. Nor is Japan's success any indication of its future prospects; it is still unclear what Korea and China have in store for Japan and America. In the past decade America watched helplessly as control over key industries shifted to foreign competitors. Giants such as IBM and GM stumbled. This era was the Vietnam of U.S. business history—demoralizing and confusing.

The only meaningful prospect for future success results from corporate strategies and government policies that encourage companies to adopt this new ideology of no-holds-barred hypercompetition. As Michael Porter comments on the results of his exhaustive four-year study of ten nations in *The Competitive Advantage of Nations*, "Companies and economies flourish because of pressures, challenges, and new opportunities, not a docile environment or outside "help" that eliminates the need to improve. Progress comes from change, not from a preoccupation with stability that obstructs it."[7] U.S. managers and policymakers must promote a dynamic environment that is the best hope for the U.S. economy and its companies.

Meeting the Challenge

The United States cannot afford to move back to aggressive attacks on its large, successful corporations by antitrust regulators. Antitrust laws often served to protect the underdog competitor from what was labeled a "predatory" firm. Yet it is this hypercompetitive predatory firm that survives in today's world. The government must untie the hands of our best hope for winning against global forces such as NEC, ABB, and others. Managers also cannot be content to focus on sustaining their current advantages. They must actively develop a series of advantages by using the New 7-S's.

Managers must abandon old strategic tools and theories that no longer apply in hypercompetitive environments. They must, for example, reconsider the use of the following strategic frameworks and maxims:

Commitment Traditionally, increasing commitment by investing in fixed equipment or plants is thought to signal intent and increase focus. But in hypercompetition a rigid commitment tends to make the firm inflexible and predictable. The more a firm is locked into a specific course of action, the more competitors can maneuver around the firm in creating new advantages. Also, long-term commitments tend to lock the company into a specific advantage rather than allow it to move flexibly from advantage to advantage. In hypercompetition the flexible, unpredictable player has the advantage over the inflexible, committed opponent.

Long-term planning Traditionally, managers are exhorted to develop long-term plans that set the company on a steady course for the future. All parts of the plan consist of and build upon each other over time. Instead managers need to plan to be opportunistic and flexible in hypercompetition; they need to plan for change rather than consistency. Good competitors will destroy your plans. (There is an old military saying: A good plan lasts only until contact with the enemy.) Because long-term success depends on a series of short-term advantages, the exact nature of which cannot always be seen at the outset, the company needs to create a process of developing a series of advantages. This is in contrast to planning for specific goals and results under traditional approaches to long-range planning. In hypercompetition managers need to ask themselves what skills or assets are necessary to ensure that the company will have the necessary flexibility to meet the demands of building a series of advantages. In particular, they need to focus on how they can best develop the New 7-S's to prepare for the long-term process of hypercompetition.

Generic strategies Traditionally, selection of generic strategies, such as being a differentiator or low-cost producer, was recommended, but in hypercompetition these positions are only a short-term strategy at best. Firms actually move between such positions in the course of the evolution of the industry. Sometimes companies occupy two positions at once. As discussed in the Introduction and Chapter 1 (cost and quality arena), the actions of competitors can move a company from one position to another without any action on the part of the company. As discussed in Chapter 2 (timing and know-how arena), consistent strategies of being a follower or first mover are too static in hypercompetition. Companies shift from being first movers to followers and then back to first movers. In hypercompetition the advantage goes to the firm that keeps moving up the escalation ladder—not to the firm that locks into a fixed position like one of the generic strategies.

Building entry barriers In hypercompetition managers seeking to build entry barriers or relying on entry barriers for protection against competitors will be frequently disappointed. As discussed in Chapter 3, even the most persistent entry barriers and strongholds are beginning to fall. In hypercompetition the best barrier to entry by new companies or expansion by existing players is for the company to move aggressively from advantage to advantage. Notice that this isn't really a defensive barrier, since companies keep on attacking, rather than defending, their current turf. This forward momentum and aggressive competition gives a clear sign to would-be competitors that entry will be a challenge. It also offers fewer windows of opportunity for competitors. In hypercompetition the advantage goes to the party with the initiative, not the player playing defense, using entry barriers to exclude players.

SWOT analysis Analyzing a competitor's current strengths and weakness and playing strengths against weaknesses may work in the short term but is not an effective long-term strategy in a dynamic environment. As discussed in the introduction, consistently playing against the weaknesses of a competitor is both predictable and a strategy that ultimately builds its weaknesses into strengths. A tennis player who serves to his opponent's weak backhand will eventually force the opponent to develop a stronger backhand. Then the first player faces a rival with a strong forehand *and* a strong backhand.

NPV analysis This method of analyzing projects to see if they generate a positive net present value (NPV) is predictable and fails to recognize the dynamic role that competitors play in shaping cash flows. Companies that use this model for capital budgeting will adopt a project only if the proposed project generates a positive NPV. In markets where opponents are willing to fight vigorously against a proposed investment, they can depress the expected cash flows for the company basing its decisions on NPV analysis and make the project look less attractive. On the other hand, if the opponent does not fight, he allows his rival to have cash flows and to undertake this investment. Thus, in a dynamic environment the hypercompetitive opponent can actually decide where the company using NPV analysis competes. Further, using NPV analysis on one project at a time (as is done in most firms) does not allow the company to see the big picture needed to develop an effective competitive strategy wherein some projects are undertaken despite their negative NPV for the larger strategic purpose of disciplining the expectations of an opponent, letting it know its NPV for certain projects will be negative because of the competitive reaction to those projects.

Power over buyers and suppliers Traditionally firms are taught to gain power over buyers and suppliers, but this ignores the reactions of the buyers and suppliers. General Motors had power over its dealers. It squeezed their margins and off-loaded inventory onto them without much concern for their risks of bankruptcy. The response was that dealers picked up Toyotas and Nissans to give themselves power over General Motors and to play each off against the other. This dynamic reaction to a temporary GM advantage destroyed the advantage. In hypercompetition the advantage doesn't go to firms that squeeze dealers and suppliers but to firms that enlist them in the effort to create new advantages through using the New 7-S's.

To revert to old strategic doctrines, no matter how successful they were in the past, can be futile. Even to stand still in this environment is to move backward. As Ernesto Martens, the CEO of Vitro, said: "Our challenge is to change who we are without losing sight of what we are all about. . . . My challenge is to convince the people here that we can no longer be complacent in the face of world competition."[8]

Our corporate and political leaders need to have the courage to address this new competitive environment by adopting a new view of competition that welcomes it and encourages it even if the business-is-war metaphor scares them or has an unpleasant sound to them.

Many companies and policymakers realized that change was needed. Forward-thinking companies have restructured themselves to become leaner. Courts and enforcers backed away from aggressive antitrust actions in the light of the decline of once-powerful corporations in hypercompetition.

The danger now is that we may misinterpret the lessons of the 1980s. We may be tempted to see these changes as a single anomaly in the environment. For managers it is tempting to think that a single restructuring or intense reengineering process can cut out the fat and set our corporations on an upward course again. It is tempting to limit the erosion of our current advantages through cooperation without hypercompetitive intent.

In politics there is a temptation to see the swing away from aggressive antitrust enforcement as a product of a Republican administration rather than the result of new realities of competition. Instead the shift to less aggressive enforcement of antitrust laws by the judicial and regulatory systems is a recognition of the new realities of hypercompetition. The dragons of monopoly power no longer roam the earth. But the threat of foreign competitors to U.S. jobs is very real. U.S. companies are no longer fighting to build monopolistic empires; they are fighting for survival. If U.S. policy fails to support its corporations in this struggle, we may wake up too late to find that the corporate giants of the world have died or moved overseas. The outcome of this struggle affects U.S. jobs, competitiveness, and the economy. The antitrust implications of hypercompetition must be addressed by regulators more explicitly. The Appendix provides some suggestions for what must be considered if America is to adjust to the new world of hypercompetition.

The challenge facing the United States today is whether it can recognize the reality of hypercompetition and rise to meet the demands of this new environment. The United States must have the courage to overcome the tired ideologies and policies that made it successful in the past but are now keeping it in that past. America's old advantages are running out. The United States now must move on to its next advantage: the creative ability of its people to disrupt markets with sudden and overwhelming force through using the New 7-S's.

Lean and Mean: Hypercompetitive Intent

The New 7-S's are the smelling salts that can wake up the sleeping giants of industry after a long period of sleep. Those large and small companies that wake up and fight will be the ones to succeed in the intense competition ahead. Instead of defending the status quo with entry barriers, the New 7-S's encourage the next generation of advantages, not sustain those of the past.

During the 1980s U.S. corporations became leaner. Now they must become meaner, adopting a hypercompetitive intent to dominate. This does not mean engaging in endless price wars, however. Chapters 1 to 4 indicated more sophisticated ways to race up the escalation ladders faster than competitors. Part III indicated that jumping to new or recently dormant arenas of competition is a good option. So too is restarting the cycles within each arena. The key is to dominate in each arena by having the superior position relative to the competition. If it moves, the firm must move, and preferably in a way that seizes the initiative (as the New 7-S's suggest). Reactive moves and playing catch-up are not enough.

The process of becoming leaner has stripped away the structures and strategies designed to support and sustain old advantages. Like mollusks that have shed their old shells, companies now have a critical decision. They can seek to create new shells, new, rigid structures and strategies to support and "sustain" a new advantage. These structures and strategies will soon become as stifling as their pursuit of their old advantage had been. Or these companies can use their newly found leanness to become aggressive hypercompetitors, flexibly and unpredictably moving from advantage to advantage.

Becoming hypercompetitive may appear to be a risky route for corporations. Certainly, stable, consistent, long-term plans sound more rational, less risky, and less costly than jumping from advantage to advantage. A natural sense of conservatism may cause some companies to opt for the seemingly safer option of shoring up and sustaining an old advantage. But becoming mean by using the New 7-S's and pursuing a series of temporary advantages, as dangerous as this may be, is far less dangerous than being trapped in a rigid company trying to sustain an advantage long after it has begun to slip away. Companies that choose this latter route could find themselves the next IBM, valiantly defending the mainframe business throughout the '80s even as it evaporates beneath them.

A Sleeping Giant Awakens

There is new evidence that U.S. companies, despite the regulations that often hold them back, can seize the initiative and win in global competition. U.S. companies are becoming more hypercompetitive without moving across the line into antitrust violations. In the first five months of 1992, *Business Week* reports, U.S. car makers seized 72.4 percent of the domestic auto and light truck market, up 1.6 points from a year earlier. At the same time, Japanese automakers lost 1.4 points.[9] In 1992 Ford Taurus moved ahead of the Honda Accord as the best-selling U.S. passenger car for the year. The Saturn is a roaring success. Lou Gerstner has a new vision for IBM that no longer defends mainframes, but moves on to what IBM is now calling "Power Architecture." Clearly the American dinosaur is not dead but is evolving to meet the new demands of its environment.

In 1993 U.S. companies began to see growing profits and investments.[10] The United States was making gains across a wide range of industries, including autos, steel, food, computers, chemicals, semiconductors, telecommunications, and banking. Analysts predicted that the largest U.S. industrial corporations were "poised for a comeback." General Motors actually led the *Fortune* 500 in sales in 1992, and old-line companies such as Gillette, Whirlpool, and Union Carbide made great gains through stronger attention to customers, technological advances, and other moves.[11]

U.S. companies increasingly are using the New 7-S's to boost stakeholder satisfaction, engage in strategic soothsaying, increase speed and surprise, shift the rules, signal, and use simultaneous and sequential strategic thrusts. They are moving ahead in the four arenas of competition by competing more aggressively on price and quality, timing and know-how, attacking strongholds, and building and using deep pockets.

Meanwhile, Japan has stumbled, and its bubble economy has been deflated. Most of what has been lost is the sense of invincibility gained during its rise after World War II—what has been called the Godzilla myth.[12] Toshiba, Honda, and other large corporations are changing their approaches to business.[13] They are discovering, as U.S. firms did during the 1980s, that all advantages are temporary. What worked in the past must be rethought to seize the advantage in the future. As always in hypercompetition, the vanquished have the chance to rise like a phoenix from defeat while the victors have the potential to lose their dominance because their hubris causes them to sustain their old ways of doing things.

Only the Dynamic Survive

Political and regulatory shifts will most likely occur too slowly to meet the immediate challenges of hypercompetition. Companies cannot wait. Of course, no one should intentionally break the law, but the dangers of standing still in hypercompetitive environments outweigh the dangers and costs of provoking an antitrust investigation by the government or a lawsuit from a competitor. The most aggressive companies realize this. Throughout its history General Electric, for example, has been no stranger to antitrust controversies.

American Airlines and Microsoft must continue to move as quickly up the escalation ladders as possible, to act decisively and aggressively, despite carrying the weight of government investigations or private lawsuits. (American had this point driven home when it began relying almost solely on price competition to win and its smaller competitors, which had been nipping at its heels, suddenly took a bite out of its rear, contributing to American's substantial losses in early 1993.)[14] The antitrust actions may have had a dampening effect, but they seem not to have affected the most aggressive companies' fundamental approach to competition. Remember, the courts are beginning to come down on the side of antitrust defendants in many situations that were previously thought to be illegal (so consult legal counsel on current law). Most of all, remember that you are helping America when you are hypercompetitive because winning in the marketplace will defend U.S. jobs and pursue dynamic efficiencies described in the Appendix.

The world has moved forward and continues to move forward into hypercompetition. For U.S. managers and policymakers the choice is clear. We can stand still and allow this wave of constant change to wash over us. We can try to resist the dynamics of the environment by clinging to concepts of sustainable advantages, by believing in the power of entry barriers. Or we can actively embrace the environment and take advantage of its opportunities. We can actively seek to disrupt current advantages, build new ones, and move competition up the escalation ladders. There is only one course that leads to long-term survival and success in hypercompetition. In a dynamic world only the dynamic survive.

ANTITRUST POLICY AND THE NEED FOR A FUNDAMENTAL SHIFT IN AMERICAN IDEOLOGY

Traditional antitrust laws were created to respond to the needs of the old realities of competition. They are based on the assumption that markets are static and companies can build sustainable advantages that result in monopolies or quasi monopolies. Antitrust laws were also designed to counter the power of large corporations that sought to sustain their advantages through oligopolies using collusive bargains.

Those laws were intended to prevent monopoly or oligopoly by encouraging perfect competition and "fair play." The idea was to achieve perfect competition by forcing firms into competitive parity. The method was to create a level playing field where a fair fight could occur and no one would dominate. This was like boxing where matches are based on pitting fighters of equal weight against each other and having rules that prohibit hitting below the belt.

Yet we know that parity is not the goal of hypercompetition. Competitive parity would mean all the players are frozen at the same rung of each of the escalation ladders in all four arenas, thereby eliminating any form of dominance or advantage. Part I clearly established the problem with this idea of parity when markets are highly dynamic. Players must continually jockey for leadership positions by racing up the ladders, restarting the cycles within each arena, and opening up new or temporarily dormant arenas unexpectedly. Size can be an advantage or disadvantage in achieving these hypercompetitive goals, but equal size is never assured.

Moreover, the antitrust laws as they are traditionally designed are no longer necessary for ensuring vigorous competition in hypercompetitive markets. Advantages are not sustainable in hypercompetition. Entry barriers are torn down and collusive behavior is impossible. Companies develop rapid product innovation, engage in intense price/quality competition, initiate market expansion or entry, form alliances with others, or build deep pockets. When firms race up each of the four escalation ladders, the market itself creates four types of dynamic efficiency. As discussed below, this dynamic process benefits consumers and gives smaller competitors a chance to disrupt the status quo at any time.

This chapter will address how antitrust laws are designed to generate static efficiency and to promote fair play in ways that tend to destroy the dynamic efficiency of the market. Antitrust laws are not only ineffective in hypercompetition; they also appear to limit the very strategies companies need to use to succeed in hypercompetitive markets. Applying traditional U.S. antitrust enforcement in an environment of hypercompetition is like driving a Model T on an expressway. The law moves too slowly to keep up with the traffic in the market, and what was once effective transportation has now become a threat to survival.

America's Most Wanted

Many of America's most successful companies have found their way onto the Most Wanted list at one time or another because of their successes. They were hotly pursued by the Department of Justice or Federal Trade Commission or hauled into court by their smaller rivals. The irony is that these highly competitive firms are charged with anticompetitive behavior for being too competitive and too good at serving the customer.

As noted in the introduction, Microsoft is one of the most successful software companies in the world, posting earnings of $708 million in the 1992 fiscal year. *Business Week* reports that the company created more than six thousand new jobs between 1989 and 1992[1] and is a fierce international competitor because it is hypercompetitive. In addition, Microsoft claims that another five hundred new companies are developing software for Windows, creating another eighteen thousand jobs.[2]

For this success Microsoft was rewarded with an FTC probe which, *Business Week* reported, considered such options as breaking the company into pieces, erecting a "Chinese wall" between divisions, or changing the way it sells software to computer makers.[3] Among other issues, *Business Week* reports that Microsoft has been criticized for allegedly announcing its new products early and using its advance knowledge of software developments to aid the development of applications programs.[4] *Business Week* reported that Microsoft could also face private lawsuits from rivals.[5] After two deadlocked votes by the FTC, which didn't end the investigation, the Justice Department began reviewing documents in 1993 to determine if it should launch its own investigation of Microsoft. If Justice decides to take on the case, analysts estimate that the probe could take as long as the FTC investigation. So the specter of federal action could hang over Microsoft, without any formal charges, for years to come.[6]

American Airlines is another hypercompetitive U.S. company under attack for antitrust reasons. As discussed at the opening of the book, American has moved aggressively from advantage to advantage, from developing the business class to launching frequent-flier programs. It has also been an aggressive competitor, restructuring pricing and using what has been called dogfighter tactics.[7] Between 1983 and 1988, while other airlines were cutting back staff, American Airlines increased its workforce by 81 percent to seventy-eight thousand employees.[8] American is also a fierce international competitor, boosting overseas flights from 12 percent to 26 percent of its total revenues between 1988 and 1992.[9] American and other U.S. airlines dominate flights between the United States and virtually every major foreign market.[10]

In May 1992 American again seized the initiative with a simplified fare structure and half-price promotion that sent competitors scurrying for the courts. *Business Week* reported that American was sued by rivals for predatory pricing, and CEO Robert Crandall appeared before a Senate committee investigating accusations that American was trying to drive out weaker competitors.[11] A federal court ultimately cleared American in 1993 of charges that it was trying to drive competitors out of business, but the rivals that filed the suit were considering an appeal.[12]

Even though competitors claimed American was too dominant, the precarious nature of American's strength was driven home by its $1.2 billion loss over the three years preceding 1993. It has been forced to concede markets to small, lean, and flexible competitors such as Southwest Airlines and Reno Air, which have been able to outmaneuver their large rival.[13]

Killing the Goose That Laid the Golden Eggs

U.S. companies such as Microsoft and American Airlines are frequently punished for the very types of activities that are necessary for survival and success against foreign competitors in hypercompetitive environments. These companies are moving aggressively up the four escalation ladders. They are racing to seek new advantages and competing intensely on price and quality as well as timing and know-how. They are building and undermining strongholds, and using the deep pockets they develop from one round of competition to build their next temporary advantage. For example, Microsoft replaced its simple DOS operating system with Windows and may erode the new Windows stronghold with its NT software. The company used the resources from MS-DOS to move to its next advantage in Windows rather than try to shore up its position with DOS, as would have been the traditional strategy of sustaining advantage. In every arena these companies have acted as aggressive hypercompetitors and have been a model for successful world-class competition. Yet this behavior is criticized by competitors as an unfair and monopolistic practice, despite the clear benefits to society of rapid product improvement.

The danger of a government policy that hunts down such companies is that it could end up destroying companies that are the nation's best hope for succeeding in global hypercompetitive markets. As one senior FTC official acknowledged in describing the challenge of the federal government's probe of Microsoft, "Everybody understands how important this industry is to us. We need to fix this thing without killing the goose that laid the golden egg."[14] Can the government force a company to be less hypercompetitive and at the same time expect it to succeed in an intensely competitive global environment?

There is an even more fundamental question policymakers must answer: Are antitrust laws needed in hypercompetition? Traditional views of antitrust are based on an assumption that markets are static and advantages are sustainable. This book has demonstrated what managers now see on a daily basis—that markets are, in fact, dynamic and advantages erode rapidly in hypercompetition. The boundaries and shape of markets are changing so rapidly that it is hard to know whether today's market will even exist tomorrow. This shift in the realities of the environment calls for an equally fundamental shift in antitrust policy.

While views adopted by the Reagan administration were more laissez-faire than traditional models of antitrust, the views of the Reaganites never completely took root in the government. Congress refused to adopt into law Reagan's proposed relaxation of criminal antitrust restrictions. Even though most are unsuccessful, hundreds of private suits are still permitted by the law, carrying the potential of treble punitive damages. States aggressively continue to enforce more restrictive policies, and the big question is whether the future will bring a return to aggressive federal enforcement supported by traditional antitrust views at a time when the public demand for populist, anti–big business revenge is growing because of the sagging economy. Yet in an age of hypercompetition, America should be asking whether we can afford the price of enforcing laws that are no longer needed.

THE OBSOLESCENCE OF ANTITRUST

Antitrust laws were originally designed as a counterweight to the power of large corporations. These laws leveled the playing field for the "little guy":

customers and small competitors. They were supposed to prevent monopolies, collusion and price fixing, predation, and exclusionary practices. These laws were created in a time of robber barons. But now, even though the robber barons are dead, America is still suffering under the same regulations that were used to constrain their power by Teddy Roosevelt in the trust-busting era of the early 1900s and by Franklin Roosevelt during the 1930s.

Today the power of large corporations, derived from sustainable advantages of these firms, is being rapidly eroded. Author Ron Chernow comments, "Years back, there was a tremendous fear about the power of American business; now there's a tremendous fear about its weakness."[15] Companies are only as successful as their next dynamic strategic action. Tiny companies such as Microsoft suddenly become powerhouses, and powerhouses such as IBM sink beneath the waves of competition. Moreover, consumers do not need as much protection in an environment where hypercompetition makes the customer king. As soon as a firm stops satisfying customers, it is replaced by one that is more customer oriented.

Who's Afraid of the Big Bad Wolf Now?

The record of antitrust actions against IBM and General Motors are cautionary tales about the declining value of current antitrust regulations in hypercompetition. These stories also provide some indication of the surprising costs of antitrust enforcement for U.S. competitiveness.

After a grueling thirteen-year antitrust lawsuit, the Department of Justice dropped its case against Big Blue in 1982. The government collected 760 million documents from IBM during the litigation, and IBM's lawyers monitored corporate meetings to keep from fueling the fires during the time that IBM was under siege.[16] But by then the damage was done. Although there were many factors that contributed to IBM's decline, the litigation certainly worked to make the company less aggressive and less flexible. The lawsuit, in the words of the chairman of a large IBM competitor, "gave the lawyers too much power and made the company risk-averse."[17] It dampened IBM's aggressiveness. IBM's delays in seizing opportunities in personal computers, RISC-based chips, and other areas have been blamed, in part, for its decline. As just one example of lost opportunities, IBM passed up a chance to purchase a 10 percent share of Microsoft in 1986 (which would have resulted in a profit of more than $2.6 billion) "because it worried about seeming to dominate the PC business too thoroughly."[18] Between 1986 and 1993 IBM cut more than one hundred thousand jobs.[19] In 1992, struggling to stay above a sea of red ink, IBM announced plans to cut another twenty-five thousand workers, shave $25 million from product development budgets, and $1 billion from administrative expenses.[20] Despite these moves, IBM posted a $4.97 billion loss in 1992.[21]

In 1936, holding more than 50 percent of the U.S. auto market, General Motor's management concluded it could not seize more of the market without triggering severe antitrust actions.[22] For more than thirty years this policy was effective. General Motors would let other competitors open new markets, always keeping its overall share of the market around 50 percent. When Volkswagen entered the U.S. market in the 1950s and 1960s, GM did not counter the new entrant forcefully as it had done successfully against VW and Fiat in Europe. As one commentator noted, "At the time, GM was very much under the anti-trust gun. Dupont had just been ordered to divest itself of its holdings of GM shares; there were anti-trust suits regarding GM's truck and bus business, its earth-moving equipment business, and its locomotive business."[23] To preserve this 50 percent limit, GM sat by as European and then Japanese competitors established their toeholds in the U.S. market. So while domestic and foreign competitors were moving aggressively into new markets, General Motors was treading on eggshells, perhaps even backpedaling to ward off lawsuits.

Certainly this was not the only factor in GM's precipitous decline, but it contributed to a culture that was slow to respond to change and seize new opportunities. In 1992 GM posted a stunning $23.5 billion loss. GM's control of more than half of the U.S. auto market in the 1960s fell to less than 35 percent in 1992. Meanwhile, foreign companies collectively gained an equivalent 35 percent share in the U.S. market[24] with active support of their home governments.

In both these cases the government and corporate executives were as sure of the invulnerability of large corporations as the builders of the *Titanic* were sure it was unsinkable. As Robert B. Coulton, a management consultant and former GM employee remarked, "General Motors was so large and so wealthy, the chairman's biggest worry used to be that the government would break up the company."[25] Both regulators and executives were shocked and surprised at how rapidly advantages can be lost in hypercompetition.

These cases illustrate that markets often are more effective than government action in ensuring that large competitors do not abuse their power. As the *Economist* comments: "After thirteen years, America's Justice Department dropped its probe into IBM because the computer industry had changed beyond all recognition, and because IBM had started to show signs of the malaise which now cripples it. A similarly long-winded investigation of Microsoft would be overtaken by technology twice as swiftly. That is why both the FTC and the Justice Department should get off Microsoft's back."[26]

Markets Replace Antitrust Law

Dominant firms cannot become enduring monopolies, and oligopolies cannot develop long-term, cozy cooperative agreements, because of the rapid and incessant progress of hypercompetition in the four arenas. Companies that use pricing and other strategies to drive competitors out of a market will find that this strategy only works as long as customers are satisfied by the low prices because as soon as the prices increase, reentry is easy. Companies use exclusionary tactics to create entry barriers, but even these do not hold for long, as discussed in Chapter 3.

Moreover, market boundaries continue to grow, making antitrust laws unnecessary. As markets globalize, it is very difficult to create a global monopoly or even oligopoly. Traditional antitrust laws fail to be effective because they were designed for a U.S.-dominated economy. When the primary market was the U.S. market and even world markets were dominated by U.S. firms, U.S. regulators could control the entire competitive dynamics of the system. But now large parts of the system are out of their control. By holding back domestic competitors to protect smaller domestic firms or domestic consumers, antitrust suits can dampen the ability of U.S. firms to act aggressively against international competitors.

Thus, once useful for constraining the power of monopolists, antitrust laws have become a dead weight suspended from the necks of some of America's most successful firms.

THE DYNAMIC EFFICIENCY AND FAIRNESS OF HYPERCOMPETITION

A group of economists who testified for IBM commented that a key weakness of the government's economic analysis in the case was that it was based on a static view of the world.

> [One] underlying error that the government's economic analysis committed was to suppose that a dynamically changing competitive market whose basic feature is technological change can be analyzed in terms of theoretical long-run equilibrium. As a result, the Antitrust Division lawyers and witnesses constantly mistook the price and product change compelled by competition for the restrictive behavior of monopoly. Indeed, the whole of the government's case was a reiteration of complaints about *lower* prices and *better* products—the antithesis of what monopoly produces.[27]

The government failed to recognize the realities of hypercompetition and actually suggested that IBM become less competitive by slowing down its activities in all four arenas of competition.

Many of the prevailing laws were based on the structure-conduct-performance model, which held that the source of competitive advantage is monopoly or market power. Monopolistic firms produce high profits by raising prices and lowering product quality. This view of how profits are generated implies that there is a basic conflict between "corporate strategy (which seeks monopoly) and the public interest (which seeks competition)."[28]

In this context, antitrust laws are needed to promote the public interest by balancing the corporate drive to create monopolies. They seek to achieve this goal by preventing monopoly, predation, actions to exclude competitors from markets, and collusion among firms.

Traditional antitrust laws—designed to create perfect competition and fair play by leveling the playing field through forcing the players to accept competitive parity and eliminating sustainable competitive advantages—fail to address the dynamic realities of hypercompetition. The problem with the traditional approach to antitrust is that it focuses on "*static* equilibrium and *costless* optimization" in face of "dynamic, noncooperative competition among heterogeneous firms where many market transactions and administrative decisions are quite costly. . . . "[29]

Hypercompetitive markets are not in equilibrium. They are in motion. At any given point in time, companies may develop a dominant share of the market. At any given point in time, companies may create a stronghold or build large resources. Companies may end up destroying less successful competitors. Thus, at any given moment in time, a market will almost never achieve a state where all the players are in competitive parity, all with equal footing. Someone will have dominance. But the dynamic motion of the market ensures that these advantages are eroded over time. Companies only stay ahead by building a series of temporary advantages.

Dynamic Efficiency

Vigorous competition leads to four types of dynamic efficiency, corresponding to the four arenas of competition described in Part I. A snapshot of competition in a market at any given time may seem to show inefficiencies, but these inefficiencies are ultimately removed by the dynamic progress of competition. By racing up the escalation ladders in each arena, companies create four types of dynamic efficiency: production efficiency, innovation efficiency, access efficiency, and resource efficiency.

In recent years antitrust laws have been more concerned with promoting the economic efficiency of markets. Because of the influence of the Chicago School of Economics, they primarily have focused, however, on two types of static efficiency: allocative efficiency and X-efficiency.[30] Allocative efficiency is concerned with ensuring that prices are as close as possible to marginal costs at a given moment in time. Unchecked, monopolistic firms can use their power to maintain excessive prices, thereby reallocating wealth from consumers to producers. This creates the inefficiency of reduced output and higher costs to consumers.

X-efficiency is concerned with maximizing the productivity of companies at a given moment in time. Inefficient management may be unconcerned about whether the company's costs are greater than competitors' costs.

These static efficiencies do not consider the long term, however. Prices and costs may be low today because a firm is not making investments necessary to lower future costs, improve future quality, enter new markets, create new know-how, or build deep pockets for the long haul.

Therefore, a different type of efficiency—dynamic efficiency—may actually be more important than these two types of static efficiency. Economist F. M. Scherer comments that "X-efficiency is much more important quantitatively than allocative efficiency, and dynamic efficiency is almost surely even more important."[31]

As early as 1942 Joseph A. Schumpeter recognized some of the weaknesses of traditional static models in explaining competition and proposed that more dynamic forces were at work. He wrote:

> The fundamental impulse that sets and keeps the capitalist engine in motion comes from new consumers' goods, new methods of production or transporation, the new markets, the new forms of industrial organization that capitalist enterprise creates. . . . A system—any system, economic or other—that at *every* given point of time fully utilizes its possibilities to the best advantage may yet in the long run be inferior to a system that does so at *no* given point in time, because the latter's failure to do so may be a condition for the level or speed of long-run performance.[32]

In other words, markets may be out of balance and lack competitive parity among the players at a given point in time yet still achieve excellent long-term performance. It is not "how efficiently resources were allocated and utilized at any moment in time, but how well entrepreneurs seized opportunities for reducing cost through technological (and other) innovations."[33]

Schumpeter and others began to develop an understanding of dynamic efficiency at work in competition, particularly among entrepreneurial firms. By looking at how competitive forces work in each of the four arenas of competition, four types of dynamic efficiency become evident in hypercompetitive markets:

Production efficiency Racing up the escalation ladder in the price and quality arena creates production efficiency. Companies are forced to work toward better quality at lower prices or risk falling behind competitors. As described in Chapter 1, competition moves toward the point of ultimate value. As this point is approached, new definitions of quality restart the competitive cycle. Companies may temporarily gain lower prices and higher quality than their competitors, but the competitors can then match or exceed these levels of quality or price. Moreover, restarting the cycle in the price and quality arena by redefining quality forces new and better products on the market all the time.

Innovation efficiency Racing up the escalation ladder in the timing and know-how arena creates innovation efficiency. Companies generate new knowledge, and that knowledge quickly diffuses. They develop new applications for that knowledge and undermine the positions of competitors, but the next round of innovations gives new or existing competitors an opportunity to seize the initiative.

Access efficiency Racing up the escalation ladder in the strongholds arena leads to access efficiency. Goods made by a company become available anywhere in the world. Customers have access to a wider variety of goods and sellers. Competitors from all parts of the world and from different industries move quickly into markets. Separate industries merge. Companies may temporarily control a market, and concentration can occur in industries. But this does not lead to long-term exploitation of customers even if one firm achieves a dominant position by using a series of temporary advantages. This domination occurs only because companies keep new entrants out by competing aggressively and constantly moving forward. Coke and Pepsi control the soft drink industry, but they compete aggressively because of the threat of new entrants in soft drinks or the merging of the industry with other beverage industries.

Resource efficiency Racing up the escalation ladder in the deep-pockets arena leads to resource efficiency. Companies seek to expand their resource base. They look for assets that are currently underutilized. They build their global reach so that they can find the best use for their resources. Even when companies build up a huge stockpile of assets, these assets are not themselves a threat to competition. Hypercompetitive companies must use these assets to build their next temporary advantage before their competitors. Small, resource-poor competitors could arrive first at the next temporary advantage through assembling resources, teaming up with other companies, or shifting the rules of competition. IBM bet the company on the 360 series computers, and the bet paid off in the 1960s. But its vast resources were unable to sustain its position when it was unable to keep up a strong position in the next temporary advantage (personal computers). Instead tiny companies such as Apple and Microsoft became giants by seizing the next advantage. Their challenge now is to invest their newly found deep pockets to build the next temporary advantage. So there is a constant struggle over the best use for resources to eliminate waste.

Fair Play

Hypercompetitive markets are dynamically efficient and allow a new type of fair play. Traditional antitrust sought to guarantee a type of fair play, which it defined as "competitive parity" wherein no bully dominated its opponents and knocked them out of the game. A new type of fair play exists in hypercompetition—no one is protected from failure based on their position at any given point in time. Size doesn't matter, as much as ingenuity does. Victory goes to the smartest and hardest working. Fairness is based on merit.

But hypercompetition is not a level playing field in the sense that all the boxers are necessarily in the same weight class. In business, if you are outweighed, you get friends to help. Moreover, there can be winners that dominate for a long while. The firms who lead on the way up the escalation ladders in each arena are those that will build profits and position. It is these firms that will create jobs. The laggards in each arena will decline and lose jobs. We need policies that ensure that U.S. firms will be the ones moving quickly forward, building position, and creating jobs.

ANTITRUST LAWS HAVE A NEGATIVE EFFECT ON HYPERCOMPETITION

Traditional antitrust laws chill and dampen the aggressive competition necessary to achieve the four types of dynamic efficiency in hypercompetition. When firms are very successful at racing up the escalation ladders, they are, ironically, vulnerable to allegations of being anticompetitive.

In hypercompetition companies often do things that might be interpreted as anticompetitive under antitrust regulations. Hypercompetitive firms create new and better quality products, a result that in turn looks like an attempt to monopolize a market when it leads to high market share and big profits. These profits are a reward for effective competition and must be used to develop the next temporary advantage, or they will be lost to a competitor. As discussed in the previous chapter, companies may make hypercompetitive use of cooperation, generating profits in one market to fund hypercompetitive behavior in another.

Dominant firms may also stay dominant by consistently staying ahead of their competitors on the escalation ladders. However, this dominance is not an attempt to monopolize a market. It is the natural outcome of hypercompetitive pressures that force firms to move up the escalation ladders faster than their competitors. If they do not do so, they fall behind and lose position. Yet when the law encourages firms to slow down their movement up the ladders to protect fair play and create competitive parity, the law destroys the natural function of the market and the dynamic efficiencies that this market process creates.

William F. Baxter, former head of the Justice Department's Antitrust Division, once commented that the purpose of the Robinson-Patman Act on price discrimination is to put lead weights in the saddlebags of the fastest riders.[34] He said, "It led companies like IBM to compete with kid gloves and often almost to preserve competitors and to raise their own prices so that their market shares didn't get too big. So in this perverse way, a section [of the law] that was ostensibly supposed to limit monopolies was causing large successful companies to engage in monopolistic behavior in order to hold their market share down."[35] He also credits restrictions on horizontal and vertical mergers in the 1960s and 1970s with the rise of conglomerates that later had to be disassembled in the 1980s and 1990s.[36] Thus, antitrust laws may have encouraged major strategic mistakes by corporate management seeking to avoid becoming too dominant and too hypercompetitive.

Does Antitrust Really Reduce Hypercompetitiveness?

Many antitrust cases against large competitors have been filed by the government. Many more private "nuisance" suits have been filed by smaller competitors. Yet the courts are becoming more permissive, and at least during the Reagan Administration, the policy of the executive branch was more laissez-faire. More and more practices previously outlawed as predatory are now accepted, and the private lawsuits are rarely won by the plaintiff. So some might ask, Where is the harm?

Even though the plaintiff is unlikely to prevail in court, these suits and investigations have an effect. The effect, however, is not to increase the competitiveness of U.S. industries. Rather, antitrust laws and enforcement have a variety of negative effects in hypercompetitive environments that harm individual competitors and U.S. competitiveness.

Antitrust laws were originally designed to promote competition. But, as discussed below, these laws have the ironic opposite effect: dampening the aggressiveness of large companies, limiting competitive actions, and creating chilling ambiguity.

Even though the intent is to protect consumers from monopolistic practices such as excessive prices and intentional production shortages, the effect of antitrust laws is often to support small competitors over large ones, sometimes even failing to recognize the damaging effect on consumers and the competitiveness of large firms. The laws tend to threaten to break up powerful, successful U.S. companies and alliances that could be used to compete head-to-head with even more powerful foreign alliances.

Antitrust laws create a series of chilling effects that tend to increase the caution of American managers, sometimes even paralyzing them. These chilling effects are caused by

- fear of nuisance suits filed by competitors
- uncertainty produced by ambiguity of the enforcement of laws
- direct and indirect costs of such suits
- removal of incentives for innovation

Each of these is discussed below.

CHILLING EFFECT 1: FEAR OF NUISANCE SUITS

Antitrust laws are a problem not only for the companies that are hauled into court but also for those that live under the threat of being hauled into court. Laws that authorize liberal antitrust suits by private competitors tend to create docile and less aggressive American competitors, weakening the position of the United States in world markets.

Lawsuits and the threat of lawsuits dampen the ability of some firms to move aggressively against competitors, to expand into new markets, and even to speak aggressively. Chief Judge Bauer notes in his opinion on Indiana Grocery's appeal of its antitrust case against the Kroger Company, that the Supreme Court has emphasized "that summary judgment may be especially appropriate in an antitrust case because of the chill antitrust litigation can have on legitimate price competition."[37]

Although recent government enforcement and court decisions are eliminating the prohibition of many pricing strategies, private lawsuits have tended to focus an inordinate amount of attention on predatory pricing, thus chilling the use of price as a weapon. Focusing primarily on static price comparisons to ensure that price is "competitively" set at marginal cost ignores the dynamic nature of markets in the cost-quality arena as well as the importance of actions in other arenas of competition.

CHILLING EFFECT 2: LEGAL AMBIGUITY AND INDECENT BEHAVIOR

Like obscenity laws, antitrust laws are so ambiguous that there is a chilling effect created by their uncertainty. As Jeffrey Harris, an economist at the Massachusetts Institute of Technology, commented, "You know predatory pricing when you see it."[38] But everyone involved has his own view of what predatory pricing is, and even the legal definition continues to be redefined by shifts in court cases and government enforcement. So companies that practice the art of aggressive and successful competition are in constant danger of being charged with indecent behavior. Companies that are at all risk-averse are forced to stay well inside the lines of the law to avoid action from competitors and the government.

The Wall Street Journal reports that the lines of the law are so hazy that even as Northwest and Continental airlines were filing a suit accusing American Airlines of predatory pricing, these two accusers were themselves accused of alleged predatory pricing by smaller competitors.[39] That companies can be accused of predatory pricing and accuse other firms of predatory pricing is a sign of how muddled the current laws have become. Companies can be hauled into court for pricing too high as well as pricing too low, so U.S. businesses are caught between a rock and a hard place when it comes to pricing policy. If the company prices are seen as too low, it could be charged by a competitor's nuisance suit with predatory pricing. If its prices are seen as too high, a company could be charged with colluding to raise prices above marginal costs based on market power or tacit collusion. Either way aggressive competitors end up in court. In the airline industry, when prices go up, companies are charged with tacit price fixing through posting prices on a computer system. When prices go down, companies are charged with predatory pricing.

Overall, then, antitrust has a chilling effect on hypercompetitive behavior, because even when companies are not being sued, no one really knows what is acceptable. The laws are so vague that they are not enforceable with consistency. This causes firms to be more conservative and risk-averse. It is hard to tell how pervasive this chilling effect has become, but when one asks managers how pervasive it is, they say that the aggressiveness of their strategic actions is restrained by the law.

CHILLING EFFECT 3: THE EXTREME COSTS OF GOVERNMENT ANTITRUST SUITS

Even though suits initiated by the government are becoming increasingly rare and are rarely lost by the defendant, they still strike fear in the hearts of managers. Just as the severity of the death penalty scares people, the costs of a criminal or civil government suit makes a lot of people more cautious than their foreign rivals.

Companies and the government are expending considerable resources on cases that ultimately prove to be unnecessary or unwinnable. The thirteen-year IBM investigation and lawsuit, for example, cost the company and the Justice Department an estimated $200 million in legal and photocopying costs alone.[40] It required more than twenty-five hundred depositions, including forty-five days by chairman Frank Carey.[41] To give an idea of the scope of the impact, every part of the organization was ordered to save documents that could be related to the case, and special collection bins were scattered throughout the worldwide organization. By the end of the investigation in 1982, just the cost of storing those forty-six thousand tons of documents alone was costing IBM $5 million per year.[42] In addition, millions of dollars were spent by the federal government in developing its millions of pages of testimony on the case.

Antitrust actions can also negatively affect stock value and damage the company's reputation (leading to higher transaction costs if other companies believe the tarnished firm will act opportunistically or be untrustworthy). In addition, private antitrust lawsuits were estimated to cost U.S. companies $250 million per year in litigation costs.[43] The magnitude of these costs is enough to make many managers worried about the impact of aggressive behavior on the top managers and even the value of the company.

CHILLING EFFECT 4: THE LOSS OF REWARDS FOR INNOVATION

In hypercompetition companies need to use the New 7-S's to gain temporary dominance and use them over and over to keep dominance. But antitrust laws often punish dominant firms, even threatening to break them up. This removes the incentive for racing up the escalation ladders and disrupting markets, thereby reducing the competitiveness of firms. The government refuses to see that it is good strategy (not monopoly power) that gives the firm its dominance. When laws try to create an even playing field by forcing firms into continual competitive parity, they chill hypercompetitive behavior by criminalizing competition and reducing the dynamic efficiency of the market process.

> Kellogg, General Mills, General Foods, and Quaker Oats were charged with antitrust violations in 1972 because of their hypercompetitive behavior. The FTC's case claimed that they "sought to stifle rival firms by introducing a 'profusion' of about 150 brands of cereal between 1950 and 1970," many of which were differentiated on the basis of minor variations in color or shape.[44]

Even though losing this type of suit is becoming less likely, there is still a chilling effect on innovation created by private lawsuits alleging exclusionary actions of this type. When antitrust laws force successful innovators to prove their innocence in court, innovation becomes more costly, and customers are forced to pay a hidden price due to the long-term loss of product innovation.

Damp and Chilled to the Bones

It is unclear whether these chilling effects merely freeze a few companies in place or chill most managers to their bones. However, the government tends to completely dismiss the cost of chilling hypercompetitive behavior.

If antitrust laws are having a chilling effect on managers, then the direct costs of antitrust litigation do not even begin to capture the full financial impact of these regulations. The costs of lost opportunities and conceding market share and jobs to foreign competitors are enormous. Although the connection between the failure of corporations and private or government antitrust actions has yet to be demonstrated, it is an issue that should receive careful attention from federal legislators and regulators. If, as many managers suspect, there is a link between antitrust actions and strategic conservatism, this should be a compelling reason for reconsidering the current structure of antitrust laws. Moreover, even if a general chilling effect is not found, it is clear that some specific hypercompetitive behavior has been historically dampened by the law.

Antitrust laws also have a direct impact on competition by restricting specific hypercompetitive tactics and slowing hypercompetitive moves by competitors. Among these dampening effects are

- limiting the hypercompetitive use of cooperation
- destroying critical mass (size) and strongholds
- making secrecy more difficult
- eliminating the use of hypercompetitive language and strategic intent

Each of these is discussed below.

DAMPENING EFFECT 1:
LIMITING THE HYPERCOMPETITIVE USE OF COOPERATION

As discussed in Chapters 4 and 10, joining forces to compete against other firms or alliances can be an effective use of cooperation in hypercompetition. Although the recent changes in the laws allowing closer domestic cooperation are in the right direction, they probably don't go far enough. Collaboration is not the preferred response to hypercompetition. But if groups of companies use collaboration in a hypercompetitive way (such as to gain the resources to take on other groups of companies using the New 7-S's), then collaboration enhances hypercompetitiveness. In competing with a Japanese keiretsu, for example, U.S. firms are at a disadvantage because of the restrictions of antitrust laws, which still prohibit joint manufacturing and some vertical integration strategies.

Traditionally, antitrust laws have tended to keep U.S. firms from joining together to compete against foreign rivals. For example, the partnership between GM and DuPont might have served as an American keiretsu, but it was broken up by the federal government in the 1940s. Had GM and DuPont been allowed to continue in their alliance, the competitive environment might have been very different in the U.S. car industry. Would GM have been more aggressive in the use of new plastics and new fuels if DuPont and GM worked more closely together? Would GM have reacted faster to its loss of U.S. market share if DuPont executives served as vigilant members of GM's board? We will never know.

With the rise of R&D consortia and a flourishing of business alliances, the government's attitude toward cooperation has relaxed somewhat recently. In 1984 Congress passed the National Cooperative Research Act, which makes it easier for firms interested in pursuing joint research and development to do so. Even so, firms cannot jointly manufacture products developed from this research without risking antitrust suits, and vertical integration of the type between DuPont and GM is still intensely scrutinized.

These consortia in the United States are often tangled in a web of red tape that makes it difficult for them to operate effectively. For example, by 1993 the U.S. Advanced Battery Consortium, created to encourage the development of batteries for electric vehicles, has been able to distribute only $81 million of a projected $264 million since its founding in 1991.[45]

New regulations signed into law in 1993 have reduced antitrust penalties for companies involved in U.S. joint manufacturing alliances.[46] But these reforms stop short of actively encouraging joint manufacturing projects. Companies would still face the uncertainty of antitrust suits, even with reduced levels of penalties. The irony is that America's Big Three automakers already have such joint manufacturing ventures with foreign competitors, without fear of antitrust action, but have been prohibited for the most part from teaming up with one another.

DAMPENING EFFECT 2:
DESTROYING CRITICAL MASS (SIZE) AND STRONGHOLDS

In the past, aggressive U.S. antitrust actions have even led to the creation of foreign competitors. A landmark ruling against the Aluminum Company of America (ALCOA) in 1945 illustrates the impact of antitrust laws on global competition. Appeals court judge Learned Hand wrote in his opinion, "ALCOA insists that it never excluded competitors; but we can think of no more effective exclusion than progressively to embrace each new opportunity as it opened and to face every newcomer with new capacity already geared into a great organization, having the advantage of experience, trade connections, and elite personnel."[47] ALCOA was being punished for being too hypercompetitive, made a criminal for "embracing each new opportunity" and aggressively defending itself against all comers.

The upshot of this punishment was that the company was broken in two—its U.S. operations continuing as ALCOA and its Canadian operations continuing as ALCAN. Now the Canadian competitor resulting from this process has become a strong foreign competitor to ALCOA, even challenging it in U.S. markets. So the U.S. government created a foreign competitor that then challenged the U.S. company. At the time it seemed to be a good idea to break up this monopoly, but this view was rather shortsighted and did not recognize the dynamics of the marketplace. Over time, global markets, government nationalization, the invention of substitute materials, vertical integration, and alliances with large aluminum users created lots of new competitors.

Only in America do we take our strengths and destroy them. Whereas some countries have an industrial policy that promotes the strongest competitors, America has a reverse industrial policy designed to break up and hold back its largest, most aggressive firms. While we are not advocating the creation of an industrial policy, America should not be binding the hands of its most powerful competitors. It should stand back and let competitive firms succeed.

DAMPENING EFFECT 3: MAKING SECRECY MORE DIFFICULT

Although winning antitrust claims in court is difficult, gaining a hearing often is not. The discovery process in private suits can give a competitor access to cost data and other strategic information that hypercompetitive firms would normally like to keep secret. Thus, the trial itself affects competition by revealing strategic information about a competitor and therefore limiting its ability to surprise and disrupt its rival.

For example, during a suit based on the Robinson-Patman Act, three defenses against charges of price discrimination are allowed: distress conditions such as bankruptcy, lower costs of producing or delivering goods, or the need to meet an equally low price of a competitor.[48] Even if sensitive corporate information is sometimes protected through the court's use of third-party audits and legal mechanisms that prevent direct transfer of information to a competitor, the company filing the suit often can use the discovery process to find out which of the defenses is being used. If the accused company is using a defense of lower costs, this reveals key information to the competitor. If it isn't using that defense, it may reveal that the company doesn't have lower costs. If the accused company does try to plead lower costs, the plaintiff's lawyers can use the discovery process to challenge how those costs are computed, revealing considerable strategic information about how the defendant computes margins and profits on products, how it allocates overhead, and other information.

DAMPENING EFFECT 4: ELIMINATING THE USE OF HYPERCOMPETITIVE LANGUAGE AND STRATEGIC INTENT

Antitrust laws have not only dampened the aggressiveness of actions but also limited how U.S. competitors can talk about strategy and set their goals. Because intent to destroy competitors is such a central part of many antitrust cases, corporate statements that show such aggressive intent can be the smoking guns of antitrust cases. Yet in hypercompetition market disruption and the destruction of a competitor's temporary advantage are key to success. So companies are forced to pretend that they are not doing what they are doing. American companies cannot use aggressive metaphors to describe their actions if those metaphors convey evidence of intent. Companies cannot "kill" competitors, and they cannot use "predatory" pricing to undercut competitors. But they *do* act aggressively, and they *do* help their competitors die a natural death. They are not allowed to price below costs, but they *do* legitimately adjust their bookkeeping methods to make sure they don't price below their recorded costs. All of this has forced the United States to become a nation of hypocrites that do things that they can't admit to.

Honda's slogan, Annihilate, crush, and destroy Yamaha! is not the type of statement a U.S. senior executive could make openly. The trouble such language can cause in the United States can be seen from the case when Harvard professor Michael Porter allegedly presented a plan for "conquering" the USFL to National Football League managers in 1984. The presentation was cited as the "smoking gun"[49] in the USFL's successful antitrust case. According to reports of court testimony, Porter's presentation included a war metaphor and references to guerrilla warfare and generalship, all of which were considered evidence of the NFL's intent to destroy the upstart league.[50] When one of the leading U.S. strategic thinkers comes under attack for merely talking about aggressive competitive actions, it is clear that the American defense of free speech does not extend to statements of good business strategy.

American Airlines CEO Robert Crandall has been called "a walking antitrust case"[51] because of his aggressive competitive statements in testimony to a Senate committee and in public statements. An American Airlines memo about Pan Am, in which Crandall scrawled a note in the margins, "Crush these guys," was brought up in the 1993 antitrust case. Defending the memo, Crandall has said he likes to use vigorous language to motivate employees. In response to questions by lawyers, he compared his statement to his comments about a caterer who served the wrong food on certain American flights. In a memo Crandall said to kill him. Of course, he said he was speaking metaphorically. The effect was that the force of Crandall's language in reference to Pan Am was then undermined.[52]

This limits the ability of U.S. firms to create a warlike culture with urgency and motivation. To be number one is a less compelling mission than to crush the competition. Yet the Japanese often believe their proverb, "business is war."

Companies are also not permitted to use "predatory" or "exclusionary" practices designed to destroy a specific competitor. They can, however, speed the competitor's death by natural causes. Companies in the United States cannot be driven out of business by their American competitors. Those that try to destroy their competitors end up in court. So we create a fantasy land wherein many companies go bankrupt, but none, at least officially, is destroyed by a competitor. Yet we know competitors do force others into bankruptcy with better products, lower prices, and new technological advances. Again, by prohibiting the use of aggressive language, companies are forced to mask their true motives for actions that are designed to weaken or destroy competitors. So they fight this competitive battle with one hand behind their backs, or they carry on without being able to say they are doing so, creating communication and motivation problems that become especially rampant in large companies where there is no way to tell the troops of the unstated intent of many strategic moves.

Finally, pricing below costs can lead to charges of "predatory pricing" or "dumping." So companies cannot talk about pricing below costs, but they can use transfer pricing and overhead allocations to manipulate costs. For example, if a company sets a low transfer price for a specific component from another one of its plants, it can significantly reduce the overall cost of the final product. Thus, it may be able to price its product below competitors but still not price below cost. Similarly, it could adjust how it charges overhead to a specific plant or product. Determining the company's true costs in such an internal environment is virtually impossible without exploring the entire internal accounting process within the company. Thus, companies may be able to price below their real cost (to enter a new market or to gain market share, for example), but they cannot talk about it, and they can't keep the books in an accurate way. They must invent fictions to cover up what they are doing.

It might seem that if companies are able to act in the way they need to in hypercompetition, there is no great loss in not being able to openly discuss aggressive strategy. The problem is that, by not openly laying out such strategies, the company loses the ability to mobilize its employees and investors. It is much more powerful and clear for a company to set a goal to "annihilate, crush, and destroy" a competitor than to pursue the same strategy without clearly stating the objective of the company. Foreign companies can do this, but American firms cannot without risk of creating evidence that will be used in a court of law. U.S. executives are forced to talk mildly even when they act aggressively. They appear meek in a world of wolves and lions, creating misimpressions. This confuses employees and forgoes the ability to send competitors effective threats via verbal signals. And it gives rivals the sense that American firms can be attacked without fierce retaliation.

The Overall Perverse Effects of Antitrust

The net result of these chilling and dampening effects is to restrain our largest and best competitors, often at the expense of customers, because the law has three perverse effects:

1. Protecting small competitors at the expense of large firms
2. Freezing the dynamics of the market process at a time when markets are naturally becoming more dynamic
3. Forcing American companies to partner with foreign firms when they are prohibited from partnering with other American firms

These effects are perverse because consumers often pay the price for the law's lack of understanding of the true nature of competition in a dynamic, not static, sense.

PERVERSE EFFECT 1: PROTECTING SMALL COMPETITORS AT THE EXPENSE OF CONSUMERS

Although government policy may be moving away from the goal of reducing industry concentration and breaking up large firms, the net effect of federal and state actions and private lawsuits is often to protect small companies at the expense of both large companies and consumers. The

Robinson-Patman Act was originally referred to as the Wholesale Grocer's Protection Act because of its intent to protect small grocers against large retail chains.[53]

An examination of private antitrust lawsuits concluded that "there is reason to suspect that most private antitrust litigation is driven by extortion motives" and "antitrust laws do offer a mechanism by which firms can benefit themselves at the expense of their rivals and the consumers of their products."[54]

Antitrust cases are brought either directly by smaller competitors or at their instigation. An antitrust case in Arkansas filed by smaller rivals against Wal-Mart seems to be more concerned with the damage done to small pharmacies trying to compete with Wal-Mart than with consumers. The federal investigation of Microsoft has been spurred on by its smaller competitors that stand to gain the most by restraining Microsoft's continued product innovation. The suit against American Airlines was brought by two smaller rivals. In each case weaker competitors are asking the government, courts, or FTC to save them because they cannot stand the competitive pressure.

Are customers hurt by Wal-Mart's low prices? Are they hurt by Microsoft's dominance of the software industry? Have they been hurt by the volume pricing discounts offered to computer manufacturers (which have been the focus of the government's investigation)? Could anyone argue that the software industry, with rapid innovation and competitive pricing, has been slowed by Microsoft's actions? Were customers hurt by the fare wars in the airline industry?

It would be hard to find a consumer in any one of these markets that would complain about these strategies. In hypercompetition there is little danger that a company can kill off its competitors and then later boost prices, so who is being helped by antitrust enforcement? As an article on the Wal-Mart case notes, "Wal-Mart's appeal to consumers could make it difficult for its challengers to win in the court of public opinion."[55] Yet an Arkansas judge ruled in October 1993 that Wal-Mart had violated state antitrust laws ordering the large discount retailer to pay nearly $300,000 to three Arkansas pharmacies.[56]

Do small companies even need government protection to thrive? They only need this protection if they are weak and ineffective competitors. But if the small firms are effective hypercompetitors, they will bring down the large companies through direct actions, by outcompeting them. While the major airlines were fighting in court over pricing policies, one of the few airlines to post a profit in the third quarter of 1992 (following the brutal summer fare wars) was a small company that managed to stay out of court.

Southwest Airlines, only the seventh largest U.S. airline, succeeded where the six larger airlines did not because of its impeccable record of delivering passengers and baggage on time, keeping its prices down, and offering dependable, no-frills service. It has lured growing numbers of customers away from larger competitors, allowing it to capture two thirds of Texas air travel. The big players, such as American, have studied Southwest's approach to see if they can apply some of its strategies.[57] Southwest's greatest protection has come not from government regulations or private lawsuits but from its own ability to identify and create new advantages over its competitors.

Even if the small players are truly weaker, it does not make sense to protect weak and ineffective small players by forcing the large players to be less aggressive. Instead it would be a more effective policy to force the smaller players to be more competitive like Southwest Airlines. If small players are using their natural advantages of flexibility and speed, they don't need antitrust protection.

PERVERSE EFFECT 2: FREEZING THE DYNAMICS OF THE MARKET PROCESS

The second perverse effect of chilling and dampening hypercompetitive behavior is that the law's goal seems to be to freeze movement along the escalation ladders at a point where the players have competitive parity. Yet in hypercompetition it is clear that the first to jump to the next rung on the ladder (or to restart the cycle) wins. By stopping this movement, the hope is to create a perfectly competitive market where price is set at the marginal cost of firms in the market and their cumulative production output equals the demand for that product at that price. This is, of course, a state of static equilibrium that can never exist in a dynamic world. Freezing movement up the escalation ladders in the four arenas of competition means the loss of the firm's dynamic efficiencies. Thus, the consumer actually pays in the long run for the short-run benefit of a price exactly equal to marginal cost.

PERVERSE EFFECT 3: FORCING U.S. PARTNERING WITH FOREIGN FIRMS

The law's preoccupation with cooperation as a collusive device has led to the perverse effect of prohibiting many types of alliances among U.S. firms, creating foreign entities and transferring U.S. technology abroad even more quickly. IBM is able to partner with Siemens and Toshiba to jointly develop *and manufacture* new RAM chips, but its joint venture with Apple and Motorola can only develop new lower-power consumer chips for laptops. If IBM wants to partner to produce these chips, it must find a foreign partner. Thus, completely integrated deals can be achieved only with foreign firms.

Even though the U.S. antitrust regulations have gone farther than ever before in allowing joint ventures among U.S. competitors, the law has not gone far enough. It still does not recognize that, in the dynamic environments of hypercompetition, the two firms can partner in one area and compete vigorously in other areas. The regulations still do not see that partnering is often designed to enhance the competitiveness of the alliance so that it may compete against other alliances.

Consumers are harmed by what amounts to an obsession with collusion conspiracy theory. Any constraint on partnering slows the development of new products, prevents the combination of two firms' manufacturing efforts from achieving economies of scale, and eliminates the creation of new sellers in the marketplace. Moreover, the transfer of U.S. jobs to overseas joint ventures also hurts consumers because no one consumes very much (except welfare) without a job.

THE UNCERTAIN FUTURE OF ANTITRUST: WHAT IS NEEDED

Fortunately, most hypercompetitive firms never run afoul of the antitrust laws. In fact, recent court decisions have increasingly recognized the realities of hypercompetition. The courts have eased restrictions on competition on price and quality (arena 1 competition). The decision in favor of American Airlines and a ruling in the cigarette industry have made predatory pricing harder to prove, for example. In a 1993 U.S. Supreme Court decision concerning predatory pricing (Brooke Group, Ltd. v. Brown and Williamson Tobacco), Justice Anthony Kennedy wrote in overturning a lower court's decision that "predatory pricing schemes in general are implausible."[58] The court held that companies must prove that the company's "predatory" actions would ultimately lead to higher prices for consumers. The DuPont titanium dioxide case allowed pricing below cost to increase volume if it is done to gain economies of scale or learning-curve effects. In other words, all you need is an excuse to get tough on pricing.

Recent court decisions are also easing restrictions on aggressive competition on timing and know-how (arena 2). The Berkey Photo v. Kodak case indicates that companies can introduce innovations even if they may damage a smaller competitor. But even though appeals courts overturned the original $87 million award against Kodak, the company spent eight years in litigation and still ended up paying $6.7 million to its smaller competitor.[59]

These decisions recognize, at least in part, some of the new realities of hypercompetitive markets. The U.S. Supreme Court's decision in the Brown and Williamson case emphasized "the realities of the market" above abstract theories.[60] These realities, according to the majority opinion in the case, recognize that lower prices tend to benefit consumers even if they hurt rivals and that predatory pricing schemes are unlikely to create a sustainable monopoly in the current business environment.[61]

While the courts are gradually shifting their view, so too is the federal bureaucracy. The rise of the Chicago School of Economics in the 1980s led to less aggressive enforcement by the FTC and the Justice Department. In fact, the antitrust division of the U.S. Department of Justice has shrunk by a third since 1980.[62] The number of antitrust suits in U.S. district courts declined from 877 in 1986 to 657 in 1989, and almost all of those suits were private.[63]

This reduction in antitrust action during the 1980s was precipitated by the Chicago School's perspective on antitrust and competition. Chicago sees profits not as "monopoly booty" but rather as "rent to unique factors," that is, rewards for good products and better resources.[64] The goal of strategy, according to the Chicago School, is not to collude or build monopolies but rather to compete aggressively to seek rents.

It argues that antitrust should be relaxed to promote active competition and open and free markets, which they believe result in a type of efficiency called static, or allocative, efficiency. In other words, the market takes care of itself by establishing its own natural equilibrium price. They claim that easy entry and exit creates "contestable" markets, which will attract entry when firms identify profit opportunities because prices are too high. This encourages companies to compete vigorously and results in low prices for consumers.

Unfortunately, the result of many free and open markets was not static efficiency. As noted earlier, hypercompetition results in some firms gaining dominance and others losing. Thus, at any given moment in time, price may not fall to the perfectly competitive price. In fact, prices may be raised to support competition in other arenas. Thus, the outcome of the laissez-faire enforcement policy of the 1980s has been considered disappointing by traditional antitrust enforcers, who want to see perfect competition and competitive parity among the players.

Unfortunately, the Chicago School may have advocated the right antitrust policy for the wrong reasons. Open and free markets do achieve efficiency, but it is not the type of static efficiency expected by traditional antitrust enforcers. It is dynamic efficiency. The Chicago School has been attacked for positing contestable markets and a hypothetical balance that was not seen during the 1980s. However, Chicago's conclusions about antitrust policy are still sound.

No Antitrust Policy before Its Time

Chicago may have also asserted its position too soon. Competition continues to heat up in many markets. Technological change creates periodic windows for entry, and global competitors get government help to overcome many barriers. Thus, consistent with the assumptions of the Chicago School, markets are becoming more contestable in the 1990s, and competitors are aggressively pursuing profit opportunities. This all results in hypercompetition with constant jockeying for dominance in four arenas of competition, not static efficiency.

Unfortunately the lack of a static efficient outcome has led to some troubling signs of a return to more aggressive enforcement. Changes in enforcement during the 1980s, and maybe even legal decisions, may have had as much to do with politics as with a new perception of competitive realities. Under President Bush antitrust enforcement began to pick up steam. Legislation proposed by the Reagan administration to permanently change the antitrust laws was not passed by Congress. The Clinton administration has given signs that it intends to pursue antitrust even more aggressively.

What Is Needed: A New Ideology of Competition

The United States must not only reconsider how it enforces antitrust, it should also reconsider the design of antitrust laws in an environment of increasing hypercompetition. As discussed in this chapter, current antitrust laws are no longer necessary to ensure competition in dynamic markets, and they now have a variety of chilling and dampening effects on dynamic competition. These laws should be redesigned to continue to achieve their original purpose of promoting competition. But the definition of competition must be changed. The view that the only "good" competition is perfect competition is dead. It is too static for the future. A new ideology, recognizing the new realities of hypercompetition, is needed. This must effectively promote hypercompetition in each of the four arenas, encouraging aggressive movement up the escalation ladders, even if this is "unfair" to the losers of these battles.

To the extent that markets remain complacent and less aggressive, the appropriate role of regulators is to increase hypercompetitiveness. Instead of punishing aggressive competitors, government should assure that the slow competitors move aggressively. Laws should continue to limit forms of cooperation that dampen competition, but not if that cooperation is being used for a hypercompetitive purpose, as outlined in the previous chapter. They should allow stronger U.S.-based global competitors to ally with each other and produce benefits for consumers in lower prices and higher levels of innovation. This would also strengthen the overall economy more than protect smaller players, which will also fall prey to large foreign firms in the absence of such change.

Even if the trend toward less aggressive enforcement continues, this is not enough. The laws need to be redesigned to meet the realities of current competition. No company could survive today using strategies and equipment designed for the markets of the 1900s or 1930s. The world is moving rapidly forward, but the law has not kept pace.

In today's competitive environment laws must be changed to recognize the realities of hypercompetition. Regulators should also have different policies for industries that are in hypercompetition and those that are not. The government could also utilize tools such as the Four Arena analysis to determine which industries are moving rapidly up the escalation ladders and which may require some intervention to keep them moving. Comparison should be made with overseas markets, especially those in Japan and Germany. Thus, the government should be required to classify industries based on whether at least one player is rapidly moving up the escalation ladders in the four arenas. Note that this does not mean all players need to be moving at the same rate on the same escalation ladder. Some may lead in different arenas, and sometimes one firm can be totally dominant on all the ladders in hypercompetition. So large aggressive players should not be the target of government intervention. They are doing a good job. Instead the weak smaller firm should be made more competitive by encouraging the use of the New 7-S's. When the small firms are more aggressive, large sluggish firms should be forced to be more aggressive or broken up to enhance their flexibility and speed. This is in direct contrast to today's policy, which slows down large aggressive players, leaves sluggish firms alone, and protects weak smaller firms. Thus, the methods of antitrust enforcement should differ for slow-moving (nonhypercompetitive) industries and for fast moving (hypercompetitive) ones.

SLOW-MOVING INDUSTRIES

In domestic markets that are not currently hypercompetitive, regulations should encourage hypercompetitive actions. The government should move to break up collusive behavior (except when it is used in a hypercompetitive way, as discussed in Chapter 10). In particular, it must eliminate collusive agreements where the funds are being used for higher dividends and inflated wages instead of new product development, cost-reduction programs, market expansion, and other hypercompetitive purposes. Actions should also be taken to force players to speed up the ladders, if the market is not doing so, by removing disincentives to competition, and making sure entry is free and open (even to foreign competitors).

Even in slow-moving industries the government needs to weigh the costs of intervention and carefully monitor movements in domestic as well as overseas markets. While the government should protect consumers, regulators should also take a broader view to consider and measure the impact of their actions on jobs, innovation, and global competitiveness. Moreover, regulators must recognize that the dynamics of the market may change naturally. If markets are nonhypercompetitive, a hypercompetitor may enter it, knowing that it can easily dominate the established laggards in the market. Substitute products may be invented, the market may merge with other markets, players may vertically integrate into the market from adjacent industries, or the boundaries of the market may expand to a worldwide market. Enforcement is unnecessary where impending changes will do the job faster and better than the government can and where the number of nonhypercompetitive markets is decreasing naturally due to technological advances, globalization, and all the other sea changes that are present or soon to come.

In some cases intervention may be warranted. The slow-moving U.S. steel industry in the 1950s and 1960s might have benefited from more aggressive government action to shake it up and encourage it to be more competitive. But if, as in Japan, the cooperation at home is used to fund more aggressive competition and expansion abroad, it should perhaps be allowed. Instead, tacitly cooperative behavior in the U.S. steel industry made it a sitting duck for foreign competitors because the profits went to higher dividends and wages, not market disruption. The ideal goal should be to create an environment in which companies compete aggressively at home and abroad, but circumstances sometimes say that forcing firms to do this may disadvantage them against global players with secure domestic strongholds.

In slow-moving industries no player is hypercompetitive—even the industry leader. In this case the leader should be encouraged to be more hypercompetitive. Breaking up AT&T has created a hypercompetitive, high-tech firm out of a large bureaucratic utility. The breakup also contributed to the development in the telecommunications industry of several strong and aggressive Baby Bell competitors, which have become successful players in global competition. By the end of the 1980s, the Bell operating companies and AT&T were spending a larger share of revenues on research and development than before the breakup. The estimated annual welfare gains from repricing services ranged from $664 million to $1.4 billion through 1988. Overall, "the efficiency gains from the opening up of the telephone industry have more than offset the possible losses that may be caused by the sacrifice of economies of scale and scope or the absence of fully compatible equipment and services."[65]

Although this may not have been the reason for AT&T's breakup, the dissolution of large firms that have lost their spirit to dominate by rushing up the escalation ladders could make a big difference in the U.S. ability to compete in global markets. In contrast, however, most antitrust suits and traditional enforcement efforts have focused not on the laggards but on the aggressive large firms.

Government action to increase competition would make domestic markets more aggressive, benefiting consumers by encouraging dynamic efficiency. It would also strengthen companies in global competition, thereby benefiting the nation.

HYPERCOMPETITIVE INDUSTRIES

In hypercompetitive environments, however, the government should recognize the dynamic efficiency of hypercompetition and take a more laissez-faire approach to regulation. It should let the dynamic efficiency of the market work and correct itself, even if it leads companies temporarily to build strong positions. Liberal permission for joint ventures, mergers, alliances, and other partnering arrangements should be granted because such arrangements are rarely collusive or monopolistic in nature. They only enhance competitiveness. In sum, the government should refrain from slowing down the winners or freezing competition at competitive parity.

The government should not hammer the nail that sticks out. If an industry leader emerges, it should be congratulated, not punished. It is interesting that on an individual level, American culture theoretically is based on rewarding individualism and personal achievement. However, on a corporate level, there is quite the reverse ideology. Yet in Japan individuals are hammered if they stick out, but corporations are not.

The Self-Destruction of Antitrust Bureaucracy

By pursuing a policy of encouraging competition in sluggish industries and limiting involvement in hypercompetitive industries, regulators would be working to move all industries into hypercompetition. Thus, in the long run the goal of antitrust regulators should be to put themselves out of business. This should be an easy task given that most industries are gravitating toward hypercompetition on their own.

THROWING FUEL ON THE FIRE

It is clear most industries will move toward hypercompetition in the next few years if they are not already there. To fuel the fires of this process, the government should turn up the heat, creating pressure that forces hypercompetition. The fuels for these changes seem to be globalization, technological change, and increased information-processing abilities.

To fuel the fires, the government can fan the flames of hypercompetition by making sure that U.S. markets remain open to foreign entry and U.S. firms have few regulatory barriers to the adoption and sharing of new technologies and information processing methods. In this way the government provides firms with the incentives to race up the escalation ladders faster than their competitors and access to the technological and informational resources necessary to do so.

CHANGING LAWS

Legislators must also reshape federal and state laws to limit private nuisance suits that dampen hypercompetitive behavior. Without this type of legislation, private lawsuits could undermine any change in direction of

U.S. regulatory policy. In addition, diverse state laws can wreak havoc with competitors such as Wal-Mart that operate across a wide range of states and compete aggressively in a variety of markets. The federal government should take federal jurisdiction over the law and supersede all state antitrust laws so that there is one uniform policy.

ASSESS THE DAMAGE OF THE CHILLING AND DAMPENING EFFECTS

Congress or the Federal Trade Commission should also conduct a study of the true costs of antitrust enforcement and legal cases. It should determine the extent of the impact of the chilling and dampening effects described above. It should assess the impact of legal costs and the cost of tying up management in lawsuits for U.S. companies. There should also be an attempt to assess whether the government can act fast enough to correct problems of antitrust enforcement in hypercompetitive environments. As suggested by the discussion above, it appears likely that the hidden costs and damaging chilling and dampening effects of the antitrust laws far outweigh the positive benefits. If so, the causes of these effects must be removed.

DECRIMINALIZE COMPETITION AND SUCCESS

In a political environment in which government officials are targeting government waste, antitrust enforcement should be carefully examined just on its costs alone. Actions to control crime are a necessary expense of society, but costly enforcement of laws that are ineffective and make criminals of successful competitors is an unconscionable expense. The salaries and expenses of the Federal Trade Commission and Justice's antitrust division totaled more than $100 million in 1992.[66] A more careful examination of the benefits of these costs should be made, especially since the markets will adjust themselves much more quickly as hypercompetition spreads everywhere.

It's Time for Robin Hood to Look beyond the Trees and See the Forest

Antitrust legislation has noble objectives. In an environment in which large and powerful corporations had many opportunities to abuse their market power, consumers and small competitors may have needed a federal Robin Hood to keep the big players in check and protect the little ones. When the competitive system did not provide this protection on its own, it was necessary to have an outside force that would work to keep players in check.

But today it is increasingly apparent that this protection is not effective, not needed, and has damaging effects. Now the arrows that are being lobbed out into the competitive arena are missing the mark, hitting innocent bystanders, and killing off the good guys—successful competitors that are the best at serving customers and the best hope for the future of U.S. competitiveness. Robin Hood may have served his purpose—protecting the little guy— at a time when he was needed. But now the customers who were supposed to be protected by the federal agencies are hurt by actions that force companies to charge higher prices, hold back on innovation, not enter new markets, and not collaborate to meet foreign competition. These consumers, who are also employees, are hurt by the loss of U.S. jobs to foreign firms. It is clearly time for Robin Hood to see beyond the trees of Sherwood Forest and realize that there is a bigger picture, a sea change in the environment, that is reducing the need for antitrust intervention.

Like companies in hypercompetition, America faces a critical choice. It can embrace the new reality of hypercompetition—designing its policy to meet the new demands of this age—or it can hold onto the past. The latter course leads to the loss of the initiative and places the nation and its corporations on a downward spiral of decline. Allowing intense and aggressive U.S. competitors to continue their behavior also will help keep jobs in the United States, benefiting U.S. workers and the U.S. economy. If, however, the debate becomes a battle over politics or over economic ideology rather than a critical examination of the realities of current markets, the United States could enter a period of endless shifting in antitrust policies that could undermine its most successful firms.

If large U.S. companies are to continue to succeed in the intense competition of international markets, the laws must be reshaped to allow and encourage the creation of temporary advantages and the disruption of competitors. The United States can no longer bind the hands of the nation's best competitors and expect them to survive the fierce combat of global competition. No one, not even American institutions like IBM, GM, Xerox, Kodak, American Express, and Sears, can sustain advantages, build monopolies, or create collusive oligopolies today. They can only resort to the New 7-S's, create temporary advantage, and fight more aggressively, as Coke, Pepsi, Intel, Microsoft, Ford, Motorola, American Airlines, and hundreds of other U.S. firms have done. The law ought not to stand in any of their ways.

Management Challenges

In the current competitive and regulatory environment, companies are forced to operate in the gray areas of the antitrust laws because of the ambiguity of the law and its constantly changing interpretation. Many say it is better to risk a private antitrust suit (government action is less likely today) than to be wiped out by the market. The truly great companies get sued occasionally and wear these civil lawsuits as a red badge of courage. They are bloodied but unbowed. Chilling effects of antitrust must be ignored, or you'll be buried by the dynamics of strategic maneuvering. Other companies will bury you if you don't bury them.

- Do you buy this philosophy? Or do you prefer a more conservative approach? What are the risks of the more conservative approach?
- How should U.S. laws be changed to encourage hypercompetitive behavior in your industry and to reduce the chilling effect of ambiguity for your firm?
- What actions do you need to take to succeed in hypercompetition, and how will those actions be viewed in the current regulatory environment? Are they in the gray area?
- How is your thinking about strategy affected directly or indirectly by the chilling and dampening effects of antitrust laws outlined above? Should you be chilled or dampened?
- What are the costs of provoking antitrust actions by competitors or the government, and how can these risks be minimized or avoided without reducing competitiveness?
- Do you feel constrained in actions or statements by the fear of antitrust actions? If so, are you losing competitive opportunities because of these constraints?
- How will you manage the ethical and legal issues associated with being hypercompetitive?

ENDNOTES

PREFACE

1. Robert Jacobson. "The 'Austrian' School of Strategy." *Academy of Management Review* 17(4): 782–805 (1992).
2. Michael E. Porter. *The Competitive Advantage of Nations*. New York: The Free Press, 1990.
3. Michael E. Porter. "Towards a Dynamic Theory of Strategy." *Strategic Management Journal*, 12 (Special Issue, Winter): 95–118 (1991).
4. Ming-Jer Chen. "Competitive Strategic Interaction: A Study of Competitive Actions and Responses." Ph.D. diss., University of Maryland, 1988.
5. Ken G. Smith, Curtis M. Grimm, and Martin J. Gannon. *Dynamics of Competitive Strategy*. London: Sage Publications, 1992.

INTRODUCTION

1. Kathy Rebello. "Microsoft: Bill Gates' Baby Is On Top of the World. Can It Stay There?" *Business Week*, February 24, 1992, 62–64.
2. Kathy Rebello. "Is Microsoft Too Powerful?" *Business Week*, 1 March 1993, 86.
3. Kathy Rebello. "Is Microsoft Too Powerful?" 88.
4. Kathy Rebello. "Is Microsoft Too Powerful?" 85.
5. Wendy Zellner and Andrea Rothman. "The Airline Mess." *Business Week*, 6 July 1992, 50.
6. Stephen D. Solomon. "The Bully of the Skies Cries Uncle." *New York Times Magazine*, 5 Sept. 1993, 14.
7. Mark Lewyn and Kathy Rebello. "The FTC vs. Microsoft." *Business Week*, 28 Dec. 1992, 30.
8. Wendy Zellner and Andrea Rothman. "The Airline Mess," 50.
9. Stratford Sherman. "How to Prosper in the Value Decade." *Fortune*, 30 Nov. 1992, 91.
10. Jeffrey R. Williams. "How Sustainable Is Your Competitive Advantage?" *California Management Review* 34 (3): 6 (1992).
11. Lois Therrien. "Brands on the Run." *Business Week*, 19 Apr. 1993, 26–29.
12. Jeffrey R. Williams. "How Sustainable Is Your Competitive Advantage?" *California Management Review* 34 (3): 8 (1992).
13. Kathleen Deveny. "Rival Hot Sauces Are Breathing Fire at Market Leader Tabasco." *Wall Street Journal*, 7 Jan. 1993, B1.

14. Scott Kilman. "U.S. Is Steadily Losing Share of World Trade in Grain and Soybeans." *Wall Street Journal*, 3 Dec. 1992, A1.
15. Lois Therrien. "Consultant, Reengineer Thyself." *Business Week*, 12 Apr. 1992, 86–87.
16. John R Wilke. "Business as War: 'Corporate Misfits' Who Run Cabletron Play a Rough Game." *Wall Street Journal*, 9 Apr. 1993, A1.
17. Alex Taylor III. "How to Murder the Competition." *Fortune*, 22 Feb. 1993, 87–88.
18. Gary Hamel and C. K. Prahalad. "Strategic Intent." *Harvard Business Review*, May-June 1989, 63–76.
19. Christopher Power. "Everyone Is Bellying Up to This Bar." *Business Week*, 27 Jan. 1992, 84.
20. "Brand New." *Economist*, 3 July 1993, 5.
21. "Who's Excellent Now?" *Business Week*, 5 Nov. 1984, 83.
22. John W. Verity. "Deconstructing the Computer Industry." *Business Week*, 23 Nov. 1992, 90.
23. Yumiko Ono and Michael Williams. "Matsushita's Overhaul Effort Puts Emphasis on Profits." *Wall Street Journal*, 7 Oct. 1992, B4.
24. Jason Zweig. "Old Is Beautiful." *Forbes*, 27 Apr. 1992, 134–135.
25. Michael Porter. *Competitive Strategy*. New York: The Free Press, 1980.
26. Michael E. Porter. *The Competitive Advantage of Nations*. New York: The Free Press, 1990, 580.
27. W. E. Fruhan, Jr. *Financial Strategy: Studies in the Creation, Transfer, and Destruction of Shareholder Value*. Homewood, Il.: Richard D. Irwin, 1979.
28. Michael Porter. *Competitive Strategy*, New York: The Free Press 1980, 7–12.
29. Gary Hamel and C. K. Prahalad. "Strategic Intent." *Harvard Business Review*, May-June 1989, 63–76.
30. Strategic Management Society. Toronto Conference, 23–26 Nov. 1991. Remarks as quoted in *Strategic Management Society Newsletter*, Dec. 1991, 2.
31. Kathy Rebello. "Microsoft: Bill Gates's Baby Is on Top of the World. Can It Stay There?" *Business Week*, 24 Feb. 1992, 64.
32. Stewart Toy. "The Yankee Invasion Has Foreign Carriers Running for Cover." *Business Week*, 6 July 1992, 54–55.
33. R. Waterman, T. Peters, and J. Phillips. "Structure Is Not Organization." *Business Horizons*, June 1980, 14–26. In James Brian Quinn and Henry Mintzberg, "Dealing with Structure and Systems." *The Strategy Process*. Englewood Cliffs, N. J.: Prentice Hall, 1988, 270–276.

PART I HYPERCOMPETITION AND ESCALATION TOWARD PERFECT COMPETITION IN FOUR ARENAS OF COMPETITION

CHAPTER 1 HOW FIRMS OUTMANEUVER COMPETITORS WITH COST-QUALITY ADVANTAGES

1. Michael Porter. *Competitive Strategy*. New York: The Free Press, 1980, 34–46.

2. K. Ohmae. "The Art of Strategic Thinking." In *The Mind of the Strategist: The Art of Japanese Business.* New York: McGraw-Hill, 1982, 22–35.
3. K. Ohmae. "The Art of Strategic Thinking," 23–24.
4. Michael Porter. *Competitive Strategy,* 44.
5. Dennis Kneale. "Rivals Go after Tylenol's Market, But Gains Are Temporary," *Wall Street Journal,* December 2, 1992, 31.
6. Terence P. Paré. "The Big Threat to Big Steel's Future." Fortune, 15 July 1991, 106–108.
7. Di Palfram. "Challenge of Open Competition." *Management Today,* Feb. 1992, 104.
8. Robert Ball. "Volkswagen's Struggle To Restore Its Name." *Fortune,* 27 June 1983, 100.
9. Cynthia Mitchell. "Paper Tiger: How Kimberly-Clark Wraps Its Bottom Line in Disposable Huggies." *Wall Street Journal,* 23 July 1987, 1.
10. Cynthia Mitchell. "Paper Tiger: How Kimberly-Clark Wraps Its Bottom Line in Disposable Huggies," 1.
11. Laurie Freeman. "P&G's Luvs Takes Lead in Diaper Derby." *AdAge,* 30 Oct. 1989, 3.
12. William Shuster. "Watches." *Jewelers Circular Keystone,* Sept. 1989, 114.
13. "Thomke to Reduce Duties at SMH." *Jewelers Circular Keystone,* May 1991, 15.

CHAPTER 2   HOW FIRMS OUTMANEUVER COMPETITORS WITH TIMING AND KNOW-HOW ADVANTAGES

1. John W. Verity. "Deconstructing the Computer Industry." *Business Week,* 23 November 1992, 90.
2. William E. Fruhan, Jr. "The NPV (Net Present Value) Model of Strategy— The Shareholder Value Model." *Financial Strategy: Studies in the Creation, Transfer, and Destruction of Shareholder Value.* Homewood, Il.: Richard D. Irwin, 1979.
3. James Brian Quinn and Henry Mintzberg. "Pilkington Brothers P.L.C." Case 3–1 in *The Strategy Process.* 2d ed. Englewood Cliffs, N. J.: Prentice Hall, 1991.
4. C. K. Prahalad and G. Hamel. "The Core Competence of the Corporation." *Harvard Business Review,* May-June 1990, 79–91.
5. See, for example, William E. Fruhan, Jr., *Financial Strategy: Studies in the Creation, Transfer and Destruction of Shareholder Value,* 13; and Enrique R. Arzac, "Do Your Business Units Create Shareholder Value?" *Harvard Business Review,* Jan.-Feb. 1986, 121–126.
6. Richard P. Rumelt. "Theory, Strategy, and Entrepreneurship." In *The Competitive Challenge: Strategies for Industrial Innovation and Renewal.* Cambridge, Mass.: Ballinger, 1987.
7. William T. Robinson. "Sources of Market Pioneer Advantages: The Case of Industrial Goods Industries." *Journal of Marketing Research* 25 (Feb.): 87–94 (1988).

8. Mark Parry and Frank Bass. "When to Lead or Follow? It Depends." *Marketing Letters* 1 (3): 187–198 (1989).
9. William T. Robinson. "Sources of Market Pioneer Advantages: The Case of Industrial Goods Industries." *Journal of Marketing Research* 25 (Feb.): 92 (1988).
10. S. A. Lippman and R. P. Rumelt. "Uncertain Imitability: An Analysis of Inter Firm Differences in Efficiency under Competition." *Bell Journal of Economics* 13 (2): 418–453 (1982).
11. Edwin Mansfield, Mark Schwartz, and Samuel Wagner. "Imitation Costs and Patents: An Empirical Study." *Economic Journal* 91 (Dec.): 907–918 (1981).
12. Robert Jacobson. "The 'Austrian' School of Strategy." *Academy of Management Review*, 17 (4): 782–805 (1992).
13. Edwin Mansfield. "The Speed and Cost of Industrial Innovation in Japan and the United States: External vs. Internal Technology." *Management Science* 34 (10): 1157–1168 (1988).
14. Fleur Templeton. "Will U.S. Biotech Mutate into Another Lost Market?" *Business Week*, 25 May 1992, 81.
15. Edwin Mansfield. "The Speed and Cost of Industrial Innovation in Japan and the United States: External vs. Internal Technology." *Management Science* 34 (10): 1161 (1988).
16. Peter F. Drucker. "Entrepreneurial Strategies." *California Management Review*, 27 (2): 9–25 (1985).
17. David J. Teece. "Profiting from Technological Innovation: Implications for Integration, Collaboration, Licensing, and Public Policy." In *The Competitive Challenge: Strategies for Industrial Innovation and Renewal*, edited by David J. Teece. Cambridge, Mass.: Ballinger, 1987, 185–218.
18. Stephanie Anderson Forest. "Twenty-five Executives to Watch: Michael Dell." *Business Week 1000*, 1992, 86.
19. A. Ries. and J. Trout. *Marketing Warfare*. New York: McGraw-Hill, 1988, 83–99.
20. Pankaj Ghemawat. *Commitment*. New York: The Free Press, 1991.
21. Edwin Mansfield, Mark Schwartz, and Samuel Wagner. "Imitation Costs and Patents: An Empirical Study." *Economic Journal* 91 (Dec.): 910 (1981).
22. Richard Reed and Robert J. DeFillippi. "Causal Ambiguity, Barriers to Imitation, and Sustainable Competitive Advantage." *Academy of Management Review* 15 (1): 97–98 (1990).
23. Edwin Mansfield, Mark Schwartz, and Samuel Wagner. "Imitation Costs and Patents: An Empirical Study," 913.
24. Bruce Einhorn. "Fake Windows, Ersatz DOS, Angry Uncle Sam." *Business Week*, 18 May 1992, 130.
25. Alan Beggs and Paul Klemperer. "Multi-Period Competition with Switching Costs." *Econometrica* 60 (3): 651–666 (1992).
26. Brian O'Reilly. "Compaq's Grip on IBM's Slippery Tail." *Fortune*, 18 Feb. 1985, 74.
27. Stephanie Anderson Forest. "Compaq Declares War on the Clones." *Business Week*, 15 June 1992, 43.

28. Stephanie Anderson Forest. "Compaq Declares War on the Clones." 43.
29. Catherine Arnst and Stephanie Anderson Forest. "Compaq: How It Made Its Impressive Move Out of the Doldrums." *Business Week*, 2 Nov. 1992, 148.
30. David Kirkpatrick. "The Revolution at Compaq Computer." *Fortune*, 14 Dec. 1992, 80–92.
31. David Kirkpatrick. "The Revolution at Compaq Computer," 80.
32. Julie Pitta. "Identity Crisis." *Forbes*, 25 May 1992, 82.
33. Based on a discussion of Sony in James Brian Quinn and Henry Mintzberg. "Sony Corporation." Case 3–2 in *The Strategy Process*. 2d ed. Englewood Cliffs, N.J.: Prentice Hall, Inc., 1991, 845–867.
34. James Brian Quinn and Henry Mintzberg. "Intel Corporation." Case 1–5 in *The Strategy Process*. 2d ed. Englewood Cliffs, N.J.: Prentice Hall, 1991.
35. Stephanie Anderson Forest. "The Upstart Chip Designer That's Chipping Away at Intel." *Business Week*, 14 Sept. 1992, 62–69.
36. John Markoff. "Race for Dominance in Chips." *New York Times*, 20 Mar. 1993, 37.
37. Motorola Advertising Supplement. *Wall Street Journal*, 24 June 1993.
38. William C. Bogner and Howard Thomas. "Core Competence and Competitive Advantage: A Model and Illustrative Evidence from the Pharmaceutical Industry." BEBR Faculty Working Paper No. 92–0174. Bureau of Economic and Business Research, Urbana/Champaign: University of Illinois, 1992.

CHAPTER 3   HOW FIRMS OUTMANEUVER COMPETITORS THAT HAVE BUILT STRONGHOLDS USING ENTRY BARRIERS

1. Michael Porter. *Competitive Strategy*, New York: The Free Press, 1980, 7–13.
2. Jaclyn Fierman. "How Gallo Crushes the Competition." *Fortune*, 1 Sept. 1986.
3. Bill Britt. "Haagen-Dazs Pushes Cold Front across World." *Marketing*, 4 Oct. 1990, 30–31.
4. Richard B. Schmitt. "Atari Tests Technology's Antitrust Aspect." *Wall Street Journal*, 14 Dec. 1988, B8.
5. Michael Porter. *Competitive Strategy*.
6. James Brian Quinn. "The Intelligent Enterprise: A New Paradigm." *Academy of Management Executive* 6 (4): 51–52 (1992).
7. "Semiconductor Exports Are Threatened." *Business Korea*, May 1992, 17.
8. Jaclyn Fierman. "How Gallo Crushes the Competition." *Fortune*, 1 Sept. 1986, 24.
9. Carrie Goerne. "Haagen-Dazs Adds Flavors to Ice Its Superpremium Competitors." *Marketing News*, 31 Aug. 1992, 8.
10. Alan Radding and Alison Fahey. "Computers Boot Up Free Samples." *Advertising Age*, 17 Dec. 1990, 12.
11. Richard B. Schmitt. "Atari to Distribute Games Playable on Nintendo Sets." *Wall Street Journal*, 13 Dec. 1988, B1.

12. James A. McConville. "Tengen Giving Peek at New Game Accessories." *HFD, The Weekly Home Furnishings Newspaper*, 25 May 1992, 94.
13. Michael Krey. "Tiny Video Game Maker May Win Atari, Nintendo War." *Business Journal (San Jose)*, 19 Nov. 1990, 5.
14. Richard B. Schmitt. "Nintendo Suit Filed by Atari Is Going to Trial." *Wall Street Journal*, 13 Feb. 1992, B1.
15. Neal E. Boudette. "Simple, Flexible, Manual." *Industry Week*, 6 Nov. 1989, 48–50.
16. Mark Robichaux. "Need More TV? TCI May Offer 500 Channels," *Wall Street Journal*, 3 Dec. 1992, B1.
17. Douglas D. Anderson. "Hyundai Heavy Industries and the Shipbuilding Industry," HSB Case 9-385-212, 1984
18. Jonathan B. Levine. "Brr-ring! America Calling." *Business Week*, 1 June 1992, 98–100.
19. Tony Shale. "The Gaijin Steam In." *Euromoney*, Jan. 1992, 16–20.
20. Henry Stuart. "Japan Hangs Out 'Do Not Disturb' Sign." *Futures*, June 1992, 48–50.
21. Brenton R. Schlender. "U.S. PCs Invade Japan." *Fortune*, 12 July 1993, 68–73.
22. Kris Herbst. "Japan: A More Open Market for Supercomputers." *Datamation*, 15 Sept. 1990, 123–125.
23. Rose Brandy and Peter Galuszka. "The Scramble for Oil's Last Frontier." *Business Week*, 11 Jan. 1993, 42–44.
24. Tim Smart. "Will US Surgical's Cutting Edge Be Enough?" *Business Week*, 21 Sept. 1992, 50–51.
25. Jennifer Reese. "Getting Hot Ideas From Customers." *Fortune*, 18 May 1992, 86–87.
26. Adrianne Linsenmeyer. "No Band-Aid Solution." *Financial World* 21 Jan. 1992, 25–27.
27. Pamela Ellis-Simons. "There's Gold in Them Thar Hicks." *Marketing & Media Decisions*, Mar. 1987, 69–76.
28. Rita Koselka. "Candy Wars." *Forbes*, 17 Aug. 1992, 76–77.
29. Robert Smiley. "Empirical Evidence on Strategic Entry Deterrence." *International Journal of Industrial Organization* 6 (2): 167–180 (1988).
30. Fahri Karakaya and Michael J. Stahl. "Barriers to Entry and Market Entry Decisions in Consumer and Industrial Goods Markets." *Journal of Marketing* 53 (4): 80–91 (1989).
31. Zoltan J. Acs and David B. Audretsch. "Small-Firm Entry in US Manufacturing." *Economica* 56 (222): 255–265 (1989).
32. Derek F. Abell. "Strategic Windows." *Journal of Marketing* 42 (3): 21–26 (1978).
33. Michael Tushman and Philip Anderson. "Technological Discontinuities and Organizational Environments." *Administrative Science Quarterly* 31(3): 439–465 (1986).
34. William T. Robinson. "Marketing Mix Reactions to Entry." *Marketing Science* 7 (4): 368–385 (1988).

35. E. R. Biggadike. *Corporate Diversification: Entry, Strategy, and Performance.* Cambridge, Mass.: Harvard University Press, 1979.
36. Donald J. Boudreaux. "Turning Back the Antitrust Clock: Nonprice Predation in Theory and Practice." *Cato Review of Business & Government Regulation* (Fall) 1990, 45–52.
37. Hal Bernton and Andrea Rothman. "Is Alaska Big Enough for These Two?" *Business Week*, 13 Apr. 1992, 74.
38. Hal Bernton and Andrea Rothman. "Is Alaska Big Enough for These Two?" 76.
39. Hal Bernton and Andrea Rothman. "Is Alaska Big Enough for These Two?" 74–76.
40. Wendy Zellner. "Striking Gold in the California Skies." *Business Week*, 30 Mar. 1992, 48.
41. Edward O. Welles. "Captain Marvel." *Inc.*, Jan. 1992, 45.
42. David A. Brown. "Fundamental Changes Likely in Services Airlines Provide during Lean 1990s." *Aviation Week & Space Technology*, 20 Apr. 1992, 32.
43. Edward O. Welles. "Captain Marvel," 47.
44. Chuck Hawkins. "FedEx: Europe Nearly Killed the Messenger." *Business Week*, 25 May 1992, 124–125.
45. Robert Smiley. "Empirical Evidence on Strategic Entry Deterrence." *International Journal of Industrial Organization* 6 (2): 176 (1988).
46. Michael Porter and Pankaj Ghemawat. "General Electric vs. Westinghouse in Large Turbine Generators (A)." Case No. 9-380-128. Boston: Harvard Business School (1980; rev. Aug. 1986).
47. "Westinghouse Agrees to Join Rolls-Royce in Power-Plant Plan." *Wall Street Journal*, 2 June 1992, A2.
48. Author's notes. Informal comments of J. Richard Stonesifer. "Challenging Conventional Thinking for Competitive Advantage." Conference sponsored by the Conference Board and Wells Rich Greene, BDDP, New York, 24 Sept. 1992.

CHAPTER 4   HOW FIRMS OUTMANEUVER COMPETITORS
WITH DEEP POCKETS

1. Arnold G. Danielson. "Southern Banking: Life After NationsBank." *Bank Management*, Sept. 1991, 14–18.
2. Martha Brannigan. "NationsBank Grows Rapidly via Innovation and a Slew of Mergers." *Wall Street Journal*, 28 Dec. 1992, A1.
3. Anat Bird, David M. Ondersma, and Thomas A. Moore, Jr. "A Superstrategy for Generating Superlative Profits." *American Banker*, 2 Dec. 1991, 12.
4. Sherrill Shaffer. "Challenges to Small Banks' Survival." *Federal Reserve Bank of Philadelphia Business Review*, Sept.-Oct. 1989, 16.
5. Martha Brannigan and Eleena de Lisser. "Two Big Rival Banks in Southeast Take On New-Age Competitors." *Wall Street Journal*, 8 July 1993, A1.

6. Michale Siconolfi. "Merrill Lynch, Pushing into Many New Lines, Expands Bank Services." *Wall Street Journal,* 7 July 1993, A1.
7. Martha Brannigan and Eleena de Lisser. "Two Big Rival Banks in Southeast Take On New-Age Competitors," A1.
8. Eleanor Johnson Tracy. "How A&P Got Creamed." *Fortune,* Jan. 1973, 104.
9. Eleanor Johnson Tracy. "How A&P Got Creamed," 104.
10. "A&P Counts the Cost of Its Pyrrhic Victory." *Business Week,* 28 Apr. 1973, 117.
11. "Can Jonathan Scott Save A&P?" *Business Week,* 19 May 1975, 128.
12. Wendy Zellner, Andrea Rothman, and Eric Schine. "The Airline Mess." *Business Week,* 6 July 1992, 50–55.
13. "American's Fare Was Fair." *Business Week,* 23 August 1993, 34.
14. Lynn G. Coleman. "'David' KOs 'Goliath,' but Giant Won't Stay Down." *Marketing News* 23 (17): 10 (1989).
15. Don Wallace. "Giant Killers: How to Fight the Big Guys and Win." *Success* 37 (3): 36–41 (1990).
16. Don Wallace. "Giant Killers, " 40–41.
17. Zachary Schiller, Neil Gross, and Lisa Driscoll. "Diamonds and Dirt." *Business Week,* 10 Aug. 1992, 22.
18. Mihir Bose. "Clifford Chance—A Very Peculiar Practice?" *Director* 43 (3): 65–70 (1990); Robert Clow. "Growing Pains." *International Financial Law Review* 9 (4): S5–S7 (1990).
19. Andrew Tanzer. "Sharing." *Forbes,* 20 Jan. 1992, 82.
20. John Carey. "One Stepper Forward for Sematech." *Business Week,* 8 June 1992, 110–112.
21. Simon Brady and Caren Chesler-Marsh. "The Madness of Mergers." *Euromoney,* Sept. 1991, 67.
22. Simon Brady and Caren Chesler-March. "The Madness of Mergers." 70.
23. Christopher Tucher. "How Ames is Digesting Its 'Whale.'" *Business Week,* Sept. 11, 1989, 62.
24. Christopher Tucher. "How Ames Is Digesting Its 'Whale.'" 62.
25. Abner A. Layne. "Pay Phones Pay Off." *High Technology Business,* Nov.-Dec. 1989, 24–27.
26. Phyllis Feinberg. "Creating Joint Ventures for David and Goliath." *Corporate Cashflow* 12 (6): 57–58 (1991)
27. Jack Meredith. "The Strategic Advantages of New Manufacturing Technologies for Small Firms." *Strategic Management Journal* 8: 255 (1987).
28. Avi Fiegenbaum and Aneel Karnani. "Output Flexibility—A Competitive Advantage for Small Firms." *Strategic Management Journal* 12: 101–114 (1991).
29. Geoffrey Colvin. "The Wee Outfit That Decked IBM." *Fortune,* 19 Nov 1990, 165–166.
30. Mike Freeman. "Growing Interest in Syndicated New Services." *Broadcasting,* 21 Sept. 1992, 60–65.
31. Thomas B. Mechling. "Food Lion: Cut-Rate Prices, Cutthroat Practices." *Business & Society Review* 72 (Winter): 39–41 (1990).

32. Mike Duff. "Hands across the Water." *Supermarket Business* 44 (2): 45–47 (1989).
33. "Buyouts and Competition Affect Supermarkets." *Chain Store Age Executive*, Nov. 1988, 71.
34. Ken Parch. "Trade Practices: Hard Times Bring Chaos to the Struggle for Power." *Supermarket Business* 47 (5): 27 (1992).

CHAPTER 5   NEW ANALYTICAL TOOLS: ANALYZING
COMPETITION USING THE FOUR ARENAS

1. Drawn from the following sources:
   J. C. Louis and Harvey Z. Yazijian. *The Cola Wars*. New York: Everest House, 1980.
   Robert D. Tollison, David P. Kaplan, and Richard S. Higgins. *Competition and Concentration: The Economics of the Carbonated Soft Drink Industry*. New York: Lexington Books, 1991.
   C. Roland Christensen. "Note on the Soft Drink Industry in the United States. Case No. 377-213. Boston: Harvard Business School, 1977.
   Constance Lynn Irwin. "Note on the U.S. Soft Drink Industry in 1986." Case No. 9-387-107. Boston: Harvard Business School, 1987.
   Constance Lynn Irwin. "Coca-Cola vs. Pepsi-Cola (A, B, C)." Case Nos. 9-387-108, 9-387-109, 9-387-110. Boston: Harvard Business School, 1987.
   Michael E. Porter. "Coca-Cola vs. Pepsi-Cola and the Soft Drink Industry." Case No. 9-391-179. Boston: Harvard Business School, 1991.
2. Robert D. Tollison, David P. Kaplan, and Richard S. Higgins. *Competition and Concentration: The Economics of the Carbonated Soft Drink Industry*. New York: Lexington Books, 1991, 2.
3. C. Roland Christensen. "Note on the Soft Drink Industry in the United States. Case No. 377-213. Boston: Harvard Business School, 1977, 4.
4. Michael E. Porter. "Coca-Cola vs. Pepsi-Cola and the Soft Drink Industry." Case No. 9-391-179. Boston: Harvard Business School, 1991, 12.
5. C. Roland Christensen. "Note on the Soft Drink Industry in the United States." Case No. 377-231. Boston: Harvard Business School, 1977, 8.
6. Constance Lynn Irwin. "Coca-Cola vs. Pepsi-Cola (B), Case No. 9–387–109. Boston: Harvard Business School (1987), 2.
7. Michael E. Porter. "Coca-Cola vs. Pepsi-Cola and the Soft Drink Industry," 9.
8. Michael E. Porter. "Coca-Cola vs. Pepsi-Cola and the Soft Drink Industry," 14.
9. C. Roland Christensen. "Note on the Soft Drink Industry in the United States," 4.
10. Michael E. Porter. "Coca-Cola vs. Pepsi-Cola and the Soft Drink Industry," 19.
11. Richard Gibson. "Coca-Cola and PepsiCo Are Preparing to Give Gatorade a Run for Its Money," *Wall Street Journal*, 29 Sept. 1992, B1.

12. C. Roland Christensen. "Note on the Soft Drink Industry in the United States," 23.
13. Robert D. Tollison, David P. Kaplan, and Richard S. Higgins. *Competition and Concentration*, 73.
14. J. C. Louis and Harvey Z. Yazijian. *The Cola Wars*. New York: Everest House, 1980, 90.
15. *The Cola Wars*, 201.
16. *Competition and Concentration*, 1.
17. Constance Lynn Irwin. "Coca-Cola vs. Pepsi-Cola (C)." Case No. 9-387-110. Boston: Harvard Business School, 1987, 2.
18. "Coca-Cola vs. Pepsi-Cola (C)," 2–3.
19. C. Roland Christensen. "Note on the Soft Drink Industry in the United States," 23.
20. *Competition and Concentration*, 1–2.
21. *Competition and Concentration*, 3–5.
22. Barbara Jorgensen. "Prices Plummet in Low-End Laser Printers." *Electronic Business*, 20 May 1991, 99.
23. Daniel Tynan. "The Buck Stops Here for Lasers." *PC World*, May 1992, 78.
24. Daniel Tynan. "The Buck Stops Here for Lasers," 78.

PART II IMPLICATIONS OF UNSUSTAINABLE ADVANTAGE: NEW CONCEPTS OF COMPETITION AND COMPETITIVE STRATEGY

CHAPTER 6 THE NATURE OF HYPERCOMPETITION: WHAT IT IS AND WHY IT HAPPENS

1. Thomas McCarroll. "How IBM Was Left Behind." *Time*, 28 Dec. 1992, 27.
2. Thomas McCarroll. "How IBM Was Left Behind," 27.
3. John Schwartz. "IBM, Please Call AT&T." *Newsweek*, 28 Dec. 1992, 46.
4. Bill Javetski. "Price War I Is Raging in Europe." *Business Week*, 6 July 1992, 44–45.
5. David Kalish. "Cat Fight." *Marketing & Media Decisions*, Apr. 1989, 42–48.
6. Sydney Ladensohn Stern and Ted Schoenhaus. "Toyland." *Across the Board*, Dec. 1990, 24–31.
7. Donald V. Potter. "Success under Fire: Policies to Prosper in Hostile Times." *California Management Review* 33 (2): 12 (1991).
8. Michael Porter. *Competitive Strategy*, 90.
9. Lois Therrien. "Recession Hell—Let's Buy Another TV." *Business Week*, 19 Oct. 1992, 35.
10. Donald V. Potter. "Success Under Fire," 1–15.
11. "Success Under Fire," 5.
12. "Who's Excellent Now?" *Business Week*, 5 Nov. 1984, 76.

13. "Who's Excellent Now?" 78.
14. "TI: Shot Full of Holes and Trying To Recover." *Business Week*, 5 Nov. 1984, 82.
15. "Levi's: The Jeans Giant Slipped as the Market Shifted," *Business Week*, 5 Nov. 1984, 79.
16. "DEC: Bogged Down by Bloated Management." *Business Week*, 5 Nov. 1984, 86.
17. "DEC: Bogged Down by Bloated Management." 86.
18. "DEC: Bogged Down by Bloated Management." 86.
19. Henry Ford. *My Life and Work*. Garden City, N. Y.: Doubleday & Company, 1925, 43.

CHAPTER 7   LIVING WITH HYPERCOMPETITION: THE NEW 7-S'S

1. A. D. Chandler. *Strategy and Structure*. Cambridge, Mass.: MIT Press, 1962.
2. Daniel Isenberg. "The Tactics of Strategic Opportunism." *Harvard Business Review*, Mar.-Apr. 1987, 96.
3. Michael E. Porter. "Towards a Dynamic Theory of Strategy." *Strategic Management Journal* 12 (Winter): 108 (1991).
4. Daniel Isenberg. "The Tactics of Strategic Opportunism," 92–97.
5. Amar Bhide. "Hustle as Strategy." *Harvard Business Review*, Sept.-Oct. 1986, 59–65.
6. Karl E. Weick. "Substitutes for Strategy." In *The Competitive Challenge: Strategies for Industrial Innovation and Renewal*, edited by David J. Teece. Cambridge, Mass.: Ballinger, 1987, 225.
7. Gary Hamel and C. K. Prahalad. "Strategic Intent." *Harvard Business Review*, May-June 1989, 63.
8. E. deBono. *Tactics: The Art and Science of Success*. Boston: Little, Brown, 1984, 143. Quoted in Karl E. Weick. "Substitutes for Strategy."
9. Danny Miller. "Environmental Fit vs. Internal Fit." *Organization Science* 3 (2): 159 (1992).
10. Pankaj Ghemawat. *Commitment*. New York: The Free Press, 1991.
11. Michael Howard. "VI: Karl von Clausewitz: Selection B: The Forgotten Dimensions of Strategy." In *The Art and Practice of Military Strategy*, edited by George Edward Thibault, Washington, D.C.: National Defense University, 1984, 84.
12. I. C. MacMillan. "Seizing Competitive Initiative." In *Competitive Strategic Management*, edited by Robert Boyden Lamb. Englewood Cliffs, N. J.: Prentice Hall, 1984, 273.
13. K. Ohmae. "The Art of Strategic Thinking." In *The Mind of the Strategist: The Art of Japanese Business*. New York: McGraw-Hill, 1982, 13.
14. Mike Freedman. "Initiative Fatigue." *Journal of Strategic Change* 1 (2): 89–91 (1992).

15. J. S. Bain. "Relation of Profit Rate of Industry Concentration: American Manufacturing 1936–1940." *Quarterly Journal of Economics* 65 (3): 293–324 (1951).
16. R. Jacobson. "The 'Austrian' School of Strategy." *Academy of Management Review* 17 (4): 782–807 (1992).
17. J. A. Schumpeter. *The Theory of Economic Development.* Cambridge, Mass.: Harvard University Press, 1934.
18. R. Jacobson. "The 'Austrian' School of Strategy," 785.

PART III DISRUPTING MARKETS AND SEIZING THE INITIATIVE THROUGH THE NEW 7-S'S

CHAPTER 8 USING THE NEW 7-S'S TO CREATE DISRUPTION

1. Anitra S. Brown. "The Genius of Gallo." *Market Watch*, May 1988, 13.
2. Marvin R. Shanken. "Gallo's Dramatic Shift to Fine Varietal." *Wine Spectator*, 15 Sept. 1991, 20.
3. Anitra S. Brown. "The Genius of Gallo," 13.
4. U. Srinivasa Rangan. "Caterpillar Tractor Co." Case No. 9-385-276. Boston: Harvard Business School, 1985, 1.
5. Christopher A. Bartlett. "Komatsu Limited." Case No. 9-385-277. Boston: Harvard Business School, 1985, 13.
6. "Komatsu Limited," 12.
7. Christopher A. Bartlett. "Caterpillar-Komatsu in 1986." Case No. 9-387-095. Boston: Harvard Business School, 1986, 2.
8. Sandra D. Atchison. "Brands on the Run." *Business Week*, 19 Apr. 1993, 26–29.
9. Christopher A. Bartlett. "Komatsu Limited" Case No. 9-385-277 Boston: Harvard Business School (1985), 3.
10. "Komatsu Limited," 11.
11. "Komatsu Limited," 12.
12. Gary Hamel. "Corporate Imagination and Expeditionary Marketing." Conference titled "Challenging Conventional Thinking for Competitive Advantage." New York: The Conference Board and Wells Rich Greene, BDDP, 24 Sept. 1992.
13. Marvin R. Shanken. "Gallo's Dramatic Shift to Fine Varietal," 22.
14. "Komatsu Limited," 8–9.
15. Lois Therrien. "How Sweet It Isn't at NutraSweet." *Business Week*, 14 Dec. 1992, 42.
16. James Brian Quinn. *Intelligent Enterprise.* New York: The Free Press, 1992, 52–58.
17. Alison Leigh Cowan . "A Weaker Market for Coolers." *New York Times*, 19 Oct. 1987, D1.
18. "Komatsu Limited," 9.

19. "Komatsu Limited," 4, 9.
20. Christopher A. Bartlett. "Caterpillar-Komatsu in 1986," 2.
21. Gary Hamel and C. K. Prahalad. "Strategic Intent." *Harvard Business Review*, May-June 1989, 63–76.
22. Jaclyn Fierman. "How Gallo Crushes the Competition." *Fortune*, 1 Sept. 1986, 24.

CHAPTER 9   APPLYING THE NEW 7-S'S: NEW ANALYTICAL TOOLS
TO SEIZE THE INITIATIVE

1. Robert D. Hof. "Inside Intel." *Business Week*, 1 June 1992, 88.
2. "Inside Intel," 90.
3. "Inside Intel," 86–94.
4. "Inside Intel," 89.
5. "Inside Intel," 87.
6. Ashish Nanda and Christopher A. Bartlett. "Intel Corporation—Leveraging Capabilities for Strategic Renewal." Working paper, Graduate School of Business, Harvard University, 25 Nov. 1992, 3.
7. "Inside Intel," 86.
8. Ashish Nanda and Christopher A. Bartlett. "Intel Corporation—Leveraging Capabilities for Strategic Renewal." Working paper, Graduate School of Business, Harvard University, 25 Nov. 1992, 8.
9. "Intel Corporation—Leveraging Capabilities for Strategic Renewal," 15.
10. "Inside Intel," 92.
11. Robert D. Hof. "Inside Intel." *Business Week*, 1 June 1992, 87.
12. Glenn W. Merry. "Polaroid-Kodak." Case No. 9-376-266. Boston: Harvard Business School, 1976, 2.
13. "Polaroid-Kodak, 8.
14. Brian Bagot. "Point-and-Shoot Cameras." *Marketing & Media Decisions*, Sept. 1989, 73–84.
15. James Brian Quinn and Henry Mintzberg. "Sony Corporation." Case 3–2 in *The Strategy Process*. 2d ed. Englewood Cliffs, N.J.: Prentice Hall, 1991, 860.
16. Ibid.
17. Mark Maremont. "Getting the Picture." *Business Week*, 1 Feb. 1993, 24.
18. Dana Gardner. "Kodak Sparks a Photo Revolution." *Design News*, 7 Dec. 1992, 58–65.
19. Howard Eglowstein. "Photography by the Numbers." *Byte*, Jan. 1993, 241
20. William George Shuster. "Watches." *Jewelers Circular Keystone*, Sept. 1989, 114–115.
21. Louis Rukeyser. "A Timely Tale of Luxury Watches: The Swiss Prove Japan Can Be Beaten," *Secured Lender* 46 (1) (1990).
22. William George Shuster. "Watches," 114–115.
23. Ibid.
24. "Watches," 114.

25. "Ambitious." *Economist*, 18 Apr. 1992, 74–75.
26. Cara Appelbaum. "High Time for Timex." *Adweek's Marketing Week*, 29 July 1991, 24.
27. Cassandra Jardine. "The Timeless Mystique of the Rolex." *Business* Feb. 1988, 114.
28. "The Timeless Mystique of the Rolex." 114–117.
29. Donald C. Hambrick and Richard A. D'Aveni. "Large Corporate Failures as Downward Spirals." *Administrative Science Quarterly* 33: 1–23 (1988).
30. Carol J. Loomis. "Dinosaurs?" *Fortune*, 3 May 1993, 39.

PART IV   THE RISE OF A NEW AMERICAN IDEOLOGY: HYPERCOMPETITIVE VALUES FOR A HYPERCOMPETITIVE AGE

CHAPTER 10   CAN COMPANIES COOPERATE THEIR WAY OUT OF HYPERCOMPETITION?

1. Michael E. Porter. *The Competitive Advantage of Nations*, 66–67.
2. Kenichi Ohmae. "The Global Logic of Strategic Alliances." *Harvard Business Review*, Mar.-Apr. 1989, 148.

CHAPTER 11   CONCLUSION: A CALL TO ARMS

1. Nancy A. Nichols. "From Complacency to Competitiveness." *Harvard Business Review*, Sept.-Oct. 1993, 166.
2. J. Schwartz. "IBM, Please Call AT&T." *Newsweek*, 28 Dec. 1992, 44.
3. Martha Brannigan and Eleena De Lisser. "Two Big Rival Banks in Southeast Take on New-Age Competitors." *Wall Street Journal*, 8 July 1993, A1.
4. John Greenwald. "Motown Turns a Corner." *Time*, 26 July 1993, 52.
5. Robert Wrubel. "Scorch, Burn and Plunder." *Financial World*, 16 Feb. 1993, 29.
6. "Scorch, Burn and Plunder, 28.
7. Michael E. Porter. *The Competitive Advantage of Nations*, 735.
8. Nancy A. Nichols. "From Complacency to Competitiveness," 163–165.
9. Kathleen Kerwin and James B. Treece. "Detroit's Big Chance." *Business Week*, 29 June 1992, 82.
10. Michael J. Mandel. "This Rebound Just May Be for Real." *Business Week*, 11 Jan. 1993, 56.
11. Edmund Faltermayer. "Poised for a Comeback." *Fortune*, 19 Apr. 1993, 174–175.
12. George J. Church. "Goodbye to the Godzilla Myth." *Time*, 19 Apr. 1993, 43.
13. Neil Gross. "Toshiba: Rethinking the Way It Does Business." *Business Week*, 27 Apr. 1992, 55.
14. Stephen D. Solomon. "The Bully of the Skies Cries Uncle," *The New York Times Magazine*, 5 Sept. 1993, 14.

APPENDIX   ANTITRUST POLICY AND THE NEED FOR A
FUNDAMENTAL SHIFT IN AMERICAN IDEOLOGY

1. Kathy Rebello. "Microsoft: Bill Gates's Baby Is on Top of the World. Can It Stay There?" *Business Week*, 24 Feb. 1992, 62.
2. W. John Moore "Taking Aim at Microsoft." *National Journal*, 4 Sept. 1993, 2163.
3. Mark Lewyn. "The FTC vs. Microsoft." *Business Week*, 28 Dec. 1992, 30.
4. Kathy Rebello. "Is Microsoft Too Powerful?" *Business Week*, 1 Mar. 1993, 82–83.
5. Mark Lewyn. "The FTC vs. Microsoft." *Business Week*, 28 Dec. 1992, 30.
6. Joe Davidson, "Justice Department Mulls Investigation of Microsoft after FTC Probe." *Wall Street Journal*, 2 Aug. 1993, B3.
7. Wendy Zellner and Andrea Rothman. "The Airline Mess: Is American's Bob Crandall Part of the Problem—or the Solution?" *Business Week*, 6 July 1992, 50–55.
8. "The Airline Mess," 53.
9. Stewart Toy. "The Yankee Invasion Has Foreign Carriers Running for Cover." *Business Week*, 6 July 1992, 54.
10. "The Yankee Invasion Has Foreign Carriers Running for Cover," 54.
11. Wendy Zellner and Andrea Rothman. "The Airline Mess." *Business Week*, 6 July 1992, 53.
12. Keith H. Hammonds. (ed). "In Business This Week: American's Fare Was Fair." *Business Week*, 23 Aug. 1993, 34.
13. Stephen Solomon. "The Bully of the Skies Cries Uncle." *New York Times Magazine*, 5 Sept. 1993, 13–38.
14. Mark Lewyn. "The FTC vs. Microsoft," 30.
15. Brian Bremner. "The Age of Consolidation." *Business Week*, 14 Oct. 1991, 86.
16. Brit Hume and T. R. Reid. "Microsoft Fighting the Blues in Government's Antitrust Quest." *Boston Globe*, 15 Aug. 1993, 78.
17. Carol J. Loomis. "Dinosaurs?" *Fortune*, 3 May 1992, 41.
18. Paul Carroll. "Inside the Disaster at IBM: The Day Bill Gates Overthrew Big Blue." *Wall Street Journal*, 16 Aug. 1993, B1–B3.
19. "Dinosaurs?" 41.
20. "Does IBM Get It Now?" *Business Week*, 28 Dec. 1992, 32.
21. Catherine Arnst and Joseph Weber. "IBM after Akers." *Business Week*, 8 Feb. 1993, 22.
22. Peter F. Drucker. *Management Cases*. New York: Harper College Press, 1977, 176–177.
23. *Management Cases*, 170.
24. Carol J. Loomis. "Dinosaurs?" 41.
25. Paul Ingrassia and Joseph B. White. "Determined to Change, General Motors Is Said to Pick New Chairman." *Wall Street Journal*, 23 Oct. 1992, A1.
26. "Too Hard on Microsoft." *Economist*, 31 July 1993, 18.

406 / Endnotes

27. Franklin M. Fisher, John J. McGowan, and Joen E. Greenwood. *Folded, Spindled, and Mutilated: Economic Analysis and U.S. v. IBM*. Cambridge, Mass.: MIT Press, 1983.
28. Lacy Glenn Thomas III. "A Survey of the Issues." In *The Economics of Strategic Planning*. Lexington, Mass: Lexington Books, 1986, 15–16.
29. "A Survey of the Issues," 26.
30. F. M. Scherer. "Antitrust, Efficiency, and Progress." In *Revitalizing Antitrust in Its Second Century*. New York: Quorum Books, 1991, 130–150.
31. "Antitrust, Efficiency, and Progress," 147. In contrast to the view presented here, however, Scherer restricts his discussion of dynamic efficiency to technological innovation ("innovative efficiency"), and he contends that antitrust laws do *not* have a negative impact on this type of dynamic efficiency.
32. Joseph A. Schumpeter. *Capitalism, Socialism and Democracy*. New York: Harper, 1942, 83.
33. "Antitrust, Efficiency, and Progress," 132.
34. Terry Calvani and Gilde Breidenbach. "Living with the Robinson-Patman Act." *Antitrust Law Journal* 59: 761 (1991).
35. Jack Shandle. "Antitrust Policy: Darwinism Is Back." *Electronics*, August 1990, 98.
36. Ibid.
37. Chief Judge Bauer. INDIANA GROCERY, INC., and PRESTON-SAFEWAY, INC., Plaintiff-Appellants, Cross-Appellees v. SUPER VALU STORES, INC., d/b/a CUB FOODS, MARKKAY OF INDIANA, INC., d/b/a CUB FOODS, and THE KROGER CO., Defendants-Appellees, Cross-Appellants. Nos. 88-1625, 88-1739, U.S. Court of Appeals for the Seventh Circuit, January 6, 1989.
38. Bridget O'Brian. "Predatory Pricing Issue Is Due to Be Taken Up in American Air's Trial." *Wall Street Journal*, 12 July 1993, A1.
39. Ibid.
40. "The Case That Won't Die." *Wall Street Journal*, 8 Apr. 1982, 24.
41. Barnaby J. Feder. "I.B.M. Says 13-Year Suit Didn't Affect Operations." *New York Times*, 10 Jan. 1982, 16.
42. Susan Chase. "IBM Has 1.9 Million Boxes of Paper That It Would Love to Toss Away." *Wall Street Journal*, 3 June 1982, 27.
43. William F. Shughart II. "Private Antitrust Enforcement: Compensation, Deterrence, or Extortion?" *Cato Review of Business & Government*, Fall 1990, 55.
44. Marshall B. Clinard and Peter C. Yeager. *Corporate Crime*. New York: The Free Press, 1980, 137.
45. Peter Coy. "Two Cheers for Corporate Collaboration." *Business Week*, 3 May 1993, 34.
46. "Clinton Signs Bill Easing Antitrust Law for Parties in Joint Production Ventures." *BNA Pension and Benefits Reporter* 20:25, 1336.
47. Judge Learned Hand. U.S. v. ALUMINUM COMPANY OF AMERICA, ET AL., No. 144, October Term, 1944. U.S. Circuit Court of Appeals for the Second Circuit, 148, F.2d, 416.

48. Marius Schwartz. "The Perverse Effects of the Robinson-Patman Act." *Antitrust Bulletin*, Fall 1986, 736.
49. Michale Janofsky. "After 7 Weeks, U.S.F.L. Rests in its Pursuit of Antitrust Goal." *New York Times*, 27 June 1986, 21.
50. Michael Janofsky. "Porter Presentation Is Trial's Exhibit A." *New York Times*, 25 May 1986, 6.
51. Bridget O'Brian. "Predatory Pricing Issue," A1.
52. Bridget O'Brian and James S. Hirsch. "American Air's Crandall Denies Rivals' Charges." *Wall Street Journal*, 29 July 1993, A3.
53. Terry Calvani and Gilde Breidenbach. "Living with the Robinson-Patman Act." *Antitrust Law Journal* 59: 761, 1991.
54. William F. Shughart II. "Private Antitrust Enforcement," 55.
55. Wendy Zellner. "Not Everybody Loves Wal-Mart's Low Prices." *Business Week*, 12 Oct. 1992, 36.
56. James Jefferson. "Wal-Mart Convicted in Ark." *The Philadelphia Inquirer*, October 13, 1993, C–1.
57. Bridget O'Brian. "Southwest Airlines Is a Rare Air Carrier: It Still Makes Money." *Wall Street Journal*, 26 Oct. 1992, A1.
58. Bridget O'Brian. "Predatory Pricing Issue," A1.
59. "Kodak to Pay Berkey Photo $6,750,000 Settling Eight-Year Civil Antitrust Suit." *Wall Street Journal*, 24 Sept. 1981, 10.
60. Roy T. Englert. "Antitrust: A Change in Direction." *Legal Times*, 26 July 1993, S40.
61. Paul M. Barrett. "Justices Reject Cigarette Firm's Antitrust Appeal." *Wall Street Journal*, 22 June 1993, A3.
62. Catherine Yang. "Annie Gets Her Antitrust Gun." *Business Week*, 23 Aug. 1993, 23.
63. Annual Report, Administrative Office of U.S. Courts, 30 June 1989 and 30 June 1986.
64. Lacy Glenn Thomas III. "A Survey of the Issues," 15–16.
65. Robert W. Crandall. *After the Breakup: U.S. Telecommunication in a More Competitive Era*. Washington, D.C.: Brookings Institution, 1991, 165.
66. Bureau of the Budget. *U.S. Federal Budget for Fiscal Year 1994*. Appendices-104 and 143.

INDEX

ABOUT THE AUTHOR

RICHARD A. D'AVENI (Ph.D., Columbia University) teaches business strategy at the Amos Tuck School at Dartmouth College and consults for several Fortune 500 corporations. He received the A.T. Kearney Award for his research on why big companies fail, and has been profiled as one of the next generation's promising new management thinkers by *Wirtschafts-Woche*, Germany's equivalent to *Business Week*.